ENCYCLOPAEDIA
OF THE
VIKING AGE

Thames & Hudson

John Haywood

ENCYCLOPAEDIA
OF THE
VIKING AGE

with 279 illustrations

For Beth, Amy, Abigail, Charlotte,
Leisha, Emily and Fionn

Designed by Liz Rudderham

© 2000 John Haywood

First published in hardcover in the United States of America in 2000 by
Thames & Hudson Inc., 500 Fifth Avenue, New York, New York 10110

Library of Congress Catalog Card Number 99-66012
ISBN 0-500-01982-7

Printed and bound in Singapore

On the title page: Carved
animal head from the
Oseberg ship burial, *c.*820

Contents

Preface

The Vikings were not the first great seafarers of northern Europe: Irish, Angles, Saxons, Frisians, Franks and other peoples all preceded them. Nor were they even the most innovative: so far as is known they developed no new techniques of navigation, and their shipbuilding was in many ways backward (they were among the last European peoples to adopt the sail). Yet in the range of their activities, the Vikings were unprecedented. In the east, they sailed down the great rivers of Russia, crossing the Black Sea to Constantinople and the Caspian Sea to reach Baghdad. In the west, they were active along the entire coastline of western Europe, even penetrating the Mediterranean to attack Italy and North Africa. Other Vikings crossed the Atlantic – leaving settlements along the way in the Faroe Islands, Iceland and Greenland – to become the first Europeans known to have set foot in North America. It is these far-flung connections that make the Vikings so fascinating. A huge hoard of Viking treasure found at Cuerdale in north-west England, an area once thickly settled by Scandinavians, contained coins and artefacts from England, Ireland, Italy, Provence, Spain, Iraq and Afghanistan. How this hoard came to be collected, why it was buried on an English riverbank, and what circumstances prevented its owners from returning to collect it we shall never know, but it does tell us that the world that the Vikings knew was vast – vaster than that known by any previous Europeans, except perhaps the Greek and Macedonian soldiers who followed Alexander the Great in his vain quest to conquer the world.

In recent years our understanding of the Vikings has been revolutionized. Not surprisingly, early medieval writers dwelled on the violent side of the Vikings. After all, it was their homes that were being burned and looted, their friends and relations that were being killed or carried off to the slave markets. The Vikings could hardly expect a sympathetic press. In the 19th century, the era of national romanticism and European colonialism, historians were more than content to accept the image of the Viking as the all-conquering sea-rover. The Scandinavian powers were in decline, and the temptation for Scandinavians to hark back to a heroic era when they bestrode the world and were feared by all was irresistible. With his brilliant operatic retelling of Nordic mythology, the *Ring des Nibelungen*, Wagner encouraged the newly unified Germans to see the Vikings as their racial forebears. Combined with Nietzsche's philosophy of the superman, frustrated imperial ambition and neo-Darwinian theories of racial supremacy, the results were tragic. Antiquarians, misidentifying Bronze Age artefacts, equipped the Vikings with their romantically barbaric, but historically inaccurate, horned helmets.

Though it has still yet to penetrate the popular consciousness fully, a more balanced appreciation of the Vikings developed in the second half of the 20th century as archaeologists uncovered evidence of peaceful Viking activity in the fields of trade, crafts, exploration and settlement. There even developed a certain tendency to underplay Viking violence, partly a result of an overreaction to the traditional view, and partly because of changing European values which, after two horrific world wars, no longer saw empire-building and conquest as praiseworthy activities. The aim of this encyclopaedia is to try to do justice to both sides of the Vikings' story, the peaceful and the violent, and to provide concise biographies of the leading personalities of the age, not only among the Vikings but also among those who opposed them with varying degrees of success.

Introduction: The Causes of the Viking Age

The Viking Age began with a series of hit-and-run pirate raids on coastal monasteries and other soft targets in Britain, Ireland and the Frankish empire at the end of the 8th century. Western Europe was enjoying a greater degree of peace, political stability and economic prosperity than it had since the fall of the Western Roman Empire in the 5th century. The tide of Muslim Arab conquests, which had seemed likely to overwhelm Christendom in the early 8th century, had been halted. Thanks to the Frankish emperor Charlemagne's conquests of the pagan Saxons, Slavs and Avars, Christendom had even begun to expand into eastern Europe. Charlemagne may have contemplated conquering the Danes, but if he did, he decided against it. In general, western Europeans showed little interest in the Scandinavians; they were certainly not seen as a threat, despite their paganism. Coasts were thought to provide secure borders, and ports and monasteries were undefended. The sudden outbreak of Viking raids was not only unexpected, it was also deeply shocking. Being pagans, the Vikings were not inhibited by any of the spiritual sanctions that protected the property and personnel of the Church in times of war between Christians. In all, the Viking Age lasted around 300 years, from c.789 until about 1100, though Scandinavian pirates were still a nuisance in some areas well into the 12th century. During that period, the Vikings played an important, and sometimes decisive, role in European history. The impact of the Vikings was probably greatest in Britain, where they broke up existing power structures, paving the way for the creation of the unified kingdoms of England and Scotland. In Ireland they founded the first towns. In the Frankish lands the Vikings exploited and accelerated the breakup of the Carolingian Empire and founded the duchy of Normandy, whose influence on the history of France, England and Italy was enormous. In eastern Europe it was the Vikings who founded the first Russian state. The Vikings were also the first settlers of Iceland and the first Europeans to reach Greenland and the New World. What is perhaps less widely recognized is that the influence of Christian Europe on the Vikings was, if anything, even greater. Scandinavian settlers in the British Isles and Normandy were assimilated by the native populations within a few generations. At home, and in the Atlantic colonies, the Vikings kept their distinctive Scandinavian identity, but by 1100 they, too, had been transformed from pagan barbarians into Christian Europeans. What then were the causes of this dramatic period of European history?

The earliest attempt at an explanation came shortly after the Viking attack on the famous Northumbrian monastery of St Cuthbert on the island of Lindisfarne in June 793. The sacking of this, one of the holiest places in the British Isles, caused widespread shock and alarm, and later chroniclers garnished their accounts of the raid with such suitable portents of imminent catastrophe as flashes of lightning, thunderbolts and fiery dragons. The Northumbrian scholar Alcuin, trying to come to terms with news of the attack, wrote, 'never before has such terror been seen in Britain as we have suffered by this pagan people'. Why, he went on to ask, had St Cuthbert not intervened to protect his monastery? Was not the attack God's punishment for some terrible sin? If somewhere as holy as Lindisfarne could not expect the protection of the saints, Alcuin concluded, then nowhere was safe. In this, at least, Alcuin was to be proven right.

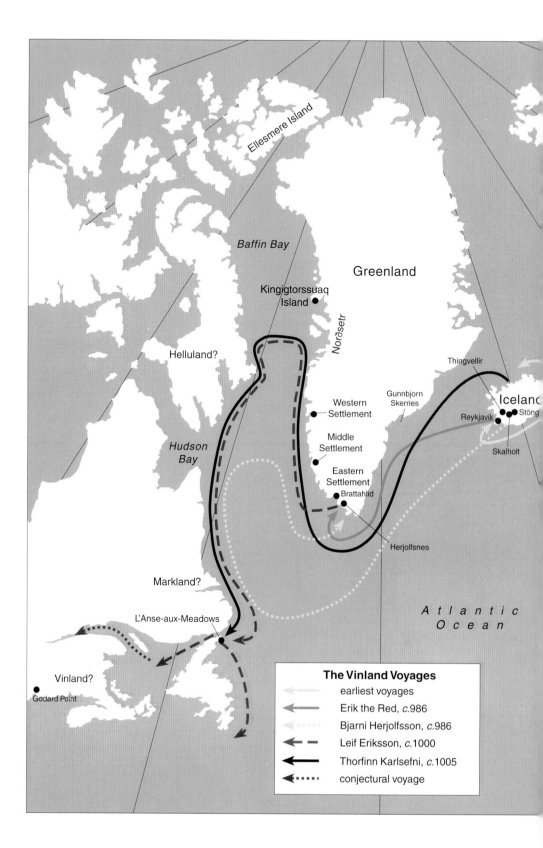

The Vinland Voyages

earliest voyages
Erik the Red, *c.*986
Bjarni Herjolfsson, *c.*986
Leif Eriksson, *c.*1000
Thorfinn Karlsefni, *c.*1005
conjectural voyage

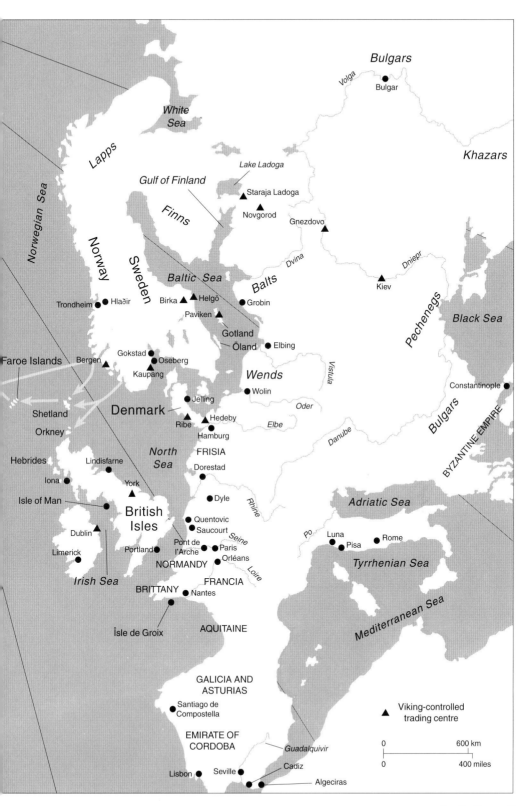

Map 1 The Viking world

9

Other early medieval writers generally concurred with Alcuin in seeing the Vikings as an expression of the wrath of God against a sinful people; modern historians, however, have sought more mundane causes for the Viking expansion.

Until recently, the Viking Age was most commonly explained in terms of a growing population's hunger for land. On the face of it, this is an attractive and plausible explanation. The population of Scandinavia was indeed growing steadily in the centuries immediately preceding the Viking Age, and it continued to do so well into the central Middle Ages. Throughout the period, new settlements were created, more land was brought under cultivation, and iron production increased steadily to meet the demand for tools. Scandinavia has little good arable land and it might be expected that the pressure of this increasing population would eventually make itself felt. Both Norway and Sweden have seen considerable emigration in periods of population growth in recent times. In the 19th century, Norway was second only to Ireland in terms of the proportion of its population that emigrated to North America. There is also considerable evidence of migrations out of Scandinavia before the Viking Age. The Cimbri and Teutones, two tribes that invaded the Roman Empire in 113 BC, originated in Jutland. Several of the Germanic peoples that invaded the empire in the 5th century AD, including the Burgundians, Goths and Vandals, believed that they, too, had Scandinavian origins; others, like the Angles and the Jutes, who migrated to Britain at this time, certainly had. So strong were these traditions, that the 6th-century Gothic historian Jordanes described Scandinavia as the 'womb of peoples' and himself believed that the Germanic migrations were the result of overpopulation.

That there was also a great deal of emigration out of Scandinavia during the Viking Age cannot be denied, but the first phase of Viking activity was dominated by raiders not settlers. Settlement of the Faroes may have begun as early as c.825, but more than half a century had passed from the time of the first attacks before any major Scandinavian settlements were made in the Scottish islands. Iceland was settled only in the 870s (though it was discovered c.860), around the same time that the Danish settlement of eastern England began. Norwegian settlement of north-west England dates to the first decades of the 10th century, as

does the Danish settlement in Normandy. Though the Vikings raided Ireland intensively, there was never any extensive Scandinavian settlement outside a few coastal enclaves. The Scandinavian Rus, who won control of a vast area of eastern Europe, remained a warrior élite ruling over a Slavic population. Land-hunger is, therefore, not an adequate explanation of the Viking expansion. It is more likely that it was the success of Viking raiding that encouraged Scandinavian settlement overseas.

A more important factor than land-hunger was trade. The economic recovery of western Europe in the 8th century led to an increase in trade with Scandinavia, which was a source of such luxuries as furs and walrus ivory. The increasing demand could not be met from Scandinavian resources alone, and already by c.750 Swedish merchants had established themselves at Slavic and Finnic settlements east of the Baltic. In a parallel development, Arab merchants were crossing the Caspian Sea to buy furs and slaves at the Bulgar and Khazar towns on the River Volga. The Arabs paid for their goods with high-quality silver coins called *dirhems*. These began to circulate in eastern Europe, giving the Swedes an incentive to press on further east in the hope of making direct contact with what was clearly a lucrative market.

It was probably while on peaceful merchant voyages that Scandinavians first learned about western Europe's rich and unguarded ports and monasteries. The Scandinavians were certainly known to the Anglo-Saxons and Franks before the outbreak of Viking raiding. Though chroniclers showed little enough interest in Scandinavians while they behaved themselves, according to Alcuin the Northumbrians were so familiar with them that they had even adopted their hairstyles. The circumstances of the earliest recorded Viking raid, on the Anglo-Saxon port of Portland c.789, suggests that the Scandinavians were well known as merchants. When three ships arrived at the port from Norway, the local royal official mistook their occupants for merchants, with fatal consequences for him and his men.

But the main causes of the Viking expansion were social and political developments within Scandinavia itself. Starting in the early first millennium AD, Scandinavian society had begun to show increasing signs of the centralization of power, first with the emergence of a warrior élite and then, in the centuries leading up to the beginning of the Viking Age, with the development of chiefdoms and local kingdoms.

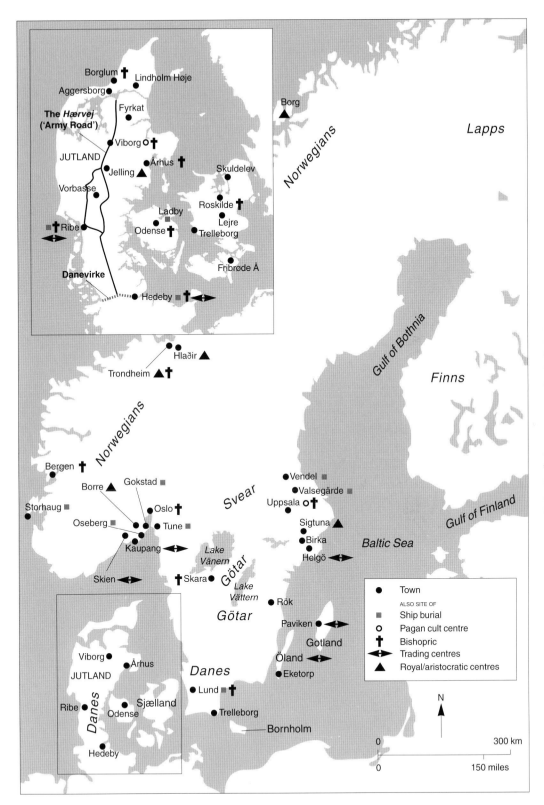

Map 2 Viking Age Scandinavia

Borglum †
Lindholm Høje
Aggersborg ●
Fyrkat
The *Hærvej*
('Army Road')
JUTLAND
Viborg ○ †
Århus †
Jelling ▲
Skuldelev
Vorbasse
Ladby
Roskilde †
Odense †
Lejre
Trelleborg
■ † Ribe ●
Fribrøde Å
Danevirke
Hedeby ■ † ◆

Borg ▲

Norwegians

Lapps

Hlaðir ▲
Trondheim ▲ †

Bergen †
Borre ▲
Gokstad ■
Storhaug ■
Oslo †
Oseberg ■
Tune ■
Kaupang ◆
Skien ◆
Lake Vänern
Skara ●
Götar
Lake Vättern
Rök
Götar

Norwegians

Svear
Vendel ●
Valsegärde ●
Uppsala ○ †
Sigtuna ▲
Birka ●
Helgö ◆

Baltic Sea

Gulf of Bothnia

Finns

Gulf of Finland

Paviken ● ◆
Gotland
Öland ◆
Eketorp

Danes

Viborg ●
Århus ●
JUTLAND
Danes
Ribe ●
Odense ●
Sjælland
Lund ● †
Trelleborg ●
Hedeby ●
Bornholm

Legend:
● Town
ALSO SITE OF
■ Ship burial
○ Pagan cult centre
† Bishopric
◆ Trading centres
▲ Royal/aristocratic centres

N ↑

0 ——— 300 km
0 ——— 150 miles

11

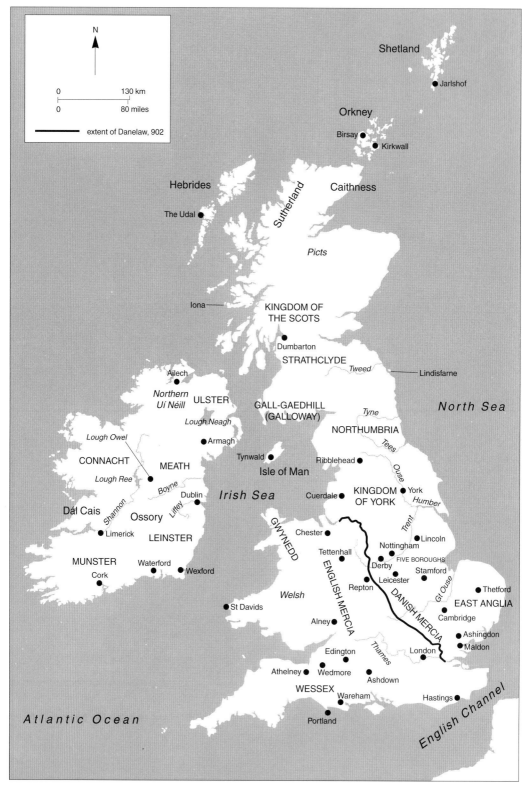

N

| 0 | 130 km |
| 0 | 80 miles |

▬ extent of Danelaw, 902

Shetland

● Jarlshof

Orkney

Birsay ●
● Kirkwall

Hebrides

Caithness

Sutherland

The Udal ●

Picts

Iona

KINGDOM OF
THE SCOTS

● Dumbarton

STRATHCLYDE

Tweed

Lindisfarne

Ailech ●

Northern
Uí Néill

ULSTER

GALL-GAEDHILL
(GALLOWAY)

Tyne

North Sea

Lough Neagh

NORTHUMBRIA

Lough Owel

● Armagh

Tynwald ●

Ribblehead ●

Tees

CONNACHT

MEATH

Isle of Man

Ouse

Lough Ree

Boyne

● Dublin

Irish Sea

Cuerdale ●

KINGDOM
OF YORK

● York

Humber

Dál Cais

Shannon

Liffey

Ossory

Chester ●

GWYNEDD

Trent

Lincoln ●

Limerick ●

LEINSTER

Tettenhall ●

Nottingham ●

FIVE BOROUGHS

MUNSTER

Waterford ●

Derby ●

Stamford ●

Cork ●

● Wexford

Leicester ●

Welsh

Repton ●

DANISH MERCIA

● Thetford

St Davids ●

ENGLISH MERCIA

EAST ANGLIA

Gt. Ouse

Alney ●

Cambridge ●

Edington ●

Thames

● Ashingdon

Athelney ●

Wedmore ●

London ●

● Maldon

WESSEX

Ashdown

Wareham ●

Hastings ●

Portland ●

English Channel

Atlantic Ocean

Map 3 Viking Age British Isles

12

In the Viking Age these were gradually swallowed up by the emerging regional kingdoms of Denmark, Norway and Sweden. In Viking Age Scandinavia all that was necessary to be eligible for kingship was to have inherited royal blood from one parent; even illegitimacy was no bar. As a result, there was a relatively large class of men who could aspire to rule; but the opportunities to do so were steadily diminishing. Competition for power became intense, and succession disputes were frequent and bloody. The losers in these disputes – if they survived – were usually forced into exile; but all was not lost. By turning to raiding to build up their wealth and reputation, they could hope to win a loyal following of warriors who would support a bid for power at home. In this way, Olaf Tryggvason won the Norwegian throne in 995. Some, like Halfdan, Ivar and the other royal leaders of the so-called Danish Great Army that invaded England in 865, may have decided that their best chance of ruling lay in winning a kingdom abroad. Other Viking rulers, such as Svein Forkbeard of Denmark, saw raiding as a way of augmenting royal income. Lacking the means to raise regular income by taxation at home, he became, in effect, a parasite on England's efficient administration, which raised vast sums in tribute to buy him off. The centralization of power in Viking Age Scandinavia also undermined the traditional autonomy of local chieftains, many of whom saw settlement overseas, especially in Iceland, as a way to preserve their independence.

As royal authority became more secure in the 11th century, the Scandinavian kingdoms began to develop effective administrations on the model of other Christian medieval European states. Kings could increasingly rely on institutionalized sources of wealth-gathering, such as taxes and tolls, and the importance of plunder declined. Freelance piracy now became an obstacle to good relations with neighbouring kingdoms and a threat to trade, and was suppressed. For the martially inclined, the 12th century brought the respectable option of participating in crusades against the pagan Wends in the Baltic or the Muslims in the Holy Land. In any case, the ambitious now also had alternatives to war to increase their wealth and status, such as entering royal service or the Church. The Viking Age in effect simply faded away.

Subject Index

THE ENCYCLOPAEDIA

Tapestry from Skog church Halsingland, Sweden, depicting members of the Æsir family of gods. On the left is one-eyed Odin, in the centre is Thor, and on the right is the fertility-god Frey.

Adam of Bremen (d. *c*.1080) Author of the *Gesta Hammaburgensis ecclesiae pontificum* ('Deeds of the Bishops of the Church of Hamburg'), the major source of information about Christian missionary activity in Scandinavia and about the customs of the pagan Scandinavians and Baltic Slavs. Adam was educated at a cathedral school in Bavaria or Franconia, and arrived in Bremen in 1066–7 at the request of archbishop Adalbert of Hamburg-Bremen (d. 1072). Adam visited DENMARK in 1068–9 and met king SVEIN ESTRITHSON, whom he cites as a major informant for his work. The archives at Bremen and reports of returning missionary bishops were also important sources.

Adam of Bremen, *History of the Archbishops of Hamburg-Bremen*, trans. F. J. Tschan (New York, 1959).

Ælfgifu of Northampton (d. *c*.1040) English concubine of CNUT, also known as Alfiva. The daughter of ealdorman Ælfhelm of NORTHUMBRIA, Ælfgifu was probably already Cnut's concubine at the time he became king of ENGLAND in 1016. She bore him two sons, SVEIN ALFIVASON and HAROLD HAREFOOT. Despite Cnut's marriage to EMMA of NORMANDY in 1018, Ælfgifu continued to enjoy high status. In 1030 she became regent of NORWAY, ruling for her son Svein, whom Cnut had made king after defeating OLAF HARALDSSON. Her vigorous efforts to centralize royal power made her unpopular, and both she and Svein were expelled in 1034–5. After Cnut's death in 1035 she supported Harold Harefoot's successful bid for the English throne.

Ælfheah (St Alphege) (954–1012) Archbishop of Canterbury and martyr. Ælfheah was a monk from the west of ENGLAND; he became bishop of

Winchester in 984 and archbishop of Canterbury in 1006. Sent by king ÆTHELRED THE UNREADY to negotiate with the Vikings in 994, he converted OLAF TRYGGVASON to CHRISTIANITY and won a promise from him not to invade England again (in return for a payment of DANEGELD). Captured at Canterbury in 1011 by Vikings who demanded 3,000 pounds of silver as RANSOM, Ælfheah refused to pay or to allow anyone else to do so. His enraged captors murdered him after a drunken FEAST. CNUT promoted the cult of Ælfheah as a means of reconciling his English subjects to Danish rule. Ælfheah was canonized in 1078.

Ælle (d. 867) King of NORTHUMBRIA (r. *c*.866–7). Following the fall of YORK to the Danish GREAT ARMY in 866 the Northumbrians repudiated king Osberht and made Ælle king, even though he was not of royal blood. The two kings united to attack the DANES at York (21 March 867). Despite breaking into the city, the Northumbrians were defeated and both kings were killed. According to legendary Scandinavian traditions, Ælle was responsible for killing RAGNAR LODBROK. In revenge, his sons invaded Northumbria, captured Ælle and killed him by carving a BLOOD EAGLE in his back. Considering that Ælle ruled only for a few months, it is most unlikely that there is any truth in this colourful story.

Æsir The larger of the two families of pagan Scandinavian gods, the Æsir dwelled in the citadel of ASGARD: they are generally associated with the sky and war. The main deities of the Æsir were the high god ODIN, BALDER, HEIMDALL, LOKI, THOR and TYR. Wars between the Æsir and the rival family of gods, the VANIR, were frequent until the Vanir were granted admission to Asgard.

A coin showing Æthelred the Unready, minted especially to pay the Danegeld.

Æthelflæd, 'lady of the Mercians' (d. 918). Daughter of ALFRED THE GREAT, Æthelflæd was married to ealdorman ÆTHELRED of MERCIA in 884. She ruled Mercia jointly with her husband, and after his death in 911 ruled alone for the remainder of her life. She gave permission for the Viking INGAMUND to settle on the Wirral c.902, and refortified Chester in 907 after he attacked it c.905. She also founded BURHS at Eddisbury and Runcorn to block Viking expansion south of the River Mersey. From 912 she cooperated closely with her brother EDWARD THE ELDER, king of WESSEX, in his campaigns to conquer the DANELAW. In 917 Æthelflæd captured Derby, and in 918 Leicester surrendered to her. In the same year, the DANES of YORK offered to submit to her, but she died before the offer could be acted upon. She was briefly succeeded by her daughter Ælfwynn, but in 919 Edward formally annexed Mercia to Wessex.

Æthelred (d. 911) Ealdorman of MERCIA (c.883–911); Æthelred also used the title 'lord of the Mercians'. He succeeded the Danish puppet king CEOLWULF II and cooperated with the West Saxons against the Vikings. Æthelred married ALFRED THE GREAT's daughter ÆTHELFLÆD in 884. In 886 he was given control of London by Alfred after its recapture from the DANES. Because of his poor health, he ruled Mercia jointly with his wife.

Æthelred I (d. 871) King of WESSEX (r. 865–71). Immediately on his accession Æthelred faced the threat of invasion by the Danish GREAT ARMY. In 867 he helped the Mercian king BURGRED besiege the DANES in Nottingham, though the ANGLO-SAXONS failed to dislodge them. In 870 the Great Army invaded Wessex, establishing a camp at Reading. Æthelred and his brother ALFRED THE GREAT defeated the Danes at Ashdown, but they in turn were defeated two weeks later at Basing. Either in this battle, or another at Merton early in 871, Æthelred was fatally wounded, dying at Easter. Though he left two sons, they were too young to rule, and the kingdom passed to Alfred.

Æthelred the Unready (Æthelred II) (c.966–1016) King of ENGLAND (r. 978–1016). Æthelred came to the throne after the murder of his half-brother Edward the Martyr. Suspicions that Æthelred may have played a part in the murder dogged his reign and undermined his subjects' trust in him. Although he was in many ways a competent ruler and skilled administrator, Æthelred is chiefly remembered for the failure of his military leadership against the Vikings, who renewed their raids on England in 980 after more than half a century of peace. Following the English defeat at MALDON in 991, large Viking FLEETS led by the likes of OLAF TRYGGVASON and king SVEIN FORKBEARD of DENMARK descended on England almost every year. Æthelred was reduced to the expedient of paying DANEGELD: 22,000 pounds of silver in 991, rising by degrees to 36,000 pounds in 1007 and 48,000 pounds in 1012. In principle, this was intended to buy time for effective defences to be organized, but in practice it was counterproductive since it merely encouraged the DANES to return and demand more. The ST BRICE'S DAY MASSACRE of Danes living in England in 1002, a reaction to a supposed plot against Æthelred's life, simply helped alienate his subjects in the DANELAW. In 1002 Æthelred married EMMA of NORMANDY in an attempt to win duke RICHARD THE GOOD away from his alliance with Svein Forkbeard. In this respect it failed, and, worse, the children of this marriage threatened the position

of his sons by his first marriage. Æthelred's authority was increasingly undermined by dissent within the royal family itself. In an attempt to meet the invaders at sea, Æthelred ordered a major shipbuilding programme in 1008, but dissension in the ranks led to the breakup of the fleet before it could be brought into action. Other intelligent military reforms also came to nothing because Æthelred, who was no warrior, could not give his forces the confident and decisive leadership they needed. By 1012 Svein Forkbeard was intent on the outright conquest of England. Though Æthelred stiffened his forces by hiring the Viking ARMY of THORKELL THE TALL, English resistance began to crumble. The new TAX that Æthelred introduced to pay Thorkell, the *heregeld*, remained an annual imposition until 1051. When Svein Forkbeard invaded in spring 1013, only London, assisted by Thorkell, refused to submit. When Æthelred fled to Normandy after Christmas 1013, London, too, surrendered and Svein was master of England. However, he died unexpectedly in February 1014 and Æthelred was invited back. Svein's son CNUT was chased out of the country, but Æthelred's triumph was short-lived. By conniving in the murder of two leading thanes from the Danelaw, Æthelred forfeited what little trust he still retained with his people. Backed by Thorkell and ERIK of HLAÐIR, Cnut returned in September 1015 to claim his inheritance. Æthelred was now ill, and when he died in April 1016 English resistance to the Danes was again collapsing. He was succeeded by his son EDMUND IRONSIDE, who rallied the English for a final struggle with Cnut. Æthelred's popular nickname, which derives from the Old English *unræd*, meaning 'ill advised', was not used during his lifetime.

agriculture The main farming activity during the Viking Age in all settled parts of Scandinavia, including Halogaland in Arctic NORWAY, was animal husbandry. Cattle, sheep, goats and pigs were all reared by Scandinavian farmers. Most of these animals were smaller than those bred today. Though their light bones rarely survive to be discovered in archaeological excavations, it is known from literary sources that chickens and, especially, geese were kept in large numbers. It is this concentration on pastoralism that explains why apparently bleak and inhospitable places such as the FAROE ISLANDS, ICELAND and GREENLAND were attractive to Scandinavian settlers: they were looking for pasture land rather than fertile soils, and even poor pasture is useful if there is a lot of it. Transhumance was practised in upland areas, with temporary shielings known as *sæter* or *aergi* occupied in the summer months, when cattle and sheep could be grazed on mountain pastures. Haymaking was a critical summer activity to stock up winter fodder for cattle. In areas with harsh winters, such as Iceland, around 2,500 kilograms of hay were needed for each cow over the winter. As was the case elsewhere in early medieval Europe, the weaker cattle were slaughtered in early winter, butchered and either salted, dried or smoked to preserve the meat. Sheep and goats usually wintered outside in the open, but in Iceland they were sometimes brought indoors in the worst weather. In DENMARK and southern SWEDEN, which have the most-fertile soils in Scandinavia, arable farming was also an important activity, and some cereals and vegetables were grown even in Arctic Norway, Iceland and Greenland. The main crops were barley, rye, oats, peas, beans and cabbage. An important non-food crop was flax for making linen. Wild fruit and nuts were gathered in season.

Left: Viking Age agriculture, from an 11th-century manuscript.

The Alfred Jewel, the handle of a pointer used as an aid for reading, made on the instructions of Alfred the Great.

Scandinavia as a whole produced a surplus of animal products, and Denmark, possibly, even a surplus of grain. In Arctic Norway, and marginal upland areas of Norway and Sweden, hunting made a significant contribution to the diet. FISHING, WHALING, SEALING AND SEABIRDING were widely practised in coastal areas.

During the early Viking Age, ploughing was still performed by the simple ard, which breaks up only the surface of the soil. By the 10th century the wheeled mould-board plough, which turns as well as breaks the soil, was coming into use in Denmark, allowing a significant increase in harvests. While the ard requires only one or two draught animals, the mould-board plough needs up to eight. This was out of the reach of most peasants and led to a shift in Denmark at the end of the Viking Age towards more communal forms of agriculture and the creation of larger fields.

Alan Barbetorte ('twist-beard') (d. 952) Duke of BRITTANY (937–52). Exiled in ENGLAND after the Viking conquest of Brittany in 919, Alan won the support of king ATHELSTAN, who gave him a FLEET to launch a campaign of reconquest in 936. Alan landed near Dol, taking the local Viking lords, who were at a wedding FEAST, by surprise. In 937 he captured the Viking stronghold at Nantes after a stiff fight; the last Vikings were expelled from Brittany in 939 after Alan captured their camp at Trans, near Dol. Alan was never able to consolidate his authority over the Breton nobility, and a civil war broke out after his death.

Alcuin (*c.*735–804) Anglo-Saxon scholar and one of the leading figures of the Carolingian Renaissance. Alcuin was educated at the cathedral school at YORK,

becoming its head in 778. At the invitation of CHARLEMAGNE, in 782 Alcuin founded the palace school at Aachen, which he led until he became abbot of the monastery of St-Martin at Tours in 796. Alcuin established the curriculum of the seven liberal arts that became basic to medieval education, revised the liturgy of the Frankish Church, and wrote several theological treatises and numerous letters to rulers and churchmen across Europe. His letters include the earliest contemporary accounts of a Viking raid, the sack of the Northumbrian monastery of LINDISFARNE in 793, and his *Life of St WILLIBRORD* gives an account of the earliest Christian mission to DENMARK.

Alfred the Great (d. 899) King of WESSEX (r. 871–99). The youngest son of Æthelwulf of Wessex, Alfred succeeded to the throne on the death of his brother ÆTHELRED I. The early years of his reign were taken up by a life-and-death struggle with the Danish GREAT ARMY, culminating in the near collapse of Wessex after a surprise attack on the royal manor at Chippenham in midwinter 878 forced Alfred into hiding at Athelney in the marshes of Somerset. From there, Alfred rallied his forces, and that May he won a decisive victory over the DANES at EDINGTON and besieged their base at Chippenham, forcing their surrender. By the treaty of WEDMORE, the Danish king GUTHRUM accepted baptism and withdrew his ARMY to EAST ANGLIA. Alfred embarked on a thorough reorganization of the defences of Wessex, building a series of fortresses or *BURHS*, reforming the army, and building a FLEET to take on the Vikings at sea. He built a close relationship with MERCIA, marrying his daughter ÆTHELFLÆD to its ruler ealdorman ÆTHELRED, and also with NORTHUMBRIA, presenting himself as leader of all the English not under Danish rule. In

886 Alfred recaptured London from the Danes after Guthrum had broken the peace the previous year. In the peace settlement, Alfred forced Guthrum to grant equal rights to the English living under his rule. The effectiveness of Alfred's defences were tested by the arrival of a large Viking army from FRANCIA in 892. But despite receiving support from the Danish settlers in the DANELAW, this new onslaught was contained. The Vikings faced constant harassment by Alfred's forces and in 896 their army broke up, most to settle in the Danelaw, others to join the Viking army on the River Seine.

A devout Christian, Alfred believed the Viking attacks were a punishment from God for the laxity of the English Church. As a result, Alfred began a programme of educational reform to raise the standard of the clergy, inviting scholars from abroad and translating into English several major works, including pope Gregory the Great's *Pastoral Care*. He was also responsible for beginning the ANGLO-SAXON CHRONICLE. In the late Anglo-Saxon period, Alfred's reputation was overshadowed by those of his successors, EDWARD THE ELDER and ATHELSTAN. Alfred's reputation began to grow in the 12th century, thanks to chronicler William of Malmesbury, and by the 16th century he had acquired his title 'the Great', the only English king to be so distinguished. Certainly, with the benefit of hindsight, Alfred's reign can be seen as decisive in English history, marking the beginning of a national KINGSHIP. In his combination of political, military and scholarly abilities, Alfred stands alone among the rulers of early medieval Europe.

R. Abels, *Alfred the Great* (London and New York, 1998).

Alney, treaty of Peace treaty between CNUT and EDMUND IRONSIDE (October–November 1016).

Following his defeat at ASHINGDON, Edmund fled to Gloucestershire, pursued by Cnut. They met on the island of Alney in the River Severn near Deerhurst, and agreed to divide the kingdom between them: Edmund was to retain WESSEX and pay off Cnut's ARMY; Cnut was to rule ENGLAND north of the Thames. The treaty was never enforced, however. Edmund died a few weeks later (30 November 1016), and Cnut became king of all England.

Althing The lawmaking assembly of ICELAND, founded by the leaders of the Norse settlers *c*.930. It met annually for two weeks each June at THINGVELLIR until 1798, after which it was moved to Reykjavik. The first meeting of the Althing established a national LAW for Iceland, based on an adaptation of the Gulathing law of south-west NORWAY by Úlfjótr. Though all freemen, except those sentenced to OUTLAWRY, could attend, the Althing was essentially an oligarchical form of government. All judicial and legislative power was in the hands of thirty-six *goðar* (local chieftains, singular *goði*), who alone had the right to vote in the *Lögrétta*, the Althing's legislative council (the number of *goðar* was increased to thirty-nine in 965 and to forty-eight in 1005). The *goðar* elected the LAWSPEAKER, a non-executive president of the Althing, who served for a three-year, renewable term. Although the Althing was ultimately controlled by the *goðar*, decision-making tended to be consensual, since the *goðar* needed to consider the opinions of their *thingmenn* ('supporters'): as freemen, the *thingmenn* could withdraw their allegiance if they so wished. From *c*.965, legal disputes that could not be resolved at the district THINGS were heard at the Althing's *fjórðungsdómar* ('quarter courts'), named after

Opposite: Thingvellir, Iceland. The Althing met in the sheltered volcanic cleft in the foreground.

An amber chessman, perhaps representing Thor, from Sjaelland, Denmark.

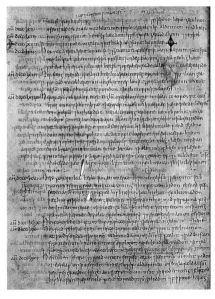

The *Anglo-Saxon Chronicle*'s account of the Danish invasion of 865.

Iceland's four geographical quarters, the Court of the North Quarter, South Quarter etc. Around 1005 a fifth court was constituted to adjudicate in cases that had become deadlocked in the quarter courts. The *goðar* were expected to argue the cases of their *thingmenn* at the Althing. In return, they could call upon the armed support of their *thingmenn* in feuds with other *goðar*. Meetings of the Althing were lively social occasions during which people could meet their friends, strike business deals and arrange MARRIAGES. As long as all the *goðar* were of roughly equal wealth, status and power, the Althing provided stable and effective government: its greatest achievement was probably the peaceful adoption of CHRISTIANITY as Iceland's official religion. But the emergence of a few leading FAMILIES in the 13th century undermined its effectiveness. The Althing's independence was restricted after Iceland was annexed by Norway in 1263, and its meetings were dominated by royal officials. The Althing was abolished in 1800.

J. L. Byock, *Medieval Iceland: Society, Sagas and Power* (Berkeley, Los Angeles and London, 1988); J. Jóhannesson, *A History of the Old Icelandic Commonwealth: Íslendinga Saga* (Winnipeg, 1974).

amber Semi-precious fossil resin collected from the North Sea coast of Jutland and the south Baltic coasts. Amber was exported from Scandinavia and the Baltic lands from as early as the second millennium BC, and is often mentioned as a Scandinavian export in Viking times. Soft and easily worked, amber was used to make beads, amulets, gaming pieces and other decorative objects. Evidence of amber-working has been discovered in almost every Scandinavian Viking Age TOWN, as well as Scandinavian settlements overseas such as DUBLIN and STARAJA LADOGA.

Amlaíb *see* OLAF

Andvari In Scandinavian mythology, a wealthy DWARF who lived below a waterfall in the form of a pike. In order to pay OTTAR'S RANSOM, LOKI caught Andvari and forced him to give up his treasure as the price of his life. When Loki insisted that he give up the magic ring Andvaranaut, Andvari cursed it so that it brought ruin on all who possessed it.

Angantyr (Ongendus) (*fl. c.*720) One of the earliest historical Danish kings. He was visited by the Northumbrian St WILLIBRORD during the first Christian mission to DENMARK *c.*725. Angantyr treated Willibrord courteously and allowed him to take thirty boys home with him to bring up as Christians, but he showed no inclination to convert himself. It was this, no doubt, that led ALCUIN, Willibrord's biographer, to describe Angantyr as 'crueller than any beast and harder than any stone'. It is not known how much of Denmark Angantyr controlled, but there is considerable archaeological evidence of the emergence of a centralized state in the Jutland area at this time, such as the founding of RIBE *c.*710, the building of the KANHAVE CANAL *c.*726, and the beginning of the DANEVIRKE *c.*737.

Anglo-Saxon Chronicle The *Anglo-Saxon Chronicle* is the single most important primary source for the history of Anglo-Saxon ENGLAND from its beginnings in the 5th century up to the Norman Conquest of 1066: without it, very little indeed would be known about the Viking Age in England. The *Chronicle* is not a single source but a group of related chronicles that all derive from a common original compiled during the reign of ALFRED THE GREAT of WESSEX, probably in the late 880s or early

A bone trial piece used by a craftsman to practise his designs, from York, 9th–10th century.

890s. Copies of this original chronicle were circulated to several different centres, where they were subsequently kept up to date by local annalists. All versions of the *Chronicle* share virtually the same information up to 890–2, but there are considerable differences between them from 893 onwards. Most versions of the *Chronicle* were discontinued soon after the Norman Conquest, but at Peterborough it was continued until 1154. Seven manuscripts of the *Chronicle*, written in the original Old English, have survived, and the existence of several others, now lost, is known from extracts quoted in later Latin sources and entries in medieval library catalogues. Though it is written mostly in a detached, dispassionate style, the *Chronicle* is not an objective record of events and it was probably begun on Alfred's orders as part of a propaganda campaign to present the Wessex dynasty as the leading defender of the Christian English from the heathen Vikings.
The Anglo-Saxon Chronicle, trans. G. N. Garmonsway (London, 1953).

Anglo-Saxons The population of England before the Norman Conquest of 1066. The Anglo-Saxons were originally three Germanic peoples from northern Germany and Jutland – the Angles, Saxons and Jutes – that invaded and settled in eastern and southern Britain in the 5th century AD. Though they were still divided into several independent kingdoms, by the 8th century the three groups were beginning to develop a common English identity. The term *Angli Saxones* was first used by early medieval continental writers to distinguish the invaders from the native Celtic population of Britain.

Ansgar, St (Anskar) (*c*.801–65) Known as the 'Apostle of the North', Ansgar was born near Amiens

and educated at the monastery of Corbie in Picardy, northern France, before becoming a monk at Corvey in Germany. After the baptism of HARALD KLAK at the court of LOUIS THE PIOUS in 826, Ansgar accompanied the king back to DENMARK to begin missionary work. After Harald was forced into exile a year later, Ansgar went to SWEDEN, where king Björn allowed him to found a CHURCH at BIRKA. Ansgar entrusted the mission in Sweden to Gautbert, concentrating on Denmark himself. In 831 he became the first bishop of Hamburg, and the following year, he was appointed papal legate for the Scandinavian and Slavonic missions. Ansgar's mission suffered severe setbacks, however; Gautbert was expelled from Birka a few years after his arrival; and in 845 Hamburg was sacked by the DANES. Ansgar became the first archbishop of Hamburg-Bremen when the two sees were united in 847–8, and in 851–2 he led a second mission to Scandinavia, founding churches at Schleswig (i.e. HEDEBY) and RIBE in Denmark and re-establishing the church at Birka. He was canonized a few years after his death in Bremen in 865. Despite Ansgar's missions, CHRISTIANITY made little headway in Scandinavia during the 9th century. Few of Ansgar's own writings have survived, but the *Life of St Ansgar* (*Vita Anskarii*) by Rimbert, his successor as bishop of Bremen, is an important historical source, not only for Ansgar's life and works but also for conditions in 9th-century Scandinavia itself.
C. H. Robinson (trans.), *Anskar, the Apostle of the North, 801–65: Translated from the Vita Anskarii by Bishop Rimbert, His fellow Missionary and Successor* (London, 1921).

antler, bone and horn Though it is a difficult material to work, antler was used in large quantities in Viking Age Scandinavia to

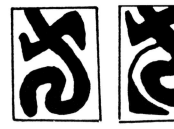

Imitation of Arabic script from lead weights found in a Viking merchant's grave on Colonsay, Scotland.

A hoard of 8th–9th-century Arab coins from Gotland.

manufacture COMBS, knife handles, needles, gaming pieces, dice and other objects. Red-deer antler was most commonly used, but reindeer, elk (European moose) and roe-deer antler was also used. Evidence of antler-working is almost exclusively confined to TOWNS, so most antler artefacts were presumably made by professional craftsmen. Bone is much easier to work than antler and was readily available in all households, where it was used to make a great variety of artefacts such as needles and pins, knife handles, spindle-whorls and ice-skates. Ox horns were sometimes made into drinking vessels.

Arabs, Vikings and the The Arabs knew the Vikings by a variety of names. Those they encountered in the east were called *ar-Rus* (RUS) or *Warank* (VARANGIANS); those in the west, *al-Majus* (pagans) or *al-Urman* (Northmen). The Arabs recognized the similarities between the two groups, and before the end of the 9th century they had come to regard the *ar-Rus* and the *al-Majus* as one and the same.

The Vikings generally did not fare too well when they tried raiding the Arab lands. A Viking raid on the emirate of Cordoba in 844 was heavily defeated, and the famous raid into the MEDITERRANEAN by BJORN IRONSIDE and HASTEIN in 859–62 lost two-thirds of its ships. Viking raids from RUSSIA against the lands of the Abbasid caliphate on the shores of the Caspian Sea enjoyed little more success. Attacks in 910 and 912–13 netted much plunder, though the second FLEET never made it home, as it was later destroyed by the KHAZARS. In 943 a Rus fleet captured the Caucasian TOWN of Barda and held it for several months in the face of Arab counter-attacks, withdrawing only after an epidemic broke out in their ranks.

These raids were very much the exception to the rule. Most contacts between the Vikings and the Arabs were peaceful. In the east, Rus merchants conducted a brisk trade in slaves and furs with Arab merchants at the BULGAR and KHAZAR towns on the River Volga. The high-quality silver COINS called *DIRHEMS* with which the Arabs paid for their goods found their way to Scandinavia in their tens of thousands. According to the 10th-century geographer Ibn Kurdadbeh, Rus merchants also regularly crossed the Caspian Sea to Jurjan, travelling on by camel to Baghdad to sell furs and swords. Some Arabs also travelled to Scandinavia itself. According to a late source, Abd al-Rahman, the ruler of Muslim Spain sent the poet al-Ghazal on a diplomatic mission to the *al-Majus* in 845, and a Jewish merchant from Cordoba, al-Tartushi, visited HEDEBY in DENMARK in the mid-10th century.

Arab accounts are the most important contemporary sources of information about the Rus. The geographer Ibn Rusteh, writing *c.*903–13, gives a detailed ethnographic account of them, including their appearance, DRESS, legal customs, religion, burial practices and methods of fighting, tribute-gathering and slave raids on the Slavs. The most sensational source is an eyewitness account of Rus merchants and a chieftain's funeral by Ibn Fadlan, who was sent on a diplomatic mission to the Volga Bulgars by the caliph al-Muqtadir in 921. Though the Arabs understandably regarded the Vikings as barbarians, it is clear that they admired their warrior bearing.

Århus Today the largest city in Jutland, DENMARK, Århus is first mentioned in literary sources in 948 as the seat of a BISHOPRIC. In the 11th century it was an important port of departure for NORWAY and

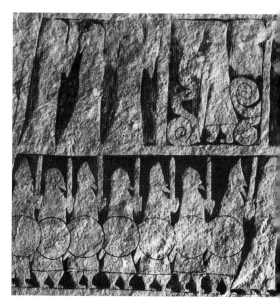
A Viking army prepares to embark on an overseas expedition. Picture stone, Gotland, c.800.

A reconstructed Viking army barracks hall, based on those at Trelleborg, Denmark.

southern SWEDEN. The Viking Age TOWN lay in the modern city centre and was protected by a semicircular earth rampart, which enclosed approximately 5 hectares. The interior was occupied by sunken-featured buildings that were used as dwellings and craft workshops. Both the rampart and the earliest buildings date from the mid-10th century. Århus may, therefore, have been founded as a fortified craft centre, perhaps as a royal initiative.

armies There is little evidence concerning the organization of the Viking armies that ravaged western Europe in the 9th and 10th centuries. The basic fighting unit was the LIÐ, a king's or chieftain's personal retinue of warriors, the size of which depended on the wealth and status of its leader. The warriors of a *lið* formed a sworn fellowship, or FÉLAG, which was bonded together by oaths of mutual loyalty. A Viking army was essentially a group of *liðr* that had united to achieve a common objective. When a campaign was over, the army simply broke up into its individual fellowships, whether to settle, to return home or to join another army somewhere else. There was no formal military discipline in Viking armies – fear of dishonour was usually sufficient to stop a warrior deserting his comrades in battle. The Viking armies of the 11th century, such as those that conquered ENGLAND under SVEIN FORKBEARD and CNUT, still included the warrior retinues of great men, but they also included a strong mercenary element that fought for pay. Local defence in Scandinavia itself probably depended mainly on the local chieftain's *lið*, supported by peasant levies.

Where possible on campaign, Viking armies took over existing FORTIFICATIONS or built their own to use as bases and to protect their SHIPS, loot and the WOMEN and CHILDREN who sometimes accompanied them in the 9th century. Though women did not fight, they served a useful function, cooking and tending the wounded. Despite their formidable reputation, Viking armies rarely went out of their way to seek battle and tended to lose as often as they won when forced to fight. They also avoided siege warfare, at which they had little skill. The Vikings' favoured battle tactic was to form a defensive shield wall or *skjaldborg* ('shield-fort') to meet the enemy attack. In attack, a wedge-shaped formation called a *svinfylkja* ('swine-wedge') was often adopted to try to break the enemy shield wall. The critical moment in a battle came if one side's shield wall was broken and it tried to disengage. The victors could then inflict heavy casualties on the vanquished as they exposed their backs in flight. The Vikings were not military innovators: their WEAPONS and tactics were similar to those used by other north Europeans at the time. Their main advantage over the defenders was their mobility. Their fast, shallow-draughted SHIPS were ideally suited for surprise attacks on coastal settlements or for transporting armies far inland along rivers. On land, the Vikings campaigned as mounted infantry, covering long distances quickly on commandeered horses, but always dismounting for battle. Usually, by the time local forces had been gathered in sufficient strength to counter-attack, the Vikings had taken their loot and gone.

Determining the size of Viking armies has proved very difficult. Contemporary annalists tended to describe the size of Viking armies in terms of the number of ships in which they arrived. Frankish, English and Irish sources agree that the numbers involved increased sharply in the 840s,

Christ in majesty, from the cover of a gospel presented to the abbey of St Emmeran by Arnulf of Carinthia.

from FLEETS of between 3 and 35 ships before this date to ones of between 100 and 350 ships thereafter. There is little evidence to suggest that these sources systematically exaggerated the size of the Viking fleets so these figures are probably broadly accurate. Despite this, interpreting them is difficult because we do not know for certain the size of the ships and their crews; and if the ships carried horses, supplies, and women and children, there would have been less room for warriors. Consideration of the size of known longships – such as the 9th-century GOKSTAD SHIP, which had a crew of more than thirty – and of the military resources of the Vikings' enemies – for example WESSEX could muster around 30,000 armed men *c.*900 – and analogy with other early medieval armies, suggests that a major Viking army of the 9th century must have numbered a few thousands (but not tens of thousands) of warriors. The mercenary armies of Svein and Cnut were probably not much larger. As Viking armies had to live off the land, they could not have remained concentrated in the field for long, and the evidence suggests that when based in any place for a long time they split up into smaller bands of a few hundred men to forage and plunder more efficiently. There were not, however, vast hoards of Viking warriors pouring out of Scandinavia. The Vikings tended to concentrate in particular places at particular times. When FRANCIA was intensively raided in 879–92, England and IRELAND enjoyed a respite; when the Vikings crossed to England in 892, Francia saw a decline in raiding. As there was rarely more than one or two large Viking armies in the field at any one time, the number of Viking warriors was actually quite limited.

P. Griffith, *The Viking Art of War* (London, 1995).

armour *see* WEAPONS AND ARMOUR

Arnór Thórðason jarlaskáld ('earl's skald') (after 1010–after 1073) An Icelandic merchant and SKALDIC poet. Arnór settled in ORKNEY *c.*1045 and served as court poet to the earls Rognvald Brusisson and THORFINN THE MIGHTY. A great deal of his verse has survived in fragments quoted in later works of Icelandic literature, including *FLATEYJARBÓK*, *HEIMSKRINGLA* and *ORKNEYINGA SAGA*. Among his works are commemorative poems for the kings MAGNUS THE GOOD and HARALD HARDRADA of NORWAY, and for his patron earl Thorfinn.

Arnulf (d. 899) Duke of Carinthia; king of the East FRANKS (r. 887–99). Arnulf was elected king at Frankfurt in November 887, after forcing his uncle, the discredited emperor CHARLES THE FAT, to abdicate. The West Franks and the kingdoms of Burgundy and Italy refused to recognize Arnulf, and after Charles's death in January 888 they chose new kings of their own, so bringing about the final breakup of the CAROLINGIAN EMPIRE. An energetic ruler, Arnulf organized effective resistance to the Vikings operating in the Low Countries, winning a crushing victory over them at the River DYLE, near Louvain, Belgium, in 891. Though other factors were also involved, the Vikings withdrew from the lower Rhine for good the following year. For most of his reign, Arnulf's authority was confined to Germany and the Low Countries, but in 894 he invaded Italy at the pope's request. Despite initial success, which saw him briefly crowned emperor, illness forced him to withdraw in 896. Arnulf's final years were marked by continuing illness and Magyar and Slav invasions of Germany.

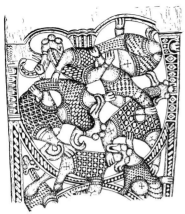

'Gripping beast' motif
in the Oseberg art style.

Silver filigree brooch in
the Jellinge style, from
Eketorp, Sweden.

Gilt mount in the
Borre style, from
Borre, Norway.

art styles The art of Viking Age Scandinavia was primarily decorative with vigorous patterns based on stylized animals. One of the most popular and longest-lasting motifs was the 'gripping beast', so-called because their paws grip anything in the vicinity, which remained in fashion from the 8th century through to the 10th. Interlace and plant motifs, adopted as a result of contact with western Europe, were popular at times, though always suitably adapted to Scandinavian taste. The Scandinavian Viking Age art styles have their antecedents in 8th-century styles such as the Broa style from GOTLAND. Although there is an obvious continuity in the development of Viking art from these earlier styles, a succession of six distinctive styles is recognized: Oseberg (800–75), Borre (850–950), Jellinge (900–75), Mammen (950–1025), Ringerike (1000–75) and Urnes (1050–1150). There is overlap between styles because an earlier style did not disappear immediately on the appearance of a new one. By the mid-12th century, animal-based decoration had gone out of fashion, to be replaced by European Romanesque art. Since the same styles were used irrespective of the medium – whether metalwork, wood, IVORY or, by the late Viking Age, stone – art styles have been an important aid to dating Viking Age artefacts. The most important examples of pictorial scenes and figurative art are to be found on the Gotland PICTURE STONES and a tapestry from the OSEBERG SHIP BURIAL.

Asgard Mythological citadel, the home of the gods. From his throne in the silver-roofed hall Válaskjálf, the high god ODIN could watch over the whole of creation. In his other hall, VALHALLA, Odin gave hospitality to all who fell in battle. Also in Asgard there was a golden-roofed hall called Gimli, where righteous men went after death. Asgard was surrounded by a massive wall, built by the GIANTS, and could be reached only by crossing Bifrost, the shimmering rainbow bridge that was guarded by the god HEIMDALL. Originally it was only the ÆSIR who lived in Asgard, but after a series of wars the VANIR, a rival family of gods, was admitted.

Ashingdon, battle of Battle fought between CNUT and EDMUND IRONSIDE on 18 October 1016 at Ashingdon, Essex. Edmund was crushingly defeated after EADRIC STREONA, the ealdorman of MERCIA, fled the battlefield, taking his men with him. The scale of the disaster is apparent from the number of men of rank killed, including a bishop, an abbot, three ealdorman and the son of an ealdorman; Edmund himself was seriously wounded. According to the ANGLO-SAXON CHRONICLE, 'all the flower of the English nation' was slain there. Shortly afterwards, Edmund made peace with Cnut by the treaty of ALNEY.

Äskekärr ship A long-distance trading ship or *knarr* discovered in the River Göta Älv on the west coast of SWEDEN, dating from *c*.980. Its dimensions – 16 metres long, 4.5 metres broad and 2.5 metres deep – are almost identical to those of the 11th-century *knarr* discovered at SKULDELEV in DENMARK. The ship's cargo-carrying capacity was about 24 tonnes. Together with the almost exactly contemporary KLÅSTAD ship from NORWAY, the Äskekärr ship is the earliest trading vessel so far discovered in Scandinavia, and the earliest to rely entirely on sail for propulsion.

Askold and Dir (*fl. c*.860–82) Two RUS chieftains who, according to the *RUSSIAN PRIMARY CHRONICLE*,

Ceremonial axe with
silver-and-gold inlaid
Mammen-style decoration,
from Jutland, Denmark.

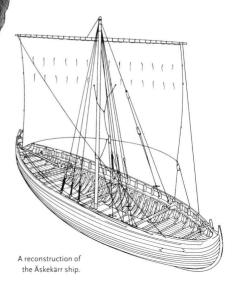

A delicate silver brooch
in the Urnes art style,
from Lindholm Høje,
Denmark.

A reconstruction of
the Äskekärr ship.

came to RUSSIA with RURIK. The two seized control of KIEV from the Polyani (a Slav tribe) around the time that Rurik took control of NOVGOROD (c.862). The *Chronicle* credits them with leading the savage Rus attack on Constantinople in 860 and with becoming Christians in 867. Askold and Dir were both killed by Rurik's kinsman OLEG when he captured Kiev and made it the Rus capital c.882.

Athelstan (c.895–939) King of WESSEX (r. 924–39) and the first Anglo-Saxon king to have effective rule over the whole of ENGLAND. The son of EDWARD THE ELDER, king of Wessex, Athelstan was brought up in MERCIA by his aunt ÆTHELFLÆD, the lady of the Mercians. On his father's death in 924, Athelstan was elected king in both Wessex and Mercia. On the death of its king, SIHTRIC CÁECH, in 927 Athelstan seized YORK and received the submission of the Northumbrians, so completing the West Saxon takeover of all England. Athelstan's growing power united against him a strong coalition of OLAF GUTHFRITHSSON, king of DUBLIN and claimant to the throne of York, CONSTANTINE II, king of the Scots, and the Britons of STRATHCLYDE. Athelstan decisively routed the allies at the battle of BRUNANBURH in 937. Regarded as a mighty king by his contemporaries, Athelstan enjoyed close relations with many European rulers, and he married his half-sisters into the royal houses of France, Germany and Burgundy. Athelstan never married and was succeeded by his half-brother EDMUND.

Aud the Deep-Minded (*fl.* late 9th century) The most famous female settler of ICELAND, where she was the founder of a great FAMILY in Laxardale, Aud was the daughter of KETIL FLATNOSE, who ruled the Hebrides in the mid-9th century, and the wife of OLAF THE WHITE, a Norse ruler in IRELAND. After the deaths of her husband and father, Aud joined her son THORSTEIN THE RED in Caithness, and then, after Thorstein was killed by the Scots, she emigrated with her retinue to Iceland, arranging advantageous marriages for her granddaughters in ORKNEY and the FAROE ISLANDS on the way. The attraction of Iceland for Aud was undoubtedly that the absence of a hostile indigenous population made it possible for a woman to claim land there and hold it securely. She settled at Breiðafjörður in western Iceland, distributing land among her retinue and freed slaves. Aud was regarded in Icelandic tradition as one of the leading figures of the settlement period and is the dominant character in the opening chapters of the 13th-century *LAXDÆLA SAGA*.

The death of Balder, from a 17th-century Icelandic manuscript.

Balder (Baldr) Scandinavian sun-god, the son of ODIN and FRIGG. According to SNORRI STURLUSON'S *EDDA*, Balder was a genial, beautiful and popular god, loved by everyone in ASGARD with the sole exception of the malicious god LOKI. Frigg had made all nature swear never to harm Balder, and the gods often amused themselves by throwing missiles at him, knowing that they could not hurt him. However, Loki learned that Frigg had overlooked the mistletoe. Placing a shaft of mistletoe in the hand of one of Balder's brothers, the blind god HODER, Loki guided Hoder's aim, which struck Balder dead. Balder was burned on a funeral pyre with his ship *Hringhorni* and his wife Nanna, who had died of grief. Odin placed the magic ring Draupnir on the pyre as a parting gift. Another of Balder's brothers, HERMOD, rode to the realm of the dead and HEL agreed to restore Balder to life only if all things living and dead wept for him. Loki alone, disguised as an ancient giantess, refused to weep and Balder remained in the underworld. In the version of the myth recorded by SAXO GRAMMATICUS, Balder is also killed by Hoder, but in this case the two are rivals for the hand of Nanna.

Balts A group of peoples that settled on the south-eastern shores of the Baltic Sea. The origins of the Balts, who speak Indo-European LANGUAGES related to Slavic, can be traced back to *c.*1800 BC. The term 'Balt' was coined only in the 19th century and is derived from the name of the sea; in Roman times they were known collectively as the Aesti. The modern Balts are the Lithuanians and the Latvians (or Letts), but in the Middle Ages they also included the Prussians (assimilated to the Germans by the 18th century), the Curonians (assimilated to the Latvians by the 16th century),

the Semigallians and the Selonians (extinct by the 16th century).

In the Viking Age the Balts had not travelled far down the road of political centralization. Each people was divided into several tribes that rarely cooperated with one another, even for warfare. The Balts built substantial earthwork fortresses, and their tools and WEAPONS were comparable with those used elsewhere in northern Europe. They were a largely self-sufficient farming people, but AMBER, slaves, furs, wax and honey were exported in exchange for silver. The Vikings both raided the Balts and traded with them. Scandinavian merchants were established at the ports of GROBIN in Courland (Latvia) by the mid-8th century and at ELBLAG in Prussia in the 9th. The *Life of St* ANSGAR mentions that the SVEAR went on tribute-gathering raids in the area in the mid-9th century. Much of the Arabic silver that flooded into GOTLAND and mainland SWEDEN in the 10th century is thought to have been paid as tribute by the Balts. However, the Balts could not be permanently subjugated by the Vikings, and by 1100 they had become pirates themselves, raiding the Swedish coast for plunder and slaves. The Balts strongly resisted attempts, beginning in 997, to convert them to CHRISTIANITY and were the last European peoples to abandon paganism, the Lithuanians not converting until 1386.

M. Gimbutas, *The Balts* (London, 1963).

Beaduheard (d. *c.*789) Reeve of king Beorhtric of WESSEX. Beaduheard has the unfortunate distinction of being the earliest named victim of the Vikings, killed at PORTLAND in Dorset *c.*789 when he mistook Norwegian pirates for merchants and ordered them to go to the nearby royal manor at Dorchester.

A berserker bites his shield in fury, from the Lewis chess set.

Inside the fort at Birka; the 'Black Earth' settlement area lies in the background.

Beocca (d. 871–2?) Abbot of Chertsey Abbey, Surrey. Beocca, his priest Edor (or Hethor) and ninety monks are said to have been killed by pagans in the second half of the 9th century. It is not clear whether the attack took place in the 850s or in 871–2, when the Danish GREAT ARMY wintered at London. By the early 11th century, both Beocca and Edor were regarded as saints. Chertsey Abbey survived the Viking attack and was flourishing at the end of the 9th century.

Bergen Originally called Bjørgvin, the city was founded in 1070 by king Olaf III (OLAF THE PEACEFUL) on a sheltered fjord on NORWAY's west coast. About 1100 a castle was built to dominate the harbour, and around the same time Bergen became the seat of a BISHOPRIC. The city quickly grew in commercial and political importance. It was Norway's capital in the 12th and 13th centuries and became the leading centre for the export of stockfish to ENGLAND and Flanders. In the 14th century, the German Hanseatic League acquired control over Bergen's TRADE; its influence lasted into the 18th century. Bergen has remained the most important port on the west coast of Norway.

berserker ('bear shirt') A ferocious Viking warrior. Before battle, berserkers worked themselves into a trancelike rage (*berserksgangr*, i.e. 'going berserk'), involving much howling and shield-biting, which gave them animal strength and ferocity. They fought without armour but their battle rage left them immune to the pain of wounds. They believed that their special powers were a gift of the high god ODIN. Berserkers frequently appear in Icelandic SAGAS – often as outlaws or bullying bodyguards, sometimes with supernatural powers – where they

provide suitable opponents against which the hero can prove himself. They are always dangerous and prone to uncontrollable rages. In a story from *EGILS SAGA*, Egil's father, a berserker, gets overexcited in a ball game and kills a maid and almost kills his son before he calms down again. *Berserksgangr* was in fact outlawed in the 12th-century Icelandic LAW book *Grágás* as a threat to public order.

The origins of the berserker are probably to be found in Germanic prehistory. The earliest use of the term *berserkr* comes from a late-9th-century poem by Thorbjorn hornklofi, *Haraldskvæði*, which describes an élite troop of *berserkir* in the service of king HARALD FAIRHAIR. However, in another poem Thorbjorn equates the berserkers with the *Úlfheðnar* ('wolf skins'). These can be identified with the German *Wolfhetan* warriors, a term known from the 8th century. There are also representations of warriors dressed in animal skins on decorative metalwork, dating from the 6th and 7th centuries, from SWEDEN and Germany. In his *Germania*, the 1st-century Roman writer Tacitus describes several similar élite groups of fanatical warriors, which are possible prototypes for the berserkers. Berserkers are sometimes represented not simply as warriors who wore animal skins but as shape shifters, as in *Hrólfs saga*, in which the champion Bjarki fought in the form of a bear while his human form slept.

Birka Viking Age port on the island of Björkö in Lake Mälaren, SWEDEN. Birka developed in the late 8th century and flourished until the late 10th century, when it was abandoned in favour of nearby SIGTUNA. The TOWN was situated on the west side of the island, and at its greatest extent covered approximately 13 hectares. The occupation deposits

Ruins of the Pictish and Norse settlements on Birsay.

known as *Svarta Jorden* ('Black Earth') are up to 2 metres thick and have produced abundant information about the buildings and the daily life of the town. Birka was protected by a rampart and hill-fort in the 10th century, and a row of wooden piles restricted access into the main harbour. The town was divided into plots of land, delineated by passageways flanked by ditches. Each plot contained one or two houses and several outbuildings used as workshops and stores. The buildings were timber framed with walls of wattle-and-daub and roofs of thatch, wood and, occasionally, turf. Many of the inhabitants were merchants, but there were also craftsmen in metals, JEWELRY and furs, and warriors. Considerable quantities of Arabic COINS suggest that Birka's most important TRADE links were with the east, especially after *c*.900, but Rhineland POTTERY and GLASS and scraps of Frisian woollen cloth are evidence of links to the west too. A complete absence of Anglo-Saxon coins suggests that Birka had been abandoned by the time ÆTHELRED THE UNREADY began paying enormous sums in DANEGELD to the Vikings in the 990s. Birka is surrounded by cemeteries containing more than 3,000 graves, about 1,100 of which have been excavated. Most burials were cremations. The richness of the grave goods are unparalleled for their quantity and quality.

St ANSGAR visited Birka in 829–30 and established a small Christian community there, but a few years later the clergy were driven out and one priest was killed. Ansgar re-established a Christian presence in 851–2. Further missionary work was undertaken by archbishop Unne of Bremen, who died there in 936, but CHRISTIANITY had little impact. Birka had a long-lasting influence on Swedish LAW, as medieval Swedish towns were governed by the *Bjärköarätt* (Birka Law). Medieval

Norwegian municipal laws, the *BJARKEYJAR RÉTTUR*, were also named after Birka.

Birsay, brough of A small island off the north-west coast of Mainland, ORKNEY. On the east side of the island is an extensive Pictish and Norse settlement. The Pictish settlement was centred on a CHURCH; an impressive symbol stone and evidence of high-quality metalworking have been discovered. The Norse settlement was built directly on top of the Pictish settlement and reused many of the building materials. The earliest Norse buildings date from the 10th century and include several well-preserved hall houses, one of which had a bathhouse. There are also the ruins of a fine early 12th-century church. Birsay is described in the ORKNEYINGA SAGA as a major political and ecclesiastical centre in the 12th and 13th centuries.

bishoprics The organization of Scandinavia into dioceses began with the appointment of missionary bishops for RIBE, ÅRHUS and Schleswig in the kingdom of DENMARK by the German king Otto I in 948. Otto's motives were largely political: he hoped to use the organization of the Church to consolidate German influence in Denmark. A bishopric was created for ODENSE, also in Denmark, by 988. The new bishoprics were placed formally under the authority of the archbishopric of Hamburg-Bremen, which had been given control over missionary activity in Denmark and SWEDEN by pope Gregory IV in the 830s (extended to the rest of Scandinavia in 1053). There is no evidence that any of these early bishops actually took up their sees, and the effective organization of Denmark into regular dioceses was begun by CNUT (r. 1019–35). He hoped to keep the Danish Church independent of German influence

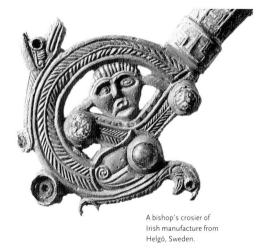

A bishop's crosier of Irish manufacture from Helgö, Sweden.

The most remote Norse episcopal seat, at Garðar, Greenland.

and had a bishop of ROSKILDE consecrated by the archbishop of Canterbury in 1022. However, he was soon forced to accept the authority of Hamburg-Bremen. By 1060 all eight dioceses of medieval Denmark – Århus, Børglum, LUND, Odense, Ribe, Roskilde, Schleswig and VIBORG – had been founded. In NORWAY and Sweden, bishops, such as king OLAF HARALDSSON's bishop Grimkell, remained itinerant members of the royal household well into the 11th century. The first regular sees to be founded in Norway were at TRONDHEIM in 1029 and BERGEN c.1100. The first Swedish bishoprics were founded at Skara c.1014 and SIGTUNA c.1060, but the diocesan organization of Sweden was not completed until c.1170. The first bishopric in ICELAND was founded at Skálholt in 1056, and the second was at Hólar in 1106. Bishoprics were founded for the FAROE ISLANDS at Kirkjubøur c.1100, and for Greenland at Garðar in 1124. The seat of an earlier bishop of Greenland who, according to the contemporary Icelandic LANDNÁMABÓK, went on a voyage to VINLAND in 1121, is unknown. Despite vigorous opposition from Hamburg-Bremen and the German monarchy, both of which resented this diminution of their influence in the region, Scandinavia became a Church province in its own right when Lund was raised to an archbishopric in 1103 or 1104. New archbishoprics were created for Norway and Sweden later in the 12th century. Until the mid-12th century most bishops in Scandinavia were either German or English.

Bjarkeyjar réttur (Bjarkøy LAWS) The earliest known municipal law codes of NORWAY. First recorded in the late 12th century, they developed out of codes governing merchants and seafarers in the late Viking Age. Only two fragments of these have survived, both from the TRONDHEIM version of the laws, dating from c.1250. The laws are named after the Swedish TOWN of BIRKA.

Bjarni Herjolfsson (*fl. c.*985) The first European known to have sighted the North American continent. An Icelandic merchant and navigator, Bjarni returned home from a voyage to NORWAY in 985–6 to find that his father had emigrated to GREENLAND with ERIK THE RED. Knowing only that Greenland was a mountainous, glaciated land with good pastures and no trees, Bjarni set out after him, but was blown off course in bad weather and found himself off the coast of a low, forested land (Labrador). Sailing north, he sighted a mountainous, glaciated but barren land (Baffin Island?), before sailing east and making landfall in Greenland, where he settled as a farmer. Bjarni was much criticized at the time for not investigating his discoveries, but he was not an explorer and can hardly be blamed for not wishing to endanger his ship and crew.

Bjorn Ironside (*fl. c.*860) A 9th-century Viking leader first mentioned by the late-11th-century Norman writer William of Jumièges, probably to be identified with Bjorn, a Viking chief who is known from contemporary Frankish sources to have been active on the Seine in 858. According to William, Bjorn was the son of king Lothbroc – perhaps the legendary RAGNAR LODBROK – who forced him into exile with his tutor Hasting (HASTEIN). Bjorn and Hasting raided in FRANCIA and the MEDITERRANEAN between 859 and 862, after which they split up. Bjorn returned to Scandinavia and later went to FRISIA, where he died. Bjorn earned his nickname 'Ironside' because his mother had given him a magic potion that supposedly made him invulnerable to WEAPONS.

The remains of a boathouse at Nordbø Rennesøy, Rogaland, Norway.

Bláland Term used by Viking Age Scandinavians to describe North Africa. Moors from North Africa and Spain who were taken prisoner during HASTEIN's and BJORN IRONSIDE's Viking raids in the MEDITERRANEAN (859–62) and who finished up on the Dublin slave market were described as blue men (Norse *blámenn*, Irish *fir gorm*).

Blathmacc mac Flaind (d. 825) A monk of Irish royal descent from IONA. Faced with frequent Viking attacks, the main body of monks at Iona retreated to the (marginally) greater safety of Kells in IRELAND in 807. Blathmacc remained behind as prior of a token community of monks who were prepared, if necessary, to face martyrdom. When the Vikings returned in 825 Blathmacc was tortured and killed after refusing to reveal the hiding place of the precious shrine of St Columba. A detailed account of Blathmacc's martyrdom, in Latin verse, was written by Walafrid Strabo, the abbot of the German monastery of Reichenau (838–49).

blood eagle Gruesome method of human sacrifice to ODIN, named after the practice of cutting open the ribcage on either side of the spine, after which the still-living victim's lungs were torn out to form the shape of an eagle's wings. The practice is known from several Icelandic sources, the earliest of which is SIGHVATR THÓRĐARSON's poem *Knútsdrápa*, composed *c*.1038, which describes the killing of Ella by the sons of RAGNAR LODBROK almost 200 years previously. Because of the lateness of the sources, many historians are inclined to conclude that the blood eagle was a literary invention, derived from the use of the eagle in poetry as a symbol of battlefield slaughter, rather than a real practice. However, the pagan Scandinavians did practise human sacrifice

and it would be perverse to believe that the Vikings were incapable of inflicting cruel tortures on their enemies. As has been pointed out, the blood eagle is no more horrifying than the old English punishment for traitors of hanging, drawing and quartering.

boat burial *see* SHIP BURIAL

boathouses It was customary in northern Europe to haul boats and SHIPS ashore for the winter. In many areas they were simply left out of doors in sheltered boat-shaped hollows, known as nousts, but more than 150 boathouses dating from the ROMAN IRON AGE to the later Middle Ages have been identified in west and north NORWAY. Most are small – less than 10 metres in length – and were probably used to store farmers' fishing boats, but there are many between 20 and 35 metres that were clearly intended to store longships. There is a close correlation between the size and proportions of Viking Age boathouses and preserved ships of the period, such as those discovered at OSEBERG and GOKSTAD, suggesting that these ships were fairly representative of those used in the region at the time. There is little evidence of Viking Age boathouses from DENMARK and SWEDEN; possible examples have been found in Denmark at Harrevig on Limfjord and on the island of Sejrø. It may be that boathouses were little used in Denmark and Sweden, or they may have been built without the stone-and-turf supporting walls that make the Norwegian boathouses so easy to identify. A boathouse has also been excavated at Westness on the ORKNEY island of Rousay.

B. Myhre, 'Boathouses and naval organization', in A. Nørgård Jørgensen and B. L. Clausen (eds), *Military Aspects of Scandinavian Society in a European Perspective*, AD 1–1300 (Copenhagen, 1997).

A fortified church at Østerlars, Bornholm. The roof is a later addition; originally the top was crenellated.

Erik the Red's farmstead at Brattahild, Greenland.

Borg An early Viking Age (8th–9th centuries) chieftain's farm on Vestvågøy, Lofoten Islands, NORWAY. An 80-metre-long hall was built on a low hill with good views over the surrounding countryside and easy access to the sea. The owners possessed gold and silver objects, and POTTERY, GLASS cups and jugs made in the Rhineland. Nearby were an open-air court site and a large boathouse. Finds of votive gold plaques suggest that Borg was also a religious centre. The FAMILY's main activities were farming and fishing, but it is known from literary sources that the chieftains of this area frequently traded with, and raided, the LAPP peoples of the Arctic.

Bornholm Danish island in the Baltic Sea. Bornholm prospered during the earlier GERMANIC IRON AGE (AD 400–800), perhaps from control of the Baltic sea lanes, but had declined by its end. The market, craft and religious centre at Sorte Muld on the south coast may have been the centre of a chiefdom that dominated the island through most of this period. Bornholm was slow to be incorporated into the kingdom of DENMARK. It was still ruled by its own king as late as c.890, and paganism still flourished there in the late 11th century. Because of its exposed position, Bornholm suffered severely from Wendish pirate raids in the late Viking Age: in the 12th century, strongly fortified CHURCHES doubled as refuges.

Borre Major Viking Age cemetery, north of OSEBERG in Vestfold, traditionally associated with the royal house of NORWAY. It contains nine large – up to 50 metres in diameter – burial mounds from the early Viking Age, the largest concentration of such mounds in Scandinavia. During the 19th century,

gravel diggers discovered a ship in one mound and recovered rich grave goods, including gilt-bronze harness mounts, dating from c.900. The size of the mounds and their rich furnishings are a sign of the growing power of the Vestfold kings in the century before the accession of HARALD FAIRHAIR.

Bragi In Scandinavian mythology, Bragi was the god of poetry. His main duty was to prepare VALHALLA for the reception of fallen heroes. He was the son of the high god ODIN and FRIGG, and the husband of IDUN.

Brattahlid (Qagssiarssuk) The site of the farmstead founded by ERIK THE RED, the founder of the Norse GREENLAND colony c.986. Brattahlid became the focus of the Norse Greenlanders' Eastern Settlement. The remains of three large stone farmsteads, a THING place and a stone CHURCH are visible today. Most of the stone structures date from the 13th or 14th centuries. The remains of a small turf church, founded (according to *Eiriks saga*) by Erik's wife Thjodhild after she was converted to CHRISTIANITY by their son LEIF ERIKSSON, have been excavated.

Bråvalla, battle of (Brávellir) Famous legendary battle, traditionally believed to have been fought near Bråviken Fjord, Östergötland, SWEDEN, between Danish king Harald Hyldetan ('Wartooth') and his nephew Ring (or Hring). Harald united DENMARK into a single kingdom, and placed his nephew Ring as subking of Sweden. The god ODIN sowed dissent between Harald and Ring. Though old and blind, Harald invaded Sweden with a countless host but was betrayed on the battlefield by Odin who, having disguised himself as Harald's charioteer, battered

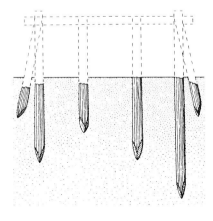

A 10th-century bridge at Ravning Enge, Jutland.

A rune-stone raised by the Swedish landowner Jarlabanke to commemorate his construction of a causeway over a marsh in Uppland, Sweden.

him to death with his club. Assuming the story has a basis in fact, the battle probably took place around the beginning of the 8th century, though dates of up to 200 years earlier have been proposed.

Brian Boru (Brian Bóraime) (926–1014) High king of IRELAND (r. 1002–14). Brian was a younger brother of king Mathgamain of Dál Cais and Munster in south-west Ireland. Brian is commonly credited with destroying Viking power in Ireland, but by the time he took part in his first battle against them, during Mathgamain's conquest of the LIMERICK Vikings in 968, their power was already waning fast. In 976 Brian unexpectedly became king of Dál Cais after Mathgamain was murdered in Munster. Brian first defeated an attempt by the Vikings to re-establish themselves at Limerick in 977, and then the following year defeated and killed his brother's murderer, Maél Muad, who had seized power in Munster. In 984 Brian began to extend his authority over the south of Ireland, imposing tributary status on the neighbouring kingdom of Ossory. By 997 Brian was strong enough to force the Uí Néill high king Maél Sechnaill II to recognize him as overlord of the southern half of Ireland. A rebellion by Leinster and the DUBLIN Vikings was easily defeated by Brian in 1000, and two years later he defeated Maél Sechnaill and replaced him as high king. By 1004 all the Irish kingdoms had become tributary to Brian (hence his nickname *bóraime*, 'of the tributes'). In 1013 Leinster and Dublin again rebelled and called in as allies a Viking force from MAN and ORKNEY. Brian defeated the coalition at the battle of CLONTARF in 1014, but was himself killed. In the aftermath of the battle, Brian's tributaries rebelled, and Maél Sechnaill was restored as high

king. Brian was rightly regarded as a great king in his own time, but his reputation has been posthumously inflated through the skilful propagandizing of the anonymous 12th-century author of the *COGADH GAEDHEL RE GALLAIBH* ('The War of the Irish with the Foreigners'), who exploited his memory to enhance the reputation of his descendants, the Ua Briain (O'Brien) dynasty of Munster.

bridges Bridge-building was unknown in Scandinavia before the late Viking Age. The earliest known bridge in Scandinavia carried the *Hærvej* (the 'Army Road') over the Vejle Å on Ravning Enge near JELLING in Jutland. The oak bridge, dated by dendrochronology to *c*.978, was 700 metres long by 5.5 metres wide, and was supported on more than 1,500 massive oak piles. There is no evidence that the bridge was ever repaired, so it was probably in use for fewer than fifteen years. Most likely, the bridge was built by HARALD BLUETOOTH, who built the chain of TRELLEBORG forts around the same time. The bridge may have been intended as a magnificent entrance to the royal centre at Jelling, but tolls may have been charged for crossing it. Other bridges in DENMARK of this period are known at Risby and Varpelev in Sjælland and Falgård in Jutland. Several bridges and causeways are known from SWEDEN in the late Viking Age. One of the best known is Jarlabanke's causeway at Täby in Uppland. Built over a boggy hollow, the causeway was 150 metres long and 6.5 metres wide, and was edged with raised stones. Two rune-stones on each bank commemorate Jarlabanke's achievement. Increasing TRADE and the need to improve communications for churchgoing and royal administration were probably the main reasons for the sudden interest in bridge-

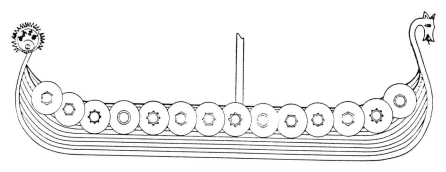

A speculative reconstruction of the longship from the burial on Îsle de Groix, Brittany, one of the few tangible reminders of the Viking presence there. Only metal parts – nails, rivets, stern decorations and shield bosses – survived the cremation.

building in the late Viking Age. It is likely that the Scandinavians learned the skills needed from the WENDS of the southern Baltic coast, where large-scale bridge-building had been practised for centuries. *See also* ROADS; TRANSPORT, LAND.

Brittany, Vikings in For most of the early Middle Ages, Brittany was an independent state whose Celtic population fiercely resisted all attempts by the FRANKS to annex it. Though Brittany suffered its share of raids in the 9th century, Viking attentions were focused on the rich valleys of the Loire and Seine, and it escaped relatively lightly. The main threat came from the Vikings on the Loire, who in 847 and 888 temporarily occupied parts of the area. But the Breton dukes were good war leaders, and the Vikings were unable to gain a permanent foothold. Several Breton dukes made temporary alliances with the Vikings when it suited them. In 866 duke Salomon allied with the Vikings, and at Brissarthe defeated and killed the Frankish count ROBERT OF ANGERS. In 875 duke Pascwethen employed Viking mercenaries in a civil war.

Following the death of duke Alan the Great in 907, Viking interest in Brittany increased. The power vacuum that now developed in the country suddenly made it very attractive to the Vikings, and from 912 it suffered constant attacks. In 913 the famous monastery of St-Winwaloe at Landévennec was completely destroyed, and its monks fled with their precious relics to FRANCIA. Within a few years most Breton monasteries had been abandoned by their terrified monks. Breton resistance collapsed completely in 919; most of the leading Breton families fled to England or Francia, and the Vikings under ROGNVALD conquered the entire country.

Their conquest seems to have been a purely military takeover: there is no evidence of any Scandinavian rural settlement in Brittany or of Viking TRADE. The Vikings' capital, Nantes, whose position at the mouth of the Loire should have enabled it to become a successful trading centre, became semi-derelict during their occupation. In 931 a Breton rebellion was put down, but it encouraged ALAN BARBETORTE, an exile in England, to launch an invasion in 936, and by 939 Brittany had been cleared of Vikings. Coastal raids continued into the 11th century, the last known being an attack on Dol in 1014.

The authority and independence of the Breton dukes never recovered from the Vikings' occupation of Brittany, and in the 11th century the region became a dependency of Normandy. The short Viking presence has left few traces in Brittany. A 10th-century SHIP BURIAL has been discovered on Îsle de GROIX, and Viking WEAPONS and other artefacts have been excavated from a circular fort at Camp de Péran near Saint-Brieuc. The fort was destroyed by fire in the 930s, possibly in the course of Alan Barbetorte's reconquest.

N. Price, *The Vikings in Brittany*, Viking Society for Northern Research, Saga Book 22 (1986–9), pp. 319–440.

Brunanburh, battle of (937) Crushing victory of ATHELSTAN, king of WESSEX, over a coalition of DUBLIN Vikings, Scots and STRATHCLYDE Britons led by OLAF GUTHFRITHSSON of Dublin, at an unidentified location, probably in northern ENGLAND. The battle was fought from dawn till dusk; when Olaf's ARMY broke it was pursued by the West Saxons and Mercians, who cut down the fugitives. Though West Saxon losses were heavy, Olaf's army was cut to pieces and he himself barely

The Alfredian *burh* at Wallingford, Berkshire, built to protect an important crossing of the Thames.

Opposite: A rich warrior burial from Birka, Sweden, containing weapons and sacrificed horses.

escaped. Among the dead were five minor Norse kings, seven jarls and Cellach, the son of king CONSTANTINE II of the Scots. Olaf's aim had been to recapture YORK, seized by Athelstan in 927, and to curb the growing power of Wessex. Athelstan's victory was therefore an important step in the creation of a unified English kingdom.

Brynhild A VALKYRIE and lover of the hero SIGURD FAFNISBANE, Brynhild lived in a hall surrounded by magic fire. She was put into a permanent sleep by ODIN as a punishment for striking down king Hjalmgunnar in battle, when the god had promised him victory. She was awakened from her sleep by Sigurd, and they became lovers. But after being given a magic potion, Sigurd forgot Brynhild and married Gudrun instead. Brynhild later married Gudrun's brother Gunnar but was enraged when she discovered that it had actually been Sigurd, disguised as her future husband, who had wooed her. In revenge for the deception, she arranged Sigurd's murder, but at once repented her action and immolated herself on his funeral pyre.

Bulgars A Turkic nomad people that migrated onto the steppes of south-east Europe in the 6th century AD. Around the middle of the 7th century the Bulgars divided into two branches. One crossed the River Danube and founded a khanate in the Balkans *c.*679. The Danube Bulgars were strongly influenced by the native Slavs and the neighbouring Byzantine Empire. By the 9th century, their LANGUAGE had been replaced by Slavic, and in 864 they were converted to Orthodox CHRISTIANITY. The Danube Bulgars were briefly conquered by the RUS under SVYATOSLAV I in 969–71, and then by the Byzantines in 1018. They regained their independence in the

13th century, only to be conquered by the Ottoman Turks in 1393. The modern state of Bulgaria is named after them. The second branch of the Bulgars settled on the middle Volga, and their capital, Bulgar, became an important Viking Age trading centre where Finnish and Rus merchants exchanged slaves, furs and wax for silver with Arab merchants. The Volga Bulgars converted to Islam *c.*922. In 1237 they were conquered by the Mongols and thereafter gradually lost their identity as a people.

Burgred (d. after 874) King of MERCIA (r. 852–74). A successful Viking attack on London in 851 led Burgred to seek closer relations with WESSEX soon after his accession. In 853 an alliance was sealed when Burgred married a daughter of king Æthelwulf of Wessex. When Mercia was invaded by the Danish GREAT ARMY in 868 the West Saxons joined Burgred in an unsuccessful siege of its base at Nottingham. The Great Army withdrew but returned in 872 and occupied REPTON the next year. Burgred was forced to abdicate and he went into exile at Rome, where he died. He was succeeded by CEOLWULF II, a Danish puppet king.

burhs Anglo-Saxon fortified settlements, built mostly in the late 9th and early 10th centuries as a response to Viking attacks. The first *burhs* were built at the end of the 8th century in the Midland kingdom of MERCIA, but their systematic use as defensive centres began under ALFRED THE GREAT (r. 871–99). In the 880s Alfred established a network of thirty *burhs* across Wessex so that no part of the kingdom was more than 32 kilometres from one. There were two categories of *burh*. The largest were planned as permanent settlements and market centres, most of which

developed into successful TOWNS. There was also a category of smaller *burhs* that were intended only as temporary forts: most of these were probably abandoned by the mid-10th century. Some *burhs*, such as South Cadbury, were sited to take advantage of surviving Iron Age FORTIFICATIONS; others, such as Bath, Chichester, Exeter and Winchester, made use of old Roman fortifications. *Burhs* such as Wallingford and Wareham had defences that were modelled on Roman forts; many others utilized natural defences. Each *burh* was given a TAX assessment and a garrison of peasant levies according to length of its walls. The formula, recorded in the *Burghal Hidage*, compiled *c*.914–18, was that four men were needed to man each pole (about 5 metres) of wall, and that one man should be supplied by each hide (the area of land needed to support one peasant FAMILY). Thus Wareham, whose defences are 400 poles (about 2,000 metres) long, was assigned 1,600 hides of land. The defences were usually built of clay or turf, topped with a timber palisade, though in a few cases these ramparts were rebuilt in stone in the 10th century. Alfred's son and successor EDWARD THE ELDER (r. 899–924) and daughter ÆTHELFLÆD, lady of the Mercians, methodically extended the system of *burhs* to consolidate their conquest of the DANELAW.

burial customs At the beginning of the Viking Age, cremation was the normal method of disposing of the dead throughout Scandinavia. The deceased were cremated on wooden pyres in their everyday clothes, together with any grave goods intended for their use in the afterlife. Afterwards, the burned remains were either simply scattered on the ground or buried in a POTTERY urn. Graves were marked by

earth mounds, cairns of stones or by stone SHIP SETTINGS. The quantity and quality of grave goods (some people were buried with none) and the size of the mound or cairn over the grave depended on the social status of the individual. The objects placed in graves were sometimes ritually 'killed': for example, a sword might be bent, and FURNITURE, broken up. In the 9th century inhumation began to be practised in DENMARK, GOTLAND and at BIRKA in SWEDEN. The wealthy were buried in timber-lined pits known as chamber graves. The body was laid out fully clothed and surrounded by grave goods and sometimes horses and even human sacrifices. According to the Arab writer Ibn Rustah, who visited Russia *c*.922, wives were sometimes interred alive with their deceased husbands. The common people were buried either in simple birch-bark shrouds or plain wooden coffins with token grave goods such as worn household tools and old jewelry. As was the case with cremations, the grave would be marked with a mound or cairn. The most famous Viking Age burials, the royal and aristocratic SHIP BURIALS, included both inhumations and cremations and were marked like other burials with mounds or cairns. Whether the ship had any particular religious significance in these burials is debated. Pagan burial practices had died out by the early 11th century, replaced by the Christian custom of inhumation without grave goods.

It is known from written sources that burial was preceded by elaborate rituals. The 10th-century Arab writer Ibn Fadlan, who witnessed the funeral of a RUS chief on the River Volga, described rituals that lasted over several days, culminating in the male relatives having ritual intercourse with a slave girl, who was then sacrificed and cremated with her master. It was normal to treat a corpse with great

C

care, as it was believed that the dead could return to haunt the living if they were not shown respect. *See also* PAGAN RELIGION.

Byrhtnoth (d. 991) Ealdorman of Essex (956–91). He was responsible for the defence of EAST ANGLIA in 991, when he was killed by Vikings under OLAF TRYGGVASON at the battle of MALDON. Byrhtnoth's death is commemorated in one of the finest and most moving Old English epic poems, *The Battle of Maldon*.

Carolingian Empire The Frankish empire founded by CHARLEMAGNE (r. 768–814), comprising most of Germany, France, Switzerland, Austria, the Low Countries, Italy and parts of Spain and Hungary. The empire passed intact to Charlemagne's sole surviving son, LOUIS THE PIOUS, but after his death it was divided according to Frankish custom between his three sons by the treaty of Verdun in 843. The empire survived through a succession of divisions until it was reunited under CHARLES THE FAT (r. 881–7), on whose death it broke up for good.

Ceolwulf II (d. 879) The last king of MERCIA (r. 874–9). According to the *ANGLO-SAXON CHRONICLE*, Ceolwulf was a puppet king of non-royal blood appointed by the DANES after the abdication and exile of king BURGRED. In 877 the Danes partitioned Mercia between Ceolwulf and themselves, the Danes taking the eastern half for settlement. After Ceolwulf's death, Mercia came increasingly under the domination of WESSEX.

Cerball mac Dúnlainge (ON Kjarval) (d. 888) King of Ossory (Irish Osraige) in south-central IRELAND (r. 842–88). Cerball showed a pragmatic attitude to the Viking invaders, warring with them when necessary but also allying with them against his Irish rivals. Cerball briefly made his minor kingdom a major player in Ireland when, in 859, he allied with IVAR I and OLAF, the Norse leaders of DUBLIN, against the powerful southern Uí Néill king Maél Sechnaill. He fought other Vikings with some success. In 862, with the king of Loígis, he destroyed a Viking *LONGPHORT* at Dunrally on the River Barrow. In 864 Cerball defeated a Viking ARMY after a raid on the monastery of Leighlin, but in 869 he was himself defeated by the Hebridean Vikings in a

Above: Silver *denier* of
Charlemagne, minted at
Bourges, France.

The Frankish king
Charles the Bald,
from a contemporary
manuscript.

sea battle off Barra. He married one of his daughters
to Olaf and another to Eyvindr Eastman, a
Hebridean Viking whose son Helgi the Lean was
one of the first settlers of ICELAND. According to
LANDNÁMABÓK, many Icelanders were proud to
claim descent from Cerball through these marriages,
and his grandson Dubthach (ON Dufthak) was
himself the founder of an Icelandic FAMILY.

Charlemagne (742–814) King of the FRANKS
(r. 768–814); 'Roman' emperor (r. 800–14); the
CAROLINGIAN EMPIRE is named after him. During a
reign of almost constant military campaigning,
Charlemagne unified most of western Europe under
his control, conquering the Saxons and Lombards
and making further territorial gains at the expense of
the Slavs, Avars, Byzantines and Spanish Muslims,
doubling the size of the Frankish realm. A devout
Christian, he vigorously suppressed Saxon paganism
and promoted Church reform and the revival of
learning known as the 'Carolingian Renaissance'.
He was also an active legislator. The exact
significance of Charlemagne's imperial coronation
in Rome in 800 is uncertain; he probably believed
that he was refounding the Western Roman Empire.
It was during Charlemagne's reign that the first
Viking raids on FRANCIA were recorded.
Charlemagne reacted vigorously to the beginning of
the raids in 799, creating a coastal defence system
with coastguards, forts and FLEETS stationed on
vulnerable river mouths to prevent forays inland.
Apart from a damaging raid on FRISIA in 810 by the
Danish king GODFRED, these defences were effective
in preventing any serious Viking attacks on the
empire until the 830s. It is quite clear from the
measures taken that Charlemagne fully appreciated
the nature of the Viking threat, but his defensive

system depended entirely on the maintenance of
strong central authority. When this began to break
down in the civil wars of the reign of his successor
LOUIS THE PIOUS, so, too, did the coast defences.

Charles the Bald (823–77) King of the West FRANKS
(r. 843–77); emperor (875–7). The youngest son of
LOUIS THE PIOUS by his second wife, Charles was
resented by his three older half-brothers, whose
inheritance rights he threatened. At the treaty of
Verdun in 843, which ended the civil war that had
broken out on Louis's death, Charles was recognized
as king of the West Franks by his surviving brothers
Lothar and Louis the German.
    Throughout his reign Charles had to contend with
the rivalry of his brothers, rebellious vassals and one
of the worst periods of Viking raiding, which he dealt
with roughly in that order of priority. This has
perplexed many modern scholars; but Charles
intended above all to defend his throne, and, judged
from this perspective, his policy towards the Vikings
is understandable. Viking raids, destructive though
they were, would have been of little consequence to
him if he had allowed his brothers or vassals to
depose and imprison him (or worse). Though his
frequent payments of tribute from 845 only
encouraged more Viking raids in the long term,
they did buy vital time in the short term for Charles
to deal with more serious threats to his authority.
His refusal to sanction the building of castles and
TOWN walls, often seen as perverse, was based on the
well-founded fear that his vassals would use them
against him as much as against the Vikings. Even
when Charles did make the Vikings a priority, the
effectiveness of his actions was often undermined by
rebellion. For example, in 858 Charles was forced to
lift a siege of the Vikings on the island of Oissel on

A 15th-century French manuscript showing king Charles the Simple marrying his daughter to the Viking leader Rollo.

the Seine when rebel vassals invited his brother Louis the German to invade and depose him. The disloyalty of his vassals also meant Charles could not rely on his ARMY; on more than one occasion it simply ran away from the Vikings. Sometimes, though, the Vikings could be more of a help than a hindrance. When the rebellious prince PIPPIN II of Aquitaine failed to prevent the Vikings from sacking Bordeaux in 848 his subjects expelled him and turned to Charles instead.

By the 860s Charles had weathered the worst crises of his reign, and he turned more of his energies to defending the Île de France – where his own estates were concentrated – against the Vikings. In 862 he ordered the construction of fortified BRIDGES over the Seine at PONT DE L'ARCHE, and on other rivers. Despite long delays in their construction, these eventually brought the area a long respite from Viking raids. In 873 Charles won a major battle over the Loire Vikings at Angers, but by this time he had his eye on greater things and failed to follow up the victory with further campaigns. Charles had acquired Lorraine in 870, and there seemed a realistic prospect that he could unite the entire CAROLINGIAN EMPIRE under his sole rule. Charles was crowned emperor in Rome in 875, but his attempt to seize the kingdom of his brother Louis, who died in 876, was defeated and the ultimate prize eluded him. Charles himself died the following year, in the midst of another rebellion by his vassals. He was succeeded by his son Louis the Stammerer.

J. L. Nelson, *Charles the Bald* (London and New York, 1996).

Charles the Fat (839–88) Frankish emperor (r. 881–7). The youngest son of Louis the German, and grandson of CHARLEMAGNE, Charles became

king of Swabia on his father's death in 876. When his brother Carloman abdicated in 879, Charles also became king of Italy. Despite proving an ineffective ruler, failing to counter Saracen raids on Italy, he was crowned emperor by the pope in 881. Charles's acquisition by inheritance of Saxony (882) and the West Frankish kingdom (884–5) briefly reunited the fragmented CAROLINGIAN EMPIRE (excepting Provence, which was held by a usurper) under a single ruler. Charles also proved ineffective at combating the Vikings, failing to press an attack on the Viking camp at Asselt on the Meuse in 882, and granting FRISIA to a Viking chief called Godafrid (882–5). After relieving their year-long siege of PARIS in 886, Charles paid the Vikings tribute and gave them permission to ravage Burgundy. This was apparently to punish the Burgundians for disloyalty, but for the Frankish nobles it was the last straw. Charles was deposed by his ambitious nephew ARNULF in November 887, so beginning the final breakup of the Carolingian Empire. Charles died, probably murdered, soon after.

Charles the Simple (Charles III) (879–929) King of the West FRANKS (r. 898–922), his reign saw the last serious Viking attacks on FRANCIA. A grandson of CHARLES THE BALD, Charles was crowned king in 893, in opposition to king ODO (r. 888–98), but withdrew his claim in 897 after defeat in the civil war that followed. He succeeded to the throne unchallenged after Odo's death the following year. Following the defeat of the Seine Vikings at Chartres in 911, Charles granted the county of Rouen to their leader ROLLO, so establishing what later became the duchy of NORMANDY and ending Viking incursions on the Seine. His attempts to strengthen royal power led to

A Viking child's toy sword, from Staraja Ladoga, Russia.

A tiny child's shoe, from Viking Age York.

his deposition in 922, his imprisonment and, in 929, his murder. Charles's nickname, 'the Simple', means sincere not simple-minded.

children As was the case in most of early medieval Europe, childhood was brief in Viking Age Scandinavia. As in many cultures, children had toys modelled on the adult world, such as miniature ships, domestic animals, tools and weapons, as well as toys such as spinning-tops. Ball games are known from literary sources. Formal education was unknown. For most parents, children were an economic necessity and there are examples from the Icelandic SAGAS of children being given to childless couples for adoption. From an early age, children were expected to work in the FAMILY enterprise, whether that be a farm, a craft or a business. At first, girls and boys were given simple tasks, gradually learning the skills that were considered appropriate to their gender, for example spinning and WEAVING for girls, ploughing or metalworking for boys. By their early teens, both boys and girls would have entered fully into adult life. In aristocratic and royal society, boys could expect to take an active part in politics and war by their mid-teens. HARALD HARDRADA was only fifteen years old when he fought with distinction for his half-brother king OLAF HARALDSSON at the battle of STIKLESTAD in 1030. At this level of society, girls were married off early to secure political alliances.

In pagan times both abortion and the exposure of unwanted children were permissible. Feeding a newborn baby implied acceptance by the parents and gave it a right to live. Except in the case of severe deformity, exposure was illegal in early Christian times, but the practice continued to be common, primarily for economic reasons. Newborn babies

were customarily given small gifts, and another was given when the child cut its first tooth. Nothing is known of pagan beliefs about the afterlife for children. No child burials have been found in pagan cemeteries in DENMARK, and very few from elsewhere in the Viking world; nor were any rune-stones raised as memorials to children. As would be expected, child burials are common in Christian cemeteries.

Christianity, conversion to Despite the Vikings' predilection for plundering CHURCHES and monasteries, this was mere opportunism on their part and there is little evidence of active hostility to Christianity itself. Nevertheless, Scandinavians met the first tentative efforts at evangelization with indifference, and it was 300 years before Christianity was firmly established: its final triumph over paganism is inextricably linked to the growth of centralized royal power.

The first Christian mission to Scandinavia took place well before the beginning of the Viking Age when St WILLIBRORD visited king ANGANTYR in DENMARK c.725. Willibrord's mission was fruitless and was not followed up until the 820s, when EBO OF RHEIMS and St ANSGAR undertook missionary journeys to Denmark, probably on the initiative of the emperor LOUIS THE PIOUS, who was anxious to increase Frankish influence in Scandinavia following the outbreak of Viking raiding. In 831 Ansgar founded the BISHOPRIC of Hamburg (linked with Bremen and promoted to an archbishopric in 847–8) as a base for the evangelization of Scandinavia. Though Ansgar and his co-workers did establish small Christian communities at HEDEBY, RIBE and BIRKA, they did not last, and by 900 Scandinavia was still almost entirely pagan.

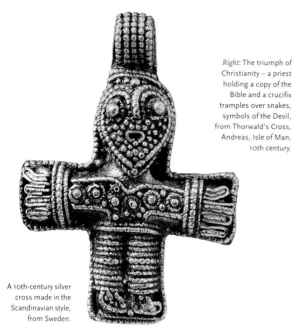

A 10th-century silver cross made in the Scandinavian style, from Sweden.

Right: The triumph of Christianity – a priest holding a copy of the Bible and a crucifix tramples over snakes, symbols of the Devil, from Thorwald's Cross, Andreas, Isle of Man, 10th century.

Christianity was making more headway among the Scandinavian colonists in the British Isles and FRANCIA as a result of contacts with the native peoples. Baptism was often demanded as the price of peace, as when ALFRED THE GREAT defeated the Danish king GUTHRUM in 878. Several of the early settlers of Iceland who had lived previously in SCOTLAND or IRELAND, such as AUD THE DEEP-MINDED, were Christians, but there were too few of them for the religion to take root.

The conversion of Scandinavia only began in earnest in the later 10th century, when Christianity began to win royal converts such as HARALD BLUETOOTH in Denmark, OLAF TRYGGVASON and OLAF HARALDSSON in NORWAY and OLOF SKÖTKONUNG in SWEDEN, all of whom actively promoted the religion to their subjects. Those with political ambitions quickly followed their kings' examples and converted, but progress was slower among the common people. As polytheists, many pagan Scandinavians initially accepted Christ simply as one more god to be worshipped alongside the traditional deities. Probably not untypical of early converts was Kjartan, a late-10th-century Icelander who announced his intention to become a Christian 'on condition that he could still put a little reliance on THOR'. Denmark can be regarded as largely Christian by 1000, Norway by 1030, but in Sweden pagan sentiment remained strong until the end of the 11th century, and there was even a brief pagan revival under Blot-Sven (r. 1080–3; *blót*, 'blood-offering'). The great pagan cult centre at UPPSALA, only a few miles from the royal Christian centre at SIGTUNA, probably remained in use as late as 1110, and private pagan devotions in the home continued for long afterwards. ICELAND officially converted as a result of a vote in the ALTHING in 1000.

Though there is no reason to doubt their sincerity, the political advantages of conversion cannot have escaped kings who were actively centralizing power in their kingdoms. By replacing diverse local customs with a single faith, Christianity helped foster a common identity. It also provided a powerful ideology of divinely ordained KINGSHIP that raised the monarch above his subjects. Conversion made relations with other Christian kingdoms easier, a particularly important consideration for Danish kings with their overbearing German neighbours. Furthermore, the Church was a steady source of experienced, literate administrators who could assist in the establishment of effective royal governments. The foundation of BISHOPRICS not only furthered the spread of Christianity but also created new administrative centres.

Chronicles of the Kings of Man and the Isles

(*Cronica regum Mannie et insularum*) The single most important narrative source for the affairs of the Norse kings of the Isle of MAN and the Hebrides from 1016 until the kingdom was ceded to SCOTLAND in 1266; the Latin chronicles also cover events in the Isle of Man up to 1377. The work of several authors, the chronicles are contemporary for events only from *c*.1237 onwards; the earlier entries were compiled from Manx oral traditions, eyewitness accounts, and Scottish and English chronicles. Despite major errors of chronology, the chronicles are generally considered a reliable source for events.

Chronicles of the Kings of Man and the Isles, ed. and trans. G. Broderick (Douglas, Isle of Man, 1995).

churches The first churches to be built in Scandinavia in the 10th and early 11th centuries

Right: The spectacular 12th-century stave church at Borgund, near Sognfjord, Norway.

Far right: The Romanesque architecture of St Magnus's cathedral at Kirkwall, Orkney.

were simple rectangular structures built of wooden staves. Fragments of painted and carved wood that have survived as a result of being reused in later buildings show that these early churches could be elaborately decorated. As the staves were set directly in the ground, these timber churches would have rotted away within twenty-five years or so, and in the course of the 11th century in DENMARK and SWEDEN they were replaced with stone buildings. In NORWAY, the tradition of building in wood persisted well into the Middle Ages. Later stave churches were provided with stone foundations, raising the building above the ground and protecting it from decay. Heavy sill timbers were laid on top of the foundations, into which the vertical staves of the church were set. One of the finest stave churches to have survived to the present day is a spectacular building – built in the 12th century at Borgund, near Sognfjord – with multiple roofs and elaborate dragon-headed finials, giving it a pagoda-like appearance. Many other churches incorporated fine wood carvings.

While Norway's stave churches are uniquely Scandinavian in character, the same is not true of stone churches. At the time of their conversion to CHRISTIANITY, Scandinavians had no traditions of stone architecture, so craftsmen had to be imported from abroad. The stone churches of the 11th and 12th centuries therefore strongly reflect the ecclesiastical and political links between Scandinavia and the rest of Europe at the end of the Viking Age. The earliest stone churches in Scandinavia were built at ROSKILDE in Denmark during the reign of CNUT. Surviving fragments of these churches show that Cnut brought masons from England to help build them. After Cnut's death in 1035, German influence over the Danish Church increased

considerably. Not only was the 12th-century cathedral at RIBE built in the German Romanesque style, it was even constructed of stone imported from the Rhineland. The earliest stone churches in Norway were built at the end of the 11th century, but none survive. However, Norway's close ecclesiastical links with the British Isles in the 12th century are much in evidence at TRONDHEIM cathedral, which was rebuilt by masons from Lincoln in the Early English Gothic style, and at Lyse abbey near BERGEN, which was founded by English Cistercian monks. A remarkable group of stone churches was built in ORKNEY during the early 12th century. One, a circular church at Orphir, is based on the plan of the Church of the Holy Sepulchre at Jerusalem; the finest, St Magnus's cathedral at Kirkwall, built by masons from Durham, is a superb example of Anglo-Norman Romanesque architecture. Of the stone churches built in the 11th century in Sweden, only fragments survive; they show both English and German influences, reflecting the origins of early missionary bishops. The conversion of the RUS to Orthodox rather than Roman Christianity is reflected in the architecture and art of the earliest surviving Russian churches, such as St Sophia at KIEV (1037–9), which were built by craftsmen from the Byzantine Empire.

class system *see* SOCIAL CLASSES

Clontarf, battle of (23 April 1014) Victory of BRIAN BORU, high king of IRELAND, over Maél Mórda, king of Leinster, and his Viking allies under SIGURD THE STOUT of ORKNEY, fought at Clontarf, north-east of DUBLIN. Although the coalition was probably engineered by their king SIHTRIC SILKBEARD, the Dublin Vikings took no part in the fighting. Though

Coin of Cnut struck in England. Cnut also had coins issued in his name in Denmark and Sweden.

Cnut and his queen, Emma, present an altar cross to New Minster, Winchester, from a contemporary manuscript.

present, Brian was too old to fight in person, and the battle was actually directed by his son Murchad. Maél Mórda and Sigurd were both killed in the battle, which lasted all day; Brian, too, was killed, cut down by a fleeing Viking leader, Brodir of MAN. Clontarf is still often presented as a decisive battle that ended the Viking threat to Ireland, but modern scholars are almost unanimously agreed that it had no long-term consequences. The battle owes its prominent position in Irish historical traditions to the successful propagandizing of the 12th-century author of the *COGADH GAEDHEL RE GALLAIBH*, whose purpose was to enhance the reputation of the Ua Briain dynasty of Munster, which traced its descent from Brian Boru. In reality, Clontarf was just another battle in the internecine struggles of the Irish kingdoms. By 1014, the Vikings had long since ceased to be a significant threat to Ireland. The Norse settlers had largely adopted CHRISTIANITY by this time, many spoke Gaelic, and their coastal TOWNS, including Dublin, had for many years already been forced to pay tribute to native Irish overlords. Despite Brian's death, the process of assimilating the Norse settlements into the political and cultural life of Ireland continued uninterrupted after Clontarf.

Cnut (Canute, Knut or Knud, known as 'the Great' in DENMARK) (d. 1035) King of ENGLAND (r. 1016–35); king of Denmark (r. 1019–35). While still in his teens, Cnut took part in his father SVEIN FORKBEARD's conquest of England in 1013. In the course of the expedition, Cnut formed a relationship with Ælfgifu of Northampton: she bore him two sons, SVEIN ALFIVASON and HAROLD HAREFOOT. On Svein Forkbeard's death early in 1014, the Danish ARMY chose Cnut as his successor, but the English

invited their king ÆTHELRED II back from exile and Cnut was forced to return to Denmark. Supported by THORKELL THE TALL and ERIK of HLAÐIR, he returned in 1015 to claim the English throne. He was stoutly resisted by Æthelred's son EDMUND IRONSIDE, who became king on his father's death in April 1016. Cnut eventually won a decisive victory at ASHINGDON in October, thanks in large part to the defection of EADRIC STREONA, the ealdorman of MERCIA, and Edmund agreed to divide the kingdom. Within a few weeks, Edmund died of injuries received at Ashingdon and Cnut became sole ruler of England. In 1018 Cnut married Æthelred's widow EMMA, though he did not repudiate Ælfgifu. Cnut taxed the English heavily, in part to pay off his army, but he was remembered as a just and pious ruler, and the English welcomed peace after twenty-five years of fruitless warfare. Cnut rewarded his leading supporters, such as Thorkell and Erik, with earldoms, and many of his HOUSECARLS received estates. However, there was no large-scale Danish immigration as there had been in the 9th century, and English nobles and churchmen continued to hold high office and, in fact, steadily increased their influence as Cnut's reign progressed.

When his brother Harald II died in 1018, Cnut returned to Denmark and was elected king the following year. In 1028 he engineered the downfall of king OLAF HARALDSSON to add Norway to his dominions. By 1030, Cnut was also recognized as overlord of SWEDEN, where COINS were issued in his name, and he probably also controlled some ports such as Jumne (WOLIN) on the southern shores of the Baltic Sea. Cnut's control of Scandinavia brought considerable commercial benefits to England, which remained his power base throughout his reign: he

Odense cathedral, founded by
Cnut II, scene of his murder and
subsequently his burial place.

ruled in Denmark through regents, and in Norway through his son SVEIN ALFIVASON, whom he appointed in 1030. Cnut's vast Anglo-Scandinavian empire made him a considerable figure on the European stage, recognition of which came in 1027 when he travelled to Rome to attend the coronation of the Holy Roman Emperor, Conrad II. Cnut was succeeded in England by HAROLD HAREFOOT, and in Denmark by HARTHACNUT, his son by Emma. Neither possessed a fraction of their father's abilities, and Cnut's empire quickly broke up.

M. K. Lawson, *Cnut* (London and New York, 1993).

Cnut II (St Cnut, Cnut the Holy) (*c.*1047–86) King of DENMARK (r. 1080–6). A son of SVEIN ESTRITHSON, Cnut succeeded his brother Harald III as king. In his youth, Cnut took part in sea raids on the WENDS, and in 1069 he joined his father's invasion of ENGLAND in support of an English rebellion against WILLIAM THE CONQUEROR. Following his father's death in 1074, Cnut hoped to inherit the throne, but his elder brother Harald was chosen king instead. The following year Cnut was offered the English throne by two Norman earls in rebellion against William. Cnut gathered a FLEET of 200 SHIPS, but by the time he reached England the rebellion had collapsed, and apart from sacking YORK he achieved nothing. Cnut allied with count Robert I of Flanders against their common enemy William, and *c.*1080 he married the count's daughter Adela. On his brother's death in 1080, Cnut was finally chosen king of Denmark. Cnut worked to free the Crown from dependence on war booty by increasing royal revenues from TAXES and tolls, but this won him few friends. Cnut was a generous patron of the Church, beginning construction of a Romanesque cathedral at ODENSE.

In 1085 Cnut revived his claim to the English throne and began to raise a large invasion fleet in Jutland. The threat of German invasion kept him from joining the fleet, and the following summer its leaders rebelled. Led by his brother Olaf, the rebels pursued Cnut to Odense, where he was murdered in the cathedral he had founded. Miracles were soon reported at his tomb in Odense, and he was canonized in 1101. The failure of Cnut's projected invasion marks the final end of the Viking Age in England.

Cogadh Gaedhel re Gallaibh ('The War of the Irish with the Foreigners') A colourful history of the Vikings in IRELAND, written in the 12th century to enhance the reputation of the Ua Briain (O'Brien) dynasty of Munster by emphasizing the wickedness of the pagan enemies they had defeated, thereby saving the country. It begins with an annalistic account of Viking raids in the 8th and 9th centuries, giving prominence to the ferocity and sacrilegiousness of pagan warlords such as TURGEIS. It then develops into a heroic epic about two Munster kings, Mathgamain and his brother BRIAN BORU, from whom the Ua Briain dynasty traced its descent. The work culminates with the battle of CLONTARF in 1014, where Brian Boru was killed defeating the Leinstermen and their Norse allies. Although the accounts of surviving contemporary annals show that the author exaggerated and possibly even invented much of his material, the *Cogadh* has had an enormous influence on perceptions of the Viking Age in Ireland and of the significance of the battle of Clontarf in particular.

The War of the Gaedhil with the Gaill, ed. and trans. J. H. Todd (London, 1867).

An antler comb from Viking Age York.

Two imitations of Frankish *deniers* issued at Hedeby *c*.825, the earliest known Scandinavian coins.

coins and coinage With the possible exception of some 8th-century pieces found at RIBE in DENMARK, coins were not minted in Scandinavia before the Viking Age. The earliest coins that can with any certainty be said to have been minted in Scandinavia were produced at HEDEBY in Denmark *c*.825. These were thinner, lighter imitations of Frankish *deniers* issued at the ports of DORESTAD and QUENTOVIC. Similar coins were later produced at other, unidentified Danish mints up to around 975. Viking rulers in the British Isles, such as HALFDAN in England, had coins struck in their own names by native coiners as early as the late 9th century, but it was more than a century before the practice spread to Scandinavia itself. Around 1000, SVEIN FORKBEARD in Denmark, OLAF TRYGGVASON in NORWAY and OLOF SKÖTKONUNG in SWEDEN began to issue coins in their own names. These were based on the Anglo-Saxon pennies that were pouring into Scandinavia at that time as a result of tribute payments to the Vikings. Danish and Norwegian kings continued to issue coins continuously after that, but the sole Swedish mint at SIGTUNA ceased functioning *c*.1030, and no new native coinage was produced until *c*.1180.

For most of the Viking Age, coins were valued chiefly as bullion rather than as a medium of exchange in their own right, and foreign coins circulated freely and in large quantities in Scandinavia. Around 250,000 foreign Viking Age coins have been discovered in Sweden alone, 100,000 of which are Islamic, and 60,000, Anglo-Saxon. Such coins are an important source of information about Viking contact with foreigners.

combs Combs are common finds in archaeological excavations of Viking Age TOWNS and cemeteries.

They vary from the plain and simple to the ornate, and were clearly owned by all levels of society. Combs were usually made by skilled urban craftsmen using ANTLER (from red deer in southern Scandinavia, elk in the north), a very difficult material to work well. A pair of backplates was prepared from a long straight piece of antler. These were attached, one on either side, to a series of thinner rectangular sheets of antler, which were then filed into teeth. There is remarkably little variation in the design of combs across the Viking world, the same styles being found from DUBLIN to NOVGOROD.

conduct, rules of The conduct that was most admired in Viking Age Scandinavian society was that which befitted a warrior: physical bravery, equanimity in the face of danger or death, self-discipline, loyalty and generosity. To behave in this way brought a man honour and respect, whatever his rank. Honour was a precious possession, and it was taken for granted that a man whose honour was slighted would seek to restore it by force. Most Viking Age Scandinavians were farmers not warriors, and they recognized the value of the pragmatic virtues embodied in *Hávamál*, a collection of wisdom verses from the *Poetic EDDA*. *Hávamál* recommends the kind of common-sense wisdom that is learned from experience. Cultivate friendship, never take hospitality for granted, and repay gifts with gifts. Do not make enemies unnecessarily or pick foolish fights. Do not drink too much, it robs a man of his wits. If you do not know what you are talking about, keep quiet: it is better to listen. Exercise caution in business and always beware of treachery and double-dealing. Always deal honestly yourself, except with your enemies: deceive them if

Constantinople – Mikligarðr ('Great City') to the Vikings – was a magnet for mercenaries and merchants.

you can! Yet here, too, the heroic virtues of the warrior are in evidence. *Hávamál* berates the coward who thinks he will live for ever if he avoids fighting, and advises that the only thing that never dies is the fame of a glorious reputation. The worst sin for a warrior or a farmer was to betray his FAMILY or friends; for this, he could be declared a *niðingr*, less than nothing, an outcast.

Constantine I (d. 877) King of the Scots (r. 862–77). A son of Kenneth macAlpin, Constantine benefited from Viking attacks on the Picts and the Britons of STRATHCLYDE to strengthen his position in SCOTLAND. His sister may have been married to king OLAF of DUBLIN. Constantine was heavily defeated by a Danish ARMY, possibly under HALFDAN, at Dollar in 875, and was probably killed in battle with the Vikings in Fife in 877.

Constantine II (d. 952) King of the Scots (r. 900–43). Constantine's reign saw the consolidation of the power of the Scottish monarchy. In the early years of his reign he was a close ally of the Northumbrians of Bernicia (i.e. Northumbria north of the Tees) against the Vikings of YORK, and twice fought with them against RAGNALD in battles at Corbridge in 914 and 918, losing the first and drawing the second. Later in his reign Constantine became more concerned about the growing power of WESSEX than about the Vikings. In 937 he invaded ENGLAND in alliance with his son-in-law OLAF GUTHFRITHSSON, the king of DUBLIN, and the STRATHCLYDE Britons, but was crushingly defeated by ATHELSTAN at BRUNANBURH. In 943 Constantine abdicated and spent the remainder of his life as a monk at St Andrews.

Constantinople, treaties of A series of agreements between the RUS and the Byzantine Empire in 907, 911 and 945. The treaties of 907 and 945 were both probably made following failed Rus attacks on Constantinople, while it is possible that the 911 treaty is simply a ratification of the 907 agreement. The 907 treaty gave Rus merchants rights to receive supplies in Constantinople for up to six months, a monthly allowance, baths and anchors, sails and other supplies for their SHIPS. They were not to live within the city walls, could not bring any WEAPONS into the city with them, and had always to be accompanied by an official. Rus merchants from KIEV were to enjoy priority treatment over those from other centres. In the 911 treaty the Rus agreed not to plunder Byzantine ships and to give whatever help was necessary to any such ships they found in difficulties. Other clauses concerned crimes committed by the Rus in Byzantine territories, RANSOM of prisoners, return of runaway slaves and terms for Rus who wanted to join the Byzantine ARMY. This last has been seen as the origin of the emperor's élite VARANGIAN GUARD of Viking mercenaries. The 945 treaty stipulates the amount of silk that Rus merchants could buy, and forbade the Rus to use Berezan at the mouth of the River Dniepr as a winter base, so preventing them from becoming a permanent presence in the Black Sea. Merchants were also required to obtain official documentation before arriving in Constantinople; those turning up without would be treated as hostile (the emphasis on documentation implies that literacy was becoming established among the Rus). The 945 document also notes the existence of a Christian community at Kiev, and provides for military cooperation against the BULGARS. It is of great interest that the names of many of the Rus signatories to the treaties have

A 17th-century manuscript from Iceland showing the eternal ash tree Yggdrasil, which supported the universe and linked the worlds of gods, men, giants and the dead.

A small part of the huge Cuerdale silver hoard.

survived. For those of 907 and 911, the names are almost all Scandinavian; that of 945 included many more Slavic names, a sign of the degree to which the Rus had been assimilated to Slavic culture by this time.

Cork Port in south-west IRELAND that originated as a monastic centre in the 7th century. Cork was raided by the Vikings in 821 and 839 and was the site of a Viking LONGPHORT from 848 to 867, when their leader Gnimhbeolu was killed. Cork was raided again in 913, and shortly after was reoccupied as part of the general resurgence of Viking activity in Ireland in the second decade of the 10th century. Though Cork was under the control of local Irish kings by the 11th century, it retained its own rulers until 1174, when its last Norse king, Gilbert MacTurger, was killed in a sea battle with the Anglo-Normans. Very little archaeological evidence of Viking Age Cork has yet been discovered.

creation myth The Vikings conceived of their universe rather vaguely as consisting of three realms, one above the other. The highest realm, ASGARD, was the home of the gods. The middle realm comprised MIDGARD, the home of humans, and JOTUNHEIM, the home of the GIANTS. Below the middle realm was NIFLHEIM, the frozen realm of the dead. The three realms were linked by the roots of YGGDRASIL, the mighty eternal ash tree that supported the universe, while Midgard and Asgard were also linked by the rainbow bridge Bifrost. Somewhere in the universe – south of Niflheim – was the fire realm of MUSPELL.

The story of the creation of the universe is told in the Eddic poem *VOLUSPÁ* and in SNORRI

STURLUSON's *Prose EDDA*. In the beginning, there existed only Muspell and Niflheim, and between them a great void called Ginnungagap, where the heat of the south met the ice of the north and began to melt it. From the melting ice emerged the frost giant Ymir and the cow Audumla. From Ymir's legs and armpit sprang the race of giants. By licking the salty ice, Audumla uncovered a third being, the primeval god Buri. By a giant woman, Buri had a son called Bor, who became the father of ODIN, Vili and Ve. The three gods slew Ymir, releasing a deluge of blood that drowned all the giants except Bergelmir and his wife. The gods carried Ymir's body to the centre of Ginnungagap and used his flesh to create soil, his bones to make mountains and his blood to make lakes and an ocean to surround the new world. Then the gods used Ymir's skull to create the vault of the sky and from his brains they made clouds. Glowing embers from Muspell were used to make the sun, moon and stars. The gods divided the world into two: the cold mountainous region of Jotunheim, which they gave to the giants, and a warm fertile realm, which they protected with a wall and called Midgard. Odin and his brothers found an ash tree and elm tree washed up on the seashore. From the ash they created the first man, Ask; from the elm the first woman, Embla. For a home, they gave them Midgard. Finally, the gods created for themselves the mighty fortress of Asgard high above Midgard.

Cuerdale hoard The largest hoard of Viking treasure, discovered in 1840 by workmen repairing the embankment of the River Ribble near Cuerdale in Lancashire. The hoard, which weighed 40 kilograms, contained 7,500 COINS, 1,000 silver ingots, and pieces of JEWELRY and HACKSILVER. The

hoard was buried in a lead-lined chest. The coins come from all over the Viking world. The majority, some 3,000 of them, were silver pennies issued at YORK by its Danish kings Sigfrid and Cnut. Fifty Arabic coins from mints from Spain to Afghanistan were probably acquired in the Baltic. Much of the hacksilver and jewelry comes from IRELAND. The latest coins in the hoard are fifty-five coins of EDWARD THE ELDER (r. 899–924), a papal coin of Benedict IV dating from 901–3, and coins of Louis of Provence dating from 901–5. These suggest that the Cuerdale hoard was buried very shortly after 905. The hoard was far too heavy to have been carried by one man. The failure to recover the hoard suggests a catastrophic end for all involved in its burial.

F. A. Philpott, *A Silver Saga: Viking Treasure from the Northwest* (Liverpool, 1990).

Danegeld A term commonly used by modern historians to describe tribute paid to the DANES by the English during the reign of ÆTHELRED II (r. 978–1016) in return for peace. It is often also used more generally to describe all such payments to the Vikings, such as the tribute paid by the Franks in the 9th century. In fact, the term Danegeld did not appear until after the Norman Conquest (1066), when it was used to describe the *heregeld* ('army TAX'), which was actually an annual land tax introduced by Æthelred in 1012 to pay for the hire of the mercenary ARMY of THORKELL THE TALL. Prior to this, Æthelred had imposed general taxes – in 991, 994, 1002, 1007 and 1008 – to raise tribute (known at the time as *gafol*) to buy off the Danes. Enormous sums were raised with apparent ease, a testament to Æthelred's abilities as an administrator and a sign of the wealth of late Anglo-Saxon ENGLAND. After the Danish conquest of England, CNUT continued to levy the *heregeld* to pay his HOUSECARLS and FLEET, and after the Norman Conquest it developed into a tax to finance military campaigns. Danegeld was last levied in 1162.

Danelaw The eastern region of ENGLAND, between the Thames and the Tees, conquered and settled by the DANES in the 9th century, in which the customary LAWS observed in local courts were strongly influenced by Danish legal customs. The word is derived from Old English *Deone lage* ('Danes law'), which is first known from a charter of 1008. The exact borders of the Danelaw during the Viking Age are uncertain, but in the 12th century it was defined as the fifteen counties of Yorkshire, Nottinghamshire, Derbyshire, Leicestershire, Lincolnshire, Northamptonshire, Huntingdonshire, Cambridgeshire, Bedfordshire, Norfolk, Suffolk,

Left: A Viking warrior on a stone cross from Middleton, North Yorkshire. Native sculptors adopted Scandinavian styles to appeal to the Danish rulers of the Danelaw.

Right: The Danevirke, a defensive rampart built to protect against the Germans and Slavs, stretches 30 kilometres across the Jutland peninsula.

Essex, Hertfordshire, Buckinghamshire and Middlesex. The first recognition that different legal customs prevailed in the Danish-ruled areas of England comes in the peace treaty between ALFRED THE GREAT and GUTHRUM, the Danish king of EAST ANGLIA, in 886–90. These differences persisted for about 200 years after the West Saxon conquest, and in 970–4 king Edgar officially granted legal autonomy to the Danelaw.

Place-name evidence shows that the Danes did not settle the whole of the Danelaw intensively and were probably a minority of the population in most areas. But, while they did not displace the majority of the native population, the Danes did take over royal and aristocratic estates wholesale and formed a new social and political élite that had a lasting influence on local customs. In local administration, the hundred (the basic unit for the administration of justice in England) was usually called a WAPENTAKE, and the hide (the area of land needed to support one peasant FAMILY) was generally known as the ploughland (OE *plogesland*). The law of the Danelaw was distinguished from English law by procedural differences, heavy fines for breach of the king's peace, and the use, unknown in England at the time, of sworn aristocratic juries of presentment to initiate the prosecution of criminal suspects in the wapentake courts. While under contemporary English law the most serious crimes could be tried by ordeal, in the Danelaw trial by combat was normal. There were also major differences in landholding in the Danelaw. At the time of the Norman Conquest there was an unusually high number of peasant freeholders, or 'sokemen', in the Danelaw compared with the rest of England. In Lincolnshire they accounted for nearly fifty per cent of the population, and in many other Danelaw

counties it was around a third. Many sokemen were driven down into serfdom during the Norman period.

C. Hart, *The Danelaw* (London, 1992).

Danes The Danes first appear in written sources in the 6th century AD. The Gothic historian Jordanes, writing in 551 but using sources thirty years older, mentions that the *Dani*, a tall and fierce people, dominated southern Scandinavia. Gregory of Tours, writing soon after 575, gives an account in his *History of the Franks* of a raid by the *Dani* on the lower Rhine in the 520s. Nothing is known for certain of the origins of the Danes, though Jordanes implies that they originated in SWEDEN. During the Viking Age the Danes inhabited the whole of modern DENMARK, and also the modern Swedish provinces of Halland, Blekinge and Skåne and the German province of Schleswig-Holstein north of the River Eider (where there remains a Danish-speaking minority today). Danish Vikings were most active in southern and eastern ENGLAND, FRISIA and northern FRANCIA: they settled in considerable numbers in eastern England (*see* DANELAW) and to a lesser extent in NORMANDY. Anglo-Saxon writers tend to use the term 'Dane' to describe all Vikings, including those known even at the time to have come from NORWAY. Frankish writers use the term interchangeably with 'Northman'.

Danevirke A complex of defensive ramparts and ditches across the neck of the Jutland peninsula near Schleswig, Germany, totalling about 30 kilometres in length. The main north–south road through Jutland, the *Hærvej*, cut through the ramparts near HEDEBY. Although clearly intended to defend Jutland against invasion from Germany, the Danevirke did

Dendrochronological analysis
of preserved timbers allows
the origins of the Danevirke
to be dated to AD 737.

not mark the southern frontier of Danish territory
in the Viking Age: that lay about 20 kilometres to
the south on the River Eider. The Danevirke was
built in several phases. The earliest phase, consisting
of the North Wall, Main Wall and East Wall, has
been dated by dendrochronology to 737. The
Frankish Royal Annals record that in 808 the Danish
king GODFRED built a wall across the neck of the
Jutland; it was broken by only one gate to allow
traffic through. Godfred's wall has not been
identified with certainty but it may be the Kovirke,
a rampart to the south of the main system that
contains the only gate so far identified in the
Danevirke. A third building phase began in the
mid-9th century. The Main Wall was rebuilt to
a height of 10 metres, the port of Hedeby was
fortified with a semicircular wall, and the
Connecting Wall was built to link Hedeby with
the Main Wall. Sections of the Connecting Wall
have been dated by dendrochronology to 968 and
*c.*951–61, making it likely that this phase of
building activity was ordered by king HARALD
BLUETOOTH (r. *c.*958–87).

The Danevirke was not, apparently, a very effective
obstacle to invasion. The Frankish emperor LOUIS
THE PIOUS successfully invaded Jutland in 815,
and the Danevirke was seized and held by the
Germans 974–*c.*983. The complex was extended
several times during the 11th and 12th centuries,
this time as a defence against Slavs as well as
Germans. It reached its ultimate development under
Valdemar the Great (r. 1157–82), who rebuilt sections
of the ramparts in brick. Reorganization of the
frontier zone in the 13th century led to a decline in
the importance of the Danevirke and it fell into
disrepair. It was last used in 1864 during DENMARK's
war with Prussia.

Denmark, kingdom of The earliest use of the term
'Denmark' appears, in the Old English form
Denemearc, in the preface to the *Old English
OROSIUS*, written in the 890s. *Denimarca* is used in
the *Chronicle of Regino of Prüm*, which was concluded
in 908. The earliest known use in Scandinavia itself
dates from the mid-10th century, when the term
*tanmarka*R or *Danmarkar* appears on the rune-stone
erected at JELLING by GORM THE OLD in memory of
his wife THYRE. The formation of the kingdom of
Denmark began several centuries earlier, however.

Denmark has a greater proportion of good arable
land than its Scandinavian neighbours. As a result, it
was, in the Viking Age, the wealthiest, the most
populous and the most politically advanced of the
Scandinavian kingdoms. The beginnings of political
centralization in Denmark can be discerned in the
ROMAN IRON AGE (*c.* AD 1–400) and the following
GERMANIC IRON AGE (*c.* AD 400–800). The earliest
named Danish king, ANGANTYR, reigned in the early
8th century, though the extent of his realm is
unknown. It is possible that the DANEVIRKE rampart,
the Samsø canal and the establishment of a market
at RIBE, all datable to the early 8th century, are
Angantyr's work. By the beginning of the 9th
century the DANES had created a kingdom that
probably included all of modern Denmark (except
BORNHOLM), part of northern Germany and the
modern Swedish provinces of Skåne and Halland. In
the early Middle Ages, Skåne and Halland formed
the Danes' 'mark', or border, which may have given
its name to the whole country (another explanation
is that the country is named after its southern border
with Germany in Jutland). Danish kings also
exercised some form of dominion over the Vestfold
in NORWAY. This territorial unit was by no means
stable. After the death of king GODFRED in 810

A gold coin issued at Dorestad
by the moneyer Madelinus.

Denmark was wracked by civil wars and succession disputes for twenty years, from which HORIK emerged as the sole ruler in the 830s. Horik provided twenty years of peace, but after he was overthrown by a family rebellion in 854 Denmark virtually disappears from the sources for a century. The kingdom was frequently divided and *c.*900–36 at least part of it was ruled by the Swedish OLAF dynasty.

Around the mid-10th century GORM THE OLD founded a new and vigorous dynasty. His son HARALD BLUETOOTH united Denmark and built the chain of TRELLEBORG forts to establish direct royal authority in all parts of the kingdom. Harald also re-established Danish influence in Norway. Converted to CHRISTIANITY in 965, Harald became the first Scandinavian ruler actively to promote the religion among his subjects: Denmark was effectively Christian by *c.*1000. Harald was overthrown by his own son SVEIN FORKBEARD. Svein strengthened his position in Denmark by launching lucrative tribute-gathering raids on ENGLAND, finally conquering the country in 1013, only to die a few months later. Denmark reached the height of its power under Svein's son CNUT (r. 1019–35), when it formed part of an empire encompassing England, Norway and SWEDEN. Cnut's empire broke up after his death, and Denmark experienced a brief period of Norwegian rule (1042–7) until the accession of SVEIN ESTRITHSON (r. 1047–74) restored the Danish line. In the course of the 11th century, Denmark was divided into local administrative districts, called *herreds*, each with its own THING. By the end of the Viking Age (*c.*1100) Denmark still suffered to some extent from internal instability. The monarchy remained elective, leading to frequent civil wars and succession disputes, and was even briefly

divided into three parts in 1156 after one particularly indecisive conflict.

E. Roesdahl, *Viking Age Denmark* (London, 1982).

dirhem The most important early Islamic COIN, the *dirhem* was an Arab copy of an earlier Persian coin. It was a thin, flat silver piece of about 29 millimetres diameter and weighing 2.9–3.0 grams. Apart from the date and the mint, *dirhems* also carried religious texts. The earliest were struck in AH 79 (AD 698–9); the last, in the 14th century. *Dirhems* were introduced into circulation in RUSSIA by Arab merchants *c.*780, and by the mid-9th century they were finding their way to GOTLAND and mainland SWEDEN in small quantities. After 910, a flood of *dirhems*, mostly from the Samanid emirate in central Asia, began to reach Sweden and Gotland: few found their way to DENMARK, fewer still to NORWAY. After 965 the flow was cut for twenty years, but it resumed at a reduced rate after 983 and ceased altogether after 1015, a result of the exhaustion of the central Asian silver mines. The fate of most *dirhems* reaching Scandinavia was to be melted down for bullion, but around 85,000 have been discovered in Viking Age coin hoards, all but 5,000 of them from Sweden and Gotland. Many thousands have also been found in the Slav lands along the southern Baltic coast. The large quantities of *dirhems* that have been found in Sweden and Gotland have been taken as evidence of a flourishing TRADE with the Arab world, but it is likely that many were acquired on tribute-gathering raids in the eastern Baltic.

disease *see* MEDICINE

dísir A race of nameless female supernatural beings. The *dísir* were normally worshipped and sacrificed to

An elaborate Swedish penannular brooch, used to fasten cloaks.

Left: A well-dressed Viking merchant of the 10th century.

Middle: A high-quality woman's leather shoe from Staraja Ladoga, Russia.

in private by pagan Viking Age Scandinavians, though they were also the objects of public cults in parts of SWEDEN and NORWAY. With the goddess FREYJA, they had power over the fertility of animals and crops, and they assisted at childbirth. Success in farming and the well-being of the FAMILY depended on their favour. It was important not to incur the wrath of the *dísir*, for they could become malevolent if offended and bring misfortune or even death.

divorce *see* MARRIAGE AND DIVORCE

Dorestad Strategically situated near the confluence of the rivers Lek and Rhine, Dorestad (present-day Wijk bij Duurstede, near Nijmegen, The Netherlands) was one of the largest TRADE centres of early medieval Europe. The earliest settlement on the site dates to the 7th century, and by 630 it was already important enough to be the site of a Frankish mint. Dorestad reached its peak in the 8th century when it covered an area of at least 40 hectares: the population was between 1,000 and 2,000. Excavations have uncovered evidence of a wide range of commercial and industrial activities at Dorestad, including textiles, metalworking, JEWELRY, bone-working, basket-weaving and shipbuilding. Finds from the site are dominated by imports – POTTERY, lava quernstones, GLASS and metalwork – from the middle Rhineland; many of these products would have been re-exported. Being more than 100 kilometres from the open sea, Dorestad was not raided by the Vikings until 834, after the Frankish coast defences had begun to break down due to civil wars. The Vikings returned in 835, 836 and 837. Though the Frankish annals speak of much killing, plundering and burning, these early Viking raids did not affect Dorestad's prosperity much, as is shown

by the peaking of output from its mints in the period 838–40. Dorestad was occupied by the DANES in 847, and in 850 the emperor Lothar granted the TOWN and other lands in FRISIA to RORIC, a Viking leader, as a fief. Though Roric was supposed to defend the town, Dorestad was sacked again in 857 and 863, after which it disappears from the sources. Archaeological evidence shows that occupation on the site did not continue into the 10th century. The decisive factor in the decline of Dorestad was probably a shift in the course of the Rhine, which robbed the site of its geographical advantages, rather than the many Viking raids, which seem only to have had short-term effects.

dress Evidence for Viking Age Scandinavian clothing comes from literary sources, fragments of textiles that have been preserved in anaerobic conditions in graves and waterlogged urban sites such as BIRKA and HEDEBY, and representations in Viking Age art, such as scenes on the PICTURE STONES from GOTLAND and the tapestry from the OSEBERG SHIP BURIAL. With only minor regional variations, the same styles of male and female clothing were worn throughout Scandinavia and in Scandinavian-settled areas overseas. Reds and greens appear to have been the favourite colours for clothing.

Women's clothing typically consisted of a long, loose-fitting shift or underdress of wool or linen, with or without sleeves and a split-neck opening that was fastened by a brooch. Shifts were often lined for comfort and warmth and decorated with embroidery. Over the top of this was worn a heavier pinafore-type dress with shoulder straps that were fastened by a pair of brooches. In most of Scandinavia and the overseas settlements these were oval in shape, but

Everyday artefacts from Viking Dublin; tableware, spoons, spindle-whorls, coins, pins and carved bone objects are all evidence of the wide range of craft activities in the city.

in Finland and parts of SWEDEN circular brooches were used, and on Gotland animal-headed ones have been discovered. Overdresses could either be sewn up into a tube or be left open at the sides, and were often tailored at the waist to emphasize the woman's figure. Outdoor clothing was a rectangular or semicircular woollen cape, folded into a triangle, worn like a shawl over the shoulders and fastened at the neck with a brooch. Capes could be decorated with woven bands or a trimming of fur. Scarves and woven bands were worn on the head and woollen hose on the legs.

Male dress was similar to that worn elsewhere in early medieval Europe. Trousers, undershirts, tunics and cloaks were the most important garments. Trousers came in a variety of styles, long and narrow, wide and pleated, or baggy knee breeches. Stocking-breeches in wool, fur or leather were also worn. Below the knees, garters or cloth strips wound around the calves were worn. Tunics often had laced cuffs and were decorated with tablet-woven braid strips, embroidery and, for the well off, gold braid. Out of doors, men wore cloaks of wool or leather, fastened on the right shoulder with a brooch. Cloaks could be trimmed with fur, decorated with braids and lined with wool or stuffed with down for warmth. Poorer people wore a woollen hooded cloak or even had to make do with a blanket with a hole in the middle for the head to go through. Brimmed hats, caps and fur hats are known. Gloves and mittens, made of wool or fur, were worn by both sexes, as were belts, to which were attached a purse, a knife and, if a housewife, keys. Purely ornamental JEWELRY was also worn by both sexes, as was, according to one Arab account, facial make-up.

Surprisingly large quantities of Viking footwear have survived, mostly from urban sites where organic materials have been preserved due to waterlogging. For example, 117 shoes have been discovered in excavations at Hedeby. Shoemaking was evidently a common urban trade. Two main types of shoe were worn by Viking Age Scandinavians. The commonest was made from a leather sole stitched to a separate upper; the other was made from a single piece of leather and sewn up over the instep. Cow's leather was normally used for shoemaking, but goatskin was used for the best-quality boots. Shoes, ankle and knee-length, or higher, boots are known. Both shoes and boots were fastened with leather straps. The uppers were often coloured, and seams sometimes had decorative stitching. Fine-quality shoes could be decorated with patterns or even inscriptions in RUNES or Latin characters. Shoes were worn over bare feet or hose.

Dublin (ON Dyflin) The first true TOWN to develop in IRELAND, and an independent Norse kingdom. Dublin grew from being a *LONGPHORT* built as a Viking raiding base and slave market in 841 into a prosperous merchant and manufacturing centre by the 10th century. The site of the original Viking *longphort* has not been identified but it is thought to have been near the confluence of the rivers Poddle and Liffey. A large cemetery at Kilmainham, 3 kilometres upstream on the Liffey, testifies to a permanent Scandinavian population at Dublin *c.*850. The founders of Dublin were Norwegian, but in 851 the city was taken by the DANES. The Danes were expelled in 853 by the Norwegian OLAF (Amlaíb), who was effectively the founder of the kingdom of Dublin. Olaf was drawn into Irish politics and power struggles, making alliances with native rulers such as CERBALL of Ossory. On the

Wattle-and-daub walls of a craftsman's house in Viking Age Dublin, preserved in waterlogged conditions.

death of Olaf's successor IVAR I in 873, Dublin became politically unstable under a succession of short-lived kings. The kingdom was weakened by a civil war in 893–4, and in 902 the Norse were expelled by the Irish.

The Norse, under SIHTRIC CÁECH, recaptured Dublin in 917. After Sihtric crushingly defeated an Irish attempt to take Dublin at Islandbridge in 919, the revived kingdom briefly became a power to be reckoned with: it frequently controlled YORK, but never securely. After a series of defeats by the Irish in the 940s the power of the Dublin Norse went into decline, and they were often forced to pay tribute to native rulers as the price of independence. In 997 Dublin came under the overlordship of the powerful king of Munster, BRIAN BORU. To try to preserve Dublin's independence, SIHTRIC SILKBEARD engineered the alliance between Leinster and the earldom of ORKNEY that was defeated at CLONTARF in 1014, but he kept out of the battle himself. This saved Dublin from the worst consequences of the defeat, but by the time Sihtric abdicated in 1036 it had become a minor power with a strong mercenary FLEET, employed by Irish, Scottish and Welsh rulers. Under Sihtric's rule, Dublin became the site of the first mint in Ireland in 997, and the seat of a BISHOPRIC in 1030. By this time, the Dublin Norse had become partially assimilated to Irish culture and were known as OSTMEN, to distinguish them from native Scandinavians. For the next century, Dublin was frequently under direct Irish rule until the Norse staged a brief recovery in the 1130s. The last Norse king of Dublin, Asgall (Ansculf) Torquilsson, was expelled in 1169 by the Anglo-Norman adventurer Richard de Clare ('Strongbow'). Asgall returned in 1171 with allies from MAN and the northern isles, including the Orkney Viking SVEIN

ASLEIFARSON, but was defeated with heavy losses: Asgall himself was captured and executed. It was the last time a Norse ARMY fought in Ireland; later in the same year Henry II of ENGLAND held court in Dublin.

Extensive excavations since the 1960s have shown that after the Vikings returned to Dublin in 917 the centre of settlement shifted to the low ridge between the Poddle and the Liffey. The settlement was protected by a low earth rampart and palisade, which was replaced c.950 by a wall of wattles topped with stakes. The earth-and-wood defences were replaced by a stone wall c.1100. The settlement was divided up into rectangular plots, defined by wattle fences, containing rectangular wattle-walled buildings with rounded corners. The wealthier inhabitants, identifiable by their larger houses and richer artefacts, lived on the higher ground, which was less vulnerable to flooding. Waterlogging has resulted in excellent preservation of organic materials, so providing much evidence of daily life in Viking Age Dublin. A wide range of craft activities was carried out, including wood-, bone-, jet- and AMBER-carving, leather-working and WEAVING. Dublin was probably also a shipbuilding centre, for one of the Viking SHIPS found at SKULDELEV in Denmark was built of Irish oak. Dublin maintained its position as Ireland's leading city after the Anglo-Norman conquest of 1169–71, when the area of settlement was greatly extended by drainage of marshland along the Liffey.

Dudo of St-Quentin (c.960–c.1043) French monk and author of *De moribus et actis primorum normanniae ducum* ('On the Manners and Deeds of the First Norman Dukes'). Dudo was a frequent visitor to the court of Richard I (RICHARD THE

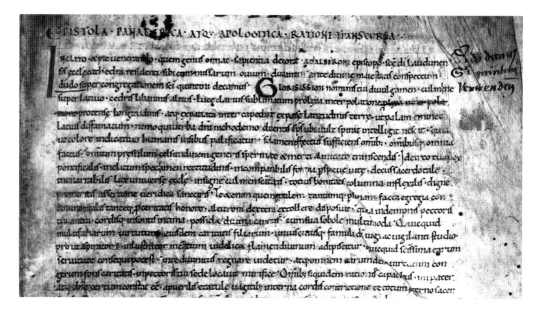

FEARLESS) of NORMANDY, who commissioned him to write the history of the country's rulers in 994. Dudo probably completed the work *c*.1015, and produced an extended version *c*.1030. Written in a painfully pompous, tortuous style with sections of verse, the history consists of a prologue and four books. Book One describes the mythical Trojan ancestry of the DANES and the adventures of a band of marauding Danish Vikings in the mid-9th century. The remaining books describe the expulsion of ROLLO from DENMARK and his exploits in ENGLAND and Flanders, his settlement in Normandy, and its history up to the death of Richard I (996). The reliability of Dudo's work is questionable, but as the only surviving inside account of the early history of Normandy it is too important to be ignored.

Dudo of St-Quentin: History of the Normans, trans. E. Christiansen (Woodbridge, Suffolk, 1998).

dwarves In Scandinavian mythology, dwarves were small, cunning, and often malicious and greedy men who lived underground. They were skilled craftsmen in metals and jewels and made many of the gods' greatest treasures, including ODIN's spear, THOR's hammer, FREYR's ship and FREYJA's necklace. They also brewed the mead of poetry and possessed healing and other magic powers. Being all males, dwarves could not reproduce sexually: they were moulded from the earth, or grew from GIANTS' blood.

Dyle, battle of the (891) Battle fought on the River Dyle near Louvain, Belgium. The East FRANKS under king ARNULF inflicted a heavy defeat on an ARMY of Danish Vikings that had arrived in Flanders from the River Seine in 890. The DANES occupied a

fortified camp in a strong position in marshland. The Frankish cavalry dismounted and stormed the camp on foot. As the Franks broke into the camp, the Danes panicked and fled to the river, where hundreds drowned trying to escape. Two otherwise unknown Danish kings, Sigfred and Godfred, were among the dead. The survivors, and their FAMILIES, withdrew to Boulogne and from there sailed to ENGLAND in 892. According to the *Annals of Fulda*, only one Frank was killed in the battle.

Opposite: A 12th-century copy of Dudo of St-Quentin's *History of the Normans*.

St Matthew, from Ebo of Rheims's personal Gospel book.

Eadred (d. 955) King of ENGLAND (r. 946–55). Eadred was the son of king EDWARD THE ELDER and the brother of king EDMUND I. Eadred faced a three-cornered struggle with the Norwegian ERIK BLOODAXE and OLAF SIHTRICSSON of DUBLIN for control of NORTHUMBRIA. With the expulsion of Erik from YORK in 954, Northumbria was brought permanently into the kingdom of England by Eadred. Eadred was a friend of St Dunstan's and supported his work of monastic reform in England.

Eadric Streona (d. 1017) Ealdorman of MERCIA (1007–17). Eadric rose to prominence in 1006, when he murdered Ælfhelm, the ealdorman of NORTHUMBRIA, on the instructions of ÆTHELRED II. His reward was the ealdormanry of Mercia and an unenviable but well-deserved reputation for duplicity and treachery. In 1015 he murdered two thanes, Sigeferth and Morcar, so that Æthelred could seize their property. After Æthelred's death in 1016 Eadric was left isolated and surrounded by enemies. He is vilified in the *ANGLO-SAXON CHRONICLE* for frequently changing side between EDMUND IRONSIDE and CNUT, but this was probably a desperate attempt to play his enemies off one against the other. Eadric's abandonment of Edmund at the battle of ASHINGDON in October 1016 was probably a decisive factor in Cnut's victory, but it did not save him. Cnut, sensibly enough, had Eadric beheaded in 1017.

East Anglia, kingdom of The Anglo-Saxon kingdom of the East Angles, it covered modern Norfolk, Suffolk and parts of Cambridgeshire and Essex. The kingdom emerged *c.*500, and under Rædwald (r. 599–624/5) it was briefly the leading Anglo-Saxon state. From *c.*650 East Anglia was dominated by the larger neighbouring kingdom of MERCIA, but

it regained full independence in 825. The first major Viking raid on East Anglia occurred in 841. In 865 the Danish GREAT ARMY landed in East Anglia and spent the winter there. In the spring the DANES took horses from the East Anglians and moved on to attack Mercia and NORTHUMBRIA. When the Danes returned to East Anglia late in 869, they defeated and killed its king, Edmund (St EDMUND), and the kingdom collapsed. Large-scale Danish settlement under GUTHRUM began in 879, after ALFRED's victory at EDINGTON. East Anglia was conquered by Alfred's son EDWARD THE ELDER in 917 and incorporated into the kingdom of WESSEX. Not all East Angles saw Edward as a liberator: some fought with the Danes against him.

Ebo of Rheims (Ebbo) (*c.*775–851) Archbishop of Rheims (816–34) and missionary. Of humble origins, Ebo was educated at the Frankish royal court and ordained as a priest. He was a counsellor and royal librarian to the emperor LOUIS THE PIOUS, before becoming archbishop of Rheims in 816. Appointed apostolic legate by pope Paschal I, Ebo led the first Frankish mission to DENMARK in 822–3, presumably with the agreement of king HARALD KLAK, who needed Louis's support to keep his throne. Despite two further missions, Ebo won few converts but helped prepare the ground for the later, though scarcely more successful, missions of St ANSGAR. In his later years, Ebo became an opponent of Louis, for which he was imprisoned in 834 and deprived of his see. Around 845–7 Ebo was appointed archbishop of Hildesheim, where he died in 851.

Eddas Two collections of Old Icelandic literature that together form the most complete and authoritative sources for pagan Scandinavian

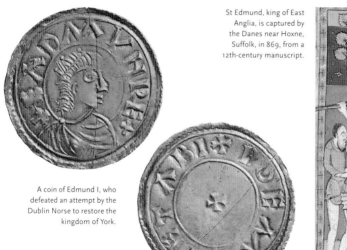

A coin of Edmund I, who defeated an attempt by the Dublin Norse to restore the kingdom of York.

St Edmund, king of East Anglia, is captured by the Danes near Hoxne, Suffolk, in 869, from a 12th-century manuscript.

mythology. The *Poetic* or *Elder Edda* is a collection of thirty-four anonymous, alliterative mythological and heroic poems. The most important of the mythological poems are VOLUSPÁ ('The Prophecy of the Seeress'), which describes the CREATION of the world and its destruction at RAGNAROK, and *Hávamál* (literally 'The Speech of Hávi [an alternative name for ODIN]', but popularly known as 'The Sayings of the High One'), a collection of gnomic and other verses offering common-sense wisdom about everyday social CONDUCT, spells and verses about the high god Odin. The heroic poetry includes a cycle of sixteen poems concerning the story of SIGURD FAFNISBANE. The different elements of the *Poetic Edda*, were composed in their present forms at various times between the late 10th and mid-13th centuries. The collection is preserved in one manuscript only, the *Codex Regius* of *c*.1300.

The *Prose, Younger* or *Snorra Edda* was written by the Icelandic poet and historian SNORRI STURLUSON *c*.1220, probably as a handbook on traditional SKALDIC verse. The *Prose Edda* consists of four sections. In the prologue, Snorri, a Christian, attempts a rational explanation of the origin of the PAGAN RELIGION: the pagan gods were simply deified ancient heroes, the descendants of king Priam, who migrated north after the fall of Troy. The second section *Gylfaginning* ('The Tricking of Gylfi'), is a comprehensive account of Scandinavian mythology, from the creation to Ragnarok, the doom of the gods. It takes the form of a contest of wits between the gods and Gylfi, a Swedish king, and quotes freely from the *Poetic Edda*. The third, and longest, part, *Skáldskaparmál* ('The Language of Poetry') is a discussion of prosody, partly in the form of a dialogue between BRAGI, the god of poetry, and

Ægir, a personification of the sea. Snorri illustrates the discussion with mythological and etymological stories and quotations from skaldic poems. The final section *Háttartal* ('list of verse forms') is a series of poems praising king Håkon IV of NORWAY and jarl Skúli that illustrate a variety of verse forms. They are accompanied by a commentary discussing metre and poetic devices such as rhyme and alliteration. Snorri's work is unique for its time in its systematic treatment of both pagan mythology and the art of poetry. As an aristocrat with a strong sense of history, FAMILY and tradition, Snorri's purpose in writing may well have been to promote traditional poetic forms at a time when continental verse forms were becoming more popular in ICELAND.

The meaning of the title *Edda* is unclear. One explanation is that it may be derived from the Old Norse *óðr* ('poetry'); another, that it is from the Latin *edo* ('I compose').

The Poetic Edda, trans. C. Larrington (Oxford, 1996); Snorri Sturluson, *Edda*, trans. A. Faulkes (London and Rutland, Vermont, 1987).

Edington, battle of (878) Decisive victory of ALFRED THE GREAT over the Danish GREAT ARMY under GUTHRUM, which ensured the survival of his kingdom of WESSEX. In May 878 Alfred left Athelney in the marshes of Somerset, where he had taken refuge from the Danish invasion, and rode to Ecgbryhtesstan (location unknown), where he gathered the levies of Somerset, Wiltshire and Hampshire. Two days later, Alfred fought the DANES at Edington in Wiltshire and put them to flight. The Danes retreated to their fort at Chippenham, and after a two-week siege by the West Saxons they agreed peace terms, confirmed by the treaty of WEDMORE.

A 15th-century wall painting, partially restored in the late 19th century, showing the martyrdom of St Edmund by the Danes.

Edmund I (921–46) King of ENGLAND (r. 939–46). Edmund was the son of king EDWARD THE ELDER of WESSEX and half-brother to his predecessor, king ATHELSTAN, who had completed the political unification of England. Following Athelstan's death in 939, OLAF GUTHFRITHSSON, the Norse king of DUBLIN, occupied YORK and the FIVE BOROUGHS of the DANELAW. Edmund recaptured the Five Boroughs after Olaf's death in 942, and in 944 he regained York, driving out the Norse kings OLAF SIHTRICSSON and Ragnald II. Edmund pursued a policy of securing peaceful relations with SCOTLAND and oversaw the beginning of the 10th-century monastic revival in England. He was murdered by an exiled criminal and was succeeded by his brother EADRED.

Edmund, St (841–69) The last Anglo-Saxon king of EAST ANGLIA (r. c.855–69). Edmund was defeated and captured in battle with the Danish GREAT ARMY under IVAR (Ingware) and Ubba near Hoxne in Suffolk, in November 869. According to later traditions, Edmund refused to deny his Christian faith or to rule as Ivar's puppet, and was tortured and executed, either by being beheaded or shot full of arrows, at Hellesdon near Norwich. Some modern scholars have suggested that he was subjected to the BLOOD EAGLE sacrifice, though the evidence for this is tenuous. Edmund was very quickly regarded as a saint. COINS inscribed 'Sc Eadmund rex' were issued in England before the end of the 9th century. In 925 ATHELSTAN founded the monastery of Bury St Edmunds to house his relics. The cult of St Edmund became popular in the DANELAW after the Scandinavian settlers began to convert to CHRISTIANITY, and it was deliberately promoted by CNUT as a means of reconciling his English subjects to Danish rule.

Edmund Ironside (Edmund II) (993–1016) King of ENGLAND (r. 23 April to 30 November 1016). The son of king ÆTHELRED II by his first wife, Ælfgifu, he earned his nickname 'Ironside' for his heroic resistance to the DANES under CNUT. Edmund, supported by ealdorman Uhtred of NORTHUMBRIA, organized the defence of England when Cnut invaded late in 1015. When Æthelred died on 23 April 1016, Edmund was declared king at London, though other parts of the kingdom declared for Cnut. He campaigned tirelessly through the summer of 1016, fighting five battles against the Danes as he pursued them across southern England. But at ASHINGDON, Essex, in October he was betrayed on the battlefield by EADRIC STREONA, the ealdorman of MERCIA, and decisively defeated by Cnut. At Alney, near Deerhurst in Gloucestershire, Edmund agreed to divide England with Cnut. Edmund was to rule everything south of the Thames; Cnut, everything to the north. A few weeks later Edmund died of wounds received at Ashingdon, and Cnut took control of the whole of England.

Edward the Elder (d. 924) King of WESSEX (r. 899–924). Edward was the eldest son of ALFRED THE GREAT. His greatest achievement was the conquest of the DANELAW as far north as the River Humber. The first three years of his reign were spent suppressing the rebellion of his cousin Æthelwold, who allied with the East Anglian DANES to raid MERCIA. Although Edward's ARMY was defeated by the Danes at the Holme in 903, both Æthelwold and the Danish king Eorhric (ON Erik) were killed. In 909 Edward invaded the kingdom of YORK: a Danish counter-attack in 910 was bloodily defeated at TETTENHALL. With the Danes of York effectively eliminated, in 912 Edward embarked on the

Einar Tambarskelve at the battle of Svöld, from an illustration to a 19th-century edition of Snorri Sturluson's *Óláfs saga Tryggvasonar*.

methodical conquest of the Danelaw, aided closely by his sister ÆTHELFLÆD of Mercia. After the unnamed Danish king of EAST ANGLIA was killed in battle at Tempsford, Bedfordshire, in 917, resistance in the Danelaw crumbled, and by the end of 918 Edward's conquest was complete. In parallel to his conquest of the Danelaw, Edward also absorbed Mercia into Wessex, seizing London, Oxfordshire and Buckinghamshire in 911, and the rest of the kingdom in 919 following the death of Æthelflæd (918). In the same year, he occupied Manchester in the kingdom of York. Edward consolidated his conquests by building fortified BURHS. The Mercians were not reconciled to the loss of their independence and they rebelled in alliance with Welsh in 924. Edward died in Cheshire in the same year, suppressing the rebellion. After a brief succession crisis he was succeeded by his son ATHELSTAN.

Egils saga Skalla-Grímssonar ('The Saga of Egil Skalla-Grímsson') One of the most important, and entertaining, of the *Íslendingasögur* (SAGAS of the Icelanders). The hero of the saga, EGIL SKALLA-GRÍMSSON, embodies the contradictory faces of the Viking Age in a single, larger-than-life character, appearing as warrior, merchant, farmer and skald. Unlike the other *Íslendingasögur*, most of the action of *Egils saga* takes place overseas, as Egil's adventures take him across most of the Viking world. It is thought, on stylistic grounds, that the saga was written by SNORRI STURLUSON, around 1230. The saga incorporates forty-eight stanzas and six long poems that it attributes to Egil, though they, too, may have been composed by Snorri.

The early chapters of the saga concern Egil's violent father Skalla-Grímr, a BERSERKER and pirate who eventually settles in ICELAND to escape a feud

with king HARALD FAIRHAIR. Egil inherits his father's ugly looks and his violent disposition, killing one of his playmates at the age of six. On his first trip abroad he makes a mortal enemy of king ERIK BLOODAXE by killing one his servants. Egil becomes a pirate and later enters the service of king ATHELSTAN in ENGLAND. The feud with Erik escalates after Egil kills one of his sons. Egil is therefore in great danger when, several years later, he is shipwrecked on a trading voyage to England and brought before Erik, now king of YORK. Erik sentences Egil to death but allows him to go free after he composes a bloodthirsty praise-poem in his honour (known as the *Hofuðslaun*, or 'Head Ransom'). After many more adventures, Egil settles down as a peaceful farmer at Borg in western Iceland until his death in advanced old age, having outlived all his adversaries.

Egil's Saga, trans. H. Pálsson and P. Edwards (Harmondsworth, 1977).

Egil Skalla-Grímsson A 10th-century Icelander who is the central character in *EGILS SAGA*. In the absence of independent sources, it is impossible to disentangle the historical Egil from the Egil of the SAGA. The saga claims that Egil was a great poet, but several scholars have questioned the authenticity of the poems attributed to him in it. According to the saga, Egil died shortly before the introduction of CHRISTIANITY to ICELAND in 1000.

Einar Tambarskelve ('paunch-shaker') (*c.*982–*c.*1050) Influential chieftain of Uppland who played a leading role in Norwegian politics in the early 11th century. Famous in SAGA tradition as an archer, Einar fought at Svöld for king OLAF TRYGGVASON against jarl ERIK of HLAÐIR.

Left: Egil Skalla-Grímsson, as imagined by a 17th-century Icelandic illustrator.

Right: A mid-11th-century illustration showing Queen Emma, with her two sons Harthacnut and Edward, receiving a copy of the *Encomium Emmae reginae* from its anonymous author.

Subsequently, he became a loyal ally of Erik and his brother SVEIN HÅKONSSON, whose sister Bergliot he married. He fought with Svein against OLAF HARALDSSON at Nesjar in 1015 and after their defeat went into exile in SWEDEN. He was reconciled with king Olaf in 1022, but in 1023 he went to ENGLAND and met CNUT, then went on PILGRIMAGE to Rome. When Cnut forced Olaf into exile in 1028 he promised Einar an jarldom. Cnut failed to deliver on his promise and Einar refused to fight against Olaf when he returned in 1030. After Olaf's death at the battle of STIKLESTAD, Einar became one of the first to recognize that the king had been a saint. In 1034 Einar went to RUSSIA to invite Olaf's son MAGNUS THE GOOD to become king of NORWAY, and after Magnus's accession the following year he became one of the king's most trusted advisors. Relations between Einar and Magnus's successor HARALD HARDRADA were difficult from the start on account of his independence of mind and great influence in the Trondelag. After Einar rescued one of his men from royal justice, Harald had him murdered at TRONDHEIM.

Eiriks saga *see* VINLAND SAGAS

Eketorp The only one of sixteen circular fortified MIGRATION period (*c*.400–550) settlements on the Swedish Baltic island of Öland to have been fully excavated. The fort consisted of fifty-three stone buildings, including houses, barns and byres. The population of between 150 and 200 lived by farming, and it manufactured its own bronze and iron tools. Eketorp and many of the other settlements were reoccupied in the late Viking Age as refuges against pirate raids by the WENDS and BALTS.

Elblag (Elbing) Viking Age trading settlement at Lake Druzno near the mouth of the River Vistula, Poland. Although the site was in the territory of the Prussian BALTS, graves in a nearby cemetery indicate a permanent Scandinavian presence at Elblag during the Viking Age. At that time the settlement was probably known as Truso.

elves Two races of supernatural beings: the light elves, who were in some way close to the gods, and the dark elves, who lived underground and were skilled craftsmen, rather like the DWARVES. Elves were worshipped and sacrificed to (*álfablót*) for a good harvest. Belief in elves survived the coming of CHRISTIANITY, though they became transformed into a kind of fairy folk.

Emma of Normandy (d. 1052) Daughter of Richard I (RICHARD THE FEARLESS) of NORMANDY, Emma was married to ÆTHELRED II, king of ENGLAND, in 1002 and adopted the English name Ælfgifu. She fled to Normandy with Æthelred in 1013 to escape SVEIN FORKBEARD. She remained in Normandy until 1018, when she returned to England to marry Svein's son CNUT. After Cnut's death in 1035, she was forced into exile in Flanders by her stepson HAROLD HAREFOOT, but returned to wield considerable influence when HARTHACNUT, her son by Cnut, finally became king of England in 1040. Following Harthacnut's death in 1042, Emma's son by Æthelred, Edward the Confessor (r. 1042–66), became king. Their relationship was not close and Edward dispossessed her of her property in 1043. She continued to live in England until her death.

Encomium Emmae reginae ('Encomium of Queen Emma') Also known more appropriately as *Gesta*

The Danes under Ivar and
Ubba invade England, from
a 'life' of St Edmund made
at Bury St Edmunds c.1130.

Cnutonis regis ('The Deeds of King Cnut'), the
encomium is concerned principally with
describing the career of CNUT. It was commissioned
by Cnut's widow EMMA in 1040–1 and written in
Flanders, probably at the monastery of St-Bertin.
Its value as a historical source is limited to some
extent because of its obvious bias. The narrative
glorifies Cnut, makes no mention of Emma's
previous marriage to ÆTHELRED II, or her children
by him, and vilifies Cnut's illegitimate son HAROLD
HAREFOOT, who had driven her and HARTHACNUT,
her son by Cnut, into exile. The purpose of the
Encomium is unclear, but it was probably
intended to advance Harthacnut's claim to the
English throne over that of Edward the Confessor,
Emma's son by Æthelred.

Encomium Emmae Reginae, ed. and trans. A. Campbell, Camden
Society 3rd Series 72, (London, 1949, reprint 1998).

England, Vikings in The Viking Age in England
began with raids, the earliest recorded anywhere
in Europe, on PORTLAND (c.789) and the monastery
on LINDISFARNE (793). A reference in a 792 charter
of Offa, king of MERCIA, to military service against
'pagans' may be evidence of other unrecorded
raids around this time. The ANGLO-SAXONS
prevented the Viking raiders penetrating inland by
blocking rivers with BRIDGES, and raiding remained
small in scale until c.835, when larger FLEETS began
arriving and won some major victories, killing, for
example, Rædwulf, king of NORTHUMBRIA, in battle
in 844. Attacks escalated further in 850 when a fleet,
said to number 350 SHIPS, established a winter camp
on the Isle of Thanet near the mouth of the River
Thames. Nevertheless, England suffered less
severely from Viking attacks in this period than
FRANCIA or IRELAND.

The decisive Viking intervention in England
began with the arrival of an exceptionally large
Danish ARMY under IVAR and HALFDAN in the
kingdom of EAST ANGLIA in 865. The Anglo-Saxon
kingdoms did not cooperate effectively against the
invaders, and by 876 the DANES had occupied East
Anglia, eastern Mercia and southern Northumbria.
Only the kingdom of WESSEX, under ALFRED THE
GREAT, successfully resisted Danish attacks.
Conquest was followed by widespread Danish
settlement in eastern England and the foundation of
small kingdoms, the longest lived of which was
based at YORK. This Danish-settled area later came to
be known as the DANELAW because of its distinctive
Scandinavian-influenced customs. Around 900
Norse settlers, many of them from Ireland, began to
settle quietly in north-west England.

Once the Vikings settled down, they lost their
main military advantage – their mobility – and they
became vulnerable to counter-attack. Alfred's
successor EDWARD THE ELDER, aided by his sister
ÆTHELFLÆD, the ruler of Mercia, conquered the
Danish-controlled areas south of the River Humber
in 912–18, while the Danish kingdom of York came
under Norse control in 919. Edward's son
ATHELSTAN captured York in 927, becoming the first
king to rule over all of England. Not all Anglo-Saxons
welcomed the rule of Wessex; some preferred the
Danes and even fought for them. After Athelstan's
death in 939 the Norse recaptured York, but could
never hold it securely, and its last Viking king ERIK
BLOODAXE was overthrown and killed in 954.
England enjoyed a respite from Viking attacks until
980, when raids from DENMARK and the Norse
settlements in Ireland and SCOTLAND began.
England's king ÆTHELRED II was a poor war leader
who was soon reduced to paying DANEGELD to buy

The Vikings' influence in England stretched well beyond the areas actually settled by them: this church doorway at Kilpeck, Herefordshire, is decorated in the late Viking Urnes art style.

off the Viking raids. Among the leaders of the Vikings were OLAF TRYGGVASON, who used the proceeds of the raids to win control of NORWAY in 995, and the Danish king SVEIN FORKBEARD. As the English defences collapsed, Svein's objective changed from exacting tribute to outright conquest. At the end of 1013 Æthelred fled the country and Svein was accepted as king of England, but he died in a matter of weeks before he could consolidate his conquest. England had to be reconquered, after an epic struggle with Æthelred's son EDMUND IRONSIDE, by Svein's son CNUT in 1016. Though many Danish aristocrats were granted English lands, Cnut's conquest was not followed by any significant Scandinavian rural settlement. Under Cnut, England became part of an empire that included most of Scandinavia, but his successors showed none of his ability and the native dynasty was restored in 1042.

The Norwegian king HARALD HARDRADA attempted to conquer England in 1066, but was crushingly defeated at the battle of STAMFORD BRIDGE, fatally weakening the English just weeks before WILLIAM THE CONQUEROR led his successful invasion from NORMANDY. The Danes supported rebellions against William in 1069–70 and 1075, and CNUT II planned another invasion in 1085. Disputes prevented the fleet from sailing, however, and Cnut's assassination in 1086 effectively marked the end of the Viking Age in England, though the Norwegian king Harald Eystein led a plundering raid along the east coast as late as 1153.

The Vikings' impact on England was considerable. Their invasions effectively eliminated the kingdoms of East Anglia, Mercia and Northumbria, leaving Wessex as the only Anglo-Saxon kingdom. When Wessex conquered the Danelaw in the 10th century,

the English were for the first time united in a single kingdom. Thus, England owes its existence as a unified kingdom indirectly to the Vikings. The extensive Danish settlements in eastern England had a long-lasting influence on local legal customs, and a wider impact on the English language through hundreds of Scandinavian loan words, including ones as basic as 'sky', 'skin', 'get', 'egg' and 'sister'. The Viking attacks on monasteries certainly caused a great deal of cultural damage, but English monasticism made a strong recovery in the 10th century. Viking raids must also have caused much short-term economic hardship for their victims through losses of livestock, seed corn and manpower. In the longer term the Vikings may have promoted urbanization, both directly through TRADE at centres like York and Lincoln, and indirectly by prompting the Anglo-Saxons to found fortified settlements called BURHS.

The Scandinavian settlers in England were assimilated into the native population within a few generations by intermarriage and conversion to CHRISTIANITY. Archaeological evidence of the Scandinavian settlement is limited. There are a few pagan burials and many works of sculpture showing the influence of Scandinavian ART STYLES, but apart from at York no Scandinavian settlements have been identified with any certainty. Excavations of Viking Age farmsteads at RIBBLEHEAD in North Yorkshire, Goltho in Lincolnshire, Bryants Gill in Cumbria and Simy Folds in County Durham, each one in an area settled by Scandinavians, have all failed to produce distinctively Viking artefacts. The most important source of evidence for Scandinavian settlement comes from place-names. In the old Danelaw counties of eastern England, Danish influence is evident in place-names ending in -by, as in

A coin of Erik Bloodaxe, a great warrior but a failure as a king in both Norway and York.

Thurkleby ('Thurkil's farmstead'), and -*thorpe*, as in Kettlethorpe ('Ketil's outlying farm'). Hybrid names incorporating a Danish personal name and the English element -*tun*, as in Grimston ('Grim's village') are also common in the Danelaw. Norse place-names are common in north-west England, especially in Cumbria. Typical Norse place-name elements include -*thveit*, as in Brackenthwaite ('bracken clearing'), -*sætr*, as in Gunnerside ('Gunnar's shieling') and -*fjall*, as in Scafell ('crag hill').

H. R. Loyn, *The Vikings in Britain* (London, 1977); J. D. Richards, *Viking Age England* (London, 1991); E. Roesdahl et al, *The Vikings in England* (London, 1981).

Erik Bloodaxe (d. 954) King of NORWAY (r. *c.*930–6); king of YORK (r. 948, 952–4). Thanks to his lurid nickname, Erik is probably one of the most famous of all Vikings, but, despite this, hard facts about his early life are in short supply. Erik's career was not by any standards a great success. Following the death of his father, king HARALD FAIRHAIR, Erik became joint ruler of Norway with two brothers, both of whom he soon killed. Erik's rule was unpopular, and *c.*936 he was forced to abdicate by his half-brother HÅKON THE GOOD. Erik was probably active in Scotland's northern isles until he was invited to become king of YORK by the Northumbrian DANES in 948. But Erik could not establish himself securely, opposed as he was not only by the English king EADRED but also by OLAF SIHTRICSSON, king of DUBLIN. Despite the support of archbishop WULFSTAN I, Erik was forced out by Eadred before the year was over and replaced by Olaf. In 952 Olaf was expelled and Erik was invited back, but his position was immediately undermined when Eadred arrested his ally, archbishop Wulfstan.

In 954 Erik was again driven from York, and while crossing the Pennines on his way to Carlisle he was ambushed and killed at Stainmore by the otherwise unknown Maccus. Osulf of Bamburgh, who had engineered Erik's downfall, was rewarded by Eadred with the ealdormanry of NORTHUMBRIA. With Erik's death, Scandinavian rule at York came to an end, and Northumbria was finally absorbed fully into the English kingdom. A surviving fragment of Erik's funeral lay, the *Eiríksmál* ('The Lay of Erik'), possibly commissioned by his widow Gunnhild, describes his tumultuous welcome in VALHALLA. Erik's fearsome reputation owes much to the medieval Icelandic SAGA tradition, especially *EGILS SAGA*, though it has almost certainly grown with the telling.

Erik of Hlaðir (Erik Håkonsson) (d. *c.*1023) Jarl of HLAÐIR (1000–*c.*1015); earl of NORTHUMBRIA (1016–*c.*1023). Erik's father HÅKON SIGURDSSON, jarl of Hlaðir, was a leading supporter of the Danish kings who had ruled NORWAY since *c.*970. When OLAF TRYGGVASON seized power in Norway in 995 Håkon was murdered and Erik went into exile in DENMARK. Around 996–7 Erik led a Viking raid to RUSSIA and sacked the merchant TOWN of STARAJA LADOGA. In 1000 Erik, with Danish and Swedish support, ambushed and killed Olaf at Svöld. Erik returned to Hlaðir to rule northern Norway in semi-independence, while SVEIN FORKBEARD brought the south back under Danish rule. He sealed the arrangement by marrying Svein's daughter Gytha. In 1015 Erik left his brother SVEIN HÅKONSSON in control of Norway and joined CNUT's invasion of ENGLAND. Erik's absence gave OLAF HARALDSSON the opportunity to seize the Norwegian throne. After Cnut's victory in England, Erik was appointed earl of

Eskimo driftwood carving of a Norse Greenlander, perhaps met on a trading voyage.

A page from a 15th-century copy of the *Saga of Erik the Red*.

Northumbria; he is last heard of in 1023, when he was a signatory to one of Cnut's charters.

Erik the Red (Eirik Torvaldsson) (d. *c*.1002?) Founder of the Norse GREENLAND colony and the father of LEIF ERIKSSON, one of the first Europeans to reach North America. Born in NORWAY, Erik emigrated to ICELAND as a child after his father was outlawed for manslaughter. Around 980 Erik was himself sentenced to OUTLAWRY for manslaughter. Seeking a safe haven, he set out with his family *c*.983 to explore Greenland, which had first been sighted about eighty years earlier and was still unnamed. Pack ice prevented Erik from approaching the coast until he rounded Cape Farewell and found a sheltered mountainous coast of ice-free fjords. Though treeless, the area had good grazing, for which reason Erik gave it its optimistic name of Greenland. In 986 Erik returned to Iceland and persuaded others to join him in founding a settlement on Greenland. Of the twenty-five ships that set out with Erik on the return journey, only fourteen made it round Cape Farewell, but this was enough to found two settlements, known simply as the Eastern Settlement and the Western Settlement. Erik established a farm at BRATTAHLID in the Eastern Settlement and was recognized as the leader of the colony. He refused to join Leif on his voyage to America *c*.1000 on the grounds of old age, and died shortly after as a result of an epidemic introduced by a ship from Norway.

Erik the Victorious (Erik Bjarnarson) (d. 995) King of the SVEAR (*c*.980–95). Erik gained his nickname for his victory at the battle of Fyrisvallarna near UPPSALA. Unfortunately, the only contemporary source to mention the battle, a SKALDIC verse by

Thorvald Hjaltason, does not say whom Erik defeated there. According to Icelandic SAGA traditions, it was Erik's nephew Styrbjorn Starki, who was demanding a share of the kingdom, along with an ARMY of DANES and JOMSVIKINGS. Several rune-stones from Skåne (now in SWEDEN but then part of DENMARK), dating from shortly before 1000, commemorate men who fell with Toke Gormsson in a battle at Uppsala, possibly Fyrisvallarna. Erik sought friendly relations with the Baltic Slavs and married a Polish princess. He was succeeded by his son OLOF SKÖTKONUNG.

Eskimos (Inuit) When the Norse settled GREENLAND's south-eastern fjords in 985–6 they found the area uninhabited. In the course of the voyages to VINLAND *c*.1000 the Norse made contact with native Americans for the first time. The Norse described these people simply as SKRÆLINGS, and it is impossible to know if they were American Indians or members of the Dorset Eskimo peoples that inhabited Labrador and Newfoundland at that time. Between 1000 and 1200 the Dorset Eskimos were replaced by the Thule Eskimos, who had originated on St Lawrence and other islands in the Bering Straits before AD 800 and had expanded west. The Thule specialized in hunting marine mammals, including seals and whales, and developed a sophisticated technology that enabled them to flourish in the high Arctic Circle until modern times. The Thule certainly traded with the Norse, whom they called the Kavdlunait, because small numbers of Norse artefacts have been found at many of their settlements in the Canadian Arctic. As the Thule migrated south along Greenland's east coast in the 14th and 15th centuries they came into conflict with the Norse settlers, though whether this

Sigurd slays the dragon Fafnir, from a 12th-century wood carving, Hylestad stave church, Norway.

contributed to the extinction of the colony is unclear. These often savage conflicts are the subject of Eskimo folktales recorded by missionaries in the 19th century, as well as of contemporary Icelandic annals.

D. Dumond, *The Eskimos and Aleuts* (2nd edition, London and New York, 1987).

Eyrbyggja saga ('The Saga of the Men of Eyrr') One of the major *Íslendingasögur* (SAGAS OF THE ICELANDERS). It tells the story of the people of Eyrr, Thórsnes and Álptafjörðr on the Snæfellsnes peninsula in western ICELAND. The story begins with the arrival of Thorolf Mostrarskegg in Iceland *c*.880, but the central character is Snorri the Priest (963–1031), a shrewd and vengeful man who, despite being a pagan priest, played a leading role in persuading the Icelanders to accept CHRISTIANITY. The SAGA ends with Snorri's death and a list of his descendants. The author of the saga is unknown, but it was written *c*.1250, probably at Helgafell in Snæfellsnes. *Eyrbyggja saga* is unique among the *Íslendingasögur* for a number of reasons: it does not concern itself with the fate of a single person or FAMILY; it has a complex structure that interweaves many separate stories and conflicts; and it gives prominence to supernatural events and ghosts.

Eyrbyggja Saga, trans. H. Pálsson and P. Edwards (Edinburgh, 1973).

Færeyinga saga ('The Saga of the Faroe Islanders') Written around 1200, the main themes of *Færeyinga saga* are the feuds between the islands' chieftains in the 10th and 11th centuries, their relations with the Norwegian kings, and the conversion of the Faroese to CHRISTIANITY. No complete manuscript of the SAGA exists; it has been reconstructed from long passages quoted in works by other authors, the largest section being preserved in *FLATEYJARBÓK*.

The Faroe Islanders' Saga, trans. G. Johnston (Ottawa, 1975).

Fafnir In Scandinavian mythology, Fafnir was the son of Hreidmar and the brother of REGIN and OTTAR. Fafnir turned himself into a dragon and killed his father to acquire ANDVARI's treasure, given by the god LOKI as ransom for killing Ottar. With the help of Regin, the hero SIGURD FAFNISBANE killed Fafnir. By tasting Fafnir's blood, Sigurd learned to understand the speech of the birds.

family The Viking Age Scandinavian family was essentially a nuclear one. The most important relationships were those between man and wife, CHILDREN and parents, and brothers and sisters. WOMEN did not sever their links to their natal families upon MARRIAGE; relationships between parents- and brothers- and sisters-in-law mattered. Sons, in particular, remained close to their parents because even after marriage they usually continued to work on the family farm. Extended family relationships were less important, but it is significant that even third cousins (in Jutland) and fourth cousins (in ICELAND) were entitled to a share of the compensation paid to compound the killing of a family member. Members of a family owed one another obligations of mutual support. Family honour had to be defended, and relatives were

Funningur, the site of
the first settlement in the
Faroe Islands, founded by
Grímur Kamban.

The interior of a
reconstructed hall where a
chieftain or king would have
feasted his followers.

expected to seek redress for the killing or injuring of
a family member, either through the courts or by
taking blood vengeance. The family was responsible
for the care and support of its members who,
through age or disability, were unable to work for
their living. Anyone without close relatives had no
one to support them in disputes, and if they became
unable to work for any reason they faced beggary. To
be expelled from one's family was, for this reason, a
fate almost as bad as OUTLAWRY and provided a
strong incentive to conform. As the family of an
outlaw could lose property and inheritance rights, it
also had an interest in restraining the behaviour of
unruly members.

Faroe Islands The spectacularly mountainous Faroe
Islands were discovered by Irish monks engaged in
the practice of *peregrinatio*, sailing into voluntary
exile for God. A few settled semi-permanently as
hermits; others may have used the islands as a
staging post for voyages as far as ICELAND. Pollen
evidence of the cultivation of oats suggests that this
may have happened in the early 7th century. The
Norse must have reached the islands in the early 9th
century, as the Irish monk Dicuil, writing *c*.825,
complained that they had forced the hermits to flee.
According to the *FÆREYINGA SAGA*, Grímur Kamban
was the first Norse settler of the Faroe Islands.
Faroese tradition has it that his settlement was at
Funningur in a sheltered bay on Eysturoy. As his
surname is of Gaelic origin, Grímur must have
spent some time in IRELAND or the Hebrides before
settling in the Faroes. Most of the settlers came
direct from the Norwegian west-coast districts of
Agder, Rogaland and Sogn. Little is known about the
early history of the settlements. As in Iceland, the
land seems to have been claimed by a few

aristocratic FAMILIES, who divided it among their
followers. An annual THING was held to resolve
disputes at Tinganes in the present Faroese capital
Torshavn. Norwegian kings claimed sovereignty over
the islands from the late 9th century, but it was not
until around 1180 that their authority was effective,
by which time the Faroese had developed their own
LANGUAGE and identity. A BISHOPRIC was founded at
Kirkjubøur *c*.1100, and, as part of the Norwegian
king's policy of strengthening his authority in the
islands, it was brought under the control of the
archbishopric of TRONDHEIM in 1152.

The main attraction of the Faroe Islands for Norse
settlers was their good grazing for sheep and cattle.
A little barley could be grown, but never enough for
the islanders to be self-sufficient. The islands also
lacked timber and iron, so TRADE was a necessity.
The main exports were wool, woven cloth and
feathers. FISHING, whaling, sealing and gathering
seabirds and their eggs provided valuable extra
supplies of FOOD.

feasts and feasting As was the case in the rest of
early medieval Europe, feasting was an important
part of the social life of the Viking Age. A great
feast could establish or enhance the reputation
of the host, and provided the occasion for striking
alliances and friendships. Kings and chieftains
were expected to feast their dependents regularly to
cement the relationship between them. To feast
someone well and send him away with good gifts
was a way of demonstrating the value placed on a
relationship. Weddings were always celebrated
with feasts.

The feasts of kings or chieftains were held in long
halls with a central hearth. Cushion-covered benches
were placed on platforms along the walls, with long

The wolf Fenrir bound, from a 17th-century Icelandic manuscript of the *Edda*.

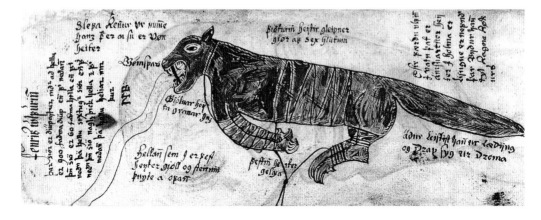

narrow tables placed in front of them, all furnished with the best tableware. Tapestries might be hung on the walls specially for the occasion. The king or chief sat on a raised dais at the centre of one wall; other guests were seated according to their social rank. Everyone would seek to impress, and would wear their finest clothes and JEWELRY. Plenty of alcoholic drinks – beer, wine or mead – and boiled or roast meat were served with fish, bread, cheese, vegetables, fruits and nuts. Entertainment was provided by SKALDIC poets, storytellers, musicians and perhaps acrobats and jugglers. Royal feasts could last several days. Writing in the 11th century, ADAM OF BREMEN tells of eight successive days of feasting laid on for the archbishop of Hamburg-Bremen by king SVEIN ESTRITHSON of DENMARK to confirm a treaty with the Holy Roman Empire.

In pagan times sacrificial feasts were held. These were called *blóts*, or 'blood-offerings'. One such feast, held in the presence of king HÅKON THE GOOD at HLAÐIR in Trondelag in the mid-10th century, is described by SNORRI STURLUSON. All the local peasants attended, bringing beer and horseflesh. The walls of the temple, inside and out, were daubed with the blood of the horses before the meat was cooked in great cauldrons. Prior to being eaten, the meat was dedicated to the gods ODIN, NJORD, FREYR and BRAGI. The feast was so important to his subjects that Håkon reluctantly agreed to eat part of the sacrificial meal, despite being a Christian.

félag (fellowship) A *félag* could be formed by a band of warriors (a LIÐ), an association of merchants, or the joint owners of property such as a ship. Members of a *félag* had mutual responsibilities towards one another. The *félagi* (companions) of a *lið*

owed loyalty to each other and to their leader, or *dróttin*, who could be a king or chieftain. There is no evidence that WOMEN could be involved in a *félag*.

Fenrir In Scandinavian mythology, a monstrous wolf, the offspring of the god LOKI and the giantess Angerboda. The gods bound Fenrir with the magic chain Gleipnir, but at RAGNAROK he will break free and kill the high god ODIN, before being slain by Odin's son Vidar.

Finns During the Viking Age the Finns inhabited a vast area of northern Europe, comprising roughly the southern quarter of modern Finland and a swathe of northern RUSSIA, from Karelia and NOVGOROD in the west to the Urals in the east. Their territory was being squeezed from the south by a northward migration of the Slavs that has continued into modern times: only a few isolated groups of Finnic peoples still survive in Russia today. The Finns speak a Finno-Ugrian language, similar to the Estonian tongue but completely unrelated to those of their Slav and Scandinavian neighbours. The Viking Age Finns were at a simpler stage of social and economic development than the Scandinavians and Slavs. Settled agriculture existed in favourable areas of Finland, but most Finns still practised primitive slash-and-burn cultivation. Cattle, horses, sheep and pigs were reared. Hunting for furs was an important activity. These were exported to Scandinavia and western Europe, apparently in return for silver and WEAPONS. Small trading TOWNS, such as Turku (Åbo) and Tampere, had begun to develop in south-west Finland by the end of the Viking Age. Furs were also the object of tribute-gathering raids by Norwegian and Swedish kings and the RUS. There is no evidence of the existence of kingdoms among the

Illustration from an Icelandic legal manuscript of a whale being flensed.

Finns in the Viking Age, but richly furnished male and female burials and hill-forts with stone and timber ramparts indicate the presence of chiefdoms and the beginning of political centralization. Animals played an important role in Finnish PAGAN RELIGION. Bears were particularly revered, and their paws, teeth and fat were believed to have healing properties. The Finns had a reputation for witchcraft and magic among Viking Age Scandinavians. CHRISTIANITY had become established in Finland by the 11th century, but it was several centuries before the Finns were fully Christianized. Despite its proximity to SWEDEN, Scandinavian cultural influences were limited in the Viking Age to styles of weapons and ornament. Scandinavian influence increased in the 12th century, when south-west Finland was conquered and settled by the Swedes.

fishing, whaling, sealing and seabirding The inshore waters along Scandinavia's North Sea and Atlantic coasts are among the world's richest fishing grounds, while the Baltic Sea is also highly productive of fish. Evidence of fishing in Scandinavia, in the form of fish traps, fish spears, fish hooks and net sinkers, exists from Mesolithic times (8000–4000 BC). Analysis of middens shows that fish and shellfish were a major FOOD source for Viking communities in easy reach of the sea, both in Scandinavia and overseas. Cod, herring and various species of flat fish were most commonly caught, but freshwater species such as eel, trout and salmon are also known. Mussels and oysters were the favourite shellfish gathered. Finds from HEDEBY suggest that commercial TRADE in herrings, for which the Baltic was later famous, existed before 1000. Commercial trade in stockfish (dried cod), NORWAY's most valuable export during the High Middle Ages, had

begun in northern Norway by c.1100: the cold, windy climate here was ideal for drying fish.

The simplest form of whaling practised was the taking of stranded whales or the towing ashore of dying whales. Laws existed in medieval Norway to determine how such finds should be shared out between the finder, the landowner and the Crown. Whales were also actively hunted in large numbers. The chieftain OHTHERE, from Arctic Norway, told king ALFRED THE GREAT how he and five others had taken sixty whales in two days hunting. According to the 13th-century *Konungs skuggsjá* ('The King's Mirror'), the normal method of whaling was to use boats to herd schools of whales ashore, where they would be killed, as is still done in the FAROE ISLANDS today. Whales were a source of meat and blubber, which was used for food and lighting, and hide, used for rope-making.

Seals were hunted mainly for their skins, which were used for waterproof clothes, shoes and bags, and their blubber, which, as well as being an important foodstuff, was used for lighting, waterproofing fabrics and as a substitute for tar in treeless areas such as GREENLAND and ICELAND. Skerries that were used regularly by basking seals were the subject of ownership disputes in 12th-century Iceland. Walruses were hunted in Arctic waters for their tusks, a source of IVORY, and skins, which were used to make ropes.

Seabirds and their eggs were gathered, often at extreme risk to the gatherers, from sea cliffs in Norway, Iceland, the Faroes and the northern isles of Scotland until modern times.

Five Boroughs The five TOWNS of Derby, Leicester, Lincoln, Nottingham and Stamford in the east Midlands of ENGLAND, which became centres of

The beginning of the saga of king Olaf Tryggvason in the 14th-century *Flateyjarbók*.

Danish power after the settlement of the GREAT ARMY in the area in 877. The towns are first described as the Five Boroughs in the ANGLO-SAXON CHRONICLE entry for 942. The Five Boroughs came under the control of WESSEX in 917–18, after EDWARD THE ELDER's conquest of the DANELAW. They were captured by OLAF GUTHFRITHSSON, king of YORK, in 940, but English rule was restored in 942. It was at one time believed that the Five Boroughs were specially fortified towns founded as an act of policy by the DANES after the settlement of 877. However, archaeological excavations have shown that all were well-established, locally important settlements when they came under Danish control. None has provided conclusive evidence of fortification by the Danes, though Derby, Lincoln and Leicester had Roman walls that could have been reused, while Nottingham and Stamford have provided evidence of defensive enclosures predating the Danish takeover. Nor is there evidence that any had a large Scandinavian urban population such as there was at York. Only at Nottingham has unequivocal archaeological evidence of a Scandinavian presence been found in the shape of two Viking warrior burials, and only Lincoln has provided clear evidence of urban growth during the period of Danish rule. But even in Lincoln's case the main period of urban growth appears to have come after the end of Danish control. It is therefore likely that the Five Boroughs were primarily defensive centres for a largely rural Scandinavian population. Nevertheless, coiners' names of Scandinavian origin appear frequently on COINS issued in the Five Boroughs in the late 10th and 11th centuries, suggesting that, if not numerous, Danes formed an influential and wealthy section of their populations.

R. A. Hall, 'The Five Boroughs of the Danelaw: a review of present knowledge', in *Anglo-Saxon England* 18 (1989), pp. 149–206.

Flateyjarbók ('The Book of Flatey') The largest and most beautifully decorated of medieval Icelandic manuscripts, *Flateyjarbók* was written by two priests, Jón Thórðarson and Magnus Thórhallsson, in 1387–90. The book is an attempt to present a continuous history of NORWAY by combining complete SAGAS and sections of sagas together, including several that have not been preserved elsewhere. For this reason, *Flateyjarbók* has always been considered one of the most important of all Icelandic manuscripts. It is estimated that the entire contents of *Flateyjarbók* must have been copied from some forty to fifty separate manuscripts.

fleets At the beginning of the Viking Age, Viking fleets were small: the early raid on PORTLAND in WESSEX c.789 involved only three SHIPS, while a raid on FRANCIA in 820 was made by a fleet of thirteen. An exception to this was the royal fleet of 200 ships raised by the Danish king GODFRED to attack FRISIA in 810. In the 830s the numbers of ships in Viking fleets began to escalate. The ANGLO-SAXON CHRONICLE records attacks on ENGLAND by fleets of 35 ships in 836, rising to 350 in 851, and between 200 and 350 in 892, though such figures are almost certainly estimates. This picture is mirrored in contemporary sources from IRELAND and Francia; smaller fleets also continued to be recorded. These figures are of relatively little help in trying to determine the size of Viking ARMIES, however, because we do not know the size of the ships involved: *if* the 9th-century GOKSTAD SHIP was typical, they had crews of thirty or more. The Danish fleets that operated against England in the late 10th and early 11th centuries were smaller – CNUT invaded England in 1015 with a fleet of 160 ships – but they would have included many of the very large

An inscribed piece of driftwood from Bergen showing a fleet of Viking warships drawn up along a beach.

drakkars, which had crews of more than sixty. Nothing is known about the organization of Viking fleets in the 9th and 10th centuries. Probably, like Viking armies, they were simply amalgamations of contingents of ships brought by individual chieftains and kings. The LEDING or *leiðangr* levy system, which was used to raise fleets in Scandinavia in the central Middle Ages, may have been in use by the end of the Viking Age. There were no specialist personnel in Viking fleets: the ships' crews were also warriors. The highest-ranking crew member was the steersman.

Fleets existed primarily for the transport of armies. Sea battles were rare and usually took place in sheltered waters such as estuaries, harbours and fjords. By modern standards, Viking ships had relatively poor sea-keeping abilities, and there was no question of mounting permanent patrols to intercept enemy fleets on the open sea. The tactics of sea battle were simple: sail alongside the enemy ship, grapple, board and clear its decks by hand-to-hand fighting; ships were rarely sunk, and they were a valuable part of the spoils of victory. The favoured defensive tactic was to lash the ships together side by side to make a raft of decks across which soldiers could move freely. This meant that individual ships could not be isolated by the enemy fleet and, except at either flank, they had to be attacked by the enemy prow-on. This made boarding more difficult, for the prow, being the highest part of the ship, was the strongest defensive position. The advantage in battle went not so much to the side with the most ships but with the largest. Larger ships were harder to board and their crews could rain spears and arrows down onto a smaller ship alongside. Usually, sails and masts were lowered before going into battle. Among the most important sea battles of the Viking

Age were HARALD FAIRHAIR's victory at HAFRSFJORD *c.*885–90 and the defeat of OLAF TRYGGVASON at Svöld in 1000.

Floki Vilgerdarson (*fl. c.*860–70) One of the first Norse explorers of ICELAND. From Rogaland in NORWAY, Floki set out to explore the island, which had been discovered accidentally by GARDAR THE SWEDE, with a view to settling on it. Not the most far-sighted of pioneers, Floki spent the first summer hunting seals at Vatnsfjörður, on Breiðafjörður in the east of the island, but he neglected to gather any winter fodder, with the result that all his livestock starved to death. This doomed his attempt at settlement, but the slow breakup of pack ice the following spring delayed his departure and he was forced to spend another winter at Borgafjörður. Thoroughly disillusioned, Floki decided to call the new land Iceland. Though other members of the party gave more favourable reports when Floki returned to Norway the next summer, the name stuck. Floki got over his initial disappointment and later returned to Iceland to settle permanently in Flokadalur in the north.

food and drink The diet of Viking Age Scandinavians was based on meat, fish, dairy products and cereals. A wide variety of meat was eaten: beef and veal, horsemeat, pork, mutton and lamb, goat and goose, and in some areas venison, seal and whalemeat, and game birds. Most meat was boiled or stewed in iron or SOAPSTONE cauldrons, or in water-filled pits heated by immersing red-hot stones from the fire. It was also spit-roasted or cooked on a gridiron over a fire. Various herbs such as juniper berries, cumin, mustard, horseradish and garlic were used to flavour the meat. Blood and offal were stuffed into

Kitchen utensils and storage vessels from the 9th-century Oseberg ship burial.

intestines to make sausage-shaped puddings. Meat and fish were sometimes dried, pickled or salted; ice was also used as a preservative. Milk was drunk, churned into butter, or separated into curds, which were eaten or made into cheese, and whey, which was drunk or, being slightly acidic, used for pickling. Butter was heavily salted as a preservative. Oats were made into porridge; barley and rye, into unleavened bread cooked in a round flat pan over the hot ashes of the fire. Ovens for baking bread were extremely rare in Scandinavia before the end of the Viking Age. Wheat bread was a luxury for the rich. Malted barley was used to brew ale, which was drunk in large quantities. Another popular drink was mead, a wine brewed from honey. Grape wine was an expensive imported luxury. Vegetables did not form a substantial part of the diet: cabbage, onions, beans and peas were most important. Wild fruits and nuts were eaten in season.

Normally, Viking Age Scandinavians ate two meals a day, *dagverðr* ('day meal') in the early morning and *náttverðr* ('night meal') in the early evening. Tableware was basic: food was served off round or rectangular wooden platters, or in wooden or soapstone bowls. Meat was cut with a knife; stews, broths and porridge were eaten with wooden or horn spoons. Drink was served in wooden or, in rich households, silver or imported GLASS cups and drinking horns. Drinking horns were probably used mainly at FEASTS and other social occasions: as they could not be put down without spilling the contents, they were clearly intended to be drained in one draught, no doubt to encourage drunkenness.

fortifications Several different types of fortification were used in Viking Age Scandinavia: they are more common in DENMARK and SWEDEN than in

NORWAY, where the difficult topography made them less necessary. The most common fortifications were camps used as temporary refuges in times of war by the inhabitants of the surrounding countryside to protect themselves and their livestock. These are often prehistoric fortifications that were simply repaired and reinforced in Viking times. The largest known refuge camp, Torsburgen on GOTLAND, was built originally in the MIGRATION PERIOD (AD 400–550). Situated on a low cliff-girt plateau, its 2-kilometre-long ramparts form an enclosure of more than 112 hectares, large enough to accommodate most of the Viking Age population of Gotland. On Öland, fortified villages of the Migration period, such as EKETORP, were reused in late Viking times as refuges, as were hill-forts from the same period on BORNHOLM. Smaller refuge forts are known from the Viking Age TOWNS of BIRKA and HEDEBY, but these fell out of use when the towns were fortified with earth ramparts topped with timber palisades in the 10th century. The Danish town of ÅRHUS was fortified around the same time, but urban defences remained rare in Scandinavia until after the end of the Viking Age. Few Viking Age fortifications in Scandinavia were built simply to accommodate a military garrison, the only certain examples being the circular earthwork TRELLEBORG FORTS built by HARALD BLUETOOTH in the late 10th century to consolidate royal power in Denmark. Castles were not built in Scandinavia until the 12th century. Linear earthwork barriers are common in some parts of early medieval Europe, but the only example known in Scandinavia is the DANEVIRKE rampart, which cuts across the neck of the Jutland peninsula near Schleswig. Though built originally in 737, it was repaired and extended several times during the Viking Age. Particularly in the late Viking

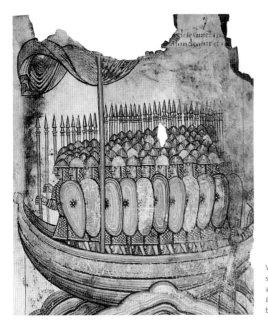

Viking warriors on their way to sack Angers on the Loire, from a late-11th-century copy of the *Life of St Aubin*, a 9th-century bishop of Angers.

Age, when Wendish piracy was becoming a problem, SEA BARRIERS of wooden stakes and deliberately sunken ships were built to protect vulnerable harbours and fjords. Another response to Wendish piracy was the construction, in the 12th century, of fortified CHURCHES on Bornholm and Öland as refuges.

It is known from literary sources that the Viking ARMIES campaigning in western Europe built fortified camps, and the Norse towns in Ireland developed from coastal forts called *LONGPHORTS*, built by early Viking raiders to protect their ships. Only one of these camps, at REPTON in ENGLAND, has been identified with certainty and excavated. Another excavated site, Camp de Péran in BRITTANY, was possibly built by Vikings, and was certainly occupied by them. Viking towns overseas, where they faced a hostile native population, were more likely to be fortified than those in Scandinavia. The RUS towns of KIEV and NOVGOROD had strong earth-and-timber ramparts, while Norse towns in Ireland such as DUBLIN, WATERFORD and WEXFORD were also heavily defended. Dublin's earth ramparts were replaced by stone walls *c.*1100. At YORK, Roman and Anglo-Saxon defences were restored and extended to protect the Viking town, while in the FIVE BOROUGHS of the DANELAW the Danish settlers probably also made use of earlier fortifications.

'Forty Years Rest' A term coined by the author of the *COGADH GAEDHEL RE GALLAIBH* ('The War of the Irish with the Foreigners') to describe the lull in Viking activity in IRELAND from the death of IVAR I, leader of the DUBLIN Vikings, in 873 to the arrival of SIHTRIC CÁECH and his great FLEET at WATERFORD in 914 and the subsequent re-establishment of Norse power in Ireland.

France *see* FRANCIA, VIKINGS IN

Francia, Vikings in Francia, the land of the FRANKS (roughly corresponding to most of modern France, Belgium, The Netherlands, Luxembourg and western Germany), was first raided by Vikings in 799. The emperor CHARLEMAGNE reacted vigorously, creating coastguard units and stationing FLEETS on major rivers. Except for the exposed coast of FRISIA, Francia experienced no serious Viking raids until the 830s, when the civil wars between the emperor LOUIS THE PIOUS and his sons had begun to undermine royal authority and with it the effectiveness of the coastal defences. In 842 the Vikings established a permanent base on the island of Noirmoutier, near the mouth of the River Loire, and thereafter were a permanent presence on Frankish territory for the next seventy years.

The main areas of Viking activity in Francia were the valleys of the rivers Seine and Loire, Flanders, Frisia and the Rhineland, all areas where navigable rivers offered the Vikings easy routes inland. Preoccupied by dynastic conflicts, Francia's Carolingian rulers were rarely able to concentrate on dealing with the Viking threat and were often reduced to buying them off with tribute. Towns were left exposed to attack because rulers such as CHARLES THE BALD were reluctant to allow them to build defences in case they should be turned into strongholds by rebel princes and nobles. For some of these rebels, such as PIPPIN II OF AQUITAINE, the Vikings were even welcome as allies. Viking raids reached their peak in the period 879–92, when the Rhineland, the Ardennes, Flanders and the Seine valley were systematically ravaged. But the Franks were finally getting the measure of the Vikings. Able warrior kings such as ODO of West Francia (France)

Frankish warrior in 9th-century fresco at Malles, Italy. Though usually better armed than the Vikings, Frankish resistance was undermined by factional disputes.

and ARNULF of East Francia (Germany) actively sought to bring the Vikings to battle and built fortresses and TOWN walls across the whole of the region between the Seine and the Rhine. Faced with resistance wherever they went, and a severe famine in the winter of 891–2, the main Viking force in Francia withdrew to England in 892, where it fared no better. The worst of the Viking Age in Francia was now over, but there remained Viking ARMIES on the Seine and the Loire. The integration of the Seine Vikings into Frankish society was begun when their leader ROLLO was made count of Rouen by CHARLES THE SIMPLE in 911. NORMANDY, as Rollo's territories came to be known, created problems of its own, but at least these were the familiar ones of dynastic and territorial ambition that kings faced from any over-mighty subject. The problem of the Vikings on the Loire was solved when the Bretons captured their base at Nantes in 937. The last Viking raids on Francia occurred in the early 11th century.

The Vikings have often been blamed for causing the breakup of the Frankish CAROLINGIAN EMPIRE, but the driving force for this was internal and dynastic: the Vikings certainly profited from the empire's internal divisions but they did not cause them. Carolingian rulers did not regard the Vikings as being nearly as serious a threat as their dynastic rivals. However, the Franks did not share their rulers' priorities. They increasingly perceived royal countermeasures against the Vikings as half-hearted or even cowardly, and by demonstrating the ineffectiveness of royal power the Vikings probably hastened its decline. The most important long-term consequence of Viking activity in Francia was the establishment of the duchy of Normandy, the importance of which to the future history of France, England and Italy can hardly be understated.

As in other areas of western Europe, Frankish monasteries – and their monks – suffered severely from Viking attacks, and many were abandoned. Monasteries were the main cultural centres of early medieval Europe, and the revival of learning fostered by Charlemagne, known as the 'Carolingian Renaissance', had collapsed before the end of the 9th century. Severe economic damage must also have been caused in the short term by Viking plundering both in the towns and the countryside. Wooden buildings were easily rebuilt, and the fertility of the soil could not be taken away, but losses of livestock, seed corn and manpower would have caused years of hardship for peasant farmers. Two major towns, QUENTOVIC and DORESTAD, were completely abandoned in the Viking Age, but the culprit here appears to be silting of the rivers that gave access to them, rather than Viking attacks. Some Frankish merchants saw in the plunder-laden Vikings an opportunity and traded with them, though this could be a dangerous business: Franks who had entered a Viking fort in Flanders to trade in 882 were captured and ransomed. Overall, however, the Vikings do not seem to have had the stimulating impact on TRADE in Francia that they had in the British Isles. Nor did the Vikings have any cultural impact on Frankish civilization; even in Normandy, the Scandinavian settlers were quickly assimilated to the native population, leaving little trace of their presence behind.

J. M. Wallace-Hadrill, 'The Vikings in Francia', in *Early Medieval History* (Oxford, 1975).

Franks The most successful of the Germanic barbarian peoples that invaded the Roman Empire in the 4th and 5th centuries. The Franks were a tribal confederation that emerged in the

The fertility-goddess Freyja, from Hagebyhögn, Sweden.

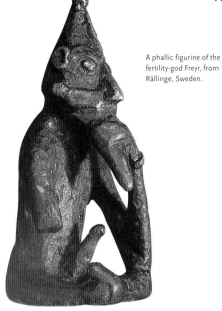

A phallic figurine of the fertility-god Freyr, from Rällinge, Sweden.

early 3rd century AD from the Chamavi, Chattuari, Salians, Tencteri and other peoples on the east bank of the lower Rhine. The Franks began to settle on Roman territory west of the Rhine in the late 4th century, but their expansion was unspectacular until the reign of Clovis (r. 482–511), who made them the masters of most of Gaul and much of Germany. Under CHARLEMAGNE (r. 768–814) the Franks conquered most of Christian western Europe. It was from the breakup of Charlemagne's empire, known as the CAROLINGIAN EMPIRE, in 887–8 that the medieval kingdoms of France and Germany emerged.

Freyja The most famous of the Scandinavian pagan goddesses, Freyja was the sister of the fertility-god FREYR, and presided over love, sensual pleasure, marriage and fertility. She shared half of the dead with the high god ODIN. In the myths associated with her, Freyja had a licentious character. In order to obtain the magic necklace Brísingamen, she agreed to sleep a night with each of the four DWARVES who had crafted it. LOKI accused her of having slept with all the gods, including her brother Freyr, and she was lusted after mightily, but in vain, by the GIANTS. Freyja was married to an obscure god called Oðr, who may originally have been Odin. During his frequent absences Freyja wept tears of gold. Freyja travelled in a chariot drawn by cats, or changed herself into a falcon.

Freyr (Frey) A leader of the VANIR family of gods, Freyr was the son of NJORD and the giantess Skadi, and the brother of FREYJA. Freyr was a fertility-god who controlled the sun and rain and the fruitfulness of the earth: he was invoked for a good harvest and peace. Freyr's associations with fertility are most

obvious in the mythical story of his successful wooing of the beautiful giantess Gerðr ('Earth'): the Swedish YNGLING DYNASTY claimed descent from this union. Freyr's most famous possession was the magic ship Skíðblaðnir. Built by the DWARVES, it was large enough to hold all the gods but could be folded to fit in a pocket. Skíðblaðnir always sailed on a true course and always had a following wind. He also owned the golden boar Gullinbursti, whose bristles could light up the darkest night. Freyr was one of the gods worshipped at the Swedish cult centre of UPPSALA, where human sacrifices were made to him. His idol was a phallic one, and a horse's phallus was used in one of the rituals associated with him.

Fribrødre Å A late-Viking Age shipyard, situated in a silted-up creek on the Danish island of Falster. Excavations have shown that old SHIPS were broken up on the site and the good timbers salvaged for reuse in new ships: large quantities of wood shavings show that new planks were also manufactured there. Many of the broken-up ship parts discovered at Fribrødre Å show Slavic characteristics. This, finds of Slavic POTTERY, and Slav elements in local place-names suggest that the site was a WENDISH colony under Danish control. The shipyard operated in the last years of the 11th century.

Frigg The wife of the Scandinavian pagan high god ODIN and the queen of ASGARD, Frigg was a mother goddess associated with pregnancy and women in labour. She was accused by LOKI of being unfaithful to her husband during one of his long absences. Frigg shares many characteristics with the fertility-goddess FREYJA, from whom she may be derived.

A reconstruction of a bed from the 9th-century Oseberg ship burial.

Frisia Area of north-west Europe inhabited by the Frisians, a Germanic people first recorded in the 1st century BC. In the early Middle Ages, Frisia extended along the North Sea coast of Europe from the mouth of the River Rhine to that of the River Ems. Though conquered by the FRANKS in 734, the Frisians retained a distinct identity until the 19th century. From the 7th to the 10th century, the Frisians played a prominent role in TRADE between the Rhineland and the lands around the North Sea and the Baltic, and they controlled several important market centres, such as the Rhine port of DORESTAD. Until their conquest by the Franks, the Frisians also had a reputation for piracy. Frisia was desperately exposed to attacks from Scandinavia: the first recorded, a raid by the Danish or Geatish king HYGELAC *c.*516–34, long preceded the beginning of the Viking Age. Frisia was raided regularly by the Vikings from 810, when the Danish king GODFRED collected 100 pounds of silver in tribute from the Frisians, until the early 11th century. Despite the construction of a chain of forts (*see* Frankish RING-FORTS) along its coast, with its many islands and navigable waterways, Frisia was impossible to defend effectively. Frankish rulers made the best of a bad job by granting Frisia as a fief to the Viking chiefs RORIC, from 850–73, and Godafrid, from 882–5, in the hope, largely disappointed as it turned out, that they would make at least some effort to keep other Vikings out.

furniture Viking Age houses were sparsely furnished by modern standards. The most basic furnishings were wooden benches that lined the walls of the house. These were built as an integral part of the house and were used as both seats and beds. The centre of one of the benches was reserved as the 'high seat' of the house's owner. Honoured guests were seated on the bench opposite the high seat. The high seat was flanked by carved pillars, which must have had some symbolic importance as many of the settlers of Iceland took them on voyages and, upon sighting land, cast them overboard, resolving to settle wherever they were washed ashore. Trestle tables were set up in front of the benches for meals. Smaller tables with fixed legs are also known.

Richer people slept in separate bed closets, as at the Icelandic farm of STÖNG, that could be shut off from the rest of the house by a door. Movable beds are also known from the rich SHIP BURIALS at OSEBERG and GOKSTAD. Some of these had elaborately carved bedposts. Down-filled bed coverings, pillows and mattresses are known from burials in DENMARK and NORWAY. Presumably, furs and blankets were also used, but none have survived. A child's rocking-cradle is known from urban excavations at LUND. Several chairs with woven seats are known from Norwegian ship burials and from Lund. A three-legged stool has also been found at Lund. Viking Age Scandinavians did not use cupboards for storage. Many items, especially WEAPONS, were simply hung on the walls. Clothes were kept in wooden chests, and valuables, in lockable strong boxes. Oak, beech and pine were the most common woods used for furniture-making; maple and birch were also used.

A board for the Viking game of *hnefatafl*, from Balinderry, Ireland.

games, pastimes and sports The lives of most Viking Age Scandinavians were governed by the demands of the farming year. Though ploughing, sowing, haymaking and harvest times were very busy, at other times of the year peasant farmers and their FAMILIES enjoyed a considerable amount of leisure time, which they occupied with a wide range of indoor and outdoor pastimes. Dice and board games using counters were popular. The best known is *hnefatafl* ('king's table'), a tactical game where one side must surround the other side's king to win. Gaming pieces of GLASS, IVORY, AMBER and other materials are relatively common finds in excavations of Viking sites. Later in the Viking Age, chess and backgammon became very popular. Singing, music played on harps and pipes, storytelling, reciting poetry and solving riddles were all suitable indoor occupations for dark winter nights around the fire. In the halls of the chieftains there was room for dancing and shows by clowns, jugglers and acrobats. Foot races, jumping, swimming and wrestling were popular outdoor sports in summer; skiing and ice-skating were enjoyed in winter. Games involving bat and ball were also played in winter on frozen lakes, though the rules are not known. Hunting and fishing were enjoyed for their own sake and for the supplementary FOOD they could provide. Falconry was a field sport for the rich. Also of a practical nature were martial-arts sports such as sword-fighting, spear-throwing and archery, and feats of strength such as stone-throwing. Archery was a particularly well-organized competition sport in late-Viking Age NORWAY. The most popular spectator sports were horse-racing and horse-fighting. In horse-fighting, stallions were goaded into fighting each other for possession of a tethered mare. Vikings were often bad losers, and the SAGAS refer to many

fights breaking out over the result of a board game, ball game or horse-fight. Little is known about CHILDREN's games; many of them were no doubt imitations of adult games and activities.

Gardar the Swede (Garðarr Svávarsson) (*fl. c.860*) Probably the first Norseman to visit ICELAND. Gardar was blown off course during a voyage from NORWAY to the Hebrides *c.860* and eventually reached Iceland near the Eastern Horn. He decided to follow the coastline westwards, eventually circumnavigating Iceland and thus proving that it was an island. Gardar's exploration took the best part of year, and he spent the winter on Iceland's north coast at Husavik. When he set sail in the spring, he was forced to abandon a man called Nattfari, together with a male slave and a bondswoman, when a boat went adrift. Nattfari survived and was still there when the settlement of Iceland began in earnest *c.870*. Naming his discovery Gardarsholm (Gardar's Island) after himself, Gardar returned to Norway. Gardar's son, Uni, was sent to Iceland by king HARALD FAIRHAIR with a commission to bring it under royal control: he was eventually killed by the father of a girl he had got pregnant.

Garm In Scandinavian mythology, Garm is the watchdog of NIFLHEIM, the realm of the dead. At RAGNAROK, Garm's howling will call the underworld to battle. Garm and TYR will die of wounds that they will inflict on each other.

Gefion A minor Scandinavian goddess responsible, in legend, for creating the Danish island of Sjælland. Sent by ODIN to find land, she was offered as much as she could plough by king Gylfi of SWEDEN. Gefion

The title page of the earliest printed edition of Saxo's *Gesta Danorum*.

Coloured glass beads from Viking Age York. Such beads were popular as decorations throughout the Viking world.

changed her four GIANT sons into oxen and, hitching them to a plough, ploughed around Sjælland, separating it from Sweden. She made her seat at LEJRE.

Germanic Iron Age Period of Danish prehistory, AD 400–800, immediately before the Viking Age. It is usually divided into the Early Germanic Iron Age (400–550) and the Late Germanic Iron Age (550–800). Apart from the migration of the Jutes and Angles from Jutland to Britain in the Early Germanic Iron Age, DENMARK largely escaped the disruption that affected much of the rest of Europe at this time. There is considerable archaeological evidence of the increasing centralization of power in the Late Germanic Iron Age, for example, the foundation of a market at RIBE, and major construction projects such as the KANHAVE CANAL on Samsø and the first phase of the DANEVIRKE rampart across the neck of the Jutland peninsula. This process was one of the major factors in the outbreak of Viking raiding at the end of the period.

Germany, Vikings in *see* FRANCIA, VIKINGS IN

Gesta Danorum ('The Deeds of the Danes') Written *c.*1200 in Latin by the Danish historian SAXO GRAMMATICUS, the *Gesta Danorum* is a sixteen-volume national history of the DANES from legendary times to the late 12th century. Saxo was working within a well-established medieval tradition of writing national histories: he certainly knew Bede's *Ecclesiastical History of the English People* and DUDO OF ST-QUENTIN's history of the Normans, and he may have been aware of Jordanes' history of the Goths, and Geoffrey of Monmouth's history of the Britons, among others. Saxo also knew Virgil's

Aeneid, and set out to glorify the early history of the Danes in the same way that Virgil had done for the Romans. The first nine volumes cover a period of almost 2,000 years up to the mid-10th century AD. These volumes of the *Gesta* contain a wealth of mythological and legendary material, including the story of Amleth, the prototype for Shakespeare's Hamlet. Saxo treats the pagan Scandinavian gods unsympathetically, presenting them as malign, lustful human tricksters who successfully pass themselves off as gods. This contrasts with the contemporary Icelandic writer SNORRI STURLUSON who, in his *Prose EDDA*, treated them as human heroes who came to be regarded as gods because of their great achievements. How much historical truth there may be embedded in the traditions Saxo recorded is impossible to tell; only at the end of the eighth volume does Saxo begin to reach secure historical ground with the story of Gøtrik (GODFRED), an independently attested contemporary of CHARLEMAGNE who led some of the first Viking raids on the Frankish empire. The ninth volume is taken up mainly by the career of the legendary Viking RAGNAR LODBROK and ends with the death of GORM THE OLD, the father of HARALD BLUETOOTH, the first Christian king of DENMARK. The final seven volumes cover the historic period up to Saxo's own times. Today, it is for its record of the legendary historical traditions of Denmark that the *Gesta* is chiefly valued, and it is only the last three volumes, covering the period *c.*1134–87, that have any worth as an independent historical source. The *Gesta Danorum* had little influence until the appearance of the first printed edition in 1514, and the first Danish translation in 1575 made Saxo's vision of the Danish past widely available. In the 19th century, the *Gesta* became a source of inspiration for many Danish

Viking Age hoard of Slav and Scandinavian jewelry found at Gnezdovo, Russia.

Romantic poets, and it is still widely read, though even in translation Saxo's florid Latin style can make tiresome reading.

Saxo Grammaticus: The History of the Danes, Books I–X, ed. H. Ellis Davidson, trans. P. Fisher (Woodbridge, Suffolk, 1996).

giants Ancient mythological beings, associated with chaos, destruction and winter. The giants were the oldest form of life on earth, being descended from the frost giant Ymir, the first living thing. Ymir was slain by ODIN and his brothers, who shaped the landscape from his body, and the giants and the gods remained implacable enemies ever after. The population of giants was kept in check by the god THOR, who took a heavy toll of giantesses in particular. At RAGNAROK, however, the giants, allied with LOKI, HEL and a host of monsters, will finally destroy the gods, though they, too, will perish. The giants were also hostile to humans, whom they sometimes ate, and killing a giant was regarded as a suitable accomplishment for a legendary hero. Giants were afraid of light and lived in caves and icy places. Part of the cosmos, JOTUNHEIM ('Giantland'), was also reserved for them.

glass Most of the finer glassware discovered during excavations of sites in Viking Age Scandinavia was probably imported from western Europe (vessels) or Russia (rings), but glass beads were made in Scandinavia itself. A glass furnace, crucibles and other evidence of glass-making have been found at the Danish TOWN of HEDEBY, and two workshops used by beadmakers have been excavated at RIBE. Beads were also made at PAVIKEN on GOTLAND, KAUPANG in NORWAY and ÅRHUS in Jutland. The main raw material for bead-making was shards of broken glass drinking cups, which were imported

from the Rhineland. Cubes of brightly coloured glass, sometimes covered with gold leaf, called *tesserae*, were also imported from northern Italy, where they were made primarily for use in church mosaics. The simplest monochrome beads were made by spinning a small amount of molten glass around an iron rod. This was allowed to solidify slightly before being rolled on a hard surface to form a cylindrical or spherical bead, which was then slipped off the rod and allowed to harden. Simple polychrome beads were made by applying strips of molten coloured glass to the surface of monochrome beads before they hardened. Polychrome mosaic beads were made by the more complex process of fusing and slicing rods of differently coloured glass.

Gleipnir In Scandinavian mythology, the magic chain used by the gods to bind the monstrous wolf FENRIR. It was made by the DWARVES from the sound of a cat's step, the roots of a mountain, a fish's breath, a woman's beard, a bird's spittle and a bear's sinews.

Gnezdovo A late-9th–10th-century archaeological complex near Smolensk, RUSSIA, on the upper River Dniepr, midway on the main route from Scandinavia to the Byzantine Empire. It has a fortress with a large extra-mural settlement and Europe's largest early medieval cemetery, with over 3,000 burial mounds. Grave offerings indicate that the majority of Gnezdovo's population were Slavs or BALTS, but with a wealthy élite Scandinavian minority. The total population of the TOWN at any one time was probably around 2,000. There is considerable evidence of craft activities, including iron-smelting and bronze-casting. Russia's largest Viking Age silver hoard was discovered at Gnezdovo in 1868. It

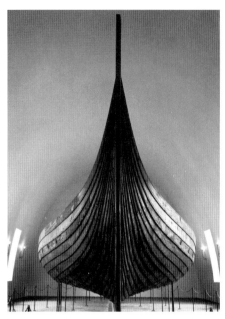

The Gokstad ship, a Norwegian chieftain's vessel built c.895–900.

Skyhill on the Isle of Man, scene of Godred Crovan's victory over the Manx in 1079.

consists mostly of JEWELRY of Scandinavian and Slav style, but with some objects from the Middle East and Central Asian steppes. Gnezdovo was abandoned around the end of the 10th century in favour of Smolensk.

Godfred (d. 810) Danish king (r. c.804–10). It is not known how long Godfred had been king when he is first heard of in 804, nor are the boundaries of his kingdom known, though he probably controlled Viken in southern NORWAY as well as part of or all of DENMARK. The completion of CHARLEMAGNE's conquest of the Saxons in 804 brought Frankish power to the borders of Denmark. Though there is no evidence that Charlemagne planned to conquer Denmark, Godfred was understandably alarmed by the possibility. He gathered an ARMY at HEDEBY and arranged a conference with Charlemagne, which, for some reason, he did not attend. In 808 Godfred attacked the Abodrites, Slav allies of Charlemagne, burning the trading TOWN of RERIC and evacuating its merchants to Hedeby. Expecting Frankish retaliation, Godfred ordered the refurbishment or extension of the DANEVIRKE rampart, which protected access to the Jutland peninsula. In 810 Godfred attacked FRISIA with a FLEET of 200 SHIPS, imposing a tribute of 100 pounds of silver. The contemporary *Frankish Royal Annals* accused Godfred of claiming Frisia and Saxony as his own and of planning to march on the imperial capital at Aachen. In the event, Godfred was murdered by one of his retainers, and his successor, his nephew Hemming, immediately made peace with Charlemagne.

goði A local Icelandic chieftain. Though the title literally means 'priest', and its use in that context is recorded in DENMARK, the role of the Icelandic *goði* (plural *goðar*) was as a secular local leader. The first Icelandic *goðar* were members of the leading FAMILIES of the settlement period (c.870–930). At first there were thirty-six *goðar*, though the number was increased to thirty-nine in 965 and forty-eight in 1005. Succession to a *goðorð* (the office of *goði*) was normally hereditary, but it was not a closed class and men could fall out of it or rise into it. In the absence of a head of state or central government, it was in effect the *goðar* who ruled ICELAND. Though all freemen could attend the ALTHING, the supreme legislative assembly, only the *goðar* could vote, and it was they who selected judges for the courts of law. *Goðar* also presided over their local THINGS. Decision-making was consensual and the *goðar* needed to take account of the feelings of their supporters, or *thingmenn*, because, as freemen, they could withdraw their allegiance if they wished and transfer it to another *goði*, who might better protect their interests. This happened fairly frequently, and as a result a *goði*'s supporters could be spread over a wide area. Icelandic chieftaincies, therefore, were political rather than territorial entities. So long as the *goðar* were of roughly equal wealth and status the political system worked well, but the emergence of a small group of pre-eminent chieftains (known as *storgoðar*, 'great chieftains') in the 13th century led to power struggles, civil war and, in 1263, takeover by NORWAY. The office of *goðorð* was abolished shortly afterwards.

Godred Crovan (Irish *crob bán*, 'white hand'; also known in Manx tradition as King Orry) (d. 1095) King of MAN and the Isles (r. 1079–95); king of DUBLIN (1091–4). Though not the first Scandinavian king of Man, Godred is the first about whom

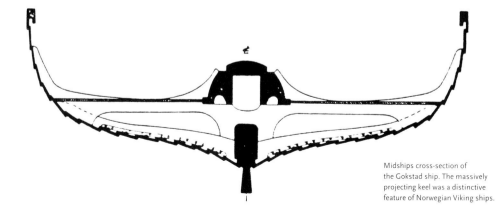

Midships cross-section of the Gokstad ship. The massively projecting keel was a distinctive feature of Norwegian Viking ships.

anything much is known. Godred spent part of his youth in Man but was probably originally from Islay in the Hebrides. In 1066 he fought with HARALD HARDRADA's Norwegian ARMY at the battle of STAMFORD BRIDGE and afterwards sought refuge with the then king of Man, Godred Sihtricsson (d. 1070). Somehow, Godred gathered a FLEET and an army, probably from the Hebrides, and invaded Man in 1079. Beaten off twice, Godred was finally victorious at the battle of Skyhill, near Ramsey, following which the Manx accepted him as king: with a short interval, his descendants ruled Man until 1265. Godred united Man and the Hebrides into a single kingdom, and for a time also ruled Dublin and gathered tribute from Galloway. The kingdom of Man and the Isles was divided into five administrative districts, which together sent a total of thirty-two representatives to the annual assembly at TYNWALD on the Isle of Man. Following Godred's death in Islay in 1095, a civil war broke out, and the kingdom was easily conquered by MAGNUS BARELEGS of NORWAY in 1098. Godred's son Olaf eventually revived the kingdom *c*.1113.

Gokstad ship burial A SHIP BURIAL, discovered in 1880 at Gokstad near Sandar in Vestfold, NORWAY. A ship had been placed in a shallow trench and a wooden burial chamber built aft of the mast. The body of the deceased was laid out on a bed in the chamber, together with grave goods. Other grave goods were placed in and around the ship before the grave was buried under an earth mound. The timber used to make the burial chamber has been dated by dendrochronology to AD 900–5 and, as Viking Age carpenters normally used unseasoned wood, the burial itself probably took place very soon afterwards.

The burial ship was clinker-built, with sixteen strakes a side. It measured 23.3 metres long by 5.2 metres broad and 2 metres deep, and was built of oak throughout. Propulsion was by a single square sail and sixteen pairs of OARS: the ship's massively projecting keel makes it likely that it was built for deep waters. A rack along the gunwale carried two shields between each oar port, suggesting that the ship carried a double crew of sixty-four. Radiocarbon dating has shown that the ship was built *c*.895–900. In contrast with the earlier OSEBERG ship, the Gokstad ship was completely undecorated – its beauty lies in its full sweeping lines. Several replicas of the Gokstad ship have been built, and one has crossed the Atlantic. Sea trials have shown it to have been a seaworthy vessel with good windward sailing abilities, but it would have taken skill to sail it, as it could become dangerously unstable at speed. It is thought that the Gokstad ship is an example of a karve, a type of ship known from SAGA literature that was built as the private travelling vessels of chieftains and their households.

As well as the ship, three boats were found in the burial, along with the remains of twelve horses, six dogs, a peacock, several beds and cooking equipment. This probably represents only part of the original grave goods, since the burial was looted at some time in the distant past. Skeletal remains found in the burial chamber indicate that the deceased was a man of sixty to seventy years old who suffered from rheumatism. Whoever he was, the quality of grave goods indicate that he belonged to the highest chieftain or royal class.

Göngu-Hrolfs saga ('The Saga of Hrolf the Tramper') The entertaining romantic tale of the hero Göngu-Hrolf's journey to RUSSIA to court the princess

A runic memorial raised to king Gorm and his wife Thyre by their son Harald Bluetooth at Jelling, Jutland.

Ingigerd on behalf of earl Thorgny of Jutland, full of fantastic and magical adventures. Because of his enormous weight, no horse could carry Hrolf and he had to walk everywhere, hence his nickname. The hero has been identified with ROLLO (Göngu-Hrolf Rognvaldsson), the Viking leader who founded the duchy of NORMANDY, but apart from the name there are no similarities between the two characters. The SAGA was written in ICELAND in the 14th century and shows the influence of the romantic literature then popular in continental Europe.

Göngu-Hrolf's Saga: A Viking Romance, trans. H. Pálsson and P. Edwards (Edinburgh, 1980).

Gorm the Old (d. 958) King of DENMARK (r. *c*.936–58). According to the 11th-century German historian ADAM OF BREMEN, Gorm was the son of Hardegon (Harthacnut) Sveinsson, a ruler from 'Nortmannia' (northern Jutland, NORWAY or possibly even NORMANDY), who overthrew the Swedish OLAF DYNASTY that ruled in Denmark in the early 10th century. The extent of Gorm's kingdom is unknown, but it probably included all of Jutland at least. Gorm was a pagan and gave Unni, the archbishop of Hamburg-Bremen, a hostile reception when he asked permission to renew missionary activities in Denmark in 936. Gorm was succeeded by his son HARALD BLUETOOTH, who had been co-ruler for some years before his father's death.

Gorm was interred under an impressive burial mound, which can still be seen at JELLING in Jutland. Dendrochronology has shown that the timber used to build his burial chamber was felled in 958, making this the most likely year of his death. Gorm's body was later removed from the mound, probably by his Christian son Harald, and reburied in a CHURCH he had built at Jelling. Surviving parts of his

skeleton show that he was about 1.72 metres tall, suffered from osteoarthritis of the lower back, and probably died in his forties.

Götar (ON *Gautar*; OE *Geatas*) A confederation of Swedish peoples, known from about the 2nd century AD. They were divided into two groups: an eastern, living between Lake Vättern and the Baltic Sea (Östergötland), and a western, living between Lake Vättern and Lake Vänern (Västergötland). They were cut off from access to the North Sea by the Norwegians and DANES, who occupied the whole of SWEDEN's west coast in the Viking Age. Virtually nothing is known about the Götar during the Viking Age, and they are not mentioned in contemporary literary sources as taking part in any Viking activities. Even western Europeans who visited Sweden, such as the missionary St ANSGAR, apparently failed to notice them. This may simply be the result of confusion over identities, but it may also be a sign that the Götar were dominated by their northern neighbours, the SVEAR (Swedes). Legendary traditions certainly refer to wars between the Svear and Götar, and some kings of the Götar, such as Alrik, who ruled Västergötland *c*.800, were members of the Svear royal family. The first king of the Svear who is known for certain to have ruled the Götar is OLOF SKÖTKONUNG (r. 995–1022), but the two peoples were not permanently united until the 12th century.

Gotland During the Viking Age the Baltic island of Gotland was an independent state or collection of chiefdoms. Gotland is first mentioned in written sources in the late-9th-century account of the merchant WULFSTAN's voyage in the Baltic in the *Old English OROSIUS*, at which time the islanders paid

A rare monument of the Götar, the Sparlösa stone (c.800) from Västergötland, Sweden.

A rare cylindrical box brooch of bronze with silver-and-gold decoration, from Gotland.

tribute to the Swedes. Gotland was only gradually incorporated into the Swedish kingdom. In the 11th century Gotland agreed to pay an annual tribute of sixty marks of silver in return for the protection of the Swedish king and the right to travel freely in his kingdom. In the 12th century military obligations were added, and in the 13th century the Swedish TAX system was extended to the island.

The culture of Viking Age Gotland differed in many ways from that of the Swedish mainland. STONE-CARVING was virtually unknown in Scandinavia until the end of the Viking Age, but throughout the period the Gotlanders erected carved PICTURE STONES as memorials to the dead. Styles of JEWELRY were also different. Gotland was evidently very prosperous at this time. Around 700 Viking Age silver hoards have been found, an enormous number for such a small geographical area: most of the silver was from the east, and was either Arabic COINS, Slavic jewelry or Russian silver bars. Gotland's central position in the Baltic made it well placed to profit from TRADE, and the dozens of small harbours and landing places that have been identified around the island's coast suggest that many Gotland farmers were also part-time merchants. Gotlanders were very active in the fur trade with RUSSIA in the 12th and 13th centuries but, although a rune-stone from Pilgårds mentions a journey by five Gotlanders to Russia, most trade in the Viking Age seems to have been conducted with the neighbouring island of Öland and the Slav lands of the south-east Baltic. Gotland was also well placed to profit from piracy, so many of the hoards may be loot or the proceeds of extortion. The island was, of course, equally vulnerable to piracy, which could help explain why Gotlanders were so keen on burying their wealth and why so many of them failed to recover it.

Great Army The name by which the particularly large Danish ARMY that invaded ENGLAND in 865 is often known, though the term as used in the *ANGLO-SAXON CHRONICLE – micel here –* was purely descriptive and not intended as a title. The arrival of the Great Army had catastrophic results for the Anglo-Saxon kingdoms. NORTHUMBRIA collapsed after YORK was captured by the Great Army in 866; EAST ANGLIA was conquered in 869; and a puppet ruler was installed in MERCIA in 874. A foray by the army into WESSEX in 870 was repulsed, but the kingdom barely survived its second invasion in 875. The army was under the leadership of several kings, none of whom apparently possessed kingdoms. HALFDAN, IVAR, Ubba and, later, Bagsecg, GUTHRUM, Oscetel and Anund are the only ones named in the *Anglo-Saxon Chronicle*, but other unnamed kings are mentioned – for example, as casualties in battles. The size of the Great Army is unknown, but its impact was such that it is reasonable to suppose that it numbered at least a few thousands. The large number of male skeletons discovered in a cemetery at the army's winter camp at REPTON indicates that it cannot, at least, have numbered only the few hundreds proposed by some modern scholars. The army apparently became less effective as its members settled down to enjoy the fruits of victory. This may have helped Wessex survive its attacks, though, of course, we do not know the extent to which the army may have been reinforced over the years by new recruits attracted by its success. The first major settlements took place in Northumbria, around York, in 875 and in eastern Mercia in 876. After ALFRED THE GREAT's victory at EDINGTON in 878, the remainder of the army settled in East Anglia under Guthrum. The area of these settlements subsequently became known as the DANELAW.

85

Drangey island off the coast of Iceland. Grettir Ásmundarson held out here against his enemies for three years, living on seabirds and their eggs, and sheep.

Runic inscription left at Kingigtorssuaq Island in Arctic Greenland by Norse hunters in 1333.

Greenland Two-thirds of Greenland, the world's largest island, lie north of the Arctic Circle, and about eighty-five per cent of its surface is covered by ice sheets. The earliest inhabitants of Greenland were Eskimos (Inuit), who arrived in the north of the island c.4000 BC. The first European to sight Greenland was probably Gunnbjorn Ulf-Krakuson, who was blown off course to the island's ice-bound east coast on a voyage from Norway to Iceland sometime around 900–30. The first attempt at Norse settlement was made by Snæbjorn Galti c.978 on some offshore islands discovered by Gunnbjorn, but the expedition ended in disaster. Around 983 Erik the Red rounded Cape Farewell and discovered Greenland's ice-free eastern fjords. The area was uninhabited and there was good pasture land. In 986 Erik returned with a fleet of settlers, and two settlements were founded: the Eastern Settlement (Eystribyggð), in the area of modern Julianhåb, and the Western Settlement (Vestribyggð), near modern Godthåb. Later a 'Middle Settlement' was founded between the two, though it was probably regarded as part of the Western Settlement. Cattle- and sheep-farming were the basis of the economy, but the settlements' most valuable products – walrus ivory and hide, falcons and polar-bear skins – came from hunting grounds (the Norðsetr) around Disco Island, north of the Arctic Circle. Hunting whales, seals and reindeer also provided valuable extra food. Iron, timber and most grain had to be imported. In the Norðsetr the Norse Greenlanders came into contact with the Eskimos, with whom they traded and sometimes fought. A rune-stone, dated 1333, found at Kingigtorssuaq Island, nearly 72° north, is the furthest north that the Norse can be said to have ventured with certainty, but iron ship rivets and other Norse artefacts have

been found on Ellesmere Island as far as 79° north. At its peak in the 12th century the Greenland colony had a population of around 4,000. The Eastern Settlement had 190 farms, 12 parish churches, a cathedral, an Augustinian monastery and a Benedictine nunnery. The smaller Western Settlement had 90 farms and 4 churches, and the 'Middle Settlement', 20 farms. The colony was governed by an assembly called, as in Iceland, the Althing. In 1261 the Norse Greenlanders accepted the sovereignty of the Norwegian king in return for trade guarantees. The colony went into decline in the 14th century: the Western Settlement was abandoned by 1341, and the 'Middle Settlement', by c.1380. The last recorded contact with the Eastern Settlement was in 1410, but archaeological evidence has shown that it survived for long after that, and that ships from Europe continued to reach Greenland occasionally. Finds of clothing in cemeteries show that the Norse Greenlanders kept up to date with 15th-century European fashions. However, a ship that visited the Eastern Settlement in 1540 found only deserted farms. A contributory factor to the extinction of the colony may have been conflict with the Thule Eskimos, who had been expanding south since the 12th century. Icelandic annals and Eskimo folktales both speak of massacres, and the small isolated community may have found it difficult to recover from these losses. The major cause, though, was the onset of the period of global cooling known as the 'Little Ice Age', which led to the collapse of the Greenlanders' farming economy, an increase in sea ice, and, consequently, a decline of contact with Europe. Skeletal remains of the last Norse Greenlanders show increasing incidences of diseases associated with poor nutrition, such as inner-ear infections, and a

Belt buckles, brooches and other fittings from the Viking ship burial on the Île de Groix.

declining life expectancy. The Norse Greenlanders were not helped by their extreme cultural conservatism, which prevented them from learning from the well-adapted Eskimos, and left them struggling to maintain a temperate European way of life in an increasingly Arctic environment.

G. Jones, *The Norse Atlantic Saga* (2nd edition, Oxford, 1986).

Grænlendinga saga *see* Vinland sagas

Grettis saga ('Grettir's Saga') One of the latest sagas of the Icelanders, written *c.*1310–20, *Grettis saga* differs from most other works of the genre by the prominent role accorded to supernatural beings such as ghosts and trolls. The central character, Grettir Ásmundarson, is a historical figure, born *c.*1000, known from other sources, but his portrayal in the saga is more akin to that of a legendary hero. Grettir is a psychologically complex character, violent but not malicious, dogged by bad luck and gifted with an almost superhuman strength that soon gets him involved with several killings of humans, wild animals, ghosts and trolls. Grettir has one surprising weakness: he is scared of the dark, the result of a curse laid on him by a ghost. Inevitably, Grettir is eventually outlawed and takes refuge on an island, where he holds out against his enemies for three years until they overcome him by witchcraft.

The Saga of Grettir the Strong, trans. G. A. Hight, edited and introduced by Peter Foote (London, 1965).

Grobin Fortified Viking Age settlement in Latvia. Excavations have provided considerable evidence of Scandinavian settlement. Two of the three cemeteries around the settlement contained grave goods of a central-Swedish type; the third, grave goods of a Gotlandic type. Further evidence of a close link with Gotland is the recent discovery of a picture stone. Grobin is probably to be identified with 'Seeburg in Kurland', which, according to Rimbert's *Life of St Ansgar*, was captured by the Svear *c.*850 during a campaign against the Curonians, a Balt tribe.

Groix, Île de An island off the coast of Brittany, site of the only known male Viking burial in France. The burial, dated to the first half of the 10th century, contained the remains of an adult male and an adolescent, probably a human sacrifice, whose bodies had been cremated in a 14-metre-long ship, which was then covered by a low barrow. The grave goods – gold and silver jewelry, bronze vessels, swords, shields, spearheads, an axe, blacksmith's tools and gaming pieces – suggest the burial of a powerful chief. Fragments of iron decoration from the stern-post of the ship, iron rivets and hundreds of nails also survived.

Gungnir The spear of the pagan Scandinavian high god Odin, forged for him by the dwarves. Gungnir was used to stir up warfare in the world: it could never miss its mark and when thrown it had the power to determine the outcome of battles. It may be from this belief that the Viking custom of opening a battle by throwing a spear right over the enemy host originated.

Guthfrith (d. 934) King of Dublin (r. 921–34); king of York (r. 927). Guthfrith became king of Dublin in 921 when his brother Sihtric Cáech left to take up the kingship of York. Guthfrith launched a furious campaign of plundering and slaving raids against the Irish but made no territorial conquests as a result of the vigorous opposition of Muirchertach,

king of the Northern Uí Néill. His attempt to seize the rival Viking stronghold of LIMERICK in 924 also failed. On his brother's death in 927, Guthfrith went to York, either to stake a claim in the kingdom or to support his young nephew OLAF SIHTRICSSON, but was quickly driven out by ATHELSTAN of WESSEX. Guthfrith fled to SCOTLAND, raised an ARMY, and returned to lay siege to York. Defeated, he surrendered to Athelstan and was allowed to return to IRELAND, where he resumed raiding. Guthfrith contracted a serious illness and died in 934; he was succeeded by his son OLAF GUTHFRITHSSON.

Guthrum (d. 890) Danish king of EAST ANGLIA (r. 879–90). Guthrum joined the Danish GREAT ARMY in 871 and took part in the conquest of MERCIA in 873–4. When the Great Army divided into two parts in 875, Guthrum, with two other kings, Oscetel and Anwend, went to Cambridge. In midwinter 878 he led a surprise attack on WESSEX that forced king ALFRED to seek refuge in the marshes at Athelney. After Alfred defeated him at the battle of EDINGTON later that year, Guthrum accepted baptism, and peace was established by the treaty of WEDMORE. Guthrum and his followers settled in East Anglia, where he ruled under his baptismal name Athelstan. In 885 Guthrum broke the peace, in retaliation for which Alfred occupied London a year later. In a peace treaty agreed shortly afterwards, Alfred recognized the borders of Guthrum's kingdom in return for his agreement to treat his English subjects equally with the DANES.

hacksilver The hacked-up pieces of silver vessels, JEWELRY and other objects plundered by Viking raiders. Hacking up plunder made it easier to share it between members of the raiding party by weight and easier to melt it down into silver ingots. Hacksilver is a common component of Viking Age treasure hoards.

Hafrsfjord, battle of Victory of king HARALD FAIRHAIR over a coalition of minor kings and earls, as a result of which he became the first king to rule most of NORWAY. The battle was fought at sea, but its course cannot be reconstructed in detail. Harald attacked the opposing FLEET as it entered the fjord and won the subsequent close-quarters fighting, clearing the decks of the enemy SHIPS. The decisive point of the battle came with the death of the enemy's champion BERSERKER Haklang. The date of this crucial battle is not known with certainty because of the problems of dating Harald's reign; most modern scholars favour a time c.885–90.

Håkon Sigurdsson (Håkon the Great) (d. 995) Jarl of HLAÐIR (r. c.963–95) and last pagan ruler of NORWAY. The son of Sigurd, jarl of Hlaðir, Håkon fought his father's murderer, king HARALD GREYCLOAK, until forced into exile in Denmark c.968. With the support of HARALD BLUETOOTH of Denmark, Håkon engineered the downfall of Harald Greycloak, and the two shared Norway between them: Harald Bluetooth receiving southern Norway, and Håkon ruling the western districts as Harald's vassal and the Trondelag in his own right. Loyal at first, supporting Harald against the German emperor Otto I in 975, Håkon later rebelled against Harald's attempts to Christianize Norway and gained outright control of the country after defeating

Hacksilver fragment from
Snäckarve, Gotland.

Coin of Halfdan,
Danish king of York.

a Danish punitive expedition at Hjorungavag, near Ålesund. In his later years, support for Håkon seems to have declined. When OLAF TRYGGVASON, a descendant of HARALD FAIRHAIR, invaded Norway in 995, Håkon was forced to flee and shortly after was murdered by one of his own men.

Håkon the Good (Håkon Haraldsson) (*c.*920–60) King of NORWAY (r. *c.*936–60). A son of king HARALD FAIRHAIR, Håkon was also known as 'Athelstan's foster-son' because he was brought up as a Christian at the court of king ATHELSTAN of ENGLAND. Håkon returned to Norway from England *c.*935 to challenge his half-brother ERIK BLOODAXE for the throne. He won the support of the powerful jarl Sigurd of HLAÐIR and was proclaimed king in the Trondelag *c.*936. When Håkon moved south into Uppland and Viken, Erik fled. Although he claimed to be king of Norway, Håkon's power was confined to the south-west of the kingdom. His nephews Tryggvi Olafsson and Guðrøðr Bjarnarson controlled the south-east, and jarl Sigurd ruled in the Trondelag in virtual independence.

Håkon enjoyed a reputation as a just ruler. He reformed the district THINGS to make them more representative and easier to consult. He has also been credited with creating the *leiðangr* (LEDING) system of ARMY and naval levies, dividing the coastal districts into *skipreiður* ('ship-providing districts'), each district having the number of SHIPS and men it had to provide laid down by LAW. A beacon system was introduced to give warning of any attack. Håkon made a fairly half-hearted attempt to persuade the Norwegians to accept CHRISTIANITY, inviting missionaries from England. He soon gave up in the face of stiff resistance, and was remembered in his funeral lay *Hákonarmál* as a defender of paganism,

though this may mean simply that he knew the limitations of his power, rather than that he abandoned Christianity. Around 955, the sons of Erik Bloodaxe began to attack Norway with Danish support. At the battle of Fitjar *c.*960 Håkon was mortally wounded; he died soon afterwards and was given a pagan burial. He was succeeded by Erik's son HARALD GREYCLOAK.

Halfdan (d. 877) King of YORK (r. 876–7). With his brother IVAR and Ubba (probably also a brother), Halfdan was the leader of the Danish GREAT ARMY that invaded England in 865. Halfdan invaded WESSEX in 870, but was soon forced to withdraw; around this time he had COINS struck in his name at London. When the Great Army split up after wintering at REPTON in 873–4, Halfdan took his followers to York, from where he raided into Bernicia (NORTHUMBRIA north of the Tees), Lothian and STRATHCLYDE. In 876, he settled his men on lands in Deira (Yorkshire), and they took up farming. Halfdan disappears from Anglo-Saxon sources soon after this. According to the 12th-century Northumbrian historian Simeon of Durham, Halfdan and Ivar were killed by the West Saxons during a raid on Devon in 878, but the contemporary ANGLO-SAXON CHRONICLE describes the leader of this expedition simply as their brother. It is more likely that Halfdan is to be identified with Alband, a Danish chief who, according to Irish sources, was killed by Oistin, the son of king OLAF of DUBLIN, at the battle of Strangford Lough in 877. Halfdan later came to be regarded as one of the sons of the legendary Viking RAGNAR LODBROK.

Halfdan the Black (d. *c.*880?) Protohistorical Norwegian king. Most traditions about Halfdan's

Far left: King Harald Bluetooth is baptized by the German missionary Poppo, a scene from the Tamdrup altarpiece, Jutland.

Left: A sincere convert, Harald prays before an altar, another scene from the Tamdrup altarpiece.

life, as recorded by medieval Icelandic historians such as SNORRI STURLUSON, are based almost exclusively on folktales and legend. He is said to have become king of Agder in southern NORWAY at the age of eighteen, and to have later acquired Vestfold and other territories. He drowned accidentally aged forty, after falling through the ice of a frozen lake. By his second wife Ragnhild, he was the father of HARALD FAIRHAIR, the first unifier of Norway. Halfdan's nickname derives from his black hair.

Harald Bluetooth (Harald Gormsson) (d. *c.*988) The first Christian king of DENMARK (r. 958–87). Harald had already been ruling jointly for some years when he became sole ruler on the death of his father GORM THE OLD in 958. At first, Harald's authority was probably effective only in Jutland, but by the end of his reign he had welded Denmark into a unified kingdom. Previous Danish rulers had probably exercised power indirectly through subordinate chieftains; by building and garrisoning the chain of TRELLEBORG FORTS, Harald was able to exercise direct rule throughout his kingdom. Through an alliance with HÅKON SIGURDSSON, jarl of HLAÐIR, Harald extended Danish control to NORWAY in 970. In 965 Harald was converted to CHRISTIANITY by POPPO, a German missionary, an event commemorated by an impressive runic stone at JELLING in Jutland. Harald became the first Scandinavian king actively to promote Christianity to his subjects. Later in his reign Harald moved the seat of royal power from Jelling to ROSKILDE in Sjælland. In 974 the DANES raided northern Germany. Rightly or wrongly, the German emperor Otto II thought Harald was behind them, and he invaded Denmark in retaliation. Despite support from jarl Håkon, Harald was forced to submit to Otto in 975: HEDEBY was under German occupation for the next seven years. If we are to believe ADAM OF BREMEN, Harald was overthrown in a rebellion led by his son SVEIN FORKBEARD in 987. Fatally wounded, Harald fled to Jumne (WOLIN in Poland), where he died shortly after.

Harald Fairhair (Harald Finehair) (d. *c.*930) King of NORWAY (*c.*880–*c.*930). Although credited with being the first king to unify Norway, little is known about Harald's reign with certainty, including its actual dates. Modern estimates date his accession to around 880 and his death to around 930. According to the SAGA of his life in SNORRI STURLUSON's *HEIMSKRINGLA*, Harald succeeded his father HALFDAN THE BLACK as king of Vestfold (west of Oslo Fjord) at the age of ten. The traditional story was told of him that his ambition was to unite Norway and he vowed not to comb or cut his hair until he achieved this, from which he gained his nickname *hárfagri* ('fairhair'). At the battle of HAFRSFJORD *c.*885–90, Harald defeated a coalition of minor kings and earls to bring most of Norway under his control. Some refugees from Hafrsfjord are said to have fled to the Scottish isles, from where they raided Norway until Harald mounted an expedition to bring that area under his control as well. Harald attempted to make provision for his many sons, dividing the kingdom and its revenues between them before his death. According to Snorri, ERIK BLOODAXE, Harald's favourite, though not eldest, son, was to be high king over them all. The settlement did not long survive him, as his sons fell out over their inheritance, each believing that he had the right to full KINGSHIP.

Harald's reign looms large in Icelandic historical traditions. According to Snorri, it was Harald's

Harald Hardrada made his reputation as an officer in the Byzantine emperor's Varangian Guard, members of which are seen here in a manuscript by the Byzantine historian John Scylitzes.

attempt after his victory at Hafrsfjord to appropriate all ÓÐAL land, and so turn freeholders into Crown tenants, that caused the first settlers to emigrate to ICELAND. However, the settlement of Iceland was in fact begun as early as 870, long before Hafrsfjord, and so cannot have been caused by Harald. Modern scholars also seriously doubt whether Harald's expedition to the Scottish isles actually took place, arguing, with some reason, that it was invented to explain why so many of the early settlers of Iceland had come from the isles.

Harald Greycloak (c.935–c.970) King of NORWAY (r. c.960–70). The son of ERIK BLOODAXE, Harald went to DENMARK after his father's death. With the help of his uncle HARALD BLUETOOTH, king of Denmark, Harald and his brothers launched several invasions of Norway, finally killing their uncle king HÅKON THE GOOD at the battle of Fitjar c.960. Harald aspired to rebuild a unified Norwegian kingdom and dealt ruthlessly with opposition, killing two of the petty kings in the Oslo region and Sigurd, jarl of HLAÐIR. Harald was a militant Christian and he aroused popular opposition by prohibiting the public worship of pagan gods. His one-time ally Harald Bluetooth eventually tired of Harald, whose actions threatened Danish influence in Norway, and he switched his support to HÅKON SIGURDSSON, son of Sigurd of Hlaðir. Harald was lured to Denmark and ambushed by a superior force at Hals on Limfjord, Jutland, and killed c.970. Norway was divided between Harald Bluetooth and jarl Håkon.

Harald Hardrada (1015–66) King of NORWAY (r. 1046–66). Harald's spectacular, if largely unsuccessful, career carried him across much of the world then known to the Vikings: it is not without

justification that he is widely regarded as the last great Viking leader. Harald's career is known mainly from his SAGA in SNORRI STURLUSON's 13th-century *HEIMSKRINGLA*. At the age of fifteen, Harald fought for his half-brother king OLAF HARALDSSON in the battle of STIKLESTAD in 1030. Defeated, Harald went into exile in SWEDEN and then to the court of prince JAROSLAV THE WISE at NOVGOROD. For three years he served Jaroslav as a mercenary, before joining the Byzantine emperor's VARANGIAN GUARD at Constantinople. Though it can be shown from contemporary Greek sources that the saga exaggerates Harald's importance, he undoubtedly made a great reputation as a warrior and a small fortune for himself during his service in the guard. In 1044 he returned to Sweden, marrying Jaroslav's daughter Elisleif (Elizabeth) on his way back through RUSSIA. There he allied with SVEIN ESTRITHSON to try to win a share of his nephew MAGNUS THE GOOD's Norwegian-Danish kingdom. When Magnus offered him joint rulership of Norway in 1046, Harald abandoned his alliance with Svein. When Magnus died the following year, Harald became sole ruler of Norway, but Svein seized power in DENMARK. Years of brutal warfare followed as Harald tried vainly to dislodge Svein from Denmark. Despite winning every battle he fought, in 1064 Harald finally recognized Svein as king of Denmark. Harald also faced frequent opposition to his rule in Norway, earning his nickname *harðráði* ('hard-ruler') for the ruthless measures he took to defend his authority. Harald had inherited a claim to the English throne as a result of a treaty between Magnus and CNUT's son HARTHACNUT in 1036. The death of ENGLAND's king Edward the Confessor in 1066 seemed the ideal opportunity to pursue that claim. Landing in the Humber Estuary with a FLEET

of 300 SHIPS in September, he defeated an English ARMY at Fulford Gate and took YORK. Only days later, another army under the English king HAROLD GODWINSON surprised Harald's force at STAMFORD BRIDGE and annihilated it. Harald himself was killed, and the severity of the losses in the battle weakened Norway for a generation. Harald was succeeded by his son Magnus II.

King Harald's Saga: Harald Hardradi of Norway, trans. M. Magnusson and H. Pálsson (Harmondsworth, 1966).

Harald Klak (Heriold) (d. 852?) King of DENMARK (r. 812–13, 819–27). Harald won power in a civil war in 812 and ruled jointly with his brother Reginfred. In 813 they mounted an expedition against rebels in Vestfold in NORWAY, which, according to the contemporary *Royal Frankish Annals*, was then part of the Danish kingdom. Harald and Reginfred were joined by their brother Hemming, a vassal of the emperor CHARLEMAGNE. This led to a rebellion, and the brothers were chased out of Denmark by HORIK and his brothers. Harald and his brothers sought and received Frankish support for a bid to regain their kingdom in 814. When this failed Harald and Hemming entered the service of Charlemagne's successor LOUIS THE PIOUS: Reginfred was killed. Harald still hoped to regain his throne and, with Louis's support, he was accepted back in Denmark as joint king with Horik and his brothers in 819. In 826 Harald was baptized at Louis's court, granted FRISIA as a fief, and sent back to Denmark with a Christian mission under ANSGAR. Despite Louis's support, Harald was overthrown the next year and again sought refuge with Louis. An attempt by Harald to regain his throne in 828 failed, after which his fate is unclear. According to the contemporary *Annals of Fulda*, he was executed by the wardens of

the Danish march on suspicion of treason in 852. A Danish pirate chief called Harald who was granted Walcheren as a fief by the emperor Lothar in 841 is described in the sources as a pagan and persecutor of Christians, so he cannot certainly be identified with Harald Klak.

Harold Godwinson (Harold II) (*c*.1020–66) The last Anglo-Saxon king of ENGLAND (r. 1066). Harold was the son of earl Godwine of WESSEX and Kent and his wife Gytha, a Danish noblewoman related by marriage to CNUT. Through his father's patronage Harold became earl of EAST ANGLIA in 1044. When Godwine was exiled by Edward the Confessor, it was Harold who led the ARMY that forced the king to reinstate him. He inherited his father's earldoms on his death in 1053. Harold became the dominant figure at court, obtaining earldoms for his brothers Tostig, Gyrth and Leofwine by 1057. In 1063 he showed his military abilities on a successful punitive expedition in WALES. When Edward died in 1066 without any heirs, Harold was chosen king, but he faced rival claimants in WILLIAM THE CONQUEROR of NORMANDY and HARALD HARDRADA of NORWAY. He also faced the hostility of his brother Tostig, who had been exiled from his earldom of NORTHUMBRIA in 1065 and was now leading Viking raids along the English coast. When Harald invaded England in September 1066 he was joined by Tostig, but both were killed when Harold surprised and defeated their army at STAMFORD BRIDGE near York (25 September). A few days later William landed on the south coast and Harold hurried south with his exhausted army to confront him. After a fierce day-long battle at Hastings (14 October), the English army broke and Harold, with his brothers Gyrth and Leofwine, was killed. By Christmas, William had

Opposite: Harold Godwinson is
crowned king of England,
from the Bayeux Tapestry.

Coin of Harthacnut; his reign saw
a rapid decline of Danish power.

been accepted as king of England. It is not known
why Harold did not allow his army time to recover
from the battle at Stamford Bridge or to gather
reinforcements. It may have been eagerness to
protect his family lands in Wessex from Norman
depredations. More likely, he did not want to give his
political enemies in England the opportunity to ally
with William against him.

Harold Harefoot (Harold I) (d. 1040) King of
ENGLAND (r. 1035–40). Harold was the illegitimate
son of CNUT and his English concubine ÆLFGIFU.
On his father's death, Harold, supported by earl
Leofric of MERCIA and the men of the royal FLEET,
became regent of England for the legitimate heir, his
half-brother HARTHACNUT, who was in DENMARK.
Harold was opposed by Cnut's widow EMMA of
NORMANDY and earl Godwine of WESSEX (the father
of king HAROLD GODWINSON), and a compromise
was reached by which she would hold Wessex for
Harthacnut. When Godwine changed sides the next
year, Harold seized the entire kingdom and Emma
fled into exile. Harold died at London in 1040 and
was succeeded by Harthacnut, who had his body
thrown into the River Thames (it was rescued and
reburied by his supporters).

Harthacnut (*c.*1020–42) King of DENMARK
(r. 1035–42); king of ENGLAND (r. 1040–2).
Harthacnut was the son of CNUT and his wife EMMA
of NORMANDY. Cnut intended Harthacnut to inherit
both Denmark and England, but his succession was
opposed in both kingdoms. On Cnut's death (if not
actually slightly before), the Norwegians threw off
Danish overlordship and chose OLAF HARALDSSON's
son MAGNUS THE GOOD as their king. Magnus
invaded Denmark, forcing Harthacnut to recognize

him as king of NORWAY in 1036. Harthacnut's forced
absence in Denmark allowed his half-brother HAROLD
HAREFOOT to seize power in England. Only when
Harold died in 1040 was Harthacnut accepted as king
in England. He quickly made himself unpopular by
levying an enormous TAX of more than £21,000 to pay
for an increase in the royal FLEET from sixteen SHIPS
to sixty-two, probably with a campaign against Magnus
in mind. He also earned a reputation as an oath-
breaker when he had earl Eadulf of NORTHUMBRIA
murdered while he was travelling on a safe conduct.
Harthacnut's unpopularity allowed his half-brother
Edward the Confessor (the son of Emma and
ÆTHELRED II) to return from exile in Normandy and
win recognition as his heir. Harthacnut died
suddenly at a seizure at a wedding feast in 1042 and
was succeeded by Edward, so bringing the period of
Danish rule in England to an end. In Denmark
Harthacnut was succeeded by Magnus the Good.

Hastein (variously Hæsten, Hasting or Anstign)
(*fl. c.*859–92) A 9th-century Viking leader, active on
the River Loire, in the MEDITERRANEAN and in
ENGLAND. The early 11th-century Norman writer
DUDO OF ST-QUENTIN described Hastein in lurid
terms as cruel, harsh, destructive, troublesome, wild,
ferocious, lustful, lawless, death-dealing, arrogant,
ungodly and much else besides – in fact an all-round
'kindler of evil', and every inch the archetypal Viking
leader of the popular imagination. Hastein was the
leader of a famous Viking expedition from the Loire
to plunder around the western Mediterranean in
859–62. Algeciras in Spain, Mazimma in Morocco,
Narbonne, Nîmes, Valence (nearly 200 kilometres
inland on the Rhône) and Arles in France, and Pisa,
Fiesole and Luna in Italy were among the many
places attacked. According to Dudo's colourful but

The site of the Viking trade centre of Hedeby, defined clearly by its semicircular rampart.

surely legendary account, Hastein mistook the Italian city of Luna for Rome and was determined to capture it. Judging the city's defences to be impervious to assault, he decided to gain entry by a ruse. Viking emissaries approached the townspeople, telling them that they were exiles seeking provisions and shelter for their sick chieftain. On a return visit the emissaries told the townspeople their chieftain was dead and asked permission to enter the city to give him a Christian burial. The townspeople agreed and a procession of Vikings followed their chief's coffin to the grave, at which point, Hastein, very much alive and fully armed, leapt out of the coffin and slew the city's bishop. In the resulting confusion, the Vikings sacked the city. When he was told that he had not, after all, sacked Rome, Hastein was so disappointed that he had Luna's entire male population massacred. This story was repeated by many later Norman writers, and the same ruse was attributed to Norman leaders such as Robert Guiscard, Bohemund of Taranto and Roger I of Sicily. Hastein completed his Mediterranean tour by sacking Pamplona in northern Spain before returning to the Loire, where he became a thorn in the flesh of both the Bretons and the FRANKS. He was probably the leader of Viking attacks on BRITTANY (866), Bourges (867), Orléans (868) and Angers (872–3). In 869 duke Salomon of Brittany paid Hastein 500 cattle for peace during the grape-harvest season. Faced with the prospect of a crushing attack by king Louis III of the West Franks, Hastein agreed to leave the Loire in 882 and moved to the Channel coast. In 890–1 Hastein was active in Flanders, and in 892 he appeared with a FLEET of eighty SHIPS in the Thames Estuary. The following year, Hastein's fort at Benfleet in Essex was stormed by the West Saxons, led by ALFRED THE GREAT, while he was absent on a plundering expedition: his wife

and two sons were taken prisoner and his ships were destroyed or captured. Alfred returned Hastein's FAMILY to him because one son was his own godson; the other was ealdorman ÆTHELRED's. These baptismal relationships suggest that this was not Hastein's first visit to England. According to the late-11th-century Norman writer William of Jumièges, Hastein ended his days in NORMANDY.

Havelok the Dane The central character of the *Lay of Havelok the Dane*, a medieval English romance written *c.*1200 in Lincolnshire, a part of eastern ENGLAND settled by the DANES in the 9th century. Havelok is the rightful king of DENMARK but, robbed of his inheritance by a usurper, he goes into exile in England. After many adventures, he marries the heiress to the English throne and regains his own kingdom, eventually uniting England and Denmark under his rule. The story has no discernible basis in fact, but has echoes of the establishment of the DANELAW and the union of England and Denmark under CNUT. An entertaining tale, but by no means a great work of literature, the *Lay* is one of the few works of vernacular English literature to survive from the period.

Hedeby (Haithabu) Danish Viking Age trading centre and port at the head of the Schlei Fjord, an inlet of the Baltic Sea, near Schleswig in modern Germany. Contemporary Frankish sources mention that king GODFRED settled merchants from RERIC at 'Sliesthorp' in 808, an event that probably began Hedeby's development as a TRADE centre, but there is evidence of the existence of a late-8th-century settlement (the Südsiedlung) a few hundred metres to the south of the centre of the Viking Age TOWN. Hedeby had its own mint – the earliest known in

A page from *Haralds saga hárfagra* in Snorri Sturluson's *Heimskringla*, itself contained in the early 14th-century *Codex Frisianus*.

Scandinavia – and probably a toll-house, but little else is known about its administration. A wide range of craft activities were conducted there, including metal-, bone-, amber- and glass-making, POTTERY and ship repair. Like in many other Viking Age towns, Hedeby's streets were paved with timbers. In the 10th century the town built substantial earth-and-timber ramparts to link it to the DANEVIRKE border rampart, and also constructed SEA BARRIERS of wooden piles to protect the harbour. A Jewish merchant from Cordoba, al-Tartushi, visited HEDEBY in the mid-10th century and wrote a description of the town. He noted its many freshwater wells, confirmed by excavations, but thought it a poor and squalid place and he hated the singing of its inhabitants, which was 'worse than the barking of dogs'. Al-Tartushi also noted the existence of a CHURCH and a small Christian community. Hedeby was under the control of the Swedish OLAF DYNASTY in the early 10th century, and under German control for a time later in the century. The town was sacked twice in the 11th century: by HARALD HARDRADA in 1050 and by the WENDS in 1066. By 1100 Hedeby had been abandoned in favour of Schleswig, where the earliest evidence of occupation is dated to 1071, probably because the latter was easier to reach in the deeper-draughted merchant ships then coming into use. At its peak, Hedeby had a population of between 1,000 and 1,500 people.

Heimdall In Scandinavian mythology, the watchman who guarded Bifrost, the rainbow bridge that led to ASGARD, the home of the gods. Heimdall was far-sighted in both night and day, and his hearing was so acute that he could hear grass growing. In the event of sudden attack, Heimdall would rouse the gods by blowing his magic horn Gjallarhorn ('echoing horn'), which he kept hidden beneath the world-tree YGGDRASIL. At RAGNAROK, Heimdall and LOKI will fight and kill one another.

Heimskringla ('The Circle of the World') An epic SAGA history of the early kings of NORWAY. Although no manuscript names him as the author, it is all but certain that *Heimskringla* was written by the Icelandic poet and chieftain SNORRI STURLUSON in the 1220s or early 1230s. The first of the sagas is the *Ynglinga saga*, which traces the descent of the Norwegian kings from the pagan gods, through the Swedish YNGLING DYNASTY, down to the end of the legendary period. In common with his approach in the *Prose EDDA*, Snorri presents Odin as a human hero from Asia who settled in Scandinavia, where his knowledge of magic and RUNES made him a great ruler. There follow sixteen sagas of the kings of Norway, from HALFDAN THE BLACK (mid-9th century) and his son HARALD FAIRHAIR to Magnus IV (d. 1177). The individual sagas vary considerably in length and detail but all are skilfully integrated into the work as a whole. Fully one-third of *Heimskringla* is taken up by *Óláfs saga helga* ('The Saga of St Olaf'), probably the most dramatic, convincingly characterized and psychologically realistic of the kings' sagas. The saga gives an account of king OLAF HARALDSSON's career, from his youthful Viking expeditions through his seizure of power in Norway, his violent promotion of CHRISTIANITY, his overthrow, and his death at the battle of STIKLESTAD in 1030. Other major sagas include *Óláfs saga Tryggvasonar* ('The Saga of OLAF TRYGGVASON'), *Haralds saga Sigurðarsonar* ('The Saga of king HARALD HARDRADA'), *Magnúss saga góða* ('The Saga of MAGNUS THE GOOD') and *Haralds saga hárfagra* ('The Saga of Harald Fairhair'). Because a great deal of *Heimskringla* consists of

A statuette of the Buddha, made in northern India in the 6th or 7th century and found at Helgö.

Broken clay moulds from a bronze-caster's workshop at Helgö.

dramatic reconstruction of events, its value as a historical source has been much debated. Snorri's main sources were SKALDIC poetry (he quotes from the works of more than seventy skalds) and earlier Icelandic historians, including Ari Thorgilsson, and a wide range of histories and genealogies, few of which now survive. Although Snorri was to some extent aware of its limitations as historical evidence, few modern historians would place as much faith in the veracity of skaldic verse as he did, though, in fairness, for the lives of many of the earlier historical kings he had few other sources on which to draw. Snorri was rather less likely to invoke the supernatural as an adequate explanation of events than most writers of his era, and his reconstruction of events, based on a keen understanding of human psychology, are certainly plausible if not necessarily correct. Where Snorri's work can be checked against independent sources, for example concerning Harald Hardrada's invasion of ENGLAND in 1066, he is found usually to be broadly accurate but often faulty in detail. Nevertheless, Snorri's achievement in weaving a multitude of historical traditions into a coherent whole makes *Heimskringla* one of the most impressive works of medieval historiography. As the greatest repository of Norway's historical traditions, *Heimskringla* played a key role in sustaining the Norwegian national identity through the centuries of foreign rule that followed its union with DENMARK in 1380 to its independence from SWEDEN in 1905.

Heimskringla: History of the Kings of Norway, trans. L. M. Hollander (Austin, Texas, 1964); *King Harald's Saga: Harald Hardradi of Norway*, trans. M. Magnusson and H. Pálsson (Harmondsworth, 1966).

Hel In Scandinavian mythology, the goddess of death and the ruler of the realm of the dead,

NIFLHEIM (also known after her as Hel), where she lived among the roots of the world-tree YGGDRASIL. She was the daughter of the malicious god LOKI and the giantess Angerboda, and had the appearance of a rotting corpse.

Helgö An island trading and manufacturing site on Lake Mälaren, SWEDEN, occupied *c.* AD 400–800. Gold-foil figurines, similar to those found at religious sites such as Gudme and Sorte Mulde in DENMARK, suggest that the island was also a pagan cult centre (its name means 'holy island') where markets were held at festival times. No other site in Sweden of the period has produced so much evidence of TRADE and manufacture. Jewelry-making was a particularly important activity: thousands of broken moulds used for casting bronze brooches have been found. IRONWORKING was also carried on. The permanent population of Helgö was small and engaged in farming. A hoard of 5th- and 6th-century Roman gold COINS suggests that at that time Helgö had trade links with the MEDITERRANEAN, possibly it was a market for furs. In the 7th and 8th centuries more exotic objects turned up, including a bronze crosier from IRELAND and a statuette of the Buddha from India. Helgö was abandoned *c.*800 in favour of nearby BIRKA.

helmets *see* WEAPONS AND ARMOUR

Hermod In Scandinavian mythology, the son of the high god ODIN. He rode Odin's eight-legged steed SLEIPNIR to HEL to try to obtain his brother BALDER's release from death. Through the trickery of LOKI, Hermod failed, but he was able to return to Odin the magic ring Draupnir, which had been placed on Balder's funeral pyre.

Hlaðir – its jarls rivalled the kings of Norway in power in the 10th century.

hirð In the late Viking Age, the *hirð* was the retinue of warriors that accompanied the kings and great magnates of the Scandinavian kingdoms, comparable to the LIÐ. The word derives from the Anglo-Saxon *hired*, meaning 'FAMILY' or 'household'. Members of the *hirð* lived as part of their lord's household and were bound to him by what amounted to a contract of mutual obligation. The contract was dissolved by the death of the lord. The *hirð* also functioned as a law court for its members and as a council for the king. Later in the Middle Ages the *hirð* developed into an aristocratic organization.

Historiae Norvegiae A short, and probably incomplete, Latin chronicle of Norwegian history, written in 1211 or very soon afterwards, probably in NORWAY. The surviving part of the chronicle covers the period from legendary times to the accession of (St) OLAF HARALDSSON in 1016. The chronicle is thought to be based on an older, lost Latin chronicle, but other sources were also used, including ADAM OF BREMEN's 11th-century *Gesta Hammaburgensis ecclesiae pontificum* ('Deeds of the Bishops of the Church of Hamburg').

Hlaðir (Lade) Centre of a powerful semi-independent Norwegian jarldom (earldom), 3 kilometres north of TRONDHEIM. As rulers of the Trondelag (the region around Trondheimsfjord), NORWAY's second largest and most northerly area of good arable land, the jarls of Hlaðir emerged in the late 9th century as potential rivals to the Vestfold kings. The first known jarl of Hlaðir was Håkon Grjotgarðson (*c*.900), who supported HARALD FAIRHAIR in return for autonomy in the Trondelag. The power of the jarls made them kingmakers in the 10th century. Håkon's son and successor Sigurd Håkonsson supported HÅKON THE

GOOD when he ousted his half-brother king ERIK BLOODAXE *c*.936. The jarldom reached the peak of its power in the late 10th century. After jarl Sigurd was killed by HARALD GREYCLOAK, Sigurd's son HÅKON SIGURDSSON allied with the DANES and overthrew Harald. At first Håkon ruled as a Danish vassal, but later he rebelled and established his jarldom as an independent power, effectively ruling all of Norway. When OLAF TRYGGVASON seized power in Norway in 995, Håkon was murdered and his son Erik Håkonsson (ERIK OF HLAÐIR) fled to DENMARK. With the support of the Danish king SVEIN FORKBEARD, Erik defeated and killed Olaf, and once again Norway was divided between Denmark and the jarls of Hlaðir. Erik left Norway to join CNUT in ENGLAND in 1015, leaving the jarldom to his brother SVEIN. Erik's absence allowed OLAF HARALDSSON to seize control of Norway: Svein fled into exile and died shortly after. After Olaf went into exile in 1028 Cnut decided to revive the practice of ruling Norway through the jarls of Hlaðir, but this plan had to be abandoned after the last of the dynasty, jarl Erik's son Håkon, drowned in 1029. After this, it was more than a century before another jarldom was created in Norway.

Hoder (Hod) In Scandinavian mythology, the blind son of high god ODIN and the god of the night. During a game, Hoder unwittingly killed his brother, the beautiful and popular god BALDER, with a dart of mistletoe placed in his hands by the malicious god LOKI. To pay for Balder's death, Hoder was killed by VALI, the god of justice. Both Hoder and Balder will return from the dead after RAGNAROK.

hogbacks Carved stones shaped like Viking longhouses that originated in Scandinavian-settled areas of northern ENGLAND in the first half of the

Below: A hogback tombstone, supported by a bear at each end, from Ingleby Arncliffe, North Yorkshire.

Above: A hogback tombstone with roof-tile pattern, from Meigle, Perthshire.

10th century and later spread to SCOTLAND. There are also single examples from WALES and IRELAND. There are no Scandinavian antecedents for hogbacks, which were probably inspired by Anglo-Saxon carved stone shrines or house-shaped reliquaries. Hogbacks are richly decorated with animals, interlace patterns, figures and, on top, tegulated patterns resembling roof tiles. The ends of many hogbacks are decorated with great beasts facing inwards. The prevalence of Jellinge-style decorations indicates that most hogbacks were carved before the end of the 10th century. Only one stone, from Brechin in eastern Scotland, has been dated on stylistic grounds to the 11th century. Although some earlier hogbacks feature pagan imagery, the fact that they are found in churchyards suggests that they were made for wealthy Christianized Scandinavian settlers, probably by native sculptors who had adopted the ART STYLES favoured by their new rulers and patrons. It is generally assumed that hogbacks were grave covers, but this is not certain because no grave has been found in association with the stones. It is, of course, more than likely that none of the hogbacks were still in their original positions when first identified. At least some hogbacks were part of composite monuments with stone crosses at each end.

R. N. Bailey, *Viking Age Sculpture in Northern England* (London, 1980).

Holger Danske (Holger the Dane, Ogier de Danemarche) A legendary hero. According to Danish folklore, Holger sleeps in the deep dungeons of Kronborg castle at Helsingør (Hamlet's Elsinore castle), or alternatively in innumerable prehistoric barrows all over the country. When DENMARK is in dire distress, and only boys and old men are left,

Holger will awake and lead the DANES in battle. The legend of Holger derives not from ancient Scandinavian tradition but from the French medieval epic poems known as *chansons de geste*. Ogier, as he is called in French, is described in these poems as the son of king Gaufrey (GODFRED) of Denmark. He is brought up as a Christian at the court of CHARLEMAGNE and becomes a mighty warrior, inflicting devastating defeats on the Saracens. Finally, bewitched by the fairy Morgana, Ogier is taken to Avalon to dwell with king Arthur. Ogier's historical prototype is probably Autcharius or Otger, a follower of Carloman, Charlemagne's younger brother, who died in 771. Ogier's surname 'de Danemarche' probably originally referred to the marches of the Ardennes rather than Denmark. Stories about Ogier, derived from the French *chansons*, appeared in Icelandic, Castilian, Catalonian and Italian folklore.

Horik (d. 854) King of DENMARK (r. 813–54). A son of king GODFRED, Horik, and his three brothers, seized power in Denmark in 813, driving out its kings, the brothers HARALD KLAK, Reginfred and Hemming. After Frankish pressure, Horik and his brothers accepted Harald back as joint king in 819, but relations broke down and they expelled him again in 827. By the 830s Horik was apparently the only survivor of Godfred's sons and was ruling Denmark alone. Relations with the Frankish emperor LOUIS THE PIOUS had been tense since 827, but Horik was careful not to provoke him, and in 836 and 838 he went so far as to execute the leaders of some Viking raids on FRANCIA. As a result of the civil wars that followed the death of Louis the Pious in 840, Horik was able to take a stronger line with the FRANKS, sending a large FLEET to sack and burn

Pedersen-Dan's statue of the Danish folk hero Holger Danske, in the dungeon of Kronborg castle.

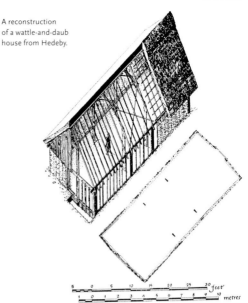

A reconstruction of a wattle-and-daub house from Hedeby.

Hamburg in 845 and ignoring demands in 847 from the emperor Lothar and his brothers Louis II and CHARLES THE BALD that he restrain his subjects from raiding Francia. Despite this, he tolerated the missionary activities of St ANSGAR, and was said to have shown great interest in CHRISTIANITY, though he never converted. In 850 Horik was forced to share his kingdom with two of his nephews. This seems to have caused another nephew, Gudurm, to return from exile in 854 to seek a share of the kingdom himself. Gudurm had spent his exile profitably engaged in piracy, and he brought with him a large force. A vicious civil war broke out in which Horik and most of the rest of the royal family, including his nephews, perished. Stability did not return to Denmark for a century.

hostages Exchange of hostages was an important element of diplomacy in northern Europe during the Viking Age. This frequently took the form of an exchange of CHILDREN, for example CNUT and THORKELL THE TALL ended a dispute in 1023 by agreeing to adopt one of the other's sons as a foster-child. Children fostered in this way could expect to be treated well and, if their foster-father was a great man, they might benefit considerably from the arrangement if the agreement held. Large numbers of hostages could be demanded from a defeated enemy as a guarantee that any peace agreement would be kept. In these one-sided exchanges, hostages could be treated mercilessly if the peace was broken, as when the English invited ÆTHELRED THE UNREADY to return from exile on the death of SVEIN FORKBEARD in 1014: the hostages given earlier to Svein had their feet and noses cut off by his son Cnut.

housecarls (*húskarlar*) The household troops of the 11th-century Danish kings of ENGLAND, they formed a unit equivalent to the HIRÐ in Scandinavia, being both bodyguards and the core of the royal ARMY. The system was introduced by CNUT in 1016 and was paid for by the *heregeld* ('army tax'). The system was maintained by the last Anglo-Saxon kings, Edward the Confessor and HAROLD GODWINSON, but from 1051 the housecarls were no longer expected to live as part of the king's household and were given grants of land instead of pay, in return for which they would fight when called. The term was originally used in a more general sense to describe hired workers.

houses The most typical dwelling in Viking Age Scandinavia and in Scandinavian-settled areas overseas was the longhouse, a farmhouse that accommodated both people and livestock under one roof (the animals provided central heating). Longhouses were around 5 to 7 metres wide, and anything from 15 to 83 metres long, depending on the owner's wealth and status. They were always three-aisled buildings with two interior rows of wooden posts, which carried most of the weight of the roof. The inside of the house was divided up into a number of separate rooms with wooden partitions. The byre was usually at the lower end of the house so that manure drained away from the living areas. There was a central hearth, and the smoke escaped through a hole in the roof or under the eaves. Many longhouses were built with slightly curved walls, making them broader in the middle than at the ends. Most farms also had many smaller buildings that were used for storage and as workshops. A common type of smaller building was the sunken-floored hut, which was half buried in the ground. These

The stone foundations of this Viking Age hall at Vallhagar, Sweden, protected the building's timber walls and posts from damp.

buildings were well insulated and were probably used for storing products that had to be kept cool. Because in TOWNS there was no need to house livestock and store crops, town houses were smaller than farmhouses. At HEDEBY, houses were rectangular, about 5 metres wide by 12 metres long, and divided into three rooms: a central living room with workshops or stores at either end. Sloping timber posts were used outside to buttress the walls against the weight of the roof. Royal and aristocratic halls were built in a similar way to longhouses but on a larger and, probably, more ornate scale. In DENMARK, halls with curved walls, up to 40 metres long by 10 metres wide, are known, for example at LEJRE and in the forts at Fyrkat and TRELLEBORG. The walls of these large buildings were buttressed with sloping timber staves to help them support the weight of the roof. There is no evidence that houses, great or small, had windows. Most floors were made simply of packed earth, though some buildings had raised floors of timber planking.

Building materials reflected the local environment. In heavily forested parts of NORWAY and SWEDEN, houses had walls of vertical hewn timber staves or of whole logs laid horizontally and notched together at the corners to make a strong joint. In less-wooded areas, such as Jutland, timber-framed buildings were walled with clay-plastered wattle and roofed with thatch. Timbers could be set directly in the earth or laid on a sill of stones to protect them from damp and rot. In treeless areas such as ICELAND and Hebrides stone and turf were used. Viking Age houses, being damp and full of smoke, were not particularly healthy to live in and made their inhabitants particularly prone to chest complaints and even carbon-monoxide poisoning.

Hygelac (Latin Chlochilaich) (*fl. c.*516–34) A 6th-century king of the DANES or Geats (Götar), leader of one of the earliest recorded Scandinavian pirate raids. At some time between 516 and 534, Hygelac was killed by the FRANKS in the course of an unsuccessful raid on the lower Rhine. The raid is recorded in several independent sources, including Gregory of Tours's 6th-century *Historiarum Libri X* (commonly known as *The History of the Franks*), and the 8th-century Anglo-Saxon epic poem *Beowulf.*

Good grazing, such as this at Fnjoskadalur, attracted the Vikings to Iceland.

I

Iceland Medieval Icelandic traditions held that the settlement of Iceland was begun by exiles from NORWAY fleeing the tyrannical rule supposedly imposed by king HARALD FAIRHAIR after his victory at battle of HAFRSFJORD. This attractively simple explanation is unlikely to be true since the battle of Hafrsfjord took place c.885–90, by which time the settlement of Iceland was already well under way. However, the Icelandic traditions probably do reflect a wider truth. The leaders of the settlements were middle-ranking aristocrats, that is, local chieftains; there were no jarls or kings among them as there were in other Norse-settled areas. These chieftains had lost much of their autonomy as a result of the growth of centralized royal power in the 9th century, so emigration to an uninhabited land where they could maintain their traditional way of life must have seemed attractive to many.

Iceland was probably discovered by Irish monks, a few of whom may have settled there as hermits before the beginning of the Viking Age. The first Scandinavian to reach Iceland, GARDAR THE SWEDE, did so by accident c.860 after being blown off course. Gardar named the island 'Gardarsholm' after himself, but the name that stuck, 'Iceland', was given by FLOKI VILGERDARSON, who led the first attempt to found a permanent settlement there in the 860s. Largely due to his own poor judgment, Floki's settlement failed, but those who followed, beginning with INGOLF c.870, succeeded. The leading settlers claimed vast areas of land, which they subdivided among their relatives and dependent followers. Despite its northerly latitude, Iceland was attractive to Norse settlement, with good grazing and extensive birch woodlands. The best land had been claimed and settled by c.930, and there was little immigration after that. According to the 12th-century LANDNÁMABÓK ('The Book of the Settlements'), the majority of the settlers came from western Norway, but there were substantial numbers from southern Norway and the Hebrides, and a few from DENMARK and SWEDEN. It has been estimated that by the end of the Viking Age the Icelandic population was c.40,000. Most of the woodland had been felled by this time, and overgrazing by cattle and sheep was causing soil erosion problems.

The early settlements were lawless, and blood feuds were rife. Leadership was provided by the GOÐAR, wealthy chieftains who presided over the local assemblies and who were well placed to resolve disputes and to give protection to lesser landowners in return for their support. Around 930, the goðar set up an annual all-Iceland assembly, the ALTHING, to resolve major disputes and to set up common LAWS, founding what is usually known as the 'Old Icelandic Commonwealth' or 'Free State' (930–1263). Iceland adopted CHRISTIANITY as the official religion in 1000 after a vote in the Althing, and in 1056 the first BISHOPRIC was set up at Skálholt. The Althing provided Iceland with stable government until the 13th century, when the concentration of power in the hands of a few leading FAMILIES led to civil wars. As a result, Iceland came under the direct rule of the Norwegian king in 1263.

The settlement of Iceland was (with that of the FAROE ISLANDS) the only permanent extension of the Scandinavian world to result from the Viking expansion. In this lies its main historical importance. Elsewhere in Europe, the Scandinavian settlers were assimilated to the local population within a few generations, leaving behind little trace of their presence beyond place-names and loan words in the native language. There was no native population in Iceland so here the settlers

retained an identity rooted in western Norway, from whose dialects the Icelandic language developed. The medieval Icelanders' pride in their origins is much in evidence in their remarkable literary tradition. Alone among the Germanic peoples, the Icelanders recorded the myths and legends of their pagan ancestors in the *EDDAS*, while their magnificent family SAGAS rank with the greatest European literature.

J. L. Byock, *Medieval Iceland: Society, Sagas and Power* (Berkeley, Los Angeles and London, 1988); G. Jones, *The Norse Atlantic Saga* (2nd edition, Oxford, 1986); J. Jóhannesson, *A History of the Old Icelandic Commonwealth: Íslendinga Saga* (Winnipeg, 1974).

Idun In Scandinavian mythology, the wife of BRAGI, the god of poetry. Idun was the goddess of spring and the guardian of the magic golden apples that gave the gods eternal youth. When Idun was kidnapped, with LOKI's help, by the GIANT THJAZI, the gods began to grow old and wrinkled until they forced Loki to rescue her.

Igor (Ingvar) (d. 945) The first truly historic ruler of the RUS (r. 913–45). Though most modern historians think it unlikely, according to the early 12th-century *RUSSIAN PRIMARY CHRONICLE*, Igor was the son of RURIK, the semi-legendary founder of the Rus state. After Rurik's death, Igor was supposedly fostered by Rurik's successor prince OLEG of KIEV, whom he eventually succeeded in 913. His reign was marked by serious military reverses for Rus forces. In 941 Oleg launched a savage but ultimately disastrous attack on Constantinople. His FLEET was attacked and destroyed by Byzantine galleys equipped with Greek fire projectors. A few Rus SHIPS, including Igor's, escaped by sailing into shallow water where the larger Byzantine vessels could not follow them. In 943 a

Rus force that attacked the Muslim lands around the Caspian Sea was forced to withdraw with heavy losses after sickness broke out in its ranks when besieged in the Caucasian city of Barda. It is not known if Igor was the leader of this force. In 945 Igor agreed a TRADE treaty with the Byzantines after threatening a second attack on Constantinople, but the terms were not as advantageous as those won by Oleg in 911 (*see* CONSTANTINOPLE, TREATIES OF). Igor was killed in 945 on a tribute-gathering expedition against the Drevljane, a Slav tribe. Because his successor, his son SVYATOSLAV, was still a child, it fell to his wife OLGA to take reprisals against Igor's killers.

Imhar *see* IVAR

Ingamund (Hingamund) (*fl. c.*905) Ingamund was among the Vikings expelled from DUBLIN when it was captured by the Irish in 902. He first tried to establish his followers in northern WALES, but was driven off by king Clydog. Ingamund then invaded MERCIA, but was defeated by the ealdorman ÆTHELRED after his Irish followers went over to the English. Ingamund asked Æthelred's wife ÆTHELFLÆD for land, and she allowed him to settle on the Wirral peninsula, near Chester. He tried to capture Chester *c.*905, but was repulsed. The settlement of the Wirral was part of a wider Scandinavian colonization of north-west England that took place around this time.

Ingolf and Hjorleif (*fl. c.*870) Two Norwegian foster-brothers who made the first successful attempt at settlement in ICELAND. According to the 12th-century *LANDNÁMABÓK*, the brothers lost their estates paying compensation to earl Atli of Gaular for killing his sons and urgently needed a safe refuge. Acting on the reports of FLOKI

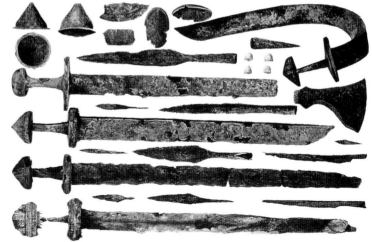

Opposite: The abbey on the Hebridean island of Iona was sacked many times by the Vikings.

Swords, spears and shield bosses from a warrior's grave at Dublin.

VILGERDARSON, Ingolf and Hjorleif made a reconnaissance voyage to Iceland's eastern fjords in the late 860s. Liking what they saw, the brothers returned *c*.870. Hjorleif settled at once on the south coast at Hjörleifshöfði. Ingolf, seeking the guidance of the gods, cast the pillars of his high seat overboard from his ship and swore to settle only where they were washed ashore. Finding the pillars took him all of three years.

During his first winter in Iceland Hjorleif was murdered by some slaves he had captured on a Viking raid in IRELAND. The slaves fled with some women to the islands that are now known after them as the Vestmannaeyjar ('Isles of the Irishmen'). They were tracked down there and killed the following year by Ingolf, who had arrived at Hjörleifshöfði to find his brother dead. Ingolf spent another two years following the coast westwards in search of his pillars, before they were eventually found at Reykjavik. Ingolf took into possession the whole of the Reykjanes peninsula west of the River Öxará as his estate. Ingolf's son Thorstein founded the first THING in Iceland at Kjalarnes.

Iona Small island off the coast of Mull in the Inner Hebrides, SCOTLAND. The monastery founded here in 563 by the Irish St Columba became one of the most famous and influential in the British Isles. Two of the finest of all early medieval illuminated manuscripts, the *Book of Durrow* and the *Book of Kells* (now both in DUBLIN), were made there. Its wealth and exposed position made Iona an early target for Viking raiders. First sacking the island in 795, the Vikings returned in 802, when they burned the abbey, again in 806, when sixty-eight monks were slaughtered, and yet again in 807. In 814 the abbot made the decision to withdraw the community to the

relative safety of Kells in IRELAND, but a token community of monks willing to risk martyrdom was left behind. When the Vikings returned in 825 the prior BLATHMACC was killed, along with several other monks. Little is known of Iona for the next 150 years, but some sort of religious community must have continued to exist on the island as several Scots kings were buried there during the period. As the Viking settlers in Ireland and the Hebrides began to adopt CHRISTIANITY, they began to regard Iona as a sacred site. OLAF SIHTRICSSON, king of Dublin, retired to become a monk there in 980. But in 986 'DANES' sacked the monastery again, killing the abbot and fifteen monks. A large hoard of 10th-century COINS discovered on the island may have been buried by one of the victims of this attack. MAGNUS BARELEGS of NORWAY made a reverent visit to Iona in 1098, and at least one of the kings of MAN was buried there. Iona steadily declined in importance through the Middle Ages. A last attack by Norwegian pirates came in 1210, a sign of the weakness of central authority during the last years of Norse rule in the isles. The abbey CHURCH became a cathedral for the diocese of the Isles in 1507, but the community was dispersed in 1561 following the Scottish Reformation. The cathedral was restored in 1905. Apart from a large collection of early Christian sculptured crosses, some showing Scandinavian influences, most of the visible remains date from the 13th century or later.

Ireland, Vikings in Viking activity in Ireland developed in much the same way that it did in ENGLAND and FRANCIA. An attack on a monastery on Lambey Island in 795 began thirty years of small-scale hit-and-run raids on coastal targets. In the 830s the Vikings began arriving with larger FLEETS, which

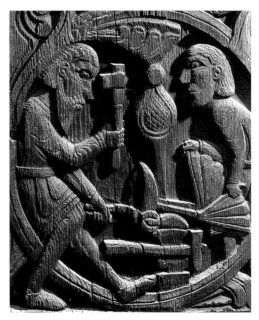

Right: The mythical smith Regin forges a sword for the hero Sigurd, from a 12th-century wood carving, Hylestad stave church, Norway.

Left: An 8th-century Irish bronze enamelled escutcheon found at Myklebostad, Norway, perhaps the souvenir of a Viking raid on Ireland.

for the first time sailed up Ireland's many navigable rivers, such as the Shannon, to attack areas far inland, causing widespread destruction. Ireland in the early 9th century was divided into five high kingdoms and a plethora of unruly subkingdoms, so there was no coordinated Irish response to the raids. By 840 the Vikings were permanently settled in Ireland, raiding all year round from their fortified bases or LONGPHORTS, the most successful of which was DUBLIN. Once the Vikings settled down they became more vulnerable to counter-attack, and Irish resistance became more effective: the death of the warlord TURGEIS in 845 and four major defeats in 847 persuaded many to seek easier pickings in Francia.

Ireland was very much the preserve of Norwegian Vikings, and they did their best to exclude competition. Although the DANES captured Dublin in 851, they were driven out just two years later by OLAF, a son of a Norwegian king. Olaf made himself king of Dublin, and became an active participant in Irish political life, forming alliances with local rulers such as CERBALL MAC DÚNLAINGE, king of Ossory. After the death of Olaf's successor IVAR I in 873, Ireland experienced a long respite from raiding known as the 'FORTY YEARS REST' while the Vikings concentrated their activities in England and Francia. In 902 it seemed as if the Irish had finally seen the last of the Vikings when they captured Dublin, but in 914 the Vikings returned in force under RAGNALD and SIHTRIC CÁECH and were soon re-established at Dublin and other ports such as WATERFORD, WEXFORD, LIMERICK and CORK. Yet they made no lasting conquests or settlements beyond these coastal enclaves. The kings of Dublin were often distracted by their ambitions to rule YORK and by wars with the other Viking TOWNS, while Irish resistance was increasingly well organized.

Traditionally, BRIAN BORU's victory over the Viking-Leinster alliance at the battle of CLONTARF in 1014 has been regarded as marking the end of the Viking Age in Ireland, but in reality Viking power in Ireland was already in sharp decline. By 1000 the Irish-Norse maintained their independence only by paying tribute and supplying troops and SHIPS to Irish kings, a price they could well afford to pay as their towns had developed into prosperous trading centres. The Irish-Norse were by this time beginning to lose their Viking identity through conversion to CHRISTIANITY, intermarriage with the Irish, and adoption of the Gaelic tongue. They became known as OSTMEN to distinguish them from native Scandinavians. The Ostmen preserved a limited independence until the Anglo-Norman conquest in the 12th century. Small-scale Viking raids from ORKNEY and the Hebrides continued to affect the Irish coasts into the 12th century.

The impact of the Vikings on Ireland is hard to assess. The Vikings have been blamed for destroying the brilliant monastic culture of early Christian Ireland, but many historians now believe that Irish monasticism was already in decline before their raids began. In many respects the Viking impact was beneficial in the long term, as they founded the first towns in Ireland, promoted TRADE and drew the island more closely into the European economy.
H. B. Clark, M. Ní Mhaonaigh and R. Ó Floinn (eds), *Ireland and Scandinavia in the Early Viking Age* (Dublin and Portland, Oregon, 1998); D. Ó Cróinín, *Early Medieval Ireland 400–1200* (London, 1995); D. Ó Corráin, *Ireland before the Normans* (Dublin, 1972).

ironworking Though it lacked the prestige of gold and silver, iron was the most important metal used in Viking Age Scandinavia, essential for farming,

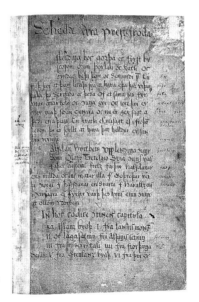

Ari Thorgilsson's *Íslendingabók*, the oldest surviving history of Iceland, written 1122–32.

construction, shipbuilding and warfare. The main source of iron was bog iron – nodules of iron oxides and decaying vegetable matter that form in bogs and marshes – but it is possible that iron ore was also being mined by the end of the period. Iron was produced in small bloomery furnaces, widely used throughout early medieval Europe, which could produce temperatures of 1,000–1,300 °C. At this temperature the impurities in the iron begin to form a molten slag, which was drained out of the bottom of the furnace, leaving a relatively pure bloom of iron behind. The iron was reheated, hammered on an anvil to remove as many of the remaining impurities as possible and converted into bars of standard size and shape for sale to blacksmiths. Between 5 and 20 kilograms of iron could be produced at a time by this method. As demand for iron increased steadily from the ROMAN IRON AGE through to the central Middle Ages, ironworkers began to colonize boggy upland areas in NORWAY and SWEDEN in search of new deposits of bog iron. Calculations based on the amount of slag found on iron-producing sites show that some areas of Småland and Gästrikland in Sweden produced nearly 10,000 tonnes of iron during the Viking Age.

Most iron was made into everyday objects such as nails and rivets, tools for farming and woodworking, cauldrons and LOCKS. The most sophisticated smithing techniques were reserved for fine WEAPONS. High-quality swords, axes and spearheads were made by forging together strips of iron of different qualities, a technique known as pattern welding. Bars of iron were drawn out and twisted together to form a flexible but strong laminate structure. This became the core of the blade. Hardened steel edges were then welded onto the core to produce a weapon that was sharp but not brittle. When polished, a pattern-welded blade had a distinctive marbled appearance, which advertised its high quality. Because of the importance of their work, skilful smiths could enjoy high social status and considerable wealth. Their graves are readily identifiable because in pagan times they were buried with their tools. These differ little from those still used by blacksmiths today. The status of the blacksmith is readily apparent in Scandinavian legends, which feature smiths, such as REGIN, with abilities to create almost magical weapons. The god THOR himself wielded a hammer, the smith's most important tool.

Íslendingabók ('The Book of the Icelanders') A short history of ICELAND from the first Norse settlements to 1118, written by Ari Thorgilsson in 1122–32. It was an abbreviation of an earlier work, now lost. The book covers the settlement, the establishment of the ALTHING and the Icelandic LAWS, the division of the country into quarters, the settlement of GREENLAND and, in the largest section, the conversion of Iceland to CHRISTIANITY and the establishment of the country's BISHOPRICS. Ari's sources were oral traditions and, for events in the 11th century, named eyewitnesses, including his foster-father Teit, who was born in 997. Despite its brevity, *Íslendingabók* established the basic chronology of Icelandic history for later historians.

The Book of the Icelanders (Íslendingabók) by Ari Thorgilsson, ed. and trans. H. Hermannsson (New York, 1930).

Ivar (OE Ingware) (*fl. c.*865) With his brother HALFDAN and Ubba (probably also a brother), Ivar was one of the original leaders of the Danish GREAT ARMY that invaded England in 865. With Ubba, he took part in the conquest of EAST ANGLIA in 869 and was responsible for the execution of its king

Left: Ivar, the leader of the Danish invasion of England in 865, from an early 12th-century life of St Edmund.

Below: The 12th-century Lewis chessmen, carved from walrus ivory.

St EDMUND. Ivar disappears from the Anglo-Saxon sources after this and nothing is known of his fate. The 12th-century *Annals of St Neots* name Ivar as the son of Lodebroch, as a result of which he has been identified with IVAR THE BONELESS, son of the legendary Viking RAGNAR LODBROK. He has also been identified with IVAR I of DUBLIN, though this is unlikely as Ivar I is known to have been Norwegian.

Ivar I (Irish Imhar) (d. 873) Norse king of DUBLIN (r. *c*.871–3). First appears in Dublin as an ally of his brother or kinsman king OLAF. In 859 the two invaded Meath in alliance with the Irish king CERBALL MAC DÚNLAINGE. Ivar, Olaf and another Norse king, Auisle, shocked Irish opinion in 863 by digging up the ancient burial mounds on the River Boyne in search of treasure. In 870–1 he joined Olaf in a successful siege of Dumbarton, the capital of the British kingdom of STRATHCLYDE. Ivar succeeded Olaf as king of Dublin *c*.871: his death in 873 marked the beginning of a long respite from Viking raids for Ireland known as the 'FORTY YEARS REST'. Ivar has been identified with another IVAR, the leader of the Danish GREAT ARMY in ENGLAND, and also with IVAR THE BONELESS, the son of the legendary Viking RAGNAR LODBROK. Neither identification seems likely as both were DANES; Ivar I was Norwegian.

Ivar II (d. 904) King of DUBLIN (r. 896–902). The grandson of IVAR I, Ivar became king after a three-way civil war between himself, his uncle Sihtric and jarl Sigfrid. The struggle weakened the Dublin Norse, and in 902 they were expelled by the Irish. Ivar went to SCOTLAND and plundered widely, sacking the ecclesiastical centre of Dunkeld in 903, but was defeated and killed by the Scots in Strathearn the following year.

Ivar the Boneless A famous but semi-legendary Viking known from 12th- and 13th-century Danish and Icelandic sources. Identifying the historical Ivar is problematic, not least because his supposed father, RAGNAR LODBROK, belongs more to the realms of legend than history. The most credible candidate is IVAR, the leader of the Danish GREAT ARMY in ENGLAND in the 860s, but he has also, improbably, been identified with IVAR I, a Norse king of DUBLIN (r. *c*.871–3). The curious nickname, in use by the 1140s, may be derived from a 9th-century story about a sacrilegious Viking whose bones shrivelled and caused his death after he plundered the monastery of Saint-Germain near Paris.

ivory Although a few objects made of elephant ivory found their way to Scandinavia during the Viking Age, most ivory used there was from walrus tusks. The main sources of walrus ivory were in northern NORWAY, the White Sea and, after *c*.1000, GREENLAND. Though walrus ivory was considered inferior to elephant ivory, it was exported in large quantities to western Europe, especially ENGLAND, Flanders and the Rhineland, from the 9th century until *c*.1300, when African elephant ivory became widely available. Ivory was used for carving religious figures, COMBS, belt buckles and gaming pieces, including the famous 12th-century Lewis chessmen.

The Viking Age settlement
at Jarlshof, Shetland.

Jarlshof A small Viking Age farming settlement near Sumburgh Head in the Shetland Islands. The site had been settled for several thousand years before the Vikings arrived in the 9th century, and they reused stones from a Pictish settlement to build their own house and ancillary buildings, which included a corn-drying room and a smithy. The house was later turned into a true longhouse, very similar to those of western Norway, by the addition of a byre. Jarlshof had the attraction for the Vikings of a sheltered harbour and convenient supplies of peat for fuel and soapstone for making domestic vessels. The farm was periodically rebuilt over the following centuries, the last time around 1600. The Norse-sounding name of the site was actually invented in the 19th century by the novelist Sir Walter Scott.

Jaroslav the Wise (ON Jarisleif) (980–1054) Grand prince of Kiev (r. 1019–54). Jaroslav was the son of grand prince Vladimir I, who appointed him to rule Novgorod. Following Vladimir's death in 1015, Jaroslav's brother Svyatopolk killed three of his other brothers and seized power in Kiev. Supported by the people of Novgorod and a force of Varangian (Viking) mercenaries, Jaroslav defeated and killed Svyatopolk to become grand prince in 1019. However, Novgorod remained his power base and normal residence.

Jaroslav consolidated the Kievan state by introducing administrative reforms, codification of the law, and military campaigns against the Poles and Pechenegs. He also made an unsuccessful attack on Constantinople in 1043. He actively promoted the spread of Christianity in the Kievan state, founded churches and monasteries, legislated for the rights of the clergy, and oversaw

the translation of Greek religious texts into the Slavic language. Using Byzantine architects and craftsmen, Jaroslav introduced an imperial style to Kiev, building the cathedral of St Sophia and the magnificent Golden Gate.

Despite his Viking ancestry, Jaroslav was culturally and linguistically a Slav, but he maintained dynastic links with Scandinavia. He was married to Ingigerd, the daughter of king Olof Skötkonung of Sweden, and their daughter Elisleif (Elizabeth) married Harald Hardrada, later king of Norway. Scandinavian exiles and mercenaries continued to find a welcome at his court, and a Swede, Rognvald, was appointed to govern the important town of Staraja Ladoga. It is difficult to tell if these Scandinavian connections still had any special significance for Jaroslav, however, because he also arranged dynastic marriages for his daughters with kings of France and Hungary, and other family members married into the Byzantine and German royal houses. Jaroslav tried to prevent a power struggle among his five sons by arranging for the division of his kingdom between them. Despite this, or perhaps because of it, a civil war broke out after his death.

Jelling Site of royal pagan and Christian monuments of the 10th century in Jutland, Denmark. The visible monuments comprise two large mounds and, between them, two rune-stones. An incomplete V-shaped stone setting was preserved beneath the southern burial mound, and evidence of a large late-10th-century wooden church has been discovered during excavations beneath the floor of the 12th-century stone church that stands alongside the rune-stones. The oldest of the monuments at Jelling is probably the smaller of the two rune-stones,

An antiquarian view of
the 10th-century Danish
royal centre at Jelling.

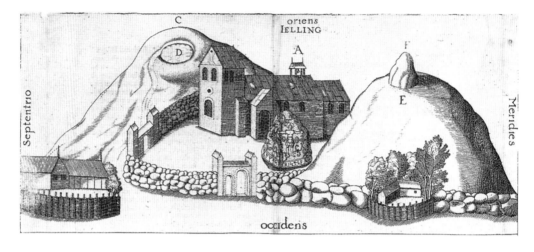

erected by king GORM THE OLD in memory of his
wife THYRE. It is not known if the stone is still in
its original position; it may originally have formed
part of the now-buried stone setting. The northern
mound originally contained a rich pagan burial
in a wooden chamber. This has been dated by
dendrochronology to 958, making it in all
probability the burial mound of Gorm himself.
The grave was broken into at a later date and the
body removed. If Thyre was also buried in the
mound, no trace of her remains or grave has been
found. Excavations of the southern mound, the
largest in Denmark, have failed to reveal any trace
of a burial. It is possible that it was built for Gorm's
Christian son HARALD BLUETOOTH, though for
what purpose is unclear.

Harald turned Jelling into an impressive Christian
site. He erected the second, larger rune-stone to
commemorate his father and mother and also his
achievement in Christianizing the DANES. It is
decorated with spectacularly vigorous carvings
of Christ on one face, and a lion entwined by a
snake on another. Harald was almost certainly
also responsible for the construction of the late-
10th-century wooden church. The bones of a middle-
aged man found in a chamber-grave under this
church may be those of Gorm, removed there
from his burial mound by Harald to Christianize
his father posthumously. The most enigmatic
monument is the stone setting. As no other
V-shaped stone setting is known elsewhere, it is
probably the surviving 'prow' of what was once an
enormous stone SHIP SETTING, more than 150
metres long.

jewelry Most of our knowledge of Viking Age
Scandinavian jewelry comes from grave finds and

treasure hoards. Because jewelry ceased to be placed
in graves after the conversion to CHRISTIANITY
c.1000, we know rather more about the types of
the earlier Viking Age than about the late. Jewelry
is normally dated on the basis of the ART STYLE used
for its decoration.

Jewelry was worn by both men and WOMEN.
As it still is today, jewelry was at once an adornment
and a way of displaying wealth, but it also served a
practical purpose, as a convenient way of carrying
wealth, as a means of exchange, for sealing a
friendship or alliance, and, at a more mundane
level, as fastenings for cloaks, dresses and belts.
The most prestigious jewelry was made of gold, but
this was in short supply in Scandinavia and most
jewelry was made of silver or bronze gilded to look
like gold. Items of gold and silver jewelry were
individually made by highly skilled craftsmen for
well-off customers. The basic design would be
pressed with a die onto a thin sheet of gold or
silver before the fine detail was added using
filigree. Cheaper bronze jewelry was mass-
produced, being cast from clay moulds made
using a single master copy. Coloured GLASS
beads were also mass-produced for use in
necklaces and pendants. Beads were also made
of AMBER, semi-precious stones and, more rarely,
gold and silver.

The commonest items of Scandinavian Viking
Age jewelry were women's bronze oval brooches
(these were never made in other metals). They were
a normal and practical part of a well-off woman's
apparel, one being worn on each shoulder to fasten
her overdress. In Finland, especially, disc brooches,
made in a variety of metals, served the same
purpose; on GOTLAND, animal-headed brooches
were used. In the mid-11th century delicate

Clockwise: A bronze oval brooch, the most typical item of Viking women's jewelry; a woman's necklace, made from glass beads, semi-precious stones, coins and other trinkets; and silver penannular brooches, made for fastening cloaks, and arm and neck rings, from Skail, Orkney.

openwork brooches in the Urnes art style and rosette brooches became fashionable. Silver neck and arm rings were also common items of jewelry. Many of these were made from melted-down Arabic silver COINS and were quite plain and made to standard weights so that their value could be readily assessed. The Arab writer Ibn Fadlan described how the Viking merchants he met on the River Volga in the 920s had these ornaments made for their wives as a way of displaying their wealth. Thor's hammers and other pagan symbols were worn as pendants, probably as amulets or good-luck charms. After the introduction of CHRISTIANITY these symbols were replaced by pendant crosses. Pendants were often hung from a brooch rather than worn around the neck. Finger rings were only rarely worn before the late Viking Age, and earrings were almost unknown.

Foreign influence on Scandinavian jewelry types was limited. Trefoil brooches, inspired by Frankish sword-belt mounts, became popular in the 9th century to fasten women's cloaks. Men's cloaks were often fastened by penannular brooches. These were worn on the right shoulder with the pin pointing upwards; adopted from the Scots and Irish by Viking settlers in the Hebrides, the fashion later caught on in Scandinavia and RUSSIA. On Gotland, copies of Slav jewelry were made. The fate of nearly all the jewelry plundered in the course of Viking raids abroad was to be melted down and recast in Scandinavian styles. There are a few examples of decorative book mounts and other metalwork being made into brooches, and necklaces of glass beads were often hung with curios from abroad, such as coins and finger rings. Slavic neck rings were converted into arm rings in SWEDEN and used as currency.

Jomsborg *see* WOLIN

Jomsvikings A semi-legendary élite band of Vikings. The Jomsvikings are mentioned in both Danish and Icelandic sources of the 12th and 13th centuries and are the subject of their own SAGA, the *Jómsvíkinga saga*, written c.1200. According to Danish traditions, king HARALD BLUETOOTH founded a fortress called Jomsborg on the Baltic coast of Wendland as a base for piracy. Strongly fortified and provided with an artificial harbour for 360 SHIPS, Harald left Jomsborg garrisoned by WENDS under the command of Danish chiefs. The Icelandic traditions are rather more romantic but less credible. The Jomsvikings were an independent Viking ARMY, founded by Pálnatóki, a Viking from the Danish island of Fyn, that hired itself out to the highest bidder. They formed a sworn fellowship (FÉLAG) of warriors aged between eighteen and fifty years old and lived by strict rules which, somewhat improbably, included a ban on WOMEN entering the fortress of Jomsborg. The power of the Jomsvikings was broken when they were defeated and slaughtered in a sea battle at Horungavag (near Ålesund) by jarl HÅKON SIGURDSSON of HLAÐIR after they had invaded NORWAY on behalf of SVEIN FORKBEARD c.990. The likely origin of the traditions associated with the Jomsborg Vikings is that Harald Bluetooth, or some other Danish king, did at some time win control over a Wendish port and subsequently maintained a garrison there. The location of Jomsborg is uncertain, but it is probably to be identified with WOLIN, which was known as Jumne in the Viking Age. However, Wolin was certainly not founded by Harald Bluetooth: its origins go back to the 8th century, and it was fortified a century or more before he was born.

Norway's Jotunheim mountains.

Jórvik *see* YORK

Jotunheim ('Giantland') In Scandinavian mythology, a cold and mountainous region on the edge of the ocean that was given to the GIANTS by the gods after the CREATION of the world. It was separated from MIDGARD, the world of humans, by a wall made from the eyebrows of Ymir, the first of the race of giants. The giants' citadel of Utgard was ruled over by UTGARD-LOKI.

Kanhave canal A 1-kilometre-long canal on the Danish island of Samsø. It links the natural harbour of Stavnsfjord on the east coast of the island with the sea to the west. The canal was 11 metres wide and could accommodate ships with a draught of up to 1.25 metres, more than adequate for most ships of the Viking Age. Timber revetments were used to prevent the banks from collapsing. These have been given a dendrochronological date of AD 726. The purpose of the canal was probably military. Samsø has a commanding position at the entrance to the Storebælt straits leading to the Baltic, and the canal would have made it easier for warships to have intercepted ships passing on either side of the island. A major engineering project, the canal is evidence of the emergence of a centralized kingdom in DENMARK in the early 8th century.

Kaupang Viking Age trading place situated on a sheltered bay close to the mouth of Oslo Fjord in NORWAY: in the Viking Age it was probably known as Skíringssalr. Large seasonal markets (*kaupang* means 'market-place') were held here from *c.*750–900. Just inland from Kaupang was the royal estate of Husby, which is possibly the reason why a trading place developed here. Finds of English, Frankish, Danish and Arabic COINS, together with Slavic, Rhenish and Frisian POTTERY, Rhenish GLASS and English metalwork are proof of Kaupang's wide international TRADE links. There is no evidence that Kaupang was permanently inhabited. Viking Age graves in nearby cemeteries, containing imported goods and agricultural tools, probably belong to local farmers who traded at Kaupang on a seasonal basis. Most of the buildings so far excavated were craftsmen's workshops. Industrial activities at Kaupang including shipbuilding, SOAPSTONE-

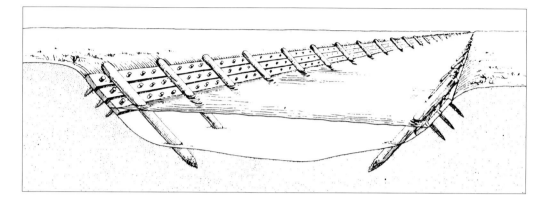

A reconstruction of the Kanhave canal across the Danish island of Samsø.

carving, metalwork and glass-bead production. Kaupang was probably abandoned because uplift of the land made it increasingly difficult to reach from the sea (it is now around 3 metres above sea level). *See also* TOWNS.

Kensington Stone A famous archaeological hoax. The Kensington Stone was supposedly found by a Swedish-born farmer near Kensington, Minnesota, in 1898. A runic inscription on the slab purports to describe the journey of eight 'Goths' (i.e. Swedes) and twenty-two Norwegians from VINLAND to Minnesota in 1362. The RUNES are a mixture of types used from the 9th century to the 11th and home-made symbols. The language used is the distinctive Swedish-Norwegian dialect spoken by Scandinavian settlers in Minnesota in the 1890s, while the date is based on the Arabic system of numeration, which was not used in 14th-century Scandinavia. Though some die-hard romantics still believe the stone to be genuine, academics quickly recognized it as a forgery, presumably made by local Scandinavian settlers, either as a joke or for reasons of ethnic prestige.

Ketil Flatnose (*fl. c.*855) Viking ruler in the Hebrides. Ketil appears in contemporary Irish sources as the leader of the *Gaill-Gaedhel* ('Foreign Gaels'), a people of Norse-Gaelic descent from the Hebrides, who were raiding in IRELAND in 857. The Icelandic SAGAS associate Ketil with king HARALD FAIRHAIR'S campaigns in the west, but as Harald had probably not even been born in the 850s, Ketil's conquests in the isles must have been an independent initiative. After his death, Ketil's family were unable to maintain their position in the Hebrides and migrated to ICELAND. His daughter AUD THE

DEEP-MINDED, his sons Bjorn the Easterling and Helgi Bjólan, and his son-in-law Helgi Magri were all remembered as leading figures in the Norse settlement of Iceland.

Khazars A Turkic-speaking people from central Asia that had settled by the 7th century on the south Russian steppes. Around AD 740 the Khazar *khagan*, or ruler, converted to Judaism, but the Khazar khanate practised religious toleration and paganism; CHRISTIANITY and Islam also flourished. The Khazar capital at Itil (Astrakhan), close to the mouth of the River Volga, was an important trading centre during the Viking Age and was enriched by dues collected on TRADE between Scandinavia, the north Slav lands and the Middle East. The Khazars also controlled the lower River Don from their second city of Sarkel and taxed RUS merchants passing through on their way to the Black Sea and Constantinople. In 912 the *khagan* allowed a Rus pirate FLEET to sail down the Volga to raid the Muslim lands around the Caspian Sea in return for half the plunder. Reports of Rus atrocities so incensed the *khagan*'s Muslim subjects that he attacked them on their return in 913 and, conveniently, got to keep all of the plunder. In 964–5 SVYATOSLAV I, the expansionist Rus ruler of KIEV, sacked Itil and Sarkel, permanently breaking Khazar power, and by the early 11th century they had disappeared as a political force.

Kiev (ON Kœnugarðr) The political centre of the early RUS state and a major Viking Age TRADE centre on the River Dniepr. According to the *RUSSIAN PRIMARY CHRONICLE*, Kiev was a fortified Slav settlement when it was seized by the Rus leaders ASKOLD AND DIR *c.*860: excavations have uncovered

Opposite: A replica of the Kvalsund ship, built in 1973.

St Sophia cathedral, Kiev, built by Byzantine craftsmen for Jaroslav the Wise in 1037–9.

the remains of a pre-Viking Age pagan temple. OLEG made Kiev the capital of the Rus state after he captured it from Askold and Dir *c*.882. Archaeological evidence indicates that Kiev's growth into a major TOWN began soon after this. Around 900 a fortress was built on Starakievskaja Gora, an escarpment overlooking the Dniepr, and a large settlement began to develop on the low-lying Podol on the riverbank below. Craft production and trade were concentrated in the Podol settlement, while the Starakievskaja Gora developed as an administrative centre, though some aristocratic graves have also been found there. After prince VLADIMIR I converted to CHRISTIANITY in 988, the defences on the Starakievskaja Gora were extended and it became an ecclesiastical centre. The Byzantine-style cathedral of St Sophia was built here in 1037–9 by JAROSLAV THE WISE, who also rebuilt some of the city's defences in stone and brick, including the Golden Gate. The demand for glazed tiles and mosaics for the new CHURCHES stimulated the development of a GLASS industry that exported products to as far away as SIGTUNA and HEDEBY. Kiev remained the leading Russian city until its sack by the Mongols in 1240.

kingship By the beginning of the Viking Age, monarchy was already the dominant force in Scandinavian society. Viking kings were primarily rulers of men rather than rulers of territory. Because of this it was quite possible for a man to be recognized as a king even if he possessed no kingdom: many of the 9th-century Viking leaders in Britain and FRANCIA were landless 'sea kings'. What was essential was the possession of royal blood, inherited from either his father's or his mother's side. It was normal practice for a king to be succeeded by one of his sons (though not

necessarily the eldest), but any male member of a royal dynasty, whether legitimate or illegitimate, was eligible for the succession. As a result, there could be several potential claimants for a throne, and succession disputes were therefore common. If rival claimants had equal support and were willing to compromise, joint kingship was a common, and surprisingly effective, expedient, but disputed successions all too often led to civil war. The competitive nature of Scandinavian kingship was one of the most important causes of Viking raiding and conquests. If he survived, the loser in a civil war had two options available to him. He could go into exile and seek the support of a neighbouring ruler to regain his throne, as the 9th-century Danish king HARALD KLAK did of the emperor LOUIS THE PIOUS, or he could take advantage of the prestige that came with royal blood to raise a war band and go plundering. The rewards of success were fame, wealth and a loyal following of warriors to support a new attempt to win power at home or to conquer a kingdom overseas. These means won Norway for OLAF TRYGGVASON and the kingdom of YORK for ERIK BLOODAXE. Returning exiles were a destabilizing influence in the Viking kingdoms and a serious problem for all established kings, no matter how popular or successful.

As well as being insecure, Viking Age kings enjoyed less than absolute power. The power of the king was limited to some extent by the need to consult the assemblies (THINGS) before making major decisions. New LAWS proposed by the king had to be approved by the assemblies before they came into force. But a clever king could manipulate the assemblies to get the result he wanted, as king Olaf of the SVEAR did in 850 to overcome pagan opposition to St ANSGAR's missionary activity.

Another potential limitation on royal power was that a new king had to be accepted by the more important assemblies. This was usually a formality, and a show of force was usually enough to suppress any opposition, as Olaf Tryggvason found with the Norwegian assemblies in 995.

The responsibilities of a Viking king were primarily military, that is, defending the kingdom against invasion and suppressing piracy. Pagan kings probably also had some religious duties. The 10th-century Norwegian king Håkon the Good reluctantly took part in a sacrifice to the gods, despite being a Christian, because his pagan subjects believed that its efficacy was in some way dependent on the king's participation. Semi-legendary traditions also record the involvement of kings of the Svear in pagan rituals at Uppsala. With the introduction of Christianity c.1000, the nature of Scandinavian kingship began to change. Kings gradually acquired a more active role as legislators, enforcers of justice and protectors of the Church. The Church in turn bestowed on Scandinavian kings the semi-sacral character enjoyed by Christian kings elsewhere in medieval Europe, and promoted the cults of royal saints such as Olaf Haraldsson of Norway and Cnut II of Denmark. Christian moral values also affected kingship, as illegitimacy became an obstacle to succession.

Royal government was rudimentary and was performed by members of the king's personal retinue, the Hirð, who were probably appointed on an *ad hoc* basis for specific tasks. The king's income came from landownership, tolls on trade, tribute and plunder from war. Because of the problems of transporting foodstuffs over long distances, kings and their retinues moved constantly from estate to estate, consuming the food where it was produced. There were favoured residences, but the Viking kingdoms did not have permanent administrative capitals.

Kjarval see Cerball mac Dúnlainge

Klåstad ship Small trading vessel discovered near Kaupang, Norway, in 1893 but not excavated until 1970. The 18-metre-long sailing ship has been dated to c. AD 990. With the nearly contemporary Äskekärr ship, the Klåstad ship is the earliest known Viking trading vessel.

Knud see Cnut

Kvalsund ship From Herøy, Sunnmøre, west Norway, the Kvalsund ship was deposited as an offering in a bog, c. AD 700, together with a smaller rowing boat. Measuring 18 metres long by 3 metres broad, the ship was clinker-built and had a strong, slightly projecting T-shaped keel. The hull had eight strakes per side, the planks being fastened together with iron rivets. The ship was probably propelled by ten pairs of oars. Though no direct evidence was found, some characteristics of the Kvalsund ship, such as the design of the rudder and its fittings, suggest that it could have been a sailing ship. Having many similarities to the 9th-century Oseberg ship, the Kvalsund ship represents an early stage in the development of the Viking ship.

A replica of the 10th-century
ship from the Ladby ship burial.

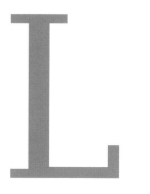

Ladby ship burial An aristocratic ship burial of the mid-10th century on Kerteminde Fjord on the island of Fyn, DENMARK, excavated in 1935. The ship was buried in a barrow situated on a prominent ridge overlooking the fjord. A dozen other Viking Age graves have been found on the ridge, though none so richly furnished as the ship burial. The ship's hull had almost completely rotted away, but its size and shape were reconstructed from the impression left in the ground and from the pattern of iron rivets that were used to fasten the planking. The ship was long and narrow: 20.6 metres long by 2.9 metres broad, and only 0.7 metres deep amidships. The length-to-beam ratio of 7:1 is the same as the smaller of the two early 11th-century warships found at SKULDELEV. The number of ribs indicates that the ship was crewed by sixteen pairs of oarsmen. Though no trace of a mast or mast-step was found, four iron shroud rings were discovered, showing that it was a sailing ship. The stem and stern were decorated with iron ornaments. Apart from the ship, grave offerings included an iron anchor and chain, eleven horses, riding gear, a pack of dogs, an elaborately decorated leash, WEAPONS, a silver belt buckle, silver and bronze tableware, and traces of gold-embroidered fabrics and furs. This presumably represents only a fraction of the original offerings, as the burial was robbed in the Middle Ages and the burial chamber and body destroyed or removed.

K. Thorvildsen, *The Viking Ship of Ladby* (Copenhagen, 1975).

Lade *see* HLAÐIR

landaurar ('land dues') According to the 12th-century ÍSLENDINGABÓK, *landaurar* was a toll of 5 ounces of silver introduced in the late 9th century by king HARALD FAIRHAIR on emigrants leaving NORWAY for ICELAND. By the 11th century it had become a lucrative toll on foreigners arriving in Norway. By a treaty agreed with the Icelanders in 1025, king OLAF HARALDSSON recognized the Icelanders' personal rights (*höldsréttur*) in Norway – including the rights to redress for injury, inheritance and TRADE, in accordance with the traditional LAWS governing merchants and seafarers, the *BJARKEYJAR RÉTTUR* – in return for payment of *landaurar* on arrival and support during war. The rights were subsequently confirmed in writing under oath in 1085.

Landnámabók ('The Book of the Settlements') The earliest and most detailed account of the discovery and settlement of ICELAND, *Landnámabók* gives the names of over 400 of the leading settlers, their origins and other biographical information, land claims and descendants. More than 3,500 personal names and 1,500 farm names are mentioned. *Landnámabók* was probably written between 1097 and *c.*1125 and is thought to have been compiled mainly by Ari Thorgilsson and his older contemporary Kolskeggr from orally transmitted FAMILY traditions. Substantial additional information was added by later copyists. The oldest redaction of *Landnámabók* is in the *Sturlubók*, written by Sturla Thórðarson in the 13th century but preserved only as a 17th-century copy of the original, which was lost in the 18th century. Other, incomplete, medieval versions are preserved in *Hauksbók* (*c.*1306–10) and *Melabók* (early 15th century). It is clear from *Landnámabók* that by far the majority of the settlers of Iceland came from western NORWAY, but with a significant number coming from southern Norway and the Norse colonies in IRELAND and SCOTLAND, as well as a few from

Landnámabók ('The Book of the Settlements') gives the names and origins of more than 400 of Iceland's earliest settlers.

DENMARK and SWEDEN. Some freed Irish or Scottish slaves were also given farms by their owners and founded families. Several of the settlers who had been living in Scotland and Ireland were Christians, but the religion soon died out in Iceland.

The Book of Settlements: Landnámabók, trans. H. Pálsson and P. Edwards (Winnipeg, 1972).

landownership Little is known about landownership in Viking Age Scandinavia. It was once widely held that Viking Age Scandinavia was a land of peasant freeholders, but it is now clear that there were considerable inequalities of landownership. Many peasant FAMILIES did hold allodial (or ÓĐAL) land in absolute ownership, but there also existed a class of royal and aristocratic landowners whose extensive estates were worked by tenant farmers. Eleventh-century runic memorials in DENMARK and SWEDEN identify many such landowners. One Swedish landowner, Jarlabanke, boasted of owning all the land in his *heruð* (local administrative district), in which case most, if not all, of its inhabitants would have been his tenants. The term *bryti* (leaseholder or steward), also known from rune-stones, is further evidence that many farmers were tenants. Excavations at the Viking Age village at VORBASSE in Denmark also suggest that many farmers were tenants. The village was completely restructured several times in its history, something that would hardly have been possible if its inhabitants had been freeholders. This, and the fact that one of the seven farms in the village was very much larger than the others, suggests that the entire community was controlled by a single wealthy landowner, the other farmers being his tenants. Landownership may have been most concentrated in Denmark, where in the central

Middle Ages only around fifteen per cent of land was owned by free peasants; at this time the figures for NORWAY and Sweden were closer to fifty per cent. Figures for the Viking Age are likely to have been higher, as many Scandinavian peasants surrendered their freeholds in the central Middle Ages to escape heavy taxation and levy service obligations.

language Viking Age Scandinavians spoke a language that they described as the *dönsk tunga* ('Danish Tongue'), and that modern linguists describe as Common Scandinavian, from which the modern Scandinavian languages are descended. The Scandinavian languages are members of the Germanic family of languages, to which English, German and Dutch also belong. The differentiation of the Germanic languages from their common ancestor probably began in the first half of the first millennium AD. Proto-Scandinavian, the earliest form of Scandinavian speech, known from a handful of short runic inscriptions dating from the period *c.*450–700, was still very similar to other contemporary Germanic dialects, but major phonetic changes in the 8th century led to the emergence of Common Scandinavian in the Viking Age. Direct evidence of Common Scandinavian consists of around 2,500 runic inscriptions, most of which are short and do not include full sentences. SKALDIC VERSES, composed during the Viking Age, but committed to writing only by later medieval Icelandic authors, cannot safely be assumed to be free of later linguistic influences. Common Scandinavian was fairly uniform, but by the end of the Viking Age clear differences had emerged between the dialects of NORWAY and the Atlantic colonies on the one hand (West Norse) and

DENMARK and SWEDEN on the other (East Norse). During the Middle Ages, Common Scandinavian gave way to Old Norwegian, Old Norse (or Old Icelandic), which developed from West Norse, and Old Danish and Old Swedish, which developed from East Norse. Further differences had emerged by the end of the Middle Ages as the languages spoken in Norway, Sweden and Denmark came under different degrees of influence from Low German, while the Icelanders and Faroese, because of their isolation, preserved a more conservative form of Scandinavian speech. Norn, the Scandinavian dialect spoken in ORKNEY and Shetland, was similar to Old Norse.

At the beginning of the Viking Age, Common Scandinavian was spoken in an area comprising all of modern Denmark, the northern part of the German province of Schleswig-Holstein, southern and central Sweden, and Norway as far north as the Lofoten Islands. During the Viking Age, Scandinavian-speaking communities were established in parts of northern and eastern ENGLAND, NORMANDY, IRELAND, SCOTLAND, Estonia, Finland, RUSSIA, the FAROE ISLANDS, ICELAND and GREENLAND. In most of these areas Scandinavian speech had begun to disappear by the end of the Viking Age as settlers were assimilated into the native population. In Greenland, Scandinavian speech survived until the Norse colony died out *c.*1500. In Orkney and Shetland, Scandinavian speech, which had completely supplanted the native Celtic language during the Viking Age, had been replaced by English by 1750. The only permanent extensions to the area of Scandinavian speech to result from the Viking expansion were Iceland and the Faroe Islands, which were uninhabited before the Norse settlement, and

south-eastern Finland, which continued under Swedish political domination until the 19th century, and where there remains a Swedish-speaking minority.

E. Haugen, *The Scandinavian Languages: An Introduction to their History* (London, 1976).

L'Anse-aux-Meadows This small Viking Age settlement at the northern tip of Newfoundland is the only certain archaeological evidence that Europeans reached the Americas before Columbus. The discovery of the site in the 1960s was dramatic confirmation that SAGA accounts of Norse voyages from GREENLAND to VINLAND had a historical basis and were not simply romantic tales about imaginary lands. The Norse origins of the site were established beyond doubt by the discovery of iron rivets and other evidence of metalworking – metals were not used by the native American Indians in the 11th century – and a bronze ring-headed pin of distinctive Scandinavian type. The settlement consisted of a cluster of turf houses and workshops, closely resembling those built by the Norse in ICELAND and Greenland, which could have accommodated about ninety people. The discovery of a spindle-whorl indicates that WOMEN were among the inhabitants, since spinning was a female occupation in Viking society. The inhabitants hunted and fished, but there is no evidence of farming. The main activity was blacksmithing and carpentry associated with ship repair. The local environment does not accord with saga descriptions of Vinland, so the settlement may have served as a base for expeditions to the south. Butternuts (a kind of walnut), which do not grow north of the St Lawrence River, have been found on the site, proving that such voyages took place. The site was occupied for only a

Opposite: A reconstruction of the Norse settlement at L'Anse-aux-Meadows, Newfoundland.

A chapter on manslaughter from the Icelandic law book *Grágás.*

few years, from around 1000 to 1020, according to radiocarbon dates.

A. S. Ingstad, *The Discovery of a Norse Settlement in America: Excavations at L'Anse-aux-Meadows, Newfoundland 1961–68* (Oslo, 1977).

Lapps (Saami) Today confined to the far north of Norway, Sweden and Finland, and Russia's Kola peninsula, the Lapps were much more widespread in Scandinavia and Russia during the Viking Age, when they ranged almost as far south as central Sweden and Norway in the west and lakes Onega and Ladoga in the east. The Lapps speak a Finno-Ugrian language, distantly related to Finnish and Estonian. Though they are known today as reindeer herders, during the Viking Age the Lapps lived primarily as hunters, fishers and gatherers, keeping reindeer mainly as draft animals, for milk and as decoys when hunting other reindeer. Hunting mainly took place in the winter, when the animal's coats were in best condition. Fishing was a summer activity. Though seasonally nomadic, the Lapps also practised limited cultivation of cereals and raised a few goats and sheep. They followed a shamanistic religion that focused on a bear cult and holy fells, lakes and rocks. Viking Age Scandinavians believed the Lapps possessed dangerous magical powers. According to the 9th-century merchant OHTHERE, who gave king ALFRED an account of his expeditions in the far north, the Lapps paid tribute to the Norwegians in furs of martens, bear and otter, reindeer hides, whalebone, sacks of down from seabirds, ships' ropes of walrus hide and seal skins for waterproof clothing. Tribute is also known to have been paid in miniver, the valuable grey winter fur of the squirrel, which was much in demand as trim for luxury garments. A great deal of straightforward TRADE was also conducted. Viking Age bronze and silver JEWELRY, iron tools and WEAPONS, and other objects of Scandinavian origin, presumably received as payment for furs, have been found on Lapp sites. By the late 11th century, the lucrative fur trade had become a monopoly of the Norwegian king.

laws Though they may often have spread destruction and disorder in their wake overseas, Viking Age Scandinavians were much concerned with creating an orderly society at home. Unfortunately, very little is known about the legal systems of Viking Age Scandinavia, as law codes were not committed to writing until the 12th century. It is beyond doubt that these later codes contain many laws that date back to Viking times, but identifying them has not proved easy. The only thing that can be said with certainty is that in all the Scandinavian countries during the Viking Age, and in the Viking colonies overseas, law was based upon the proceedings of the local THING, the assembly of freemen. As a result, there was considerable regional variation. For example, NORWAY had four law provinces – the Gulathing (west Norway), Frostuthing (Trondelag), Eiðsifathing (east) and Borgarthing (south) – each with its own lawmaking assembly (*lögthing*) and regional law code. Early Norwegian TOWNS also each had their own laws, known as the *BJARKEYJAR RÉTTUR.* Similarly, Jutland and the major Danish islands had their own law codes, as did the regions of SWEDEN. The Icelandic laws were based on the Norwegian Gulathing laws, introduced by Ulfjótr at the first meeting of the ALTHING *c.*930. Laws agreed at the meetings of the *thing* were committed to memory and handed down orally. Men knowledgeable in law, such as the Icelandic *lögmen,*

A fragment of the Norwegian Gulathing laws.

were valued as advisers to kings and chieftains. Lawmaking and trials were conducted in public, and all freemen had an equal right to have recourse to law.

Obtaining a judgment was one thing; enforcing the sentence was quite another, as this was primarily the responsibility of the litigant. For an ordinary peasant farmer this might prove impossible without the support of a chieftain or other powerful person; only with the growth of royal power at the end of the Viking Age did this begin to change. The penalties that could be imposed by law were usually financial. A great deal of highly complex law in all Scandinavian countries concerned the payment of *mannbœtr* (compensation) for killings or injuries. The scale of compensation depended on the severity of the injuries and, except in ICELAND, on the status of the victim. Theft was usually punished by hanging, as it was assumed that a thief would be too poor to pay compensation for his crime. The most serious penalty at a court's disposal, OUTLAWRY, was usually reserved for those who refused to accept judgment or to pay compensation. Placed outside the protection of the law, the outlaw's best chance of survival was to go into exile. There is evidence from all the Scandinavian countries that cases affecting the honour of the disputants could be settled out of court by single combat. WELAND, a Viking leader in FRANCIA, was apparently killed in such a combat in 863 after he had been accused of treachery. In Iceland these duels were called *hólmganga* ('island-going') because they were usually held on islands. The custom was easily abused by able warriors. Trial by ordeal was also known in DENMARK.

Later medieval writers such as SAXO GRAMMATICUS and SNORRI STURLUSON refer to legislation by early Danish and Norwegian kings, but it is the 11th century before there is any real evidence of royal lawmaking. CNUT (r. 1019–35) is credited with introducing a law code for his warrior retinue, and CNUT II (r. 1080–6) introduced laws to secure internal peace that were inspired by the contemporary 'Peace of God' movement in France and elsewhere. Systematic codification of Danish laws began only in the second half of the 12th century. King OLAF HARALDSSON (r. 1016–28) is believed to have revised the Norwegian Gulathing and Frostuthing laws, but again it is the 12th century before there was systematic codification of the law. The position in Sweden is obscure. Laws issued by Scandinavian kings came into force only when, or if, they were accepted by the local assemblies. Icelandic laws were first recorded in 1117–18: the most important collection of early Icelandic law, *Grágás* ('Grey Goose'), was compiled in the mid-13th century.

Lawspeaker (ON *Lögsögumaðr*) The president of the Icelandic ALTHING, the Lawspeaker was the only public office in the Icelandic Commonwealth. The Lawspeaker was elected for a three-year, renewable term on the opening day of the Althing, immediately after the outgoing Lawspeaker had opened proceedings. Re-elections were not unusual: the longest-serving Lawspeaker, Skapti Thóroddsson, served for twenty-seven summers (1004–30). The Lawspeaker's most important duty was to recite the Icelandic LAWS from the Law Rock, under the supervision of the *lögrétta* (legislative council). Until the codification of the Icelandic laws in 1117–18, this had to be done from memory: one third of the code was recited in each year of the Lawspeaker's term of office. If necessary the

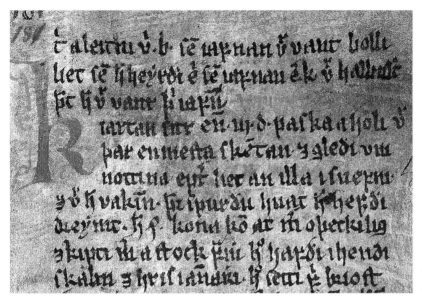

A page from a 14th-century copy of *Laxdæla saga*.

Lawspeaker could consult with five or more *lögmenn* (legal experts) before reciting the laws. The Lawspeaker had no executive authority but had a vote in the *lögrétta*, which he chaired. For his services, the Lawspeaker was paid 200 ells of homespun cloth a year (one ell equalling about 112 centimetres, or 45 inches), plus a share of fines levied by the courts. The office of the Lawspeaker was created at the first meeting of the Althing *c.*930. There is no evidence that any similar office ever existed in NORWAY, so the Lawspeaker appears to have been a uniquely Icelandic institution. The office was abolished in 1271 after the union with Norway.

Laxdæla saga ('The Saga of the Laxdalers') One of the most important *Íslendingasögur* (SAGAS of the Icelanders), written by an unknown author in the mid-13th century. Because, unusually in medieval Icelandic literature, so many of the central characters are WOMEN, it has been suggested that the author was female. The saga concerns the people of the Dales (Dalir), a district of the Breiðafjörður region of western ICELAND. The saga begins with KETIL FLATNOSE, a Viking settler in the Hebrides: the saga says he fled there to escape king HARALD FAIRHAIR, but that is unlikely for chronological reasons. After Ketil's death (late 9th century), his sons Bjorn and Helgi and daughter AUD THE DEEP-MINDED emigrate to Iceland and settle in the Dales. Under Aud's wise leadership, the Dales enjoy peace, but in time her and Bjorn's descendants come into conflict with one another. The saga climaxes with the love affairs of Guðrún Ósvífrsdóttir (a descendant of Bjorn) and Kjartan and Bolli (both descendants of Aud). After Guðrún persuades her husband Bolli to kill Kjartan, her former lover, a blood feud escalates

out of control until it is finally resolved by Snorri the Priest (d. 1031).

Laxdæla Saga, trans. M. Magnusson and H. Pálsson (Harmondsworth, 1969).

leding (*leiðangr*) The FLEET levy of the Scandinavian kingdoms in the central Middle Ages is described variously as *leding* (Old Danish), *leiðangr* (Old Norwegian) and *lethung* (Old Swedish). Each country was divided into ship-providing districts called *skipæn* (DENMARK), *skipreiða* (NORWAY) or *skiplagh* (SWEDEN). The farmers of the district were obliged by LAW to own suitable WEAPONS and to supply and equip a ship of forty, forty-two, or occasionally, fifty OARS. The origins of the levy system have been sought in the Viking Age, and it has been claimed that the conquest of ENGLAND by SVEIN FORKBEARD and CNUT at the beginning of the 11th century was achieved by the use of fleets and ARMIES raised in this way. However, there is no certain evidence for the existence of the levy fleets during the Viking Age. While it is clear that in Denmark, at least, kings were able to impose public obligations on their subjects from an early date (how else than by a labour levy could the DANEVIRKE have been built in the 8th century?), the earliest contemporary evidence for the *leding* system dates only from 1085, in the reign of CNUT II. Rather than being composed of levies, the independent evidence of contemporary runic memorials and Anglo-Saxon literary sources indicates that the Danish armies that conquered England were made up of mercenaries and the personal warrior retinues of the king and chieftains. The 13th-century Icelandic historian SNORRI STURLUSON credits HÁKON THE GOOD (r. *c.*936–60) with introducing the system of *leiðangr* in Norway by dividing the coastal districts

A coin of the Norwegian king Olaf the Peaceful, found on a Native American settlement in Maine, possibly the location of Leif Eriksson's Vinland.

into *skipreiður*. But the system that Snorri is actually describing is the Norwegian levy system of his own time. If Håkon really was responsible for introducing *leiðangr*, the system would surely not have remained unchanged for 300 years until Snorri's day. Nor is a levy system documented in Sweden before the central Middle Ages.

Leif Eriksson (Leif the Lucky) (*fl.* early 11th century) Norse navigator and probably the first European to make a landfall on the American continent: Leif was the son of ERIK THE RED, the founder of the Norse Greenland colony. The 13th-century Icelandic VINLAND SAGAS, *Eiríks saga rauða* ('Erik the Red's Saga') and *Grænlendinga saga* ('The Saga of the Greenlanders'), preserve different traditions about Leif's discoveries.

According to the *Grænlendinga saga*, which is now generally held to be the more reliable of the two SAGAS, Leif set out shortly after 1000 to explore the land sighted by the Icelander BJARNI HERJOLFSSON *c.*986 when blown off course *en route* to Greenland. Leif's first landfall was a land of bare rock and glaciers, which he called Helluland ('Slab Land'), probably Baffin Island. From there, Leif sailed south and encountered a low, forested land, which he called MARKLAND ('Forest Land'), probably Labrador. Continuing still further south, Leif spent a winter in a land with a mild climate, where grapes grew wild and rivers teemed with salmon, which he called VINLAND ('Vine Land'). This was probably somewhere between the Gulf of St Lawrence and Cape Cod, perhaps Nova Scotia, but there can be no certainty about this. In the spring, Leif returned to Greenland with a cargo of timber. Further expeditions to Vinland were made by Thorvald,

Leif's brother, by the Icelander THORFINN KARLSEFNI and by Freydis, Leif's sister. Leif later inherited his father's position as leader of the Greenland colony.

According to *Eiríks saga*, Leif went to NORWAY *c.*999, where he was converted to CHRISTIANITY by king OLAF TRYGGVASON. When Leif prepared to return home in the following year, Olaf asked him to try to persuade the Greenlanders to accept Christianity. Though sceptical of his chances of success, Leif agreed. On his return voyage, Leif was blown off course to an unknown land, where wild wheat and vines grew, which he decided to call Vinland. On his return home, Leif converted his mother to Christianity, and she subsequently built the first CHURCH in Greenland, at BRATTAHLID.

Lejre Viking Age royal and pagan religious centre, 8 kilometres south of ROSKILDE, Sjælland, DENMARK. According to the German Thietmar of Merseburg, writing *c.*1016, a religious festival involving the sacrifice of ninety-nine humans, the same number of horses and an unspecified number of dogs and cocks was held at Lejre every ninth year, in the month of January. Many legends about kings associated with Lejre are recorded in later Danish and Icelandic literary sources, and it was the reputed burial ground of several semi-legendary kings of Denmark, e.g. Harald Hyldetan (8th century?), the victor of BRÅVALLA. Excavations have not revealed any traces of a temple, and it is likely that the gods were worshipped in the open air. An 80-metre-long SHIP SETTING may have been used for religious ceremonies. The richness of other archaeological remains, including a large bow-sided hall, richly furnished graves and evidence of craft activities, underlines Lejre's importance in the Viking Age.

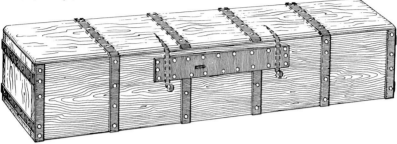

A reconstruction of a lockable chest for storing valuables, from Lejre, Denmark.

Lejre was supplanted in the 11th century by the nearby Christian centre at Roskilde.

lið Λ Viking Age Scandinavian king's or chieftain's personal retinue of warriors. The size of a *lið* depended on the wealth, status and power of its leader. The *lið* of a local chieftain may have been large enough to man only a single SHIP; the *lið* of a king may have been sufficient to man a FLEET. The members of a *lið* formed a military fellowship, or *FÉLAG*, bound by mutual loyalty. Discipline in the *lið* was probably maintained by the individual warrior's fear of dishonour if he abandoned his lord and companions in battle. The heroic ideal was that a warrior should follow his leader to his death if necessary. The Viking ARMIES that ravaged western Europe in the 9th century were simply groups of *lið*s that had come together for a common purpose. The *lið*s of chieftains probably formed the nucleus of local defence forces, supplemented by whatever local levies could be raised.

life expectancy In the absence of records of births and deaths, the life expectancy of Viking Age Scandinavians cannot be calculated with any precision. In common with other pre-industrial societies, Viking Age Scandinavians must have suffered a high rate of infant mortality. However, infant burials are very rare – in pagan times CHILDREN were apparently treated differently from adults in death – so the exact level is unknown, but of four children mentioned on a runic memorial at Hillersjö in SWEDEN only one survived to adulthood. The life expectancy of people who did survive to adulthood compares favourably with many Third World countries today. Of a sample group of 240 Viking Age skeletons from DENMARK, forty-one

per cent had survived to an age of between twenty and thirty-five, fifty-eight per cent survived to between thirty-five and fifty-five, but only one per cent had lived beyond the age of fifty-five. Mortality among WOMEN of child-bearing age was somewhat higher than for men of the same age group, no doubt as a result of complications during childbirth. Recent studies have shown that the methods used by archaeologists to determine the age of death from skeletal material can result in considerable underestimation of life span, so it may not have been quite so unusual for people to survive into old age as these figures suggest. Literary references and runic memorials suggest that premature violent death as a result of feuds, battle or accidents was not uncommon for men, though skeletal remains that show signs of physical injury are rare (not all fatal injuries leave marks on the bones, of course).

Limerick (ON Hlymrekr) After DUBLIN, the most important Scandinavian settlement in IRELAND. Excavations have so far failed to reveal any definite traces of the Viking Age TOWN. Limerick originated as a *LONGPHORT* in the 840s, when its position at the mouth of the River Shannon made it an excellent base for raiding the central lowlands of Ireland. Permanent Scandinavian settlement began when it was captured and fortified by Tomar mac Ailche (Thormódr Helgason) in 922. Relations between Limerick and the Dublin Vikings were hostile. GUTHFRITH of Dublin tried to conquer Limerick in 924 but was defeated, and in 927 Tomar briefly took Dublin during Guthfrith's absence in YORK. Dublin finally achieved the upper hand when OLAF GUTHFRITHSSON destroyed the Limerick FLEET on Lough Ree in 937. In 968 Mathgamain, king of Dál

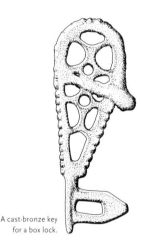

The monastery of Lindisfarne, scene of one of the earliest Viking raids in 793.

A cast-bronze key for a box lock.

Cais and Munster, captured and savagely sacked Limerick: all male prisoners of fighting age were executed, all others were sold as slaves. Limerick's king Ivar escaped to ENGLAND. Returning from exile in 969, Ivar refortified Limerick, but in 977 he was killed in battle by BRIAN BORU. Thereafter, Limerick was effectively under Irish control, though its population preserved a Norse character until the late 12th century.

Lindholm Høje Important Viking Age cemetery and settlement on a low hill on the north side of Limfjord, opposite Ålborg, Jutland. The settlement had both rectangular and bow-sided buildings (the latter similar to those found in the 10th-century forts at Fyrkat and TRELLEBORG). A road built of wooden planks ran through the settlement. There was limited evidence of bronze- and IRONWORKING, but farming was the main occupation. Part of the village fields have been excavated: they show narrow ridge-and-furrow patterns created by ploughing (or hoeing). Marks of harrows, cartwheels and even footprints were also found in the soil. The cemetery contained 700 burials, most of them cremations, dating from the 6th century to the late 11th. The earliest cremations were covered with small mounds, but in the 8th century they were placed inside square, triangular or round stone settings. During the Viking Age the cremations were surrounded with small stone SHIP SETTINGS, a symbolic alternative to burial in a real ship. In the course of the late 11th century inhumation replaced cremation as the method of burial, perhaps as a result of the influence of CHRISTIANITY. Though the cemetery is exceptionally large, it was in use for around 500 years, indicating that the village population averaged only around forty. Both

settlement and cemetery were abandoned c.1100, when they were buried by drifting sand dunes.

Lindisfarne (Holy Island) Island off the coast of Northumberland, north-east ENGLAND, location of the earliest securely dated Viking raid. The island's attraction for the Vikings was the famous monastery founded by St Aidan in 634. The raid was carried out on 7 June 793 by Vikings from Hordaland in west NORWAY. In the course of the raid, the CHURCH was looted and suffered slight structural damage; the altars were desecrated, some holy relics were destroyed, and some of the monks were killed or drowned; others were taken away captive. The monks must have had some warning of the attack because the monastery's greatest treasures, including the *Lindisfarne Gospels* and the relics of St Cuthbert, did not fall into the Vikings' hands. This attack on such a holy place was deeply shocking. The Anglo-Saxon scholar ALCUIN, writing shortly after news of the attack reached the continent, saw God's and the saints' failure to protect the monastery as a sign of divine anger for some great sin. The emperor CHARLEMAGNE took steps to RANSOM the captive monks, but it is not known if he succeeded. The community survived the raid, although in the 840s the shrine of St Cuthbert and other treasures were moved inland to Norham for safe keeping. Lindisfarne was sacked for a second time by the Vikings in 875, after which it was abandoned by the monks who, after seven years of wandering with the relics of St Cuthbert, were resettled at Chester-le-Street (County Durham). Renewed Viking attacks led to a final move to Durham in 995. Lindisfarne was reoccupied by Benedictine monks in 1081.

No visible remains of the Anglo-Saxon monastery survive; all of the standing monastic ruins on the

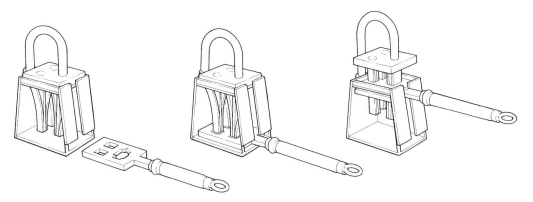

Cutaway drawings showing how a Viking Age padlock worked.

island belong to the later Benedictine abbey. Excavations at Green Shiel, in the north of the island, have uncovered a Viking Age farming settlement. Though built of stone, like other contemporary settlements in Scandinavian-settled parts of northern England (e.g. RIBBLEHEAD), there is no evidence that it was occupied by Scandinavians.

locks and keys Locks and keys for doors, strong boxes and chests are common finds on Viking Age sites. Several different types of lock, including padlocks, are known. Simple deadlocks were commonly used, but in the 11th century a distinctive type of lock, which was opened by using a sliding key to compress a system of iron leaf-springs, came into use in Scandinavia, from where it spread to ENGLAND, ICELAND and GREENLAND. Scandinavian housewives were the keepers of the FAMILY's keys and were responsible for those objects that were kept locked up. Keys and boxes fitted with locks are common offerings in female graves. Though Viking Age locks would have been quite easy to pick, they remained a powerful symbol of ownership.

Loki One of the ÆSIR family of gods, Loki is the most enigmatic of the Norse pagan deities. His parents were the GIANT Fárbauti and his wife Laufey. Intelligent, humorous, deceitful, malicious and entirely amoral, Loki was highly attractive yet sired monstrous children: he was a shape-shifter who could take on the form of any animal, male or female. By the giantess Angerboda, Loki was the father of the monstrous wolf FENRIR, the MIDGARD SERPENT and HEL, the hideous goddess of the dead; while in the shape of a mare he gave birth to ODIN's eight-legged steed SLEIPNIR. There is no evidence that Loki was ever worshipped, and his role in the

Norse pantheon has not been satisfactorily explained. He has been seen as a personification of fire, which can both help and harm. In the myths, Loki's role is often to provoke a crisis and then to resolve it by his wit and cunning. The most important myth associated with Loki is the slaying of the beautiful god BALDER. Out of malice and jealousy, Loki tricked the blind god HODER into killing his own brother Balder with a dart of mistletoe. The gods sent Odin's son HERMOD to the realm of the dead to beg Hel to release Balder. She agreed on condition that all things, living and dead, weep for the slain god. Loki alone, disguised as an ancient giantess, refused and Balder remained with Hel. The anger of the gods was so great that Loki fled and changed himself into a salmon. Kvasir (a minor member of the Æsir with a reputation for wisdom) devised a special net and caught Loki, who was bound beneath the open jaws of a venom-dripping snake. Loki's faithful wife Sigyn sits beside him, catching the venom in a bowl, but whenever she turns away to empty it, the poison drips onto his face, causing him to writhe in agony, making the earth quake. At RAGNAROK, Loki will finally break his bonds and lead his children against the gods: he and the watchman HEIMDALL will slay one another.

longphort Irish-Gaelic word for a fortified Viking landing place. The first *longphort* was built at DUBLIN in 841 and was the nucleus around which the city developed. Other Irish TOWNS, including WATERFORD, WEXFORD, CORK and LIMERICK, have their origins as *longphorts*. Other, short-lived *longphorts* were built by the Vikings in the mid-9th century at Arklow, Annagassan, Lough Ree, Dunrally, Youghal and Clondalkin, among other places.

The Frankish emperor
Louis the Pious, from a
contemporary manuscript.

The imposing Romanesque
cathedral at Lund, built *c*.1120.

Long Serpent (Ormrinn Langi) Arguably the most famous SHIP of the Viking Age, *Long Serpent* was a richly decorated *drakkar* built in 999–1000 for king OLAF TRYGGVASON of NORWAY for an expedition against the WENDS. *Long Serpent* was an exceptionally large ship for the time, described in the *FLATEYJARBÓK* as having a keel 72 ells (about 39 metres) in length; it had a crew of sixty-eight oarsmen and could carry more than 500 warriors. Unusually, the name of the master shipwright is known, Thorberg Skavhogg ('he who cuts smoothly with an axe'), a clear sign of the ship's exceptional qualities. The *Long Serpent* was king Olaf's flagship when he met his death at the battle of Svöld in 1000, and formed part of the booty captured by the victor, jarl ERIK of HLAÐIR. Its subsequent fate is unknown.

Louis the Pious (778–840) Frankish emperor (r. 814–40). It was during Louis's reign that the Vikings made their first serious inroads into the Carolingian Empire. Although the emperor CHARLEMAGNE had provided for his empire to be divided between his sons on his death, he was, in the event, survived only by Louis, who inherited the empire intact in 814. Apart from pirate raids by Vikings in the north and Saracens in the MEDITERRANEAN – which were contained by the coastal defences instituted by Charlemagne – Louis faced no serious external threats, and his reign might have been relatively uneventful had he not married for a second time in 819.

In 817 Louis had appointed his eldest son Lothar as co-emperor and heir; his younger sons Pippin and Louis the German were granted subkingdoms. This settlement collapsed as a result of Louis's marriage to Judith of Bavaria in 819, only four months after

the death of his first wife. The son that Judith bore Louis in 823, CHARLES THE BALD, could be provided with a suitable inheritance only at the expense of his elder sons. When Louis granted Alemannia to Charles in 829, Lothar, backed by his brothers, rebelled and deposed his father. Louis was restored at the assembly of Nijmegen in 830, but the problem of the division of the empire continued to fester for the remainder of his reign. Civil war broke out in 832 after Louis granted Pippin's kingdom of Aquitaine to Charles and the emperor was again deposed, only to be restored in 834. Louis's last years continued to be marked by revolts, and on his death in 840 another civil war broke out between his surviving sons Lothar, Louis the German and Charles, ended only by the tripartite division of the empire at Verdun in 843.

Throughout his reign, Louis managed to pay considerable attention to the defence of the northern coasts against the Vikings, with some success. Only one Viking raid is recorded in Louis's reign before 829 and this, by a strong force of thirteen SHIPS in 820, was repulsed twice by coastguards before it finally found a gap in the defences and sacked a village in Aquitaine. The civil wars of the early 830s seriously undermined the effectiveness of the defences, and in 834 the Vikings penetrated inland for the first time, sacking the port of DORESTAD on the Rhine. In the face of persistent raids, Louis continued to act energetically, ordering FORTIFICATIONS to be built to guard the Rhine Estuary in 835 and 837 (*see* Frankish RING-FORTS). One of these forts on Walcheren was taken by the Vikings in 837, with such heavy losses suffered by Louis that he cancelled a trip to Rome. At the same time, Louis pursued an effective diplomatic policy in DENMARK, supporting the often-exiled HARALD KLAK

A silver penny of Magnus Barelegs, king of Norway 1093–1103.

against his rivals the sons of GODFRED up to 828, and promoting Christian missions to Scandinavia. In 836 and 838 Louis even persuaded the Danish king HORIK to capture and execute pirate leaders. This may have been more effective than military measures against the Vikings, as there were no recorded raids on the Carolingian Empire from 838 until the renewal of civil war in 841.

Lund With ROSKILDE, Lund (now in Skåne, SWEDEN) was the leading royal and ecclesiastical centre of the medieval kingdom of DENMARK. Once thought to have been founded by CNUT, the earliest evidence of settlement at Lund dates to the late 10th century, when it was a village with a single east–west main street. It may have been a Christian community from the beginning: dendrochronological analysis of a wooden coffin from a medieval churchyard has given a date of c.990. In 1020 Cnut founded a mint at Lund, and c.1050 five new CHURCHES were built there. A BISHOPRIC was founded in 1060, which was subsequently raised to an archbishopric in 1103–4. The present imposing Romanesque cathedral was begun c.1120. Leather-working was a major industry at Lund: one street has been excavated that was surfaced entirely with discarded leather offcuts. Lund came under Swedish rule in the 17th century.

Lyrskov Heath, battle of Battle fought near HEDEBY in September 1043 between a Danish-Saxon alliance under king MAGNUS THE GOOD and the WENDS. The DANES and Saxons won a decisive victory, ending the Wendish pressure on DENMARK's southern frontier. No reliable casualty figures exist: ADAM OF BREMEN, writing about thirty years after the battle, gives the Wendish dead as 15,000.

Magnus Barelegs (c.1073–1103) King of NORWAY (r. 1093–1103). Magnus led the last major Viking expeditions in the Irish Sea: he gained his nickname because he often wore the Gaelic kilt. After succeeding his father OLAF THE PEACEFUL, Magnus initially ruled Norway jointly with his cousin Håkon Magnusson, becoming sole ruler on Håkon's death in 1095. One of Magnus's first acts as king was to launch an old-fashioned Viking raid on the Swedish coast. After the murder of his envoy Ingemund on the Hebridean island of Lewis in 1097, Magnus decided to establish direct royal control over the earldom of ORKNEY and the kingdom of MAN and the Isles, both long claimed by Norway. The following year Magnus led a brutal ravaging campaign through the Isles, sparing only the holy island of IONA. The earls of Orkney were deposed and replaced by Magnus's son Sigurd, and the Isle of Man was quickly conquered. Using Man as his base, Magnus went on to capture DUBLIN and to exact tribute in Galloway and Anglesey. While in Anglesey, Magnus defeated the Norman earls Hugh of Chester and Hugh of Shrewsbury, who were also campaigning in WALES. After agreeing a treaty with king Edgar of SCOTLAND, recognizing the Norwegian claim to the Isles, Magnus returned home to a short war with the Swedes. Magnus made a second expedition to the Isles in 1102 and spent the winter with the Irish high king Muirchertach II, with whom he made a MARRIAGE alliance. The next summer Magnus was killed in a skirmish in northern IRELAND while foraging for food. Magnus's achievement was short-lived: within a few years of his death, Norwegian royal authority in the Isles began a slow but irrevocable decline.

The site of the battle of Maldon; the causeway links Northey Island to the mainland.

Magnus Erlendsson (St Magnus) (*c*.1075–1117) Earl of ORKNEY (r. 1104–17). The son of earl Erlend of Orkney (r. 1064–93), Magnus joined king MAGNUS BARELEGS' ravaging expedition through the Hebrides and the Irish Sea in 1098. He antagonized the king by refusing to fight in battle with the Normans in Anglesey because he had no quarrel with them (he is said to have chanted psalms throughout the battle). Magnus later jumped ship as the king was returning to Orkney and entered the service of Malcolm III of SCOTLAND. When king Magnus was killed in 1103, Magnus returned to Orkney and was given a half-share in the earldom by his cousin Håkon Paulsson. Tension soon arose between the earls, and Håkon lured Magnus to a peace meeting on the island of Egilsay and murdered him shortly before Easter 1117. Magnus was buried at BIRSAY and miracles were soon reported at his grave. His remains were later transferred to the magnificent cathedral built at Kirkwall by his nephew earl Rognvald Kali.

Magnus the Good (Magnus Olafsson, Magnus I) (1024–47) King of NORWAY (r. 1035–47); king of DENMARK (r. 1042–7). An illegitimate son of king OLAF HARALDSSON, Magnus was taken to RUSSIA at the age of four with his father, who had been driven into exile by CNUT. Following Cnut's death in 1035, or possibly shortly before it, the Norwegians rebelled against the rule of his son SVEIN ALFIVASON and invited Magnus to return from exile. Cnut's successor in Denmark, his son HARTHACNUT, recognized Magnus as king of Norway the following year. The two rulers agreed that whoever outlived the other would rule both Denmark and Norway. Accordingly, when Harthacnut died in 1042, Magnus became king

of Denmark, appointing Cnut's nephew SVEIN ESTRITHSON as his regent. Svein soon rebelled, but the DANES remained mostly loyal, especially after Magnus's victories over the WENDS, who threatened southern Denmark, at Jumne (WOLIN) and LYRSKOV HEATH in 1043. Magnus faced a renewed threat when his uncle HARALD HARDRADA returned from Constantinople in 1044 and allied with Svein. In 1046 Magnus accepted Harald as joint ruler, and the two then turned against Svein. Magnus died in Jutland on campaign against Svein the following year: Harald became sole ruler in Norway, while Svein seized power in Denmark.

Maldon, battle of (991) Viking victory over the English, fought near Maldon, Essex. A large Viking FLEET of ninety-three SHIPS, led by OLAF TRYGGVASON attacked Kent and EAST ANGLIA, making its base on Northey Island in the Blackwater Estuary near Maldon. BYRHTNOTH, the ealdorman of Essex, took the levies of the eastern counties to confront the Vikings on the island. After an exchange of arrows and spears at long range, which caused only light casualties on either side, Byrhtnoth allowed the Vikings to cross to the mainland and to form up for battle. Byrhtnoth was killed by a spear, and the levies fled, but the warriors of his personal retinue fought to the death in a heroic last stand. The battle is commemorated in the Old English poem *The Battle of Maldon*, which praises in moving terms the loyalty of Byhrtnoth's men as they defended their fallen lord's body. The poet criticizes Byrhtnoth's 'extravagant spirit' in letting the Vikings cross to the mainland unimpeded, but he no doubt realized that if they could not be brought to battle they would simply sail away and attack somewhere else. The battle marked the beginning of a serious

St Patrick's Island, Peel,
the royal and ecclesiastical capital
of the kingdom of Man.

escalation of Viking activity around the English coasts, and the aftermath of the battle saw the first payment of DANEGELD.

The Battle of Maldon, ed. and trans. Bill Griffiths (Hockwold-cum-Wilton, Norfolk, 1995); D. G. Scragg (ed.), *The Battle of Maldon* AD 991 (Oxford, 1991).

Man, kingdom of Norse kingdom, centred on the Isle of Man in the Irish Sea; at its height *c.*1095 it also controlled the western isles of SCOTLAND. Archaeological evidence in the shape of pagan graves indicates that Viking settlement in the Isle of Man began in the later 9th century. The native Celtic-speaking Christian population was subjugated but not exterminated. Following their conversion to CHRISTIANITY in the 10th century, the Norse settlers erected a fine series of carved memorial crosses showing a blending of Scandinavian and Celtic ART STYLES (*see* MANX CROSSES). Nineteen silver hoards dating from 960–1070 suggest that Man prospered by its proximity to DUBLIN, and from the 1030s COINS, modelled on those of Dublin, were minted on the island. Though the names of some earlier kings are known, the recorded history of the kingdom of Man really begins with GODRED CROVAN, who won control of the island at the battle of Skyhill in 1079. Godred united Man and the Hebrides into a single kingdom, and for a time also ruled Dublin and gathered tribute from Galloway. The kingdom of Man and the Isles was divided into five administrative districts, which together sent a total of thirty-two representatives to the annual assembly at TYNWALD in the Isle of Man. Following Godred's death in 1095, a civil war broke out and the kingdom was conquered by MAGNUS BARELEGS of NORWAY in 1098. Godred's son Olaf I (r. 1113–53) eventually revived the kingdom *c.*1113, but

recognized Norwegian sovereignty. In 1156 Godred II (r. 1153–87) lost control of the southern Hebrides to the Scottish-Gaelic chieftain SOMERLED, and the kingdom was permanently weakened. The rest of the Hebrides were under effective Scottish control by 1263, and Man itself was ceded to Scotland by Norway in 1266, a year after the death of Magnus Olafsson, its last Norse king.

C. E. Fell, P. Foote, J. Graham-Campbell and R. Thomson (eds), *The Viking Age in the Isle of Man* (London, 1983); *Chronicles of the Kings of Man and the Isles*, ed. and trans. G. Broderick (Douglas, Isle of Man, 1995).

Manx Chronicle *see* CHRONICLES OF THE KINGS OF MAN AND THE ISLES

Manx crosses Nearly fifty carved stone memorial crosses erected between the mid-10th and early 11th centuries by the Scandinavian settlers of the Isle of MAN after their conversion to CHRISTIANITY. Most take the form of a rectangular slab of local slate on which a wheel-headed cross has been carved in low relief: a few free-standing crosses are also known. The ornament of the earliest crosses shows strong Celtic and northern English influences, but Scandinavian decorative motifs – primarily in the Jellinge and Mammen ART STYLES – dominate later examples. Several crosses include scenes from the legend of SIGURD FAFNISBANE; others, such as Thorwald's Cross at Andreas, show scenes from RAGNAROK and other pagan myths. Overtly Christian scenes are rare. Though the memorial inscriptions on the crosses are in Norse and carved in RUNES, several commemorate people with Celtic names, suggesting that there was intermarriage between the Norse and native populations. The crosses were probably the work of Norse sculptors,

Runic slab from Andreas, Isle of Man, showing the hero Sigurd roasting the heart of the dragon Fafnir.

Gaut's Cross, Kirk Michael, Isle of Man, 10th century.

one of whom, Gaut Björnsson (*fl. c*.950), is known by name from inscriptions he left on two of his crosses.

Markland ('Forest Land') Forested land in North America, probably Labrador, first discovered by BJARNI HERJOLFSSON or by LEIF ERIKSSON *c*.1000 in the course of his voyage from GREENLAND to VINLAND. Although not attractive for settlement, Markland had lasting significance for the Norse Greenlanders as a source of timber. Voyages from Greenland to Markland to collect timber continued until at least 1347.

marriage and divorce Among pagan Viking Age Scandinavians marriage was essentially a business contract between two FAMILIES. A marriage was arranged in two stages: the betrothal and the wedding. The initiative had to come from the man or his father, who would make the proposal of marriage to the woman's father or guardian. If the latter was agreeable, the groom promised to pay the bride-price (*mundr*). In ICELAND the minimum payment was 8 ounces of silver; in Norway it was 12. In return, the bride's father promised to hand over her dowry at the wedding. Both the bride-price and the dowry remained the property of the bride after the wedding. The two men shook hands on the agreement in front of witnesses and agreed a date for the wedding, usually within a year. The woman's consent to the marriage might be sought but it was not necessary. Widows had more freedom than single WOMEN, as they needed only to seek their fathers' approval before remarrying. Only in the 12th century, well after the introduction of CHRISTIANITY, did a woman's consent to marriage become necessary. The wedding itself took the form of a FEAST, usually held at the bride's family home.

The marriage was considered legally binding when the couple had been seen going to bed by a minimum of six witnesses.

If a marriage was an unhappy one it could be ended by a divorce, though this does not seem to have happened very often. On the face of it, divorce was a simple procedure. All that was required of the party who was seeking a divorce was that they summon witnesses and declare himself or herself divorced. In practice it may have been more complicated than this if there was property at stake. A wife's adultery was a serious matter, and in some areas the husband had the right to kill both her and her lover if they were caught together. There was no penalty for a man if he kept a concubine or had CHILDREN outside his marriage. This was very common in the higher levels of society, even after the conversion to Christianity, and overseas, where captive native women were often taken as concubines by Viking men. It was probably the widespread practice of concubinage that led some outside observers, such as ADAM OF BREMEN in the 11th century, to accuse the Scandinavians of practising polygamy, but monogamy appears actually to have been the rule, as even pagan marriage contracts recognized only one legal wife.

medicine In pagan times the practice of medicine was largely, and midwifery always, the preserve of WOMEN, both in the home and on the battlefield. Women practising surgery on battle wounds are mentioned several times, for example at the siege of PARIS in 885–6 and at the battle of STIKLESTAD in 1030. Preventative medicine was more a matter of magic than science, consisting mainly of charms and spells (spoken or written in RUNES) and

Offa's Dyke, a border rampart
built along Mercia's border with
the Welsh. Offa also organized
defences against early Viking raids.

protective amulets. Medical treatments included
bone-setting, cleaning and cauterizing wounds,
bandaging, lancing boils and the use of herbal
potions and ointments. Angelica was a widely used
medicinal herb for digestive and other ailments, and
the antiseptic qualities of some mosses were
recognized. Water was heated before being used in
medical treatments, possibly, but not certainly, to
sterilize it. Charms and spells were used to reinforce
the efficacy of these rudimentary treatments. The
severity of battlefield wounds was diagnosed by
giving patients a meal of onion porridge. If the
wound subsequently began to smell of onions it was
a sign that the bowel was perforated and that the
patient would soon die of peritonitis. With the
coming of CHRISTIANITY, foreign monks introduced
more-advanced surgical techniques to Scandinavia
and founded the first hospitals. The earliest
Scandinavian hospitals are recorded in DENMARK in
the late 11th century. Male physicians became more
common, though none were trained in Scandinavia
before the 15th century.

Mediterranean and Spain, Vikings in the It was
only natural that once the Vikings were established
as a permanent presence on the River Loire in the
840s they would sail farther south and test the
possibilities of the Iberian peninsula. When they
did, they found local resistance to be discouragingly
effective. In 844 a Viking FLEET of 100 SHIPS from
the Loire attacked the northern Spanish Christian
kingdom of Galicia and Asturias before moving
south to sack Lisbon, Seville, Cadiz and Algeciras in
the emirate of Cordoba and Asilah in Morocco. The
expedition ended disastrously when the emir of
Cordoba trapped the Viking fleet on the River
Guadalquivir near Seville, destroying thirty ships,

killing 1,000 Vikings and capturing 400 more, most
of whom were executed. After this, the Vikings
stayed away until 859, when HASTEIN and BJORN
IRONSIDE led another fleet, this time of sixty-two
ships, from the Loire through the Strait of Gibraltar
into the Mediterranean, where it remained for
nearly two years, plundering the coasts of Spain,
Morocco, Provence and Italy. Though celebrated
as a great feat of arms and seamanship, this
expedition, too, was a costly failure. A Moorish
fleet from Spain caught Bjorn and Hastein as they
returned through the strait, and only twenty ships
made it back to the Loire. The Vikings never
returned to the Mediterranean, and there were no
more large-scale attacks on Christian or Muslim
Spain, though a few pirate raids are recorded into
the early 11th century.

Mercia, kingdom of Anglo-Saxon kingdom covering
the English Midlands, that is, the area bounded by
the Welsh border, the River Humber, EAST ANGLIA
and the River Thames. Mercia emerged in the 6th
century, and under its greatest king, Offa (r. 757–96),
it dominated ENGLAND south of the Humber.
Decline set in after Offa's death, and from 825 it
came under the domination of WESSEX. The Danish
GREAT ARMY invaded Mercia in 867, but withdrew in
868 after it had been besieged at Nottingham by the
Mercians and West Saxons. The DANES returned in
872, and after they established a fortified camp at
REPTON in 873–4, king BURGRED abdicated and
retired to Rome. The Danes appointed CEOLWULF II
(r. 874–9) as a puppet king to keep the kingdom at
their disposal until they were ready to occupy it. In
877 the Danes appropriated the eastern half of the
kingdom (which became part of the DANELAW) for
settlement and granted the rest to Ceolwulf. After

The Midgard Serpent prepares
to take the bait – an ox's head at
the end of Thor's fishing line.

Ceolwulf's death, 'English' Mercia came under
the control of the ealdorman Æthelred and, after
his death in 911, of his wife Æthelflæd. On
her death in 918 Æthelflæd left Mercia to her
daughter Ælfwynn, but the following year king
Edward the Elder annexed it to Wessex after
his conquest of the Danelaw.

Merovingian period The last period of Norwegian
prehistory before the Viking Age, *c.* AD 550–800. It is
named after the dominant European power of the
time, the Frankish Merovingian dynasty (460–751).
It is equivalent to the Swedish Vendel period and
the Danish late Germanic Iron Age.

Midgard In Scandinavian mythology, Midgard
was the world inhabited by humans, located in the
middle of the universe between the fiery realm of
Muspell and the icy realm of the dead Niflheim.
Midgard was created, with the heavens and the sea,
by Odin and his brothers from the body of the giant
Ymir, and was connected to the realm of the gods,
Asgard, by the rainbow bridge Bifrost. Midgard
was round and surrounded by a deep ocean, in
which dwelt the frightful Midgard Serpent. On
the same plane of the cosmos as Midgard, but
separated from it by a wall made of Ymir's eyebrows,
was Jotunheim, the land of the giants. *See also*
CREATION MYTH.

Midgard Serpent (*Miðgarðsormr*) An enormous
mythological serpent, also known as the 'World
Serpent'. The Midgard Serpent was the offspring
of Loki and giantess Angerboda. Odin flung it into
the depths of the sea that surrounds Midgard,
where it lies coiled around the world biting its tail.
Thor once tried, unsuccessfully, to catch the

Midgard Serpent, but at Ragnarok he will kill it
with his hammer before falling dead from the
effects of its venom.

Migration period The period of Swedish prehistory
from *c.* AD 400–550 (also used for the same period of
German history). Fortified local power centres, such
as Eketorp on Öland, and impressive burial
mounds at Gamla Uppsala are evidence of the
emergence of powerful, well-organized chiefdoms in
Sweden in this period. It is equivalent to the early
Germanic Iron Age of Danish prehistory.

Mikligarðr The 'Great City', the Viking name
for Constantinople (Istanbul), the capital of the
medieval Greek Byzantine Empire. Among the
attractions of Mikligarðr to the Vikings were the
opportunities to trade furs and slaves for Byzantine
silks, and the chance to serve as mercenaries in the
Byzantine emperor's élite Varangian Guard.

Mjöllnir (Miollnir) The hammer of the thunder-god
Thor, Mjöllnir was essential to the defence
of Asgard and gave protection to humans against
evil and violence. Forged by the dwarves, the
hammer, when thrown, had the property of always
hitting its target before returning to the thrower's
hand. Marriages and newborn children were
consecrated by Mjöllnir. Thor's hammer amulets
were commonly worn by pagan Vikings as good-
luck charms.

monasticism in Viking Age Scandinavia Though
missionary activity began in earnest in the
9th century, there had been little development
of monasticism by the end of the Viking Age.
Tradition credits Cnut with introducing English

Mjöllnir amulets were popular Viking good-luck charms.

A head of a monk from Urnes stave church, Sognefjord, Norway.

Benedictine monasticism to DENMARK, but there is no contemporary evidence to verify this. David (d. 1082?), a Benedictine abbot from ENGLAND, is supposed to have founded a monastery at Munktorp in central SWEDEN, but, again, there is no conclusive evidence for this. A chapter of Benedictine monks from Evesham in England was introduced to ODENSE cathedral in Denmark by king Erik the Evergood c.1095. Benedictine monasteries were founded at Selja, near BERGEN, and Niðarholmr, near TRONDHEIM in NORWAY c.1100, and at LUND, in Skåne, in 1104. The Augustine (or Austin) canons were established at Vestervig in Jutland and Dalby in Skåne some years before 1100. The main development of monasticism in Scandinavia took place between 1100 and 1200.

Muirchertach of the Leather Cloaks (d. 943) King of the Northern Uí Néill (r. 919–43), high king designate (938–43). He was remembered in Norse as well as Irish tradition for his victories over the Vikings. Muirchertach faced a resurgence of Viking activity following their return to DUBLIN in 919 and the defeat and death of his father, king NIALL GLÚNDUBH, at the battle of Islandbridge in September of the same year. He first defeated the Dublin Vikings at Armagh in 921, then at Carlingford in 925, when he beheaded 200 prisoners, then at Anagassan in 926, and again at Armagh in 933, when he killed 200 raiders and recovered all their loot. In alliance with Donnchadh Donn, his rival for the high KINGSHIP, he sacked Dublin itself in 938. Captured the following year by the Dublin Vikings in a revenge attack on his stronghold of Ailech (Donegal), he was quickly ransomed. In 941 he toured IRELAND to establish his claim to the high kingship. Later in the year, he

ravaged Viking settlements in the Hebrides in retaliation for pirate raids. Muirchertach was killed in battle with Blacaire Guthfrithsson, king of Dublin, at Clonkeen near Armagh in February 943.

Muspell (Muspelheim) In Scandinavian mythology, the realm of fire, ruled over by the GIANT Surt. It was heat from Muspell that melted the ice of NIFLHEIM into mist and made possible the CREATION of the earth. Hurled by Surt, the fires of Muspell will also complete the destruction of the world at RAGNAROK. Pagan Scandinavian cosmology is vague about where exactly Muspell fits into the cosmos, but it is somewhere south of Niflheim.

N

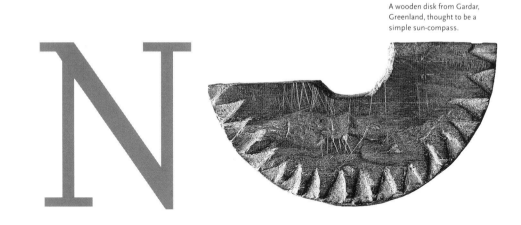

A wooden disk from Gardar, Greenland, thought to be a simple sun-compass.

Nadodd (*fl. c.*860) Probably the second Norseman to visit ICELAND. Nadodd was a Norwegian Viking with so many enemies that he had decided to settle in the FAROE ISLANDS for safety. Blown off course after leaving NORWAY, Nadodd made a landing at Reyðarfjörður on Iceland's mountainous east coast. He climbed a mountain to look for signs of human habitation or smoke, but saw none. Leaving in a snowstorm, he named the new land Snæland (Snowland), but gave good reports of it when he reached the Faroes.

Naglfar ('nail-farer') In Scandinavian mythology, a ship built from the untrimmed nails of dead people. At RAGNAROK it will be let loose from its moorings to carry the GIANT Hrym to the last battle with the gods. It was considered inadvisable to allow anyone to die with untrimmed nails, as they would contribute material for building *Naglfar*: both gods and men hoped the ship would take as long as possible to complete.

navigation Little is known about how the Vikings navigated their SHIPS. Where they could, they simply followed the coast, keeping a safe distance out to avoid shoals and reefs, and navigating by prominent landmarks on shore. Most of the Danish raids on ENGLAND and FRANCIA could have been carried out in this way. However, the Vikings, especially the Norwegians, did make long open-sea voyages across the Atlantic, during which they were out of sight of land for several days at a time. These voyages were probably made without the aid of any navigational instruments. The magnetic compass was certainly unknown, while stories about the use of a 'SUN STONE' (*sólarsteinn*), a crystal that could locate the sun in cloudy weather, are most likely legendary.

A broken wooden disk, marked with radial lines, found in GREENLAND has been interpreted by some as a simple sun-compass, but this is not universally accepted.

Viking navigators knew how to use the altitude of the sun at midday and the stars to judge latitude. This was a useful aid to navigation if the latitude of the destination was known. Sounding for depth, widely used by the ANGLO-SAXONS during the Viking Age, was probably used by Viking navigators in the Baltic Sea, but apparently not in the deeper Atlantic waters. The most important source of navigational information came from an ancient stock of orally transmitted practical knowledge of sea and weather conditions. A build-up of cloud formations might indicate the presence of land beyond the horizon; observing the direction of the flight of seabirds could give similar information. A slackening of the sea in stormy weather could indicate that the ship had sailed into the lee of an island obscured by cloud, rain or darkness. Because of the risk of running aground, Viking navigators tried to avoid sailing along coasts at night. If they did, experienced navigators could sense the proximity of the coast by the strength of waves reflected by the shore onto the sides of the ship. Though charts were not used, tolerably accurate sailing directions were transmitted orally.

Despite this, the Viking seafarer had little control over his course in bad weather, and shipwreck was a common hazard. Sometimes a mariner who had been blown off course made an unexpected landfall on an unknown shore – the Norse discoveries of ICELAND, Greenland and North America were all made in this way – but the fate of Alvard, a seafarer commemorated on an 11th-century rune-stone from BORNHOLM, was no doubt more typical: 'Sasser had

A 14th-century copy of
Njáls saga in a sturdy,
utilitarian, wooden cover.

this stone set in memory of Alvard, his father. He
drowned at sea with all the crew. Christ help his soul
eternally. May this stone stand in his memory.'

Niall Glúndubh ('Black Knee') (*c.*870–919) Northern
Úi Néill (O'Neill) king of Ailech (r. 896–919); high
king of IRELAND (r. 916–19). Niall shared the
KINGSHIP of Ailech in Donegal with his brother
Domnall until the latter's death in 915. Niall
campaigned frequently in Meath and Connacht,
establishing a strong position in north-central
Ireland, and in 916 he succeeded Fland Sinna of the
southern Úi Néill as high king. The re-establishment
of the Vikings at WATERFORD brought Niall south
with an ARMY in 917 but, apart from an indecisive
confrontation near Cashel, he achieved nothing. He
encouraged the Leinstermen to attack the Norse king
SIHTRIC CÁECH at his camp at Cenn Fuait (about 25
kilometres inland from Waterford), but they were
soundly defeated, and later in the year Sihtric
recaptured DUBLIN. In September 919 Niall
attempted to drive Sihtric out of Dublin, but was
crushingly defeated at Islandbridge. Niall and five
other Irish kings were killed.

Nidaros *see* TRONDHEIM

Niflheim The Scandinavian underworld where the
souls of the dead went if they died of disease or old
age. Niflheim was a dark and dreary place of ice and
mist, surrounded by a high wall with a well-barred
gateway that is the barrier dividing the living from
the dead. Twelve icy rivers flowed out of Niflheim.
The realm was ruled by the goddess HEL, who
dwelled among the roots of YGGDRASIL, the world-
tree. The roots of the tree were gnawed at by
Niðhoggr ('corpse-tearer'), a frightful serpent that
consumed the corpses of the dead. Niflheim is
surrounded by a vast abyss and is linked to
MIDGARD, the world of humans, by a single
echoing bridge, guarded by a giantess who
challenges those who cross.

Njáls saga ('Njal's saga') The longest and greatest of
the *Íslendingasögur* (SAGAS of the Icelanders), *Njáls
saga* was written *c.*1275–90 by an unknown author.
Its terse narrative and psychological realism make
Njáls saga an astonishingly modern-seeming work,
especially when compared with the chivalric
romances then popular in western Europe. The saga
ranges widely in time and space, from the settlement
period to the battle of CLONTARF in 1014, and from
ICELAND to Scandinavia and the British Isles. The
main theme of the saga is the relationship between
Njal, a wealthy, peace-loving farmer whose wisdom
and knowledge of LAW make him a very influential
man, and his friend Gunnar. Their friendship is
tested when Gunnar's wife, the manipulative,
dishonest and vindictive Hallgerðr, falls out with
Njal's wife Bergthora. Njal and Gunnar refuse to
take up the quarrel but, egged on by the two women,
their relatives get involved in a round of tit-for-tat
killings. Despite their wives' feuding, the two men
remain friends and make peace. When Gunnar is
outlawed for his involvement in another blood-feud,
Njal advises him to leave the country, but he refuses
and is killed by his enemies after a heroic last stand.
With Gunnar's restraining influence gone, the feud
reopens: Njal's attempts to make peace are in vain,
as both families are determined on bloodshed. The
saga reaches its climax when Njal and his family are
trapped in their hall by their enemies and burned
alive. But the burners are themselves relentlessly
hunted down and killed by Njal's son-in-law Kári,

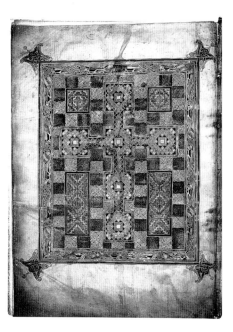

The *Lindisfarne Gospels*,
made at Lindisfarne *c.*698, are
the greatest cultural achievement
of the Kingdom of Northumbria.

who alone escaped from the inferno. The saga ends
with a reconciliation between Kári and Flosi, the last
survivor, and leader, of the burners.

Njal's Saga, trans. M. Magnusson and H. Pálsson
(Harmondsworth, 1960).

Njord In Scandinavian mythology, a god associated
with fertility and the sea. Njord ruled the winds
and protected sailors. One of the VANIR family of
gods, Njord was married to Skadi, the daughter
of the GIANT THJAZI. Their children were FREYR
and FREYJA.

Normandy, duchy of Region of northern France
that came under Viking rule in the 10th century,
the name of which is derived from *Nordmannia*
('Northman's Land'). The origins of Normandy
can be traced to the arrival of a large Viking
army on the Seine in 885. In 890 most of
this force moved on to Flanders, and eventually
to England, but some Vikings remained behind
and continued to raid in the area. After the Seine
Vikings unsuccessfully besieged Chartres in 911,
their leader ROLLO reached a peace agreement with
the Frankish king CHARLES THE SIMPLE at ST-CLAIRE-
SUR-EPTE. In return for his homage, conversion to
CHRISTIANITY and an undertaking to defend the
Seine against other Viking invaders, Rollo was made
count of Rouen (the title of 'duke' was adopted by
Norman rulers only in 1006). Though the
establishment of Normandy would certainly cause
some major problems for later kings of France, the
treaty achieved its immediate objective: permanently
ending the threat to the Seine. Rollo was granted
further lands around Bayeux in 924, and his son
WILLIAM LONGSWORD gained the Cotentin
peninsula in 933, but the powerful counts of

Flanders defeated their attempts to expand
eastwards. A political crisis followed the murder of
William Longsword in 942 and the subsequent
accession of his ten-year-old son RICHARD THE
FEARLESS, but by 946 the threat to the survival of
Normandy had been averted. Under Richard and his
successor RICHARD THE GOOD, Normandy became
progressively assimilated into the political life of the
West Frankish kingdom (France).

Normandy may owe its creation and name to the
Vikings but they had very little influence on the
region in the long term. Place-name evidence
suggests that Scandinavian settlement was fairly
dense around Fécamp, Rouen, Caen and the
Cotentin peninsula, but elsewhere it was sparse: the
Scandinavian settlers were certainly a minority in
Normandy as a whole. Place-names indicate that
most settlers were Danish, though many may have
previously settled in the DANELAW in ENGLAND, and
others in the Cotentin were Irish-Norse. There is
almost no archaeological evidence of Scandinavian
settlement, indicating that the settlers quickly
adopted Frankish material culture and BURIAL
CUSTOMS. One of the most important finds is a
richly furnished female grave from Pîtres. Finds of
several swords of Anglo-Saxon pattern strengthen
the case for immigration via England. A new wave of
pagan settlers arrived *c.*942 and, led by one Turmod,
started a brief pagan revival, but most of the original
settlers had become at least nominally Christian by
this time, and monasteries such as Jumièges,
abandoned in the previous century, were being
reoccupied. A final influx of pagan Viking warriors
created a brief stir in the early 960s. TRADE links
with Scandinavia were never important and had
been abandoned by the early 11th century, by which
time Norman COINS cease to appear in Scandinavian

Geirangerfjord, Norway.
Deep, sheltered fjords like
this were Viking Age Norway's
most important highways.

hoards. Scandinavian speech probably survived until the early 11th century, as the presence of a Norwegian poet at the ducal court in 1025 suggests that there were still people there who could understand him. By the time WILLIAM THE CONQUEROR led his invasion of England in 1066, however, the Normans had become completely assimilated to French culture and language.

D. Bates, *Normandy before 1066* (London, 1982).

Norns Supernatural female beings whose role in Scandinavian pagan mythology is to determine the fate of each human being, the gods and the whole world. They represented the highest powers of the universe. Their fate-making is described in poetry as spinning a thread or making a mark on wood. The Norns visited every newborn child to decide the outcome of its life: their decisions, which could be quite arbitrary, were final and could not be changed.

Northumbria, kingdom of Anglo-Saxon kingdom formed c.600 from a coalition of two rival kingdoms, Deira (between the rivers Humber and Tees) and Bernicia (between the Tees and the Firth of Forth). The kingdom reached the peak of its power in the mid-7th century under kings Edwin (r. 633–41) and Oswy (r. 641–70). In the 7th and 8th centuries Northumbria enjoyed a cultural 'golden age', with remarkable achievements in book illumination, stone sculpture and literature. Monasteries at Jarrow and LINDISFARNE and the major ecclesiastical centre at YORK became cultural centres of Europe-wide standing. These rich monasteries were the targets of some of the earliest known Viking raids, beginning with Lindisfarne in 793 and Jarrow in 794. Though its king Rædwulf was killed in battle with Vikings in 844,

Northumbria seems to have escaped relatively lightly until the 860s. Fatally, the Northumbrians chose to have a civil war at just the moment when the Danish GREAT ARMY arrived in ENGLAND. After the DANES, under HALFDAN and IVAR, captured York unopposed in 866, the two rival kings ÆLLE and Osberht united and attempted to storm the city in March 867. The attack was repulsed, both kings were killed, and the kingdom collapsed. By 876, York had become the capital of a Danish kingdom that covered most of Deira. Bernicia, however, maintained its independence under a line of kings based at Bamburgh. The last Northumbrian king, Aldred, was deposed in 927 when Bernicia was annexed by WESSEX. Northumbrian identity remained strong into the 11th century.

Norway, kingdom of Unlike the kingdoms of DENMARK and SWEDEN, which are named after their peoples, Norway is named after the 'North Way', a sheltered sea route to the north through the Skerry Guard, a chain of coastal islands and reefs. The first evidence of the development of kingdoms in Norway are the rich late-8th-century burials at BORRE and OSEBERG in Vestfold. At the beginning of the Viking Age, Norway was divided up into around a dozen chiefdoms and small kingdoms, some of them, in the south, under Danish domination. Danish influence declined in the 9th century, and c.885–90 HARALD FAIRHAIR, the king of Vestfold, succeeded in bringing most of the country under his control at the battle of HAFRSFJORD. Harald is traditionally regarded as the founder of the kingdom of Norway for his achievement, but local identities remained strong and it would be more than a century before the country was securely unified. The powerful jarls of HLAÐIR in the Trøndelag resisted the attempts by

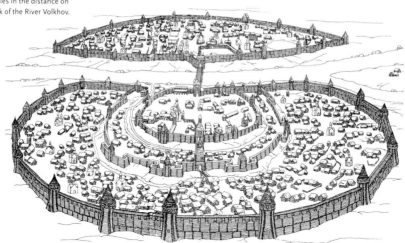

A reconstruction of medieval Novgorod, seen from the west. The 'Market Side', occupied by merchants, lies in the distance on the east bank of the River Volkhov.

Harald's successors to centralize power. In 970 king HARALD GREYCLOAK was killed fighting an alliance of HÅKON SIGURDSSON of Hlaðir and the Danish king HARALD BLUETOOTH, and Norway came under nominal Danish rule. Håkon became the effective ruler of Norway until he was overthrown in 995 by OLAF TRYGGVASON, a descendant of Harald Fairhair. Olaf became the first king to exercise effective power throughout Norway and he pursued an aggressive policy of Christianization. Olaf ruled for only five years before he was killed in battle against jarl Håkon's son ERIK and the Danish king SVEIN FORKBEARD. Erik and Svein divided Norway between them, but in 1016 the country was reunited by OLAF HARALDSSON (St Olaf), another descendant of Harald Fairhair. Olaf completed the Christianization of Norway, but was never a popular ruler. In 1028 CNUT forced him into exile and Norway again came under Danish rule. When Olaf tried to return in 1030 he was killed in battle at STIKLESTAD. Danish rule was resented, and a rebellion in 1035 brought Olaf's son MAGNUS THE GOOD to power. Magnus and his successors consolidated royal authority, and by the end of the 11th century Norway was a securely unified kingdom. The medieval Norwegian kingdom reached its peak in the mid-13th century, when it controlled the earldom of ORKNEY, the FAROE ISLANDS, ICELAND and GREENLAND.

Novgorod (ON Holmgarð, 'island town') The settlement of Novgorod ('new town'), on the River Volkhov in north-east RUSSIA, began c.930, when Scandinavians and Slavs moved there from the fortified island of RYURIKOVO GORODISCE, the original Holmgarð 2 kilometres to the south. Merchants' and craftsmen's quarters huddled

around the fortress on the west bank, while a colony of foreign merchants grew up on the east bank around a royal palace. By the 11th century Novgorod had developed into a rich TRADE, royal and ecclesiastical centre, and it remained the chief city of north-east Russia until the beginning of the 18th century. Novgorod has seen extensive archaeological excavations. Waterlogged conditions have resulted in excellent preservation of organic materials, including 11th-century (and later) merchants' letters and accounts, written on birch-bark in Old Russian using the Cyrillic alphabet. Few specifically Scandinavian objects have been discovered, suggesting that the population was mostly Slavic.

Odin brandishing his spear Gungnir, from the Norse cross at Gosforth, Cumbria.

oars Oars were an important auxiliary means of propulsion for Viking warships, especially in battle and when sailing up rivers. TRADE SHIPS carried a few pairs of oars, which were used mainly for manoeuvring into or out of harbour. The earliest evidence for the use of oars in Scandinavia is a rowlock dated to *c*.30 BC–AD 250 found in a bog in Hordaland, western NORWAY; before this paddles were used.

óðal Allodial land acquired or rightfully inherited from ancestors; that is, land held by absolute right, free of obligations to anyone else. The term is confined to NORWAY, SWEDEN and the Norse colonies in the northern isles (but not MAN) and ICELAND. HARALD FAIRHAIR's attempt to abrogate *óðal* rights in Norway was traditionally held to be the cause of Norse emigration to Iceland in the late 9th century. *See also* LANDOWNERSHIP.

Odense Today the main TOWN of Fyn, DENMARK. Although no evidence has been found for settlement until well after 1000, the presence of a 10th-century TRELLEBORG FORT at nearby Nonnebakken (now destroyed), and its choice as a BISHOPRIC in 988, suggest that Odense must already have been a location of some importance in the late Viking Age. CNUT II (Cnut the Holy) was murdered here in 1086.

Odin Odin was the high god of the pagan Scandinavian pantheon, whom the other gods served as 'children serve their father'. He was a member of the ÆSIR family of gods and the grandson of the primeval god Buri. He was the Scandinavian equivalent of the pagan Anglo-Saxon god Woden and the early Germanic Wotan. Odin's wife was the goddess FRIGG and he was the father of the gods BALDER, Bali, HODER, THOR, TYR and Vali. It was Odin who shaped the world from the body of the GIANT Ymir; who set the sun and moon on their courses; and who brought the first man and woman to life. Odin was a frightening deity, furious, violent, cruel, cynical, deceitful and fond of human sacrifices. He was the god of battles, and the VALKYRIES brought the souls of the bravest warriors to dwell with him in VALHALLA. Odin's obsession was wisdom and he travelled widely in its pursuit. From his high seat, Hlidskjalf, he could see and hear everything in the universe. On Odin's shoulders sat two ravens, Huginn ('thought') and Muminn ('memory'), which flew out over the world and returned to whisper all they knew in his ears. Odin was prepared to make great personal sacrifices to gain knowledge. To drink from the fountain of Mimir, which conferred ultimate wisdom, Odin gladly gave up one of his eyes. On another occasion Odin hanged himself, impaled on a spear, for nine days from the world-tree YGGDRASIL to discover the secret of the RUNES. Through his magic skills and shape-changing ability, Odin won the mead of poetry for the gods and humans from the giant Suttung, who had stolen it from the DWARVES. Among Odin's possessions were the magic ring Draupnir, the spear GUNGNIR and the eight-legged horse SLEIPNIR, which could gallop as well on air and water as on land. Odin will lead the gods into the last battle at RAGNAROK, where he will be swallowed by the monstrous wolf FENRIR.

Odo (Eudes) (d. 898) King of the West FRANKS (r. 888–98). Odo was the son of count ROBERT OF ANJOU. While count of PARIS, he made his

reputation by his successful defence of the city against the besieging Vikings under Sigfred in 885–6. After the deposition of the emperor CHARLES THE FAT, Odo was elected king of the West Franks, the first who was not of Merovingian or Carolingian blood. His reign saw a decline in Viking activity in FRANCIA. Because of internal opposition, however, Odo's position was never secure, and between 893 and 897 he had to fight off a challenge by the future king CHARLES THE SIMPLE. Odo won a victory over the Vikings at Montfaucon in 888, but their losses were not serious enough to prevent them from threatening Paris again in 889. A resolute show of force by Odo and an offer of tribute secured their withdrawal, and in 892 most of the Vikings on the Seine left for ENGLAND.

Ogier the Dane (Ogier de Danemarche) *see* HOLGER DANSKE

Ohthere (ON Ottar) (*fl.* late 9th century) A merchant and farmer from Halogaland in Arctic NORWAY who visited ALFRED THE GREAT's court *c.*890 and gave the king an account of TRADE and travel in Scandinavia that was included in the *Old English Orosius*. Ohthere described to Alfred a voyage he had made to the White Sea in search of walruses. Ohthere was reckoned a wealthy man in his homeland. The bulk of his wealth was derived from reindeer herds and from the tribute in skins, furs and feathers paid by the Lapps, though he kept a few cattle, sheep and pigs and ploughed what little of the region's stony soil he could. He also gave details of the voyage south from Halogaland via 'Sciringesheal' (probably KAUPANG) to HEDEBY. While at court, Ohthere presented king Alfred with a gift of walrus IVORY.

Olaf (Irish Amlaíb) (d. *c.*871) King of DUBLIN (r. 853–*c.*871). Olaf is described in Irish sources as the son of the king of Laithlinde, a Viking kingdom in western NORWAY or the Hebrides. He is often identified with OLAF THE WHITE, a Viking known from later Icelandic sources, who was said to have captured Dublin sometime in the 9th century. In alliance with his brother or kinsman IVAR I (Irish Imhar) he recaptured Dublin from the DANES in 853, going on to make it the main centre of Viking activity in the Irish Sea area. Olaf was gradually drawn into Irish political life and, with Ivar, allied with CERBALL MAC DÚNLAINGE to invade Meath in 859; he later married one of Cerball's daughters. Olaf formed another alliance with a native kingdom in 862, when he joined the northern Uí Néill in an attack on their neighbours, the southern Uí Néill. In 863 he shocked the Irish by digging open the prehistoric burial mounds on the River Boyne with Ivar and Auisle, another kinsman, to search for treasure. Effective Irish resistance in the 860s forced Olaf to look elsewhere for plunder, and in 866 he ravaged Pictland. An Irish attack on Dublin led Olaf to sack Armagh in retaliation in 869, killing or capturing 1,000 people. In 870–1 Olaf and Ivar plundered Dumbarton, the fortress capital of STRATHCLYDE, after a four-month siege. Much treasure and a huge number of prisoners were captured. Olaf was probably killed while raiding in SCOTLAND *c.*871, though a late Irish source says he returned to Norway to support his father Guthfrith in a civil war. He was succeeded by Ivar.

Olaf, St *see* OLAF HARALDSSON

Olaf Cuarán *see* OLAF SIHTRICSSON

An early medieval figure of
Olaf Haraldsson, identified
by his symbol, an axe.

Coin of king Olaf
Guthfrithsson, issued at
York, bearing the pagan
symbol of the raven.

Olaf dynasty An obscure dynasty of Swedish origin
that ruled in DENMARK *c*.900–36. Olaf, the founder
of the dynasty, seized power by force of arms,
overthrowing an even more obscure Danish king
called Helgi. Olaf was succeeded by his sons Gnupa
and Gerd, and then by Sigtryg, Gnupa's son.
Gnupa converted to CHRISTIANITY in 934 following
a punitive invasion of Denmark by king Henry the
Fowler of Germany. According to the 11th-century
German historian ADAM OF BREMEN, the dynasty
was overthrown by Hardegon (Harthacnut)
Sveinsson from 'Nortmannia' (northern Jutland,
NORWAY or possibly NORMANDY), who was probably
the father of GORM THE OLD. The extent of Olaf's
kingdom is unknown, but rune-stones found near
HEDEBY, which mention Gnupa and Sigtryg, suggest
that it was centred in southern Jutland.

Olaf Guthfrithsson (d. 941) King of DUBLIN
(r. 934–41); king of YORK (r. 939–41). Olaf succeeded
his father GUTHFRITH as king of Dublin in 934. He
established dominance over the Norse in IRELAND
when he defeated the LIMERICK Vikings in a naval
battle on Lough Ree in 937. Later that year, he allied
with CONSTANTINE II, king of the Scots, and the
STRATHCLYDE Britons to try to recapture the
kingdom of YORK, taken by ATHELSTAN of WESSEX in
927, but was crushingly defeated at BRUNANBURH.
Following Athelstan's death in 939, Olaf tried again,
capturing not only York but the FIVE BOROUGHS as
well. Olaf was succeeded at York by his cousin OLAF
SIHTRICSSON, and in Dublin by his brother Blacaire.

Olaf Haraldsson (Olaf II, St Olaf or Olaf the Stout)
(*c*.995–1030) King of NORWAY (r. 1016–28). Olaf
completed the conversion of the Norwegians to
CHRISTIANITY. He was the son of Harald Grenske, a

minor king in south-east Norway, and a descendant
of HARALD FAIRHAIR. Olaf began a career as a Viking
raider at the age of twelve, fighting in ENGLAND as a
mercenary both for THORKELL THE TALL and
ÆTHELRED II. While wintering in NORMANDY in
1013, he was baptized by the archbishop of Rouen. In
1015 he took advantage of the DANES' preoccupation
with England to invade Norway. Having defeated the
pro-Danish forces under jarl SVEIN HÅKONSSON at
Nesjar on Oslo Fjord, he was acknowledged king
throughout most of Norway by the end of 1016. Olaf
reconquered the territories lost to the Swedes after
the death of OLAF TRYGGVASON in 1000 and set
about continuing his work of converting the
Norwegians to Christianity. Although, thanks to
Olaf Tryggvason, Christianity was well established in
the coastal areas of Norway, the interior remained
largely pagan. Olaf's methods of evangelization were
brutal but effective. Those who converted enjoyed
royal favour; those who refused faced death,
mutilation or blinding. With his bishop, Grimkell,
Olaf took the first steps towards establishing an
ecclesiastical organization for Norway by proclaiming
the Moster LAW on religious observance in 1024.
Olaf was also remembered for his reforms to the
regional law codes.

The growing threat of invasion by the Danish king
CNUT led Olaf to make peace with the Swedish king
OLOF SKÖTKONUNG in 1019: Olaf married Olof's
illegitimate daughter Astrid. In 1026 Olaf invaded
Skåne with Olof's successor ÖNUND JACOB and
defeated Cnut at the Helgeå (Holy River). But Olaf's
success in strengthening royal authority and violent
imposition of Christianity had caused growing
discontent among the leading chieftains in Norway.
Attracted by the prospect of a return to the days of
indirect rule, they allied with Cnut and Håkon

Altarpiece from Nidaros cathedral, Trondheim, showing scenes from the life and death of Olaf Haraldsson.

Eriksson of HLAÐIR and forced Olaf into exile in RUSSIA in 1028. The accidental death by drowning of Håkon the following year gave Olaf the opportunity to try to win back his throne. Raising a small ARMY in SWEDEN, Olaf invaded the Trondelag, where he was defeated and killed by a large peasant force at STIKLESTAD (29 July 1030). His body was secretly buried at TRONDHEIM by some loyal peasants. Miracles were soon reported at Olaf's burial place, and a year after his death he was pronounced a saint by bishop Grimkell. The growth of the cult of St Olaf was greatly aided by the unpopularity of Danish rule and a series of bad harvests, which were seen as a sign of divine anger. Olaf's reputation grew steadily with time, and by the 12th century he was regarded as the epitome of the just king and the creator of the unified Christian Norwegian kingdom.

Olaf Sihtricsson (Olaf Cuarán, 'sandal') (d. 981) King of DUBLIN (r. 945–80); king of YORK (r. 941–4, 949–52). Olaf was the son of SIHTRIC CÁECH, king of Dublin and York. On his father's death in 927, he was expelled from York by ATHELSTAN of WESSEX and fled to Dublin. He eventually became king of York in 941 as successor to his cousin OLAF GUTHFRITHSSON. In 942 Olaf lost the FIVE BOROUGHS to king EDMUND I of ENGLAND, and in 943 he was baptized as part of the peace settlement. The following year he was driven out of York with another king, Ragnald Guthfrithsson, and in 945 was accepted as king of Dublin. Olaf regained York in 949, but was driven out again in 952, this time for good, by the Norwegian ERIK BLOODAXE. In 980 the Uí Néill king Maél Sechnaill defeated Olaf at Tara and went on to capture Dublin, as a result of which Olaf retired to

become a monk on IONA. He was succeeded by his sons Járnkné (r. 980–9) and SIHTRIC SILKBEARD (r. 989–1036).

Olaf the Peaceful (Olaf III) (d. 1093) King of NORWAY (r. 1067–93). Olaf fought at the battle of STAMFORD BRIDGE, at which his father HARALD HARDRADA was killed in 1066. He negotiated peace with the English king HAROLD GODWINSON after the battle and returned to Norway to rule jointly with his brother Magnus II: he became sole ruler on Magnus's death in 1069. In 1068 he agreed a peace treaty with SVEIN ESTRITHSON, by which the Danish king gave up his claims to Norway, so beginning twenty-five years of peace. Olaf oversaw reforms in the organization of the Norwegian Church and improved relations with the papacy, while maintaining close personal control over the clergy. Olaf encouraged urban growth, founding BERGEN c.1070.

Olaf the White (fl. mid-9th century?) A Norse king of DUBLIN who is known from the medieval Icelandic SAGA tradition. He was the husband of AUD THE DEEP-MINDED and the father of THORSTEIN THE RED. Olaf the White is probably, but not certainly, to be identified with OLAF (Amlaíb), who is known from contemporary Irish sources to have ruled at Dublin 853–c.871.

Olaf Tryggvason (Olaf I) (c.968–1000) King of NORWAY (r. 995–1000). A grandson of HARALD FAIRHAIR, Olaf was brought up in exile, probably in RUSSIA: he later became a Viking leader in the Baltic. In 991 Olaf led a large Viking FLEET to ENGLAND and was bought off with a large payment of DANEGELD after defeating and killing the ealdorman

Illustration from the *Flateyjarbók*, showing the legendary exploits of Olaf Tryggvason, seen here killing a boar and a sea-ogress.

BYRHTNOTH at the battle of MALDON. Olaf returned to England in 994 as the ally of SVEIN FORKBEARD of DENMARK, but was bought off again by another large payment of Danegeld. In return, Olaf accepted CHRISTIANITY and promised king ÆTHELRED II that he would never attack England again. Surprisingly, this was a promise that Olaf kept. Olaf used his new-found wealth and reputation to launch an invasion of Norway in 995. On Olaf's arrival in the Trondelag, jarl HÅKON SIGURDSSON of HLAÐIR, the ruler of Norway, was murdered and Olaf was accepted as king. In 996 Olaf began to force Christianity on the Norwegians; opposition was dealt with violently. By 999 he had Christianized most of the coastal districts of Norway. Olaf also successfully pressurized the Icelanders into accepting Christianity. Spreading the Christian faith was part of Olaf's efforts to strengthen the Crown; he also introduced the office of district governor, and he was the first Norwegian king to issue COINS. Olaf's reign was destined to be short. Neither Svein Forkbeard nor ERIK OF HLAÐIR (jarl Håkon's son) were reconciled to the loss of influence in Norway. They were joined in an alliance by the Swedish king OLOF SKÖTKONUNG, who had designs on Norwegian territory. When returning to Norway from a campaign in the Baltic in 1000, Olaf was ambushed by the allies at Svöld (location unknown) and defeated in a sea battle. When all was lost, Olaf jumped overboard from his flagship, the LONG SERPENT, and sank without a trace. After his death, stories circulated that he had made his escape by swimming underwater to another ship and had gone to Wendland, but as the SAGA of his life puts it, 'king Olaf Tryggvason never came back again to his kingdom of Norway'.

Oleg (ON Helgi) (d. *c.*913) Ruler of the RUS (*c.*879–913). Possibly a kinsman of RURIK, the semi-legendary founder of the Rus state, Oleg became ruler of NOVGOROD *c.*879, but moved his capital to KIEV after he captured the TOWN from rival Rus leaders ASKOLD AND DIR *c.*882. According to the 12th-century *RUSSIAN PRIMARY CHRONICLE*, Oleg attacked Constantinople in 907. The attack is not recorded in Byzantine sources and may have been invented by the chronicler to explain TRADE treaties agreed between the Rus and the Byzantine government in 907 and 911 (*see* CONSTANTINOPLE, TREATIES OF). Oleg died not long after these treaties were made. The *Russian Primary Chronicle*'s account of his death is plainly legendary. Having been told by a soothsayer that his favourite horse would cause his death, Oleg vowed never to ride or see it again. After five years, the horse died, but when, mocking the soothsayer, Oleg went to view its skeleton he was fatally bitten by a snake that crawled out from among its bones. It may be that Oleg really died in battle. The 10th-century Arab writer al-Masudi records the defeat by the KHAZARS of a Rus ARMY returning from a raid in the Caspian Sea near Itil (Astrakhan) on the River Volga in 913. Among the slain was the leader of the Rus; although not named by the author, he may well have been Oleg, for he disappears from history around this time. Oleg was succeeded by his foster-son IGOR.

Olga (ON Helga) (d. 969) RUS queen, wife of IGOR of KIEV. According to (no doubt) legendary stories recorded in the 12th-century *RUSSIAN PRIMARY CHRONICLE*, Olga was the archetypal Viking queen. Both ruthless and cunning, she wreaked a terrible vengeance on the Drevljane (a Slav tribe) after they had killed her husband when he was on a

An animal in the Urnes art style, inscribed by a Viking sheltering in the Neolithic burial chamber of Maes Howe, Orkney.

Coin of Olof Skötkonung, the first Swedish king to issue coinage.

tribute-gathering expedition against them in 945. She remained influential during the reign of her son SVYATOSLAV, defending Kiev against an attack by PECHENEG nomads in 967 while he was absent on campaign. Olga visited Constantinople in 957, and was the first member of the Rus royal house to be converted to CHRISTIANITY.

Olof Skötkonung (the 'tributary king') (d. 1022) King of the SVEAR (r. c.995–1022). The son of king ERIK THE VICTORIOUS, Olof was the first king known for certain to have ruled both the Svear and the GÖTAR. For most of his reign Olof pursued a pro-Danish policy, and he may actually have been a tributary of SVEIN FORKBEARD, who became Olof's stepfather after he married Erik's widow. Olof supported Svein and jarl ERIK of HLAÐIR against OLAF TRYGGVASON at the battle of Svöld in 1000. Olof gained the Böhuslan coast (now in SWEDEN) from NORWAY and the revenues of the Trondelag for his trouble, but lost them when OLAF HARALDSSON (St Olaf) seized power in Norway in 1016. Olof agreed peace terms and married his illegitimate daughter Astrid to the Norwegian king in 1019, an act that signalled the end of his alliance with Denmark. Olof's legitimate daughter, Ingigerd, married JAROSLAV THE WISE, prince of KIEV. Olof was a Christian, but the traditional date of his conversion, 1008, is too late, for he used Christian imagery on his COINS from the beginning of his reign. Though Olof supported missionary activity and founded the first BISHOPRIC in Sweden (at Skara in 1014), the strength of pagan sentiment was such that he did not pursue a policy of forcible conversion. Olof's union of the Svear and Götar was not permanent: it was the 12th century before a truly united Swedish kingdom developed.

Önund Jacob (d. 1050) King of the SVEAR (r. c.1022–50). The son of OLOF SKÖTKONUNG, Önund allied with OLAF HARALDSSON of NORWAY against CNUT of DENMARK. In 1026 they invaded Skåne and defeated Cnut at the battle of Helgeå (Holy River). But it was only a temporary setback for Cnut, who drove Olaf out of Norway in 1028, isolating Önund. Cnut went on to campaign in SWEDEN, forcing Önund to acknowledge his lordship c.1030 and even to issue COINS at the Swedish royal centre of SIGTUNA that bore the legend 'Cnut king of the Svear'. Cnut's death in 1035 allowed Önund to recover his independence. Following Önund's death, Sweden entered a period of political instability, from which it did not emerge for a century.

Orkney, earldom of Norse earldom comprising in the 11th century the Orkney and Shetland Islands and Sutherland and Caithness on the Scottish mainland. The origins of the earldom are obscure. According to medieval Icelandic historical traditions, Orkney was conquered in the late 9th century by king HARALD FAIRHAIR of NORWAY, who granted the islands to his ally ROGNVALD OF MØRE as compensation for the death of his son Ivar on the campaign. Independent Irish sources, suggest that it was Rognvald himself who conquered the islands at about the same time as the DANES captured York (866), much too early for Harald to have had a hand in events. Archaeological evidence generally supports the conclusion that the main period of Scandinavian settlement in Orkney was around the middle of the 9th century. The story of Harald's expedition, if not actually true, certainly does reflect an early interest in Orkney by the Norwegian kings. Although up to the end of the

11th century the earls of Orkney were effectively independent rulers, they did acknowledge Norwegian sovereignty.

SIGURD THE MIGHTY (d. *c.*892) began the expansion of the earldom, conquering Caithness and Sutherland. Considerable Norse settlement in Caithness followed. The maximum expansion of the earldom took place under SIGURD THE STOUT (r. *c.*985–1014), who brought the Norse settlements in the Hebrides under his control, and THORFINN THE MIGHTY (r. *c.*1020–65), who probably conquered Ross *c.*1030–5. Thorfinn is also known to have ruled in the Shetland Islands: whether he was the first Orkney earl to do so is unclear, as it is possible they had formerly been ruled from Norway. Many Orkney earls, including Thorfinn, found the islands a convenient base for Viking raiding in the Irish Sea area, and Norse pirates such as SVEIN ASLEIFARSON continued to harass the British coasts into the second half of the 12th century. By this time, the earldom was a declining power. Shetland was brought back under direct rule by Norway in 1195, and Sutherland, Caithness and Ross were conquered by the Scots in 1199–1202: the Hebrides had already been lost to the kingdom of MAN in the late 11th century. After the Union of Kalmar in 1397, Orkney, along with Shetland, came under Danish sovereignty, until they were both ceded to Scotland in 1469.

Orkney and Shetland are unique among the areas settled by Scandinavians during the Viking Age in that the native population (the Celtic Picts in this case) became assimilated to Scandinavian culture and language and not vice versa, as happened in other areas. So complete was this assimilation – a sign, probably, that the Scandinavian settlers were very numerous – that almost all place-names in

Orkney, Shetland and even Caithness are of Norse origin. Orkney and Shetland developed their own Norse dialect, known as Norn. By the beginning of the 15th century, however, the Scots dialect of English was being used in official documents, and by the mid-18th century Norn had died out. Physical reminders of the Norse age in Orkney and Shetland are relatively numerous. Several settlements, such as BIRSAY in Orkney and JARLSHOF in Shetland have been excavated, and the ruins of fine early Norse CHURCHES, built soon after the Christianization of the islands in the 11th century, survive at Orphir and Egilsay in Orkney. Most impressive of all is the early 12th-century cathedral of St Magnus (MAGNUS ERLENDSSON) at Kirkwall, Orkney, which is, after Durham cathedral, perhaps the finest Romanesque building in the British Isles.

B. E. Crawford, *Scandinavian Scotland* (Leicester, 1987).

Orkneyinga saga ('The Saga of the Orkney Islanders') Also known as *Jarla saga* ('The Saga of the Earls [of Orkney]'), *Orkneyinga saga* was compiled by an unknown Icelandic author *c.*1200. In its original form, the SAGA, which draws on a multiplicity of oral traditions and written sources, told the history of the earldom of ORKNEY from its foundation to 1170. The original text was supplemented *c.*1234–5 with additional information on genealogy, the miracles of the martyred earl St Magnus (MAGNUS ERLENDSSON), and Norse settlements in Caithness on the Scottish mainland, which bring the story up to the early 13th century. Judged on its literary merits alone, *Orkneyinga saga* is not one of the great sagas, but the author clearly wanted to draw as far as possible on reputable sources, making it an invaluable and fascinating record of the earldom's historical traditions (it is not

The excavation of the Oseberg ship burial in 1904.

without errors, however). The author also quotes extensively from SKALDIC poetry composed for the Orkney earls, including verses by the 11th-century skald ARNÓR THÓRÐASON JARLASKÁLD (*c*.1010–*c*.1073), court poet to Rognvald Brusisson and THORFINN THE MIGHTY.

Orkneyinga Saga: The History of the Earls of Orkney, trans. H. Pálsson and P. Edwards (London, 1978).

Orosius, Old English The *Old English Orosius* is a translation into Old English of the early Christian writer Orosius's *Historiae adversus Paganos* ('Histories against the Pagans'), made on the instructions of ALFRED THE GREAT of WESSEX in the 890s. Orosius, a 5th-century Spaniard, wrote his work after the Visigothic sack of Rome in 410 to refute the claims made by pagans that the Roman Empire's decline was due to the abandonment of the traditional gods for CHRISTIANITY. Orosius was probably selected for translation because his belief in the inevitable triumph of Christianity was a matter on which the ANGLO-SAXONS may have needed some reassurance in the late 9th century. The main interest of the *Old English Orosius* for historians of the Vikings lies in an appendix containing unique firsthand descriptions by two Scandinavian merchants, OHTHERE and WULFSTAN, visitors at Alfred's court, of voyages in the White Sea and the Baltic. Though brief, these accounts are valuable sources of information on AGRICULTURE, customs, TRADE routes and trade centres in Scandinavia and the Baltic region in the 890s.

N. Lund, *Two Voyagers at the Court of King Alfred* (York, 1984).

Oseberg ship burial A magnificent 9th-century SHIP BURIAL from Oseberg farm, near Slagen in Vestfold, NORWAY, excavated in 1904. Because the heavy blue-clay soil and compacted turf burial mound produced near anaerobic conditions, preservation of the burial was remarkable: even textiles had survived. Although the grave was robbed at some time, it contained the richest assembly of artefacts of any Viking Age burial yet discovered in Scandinavia.

The single most impressive object is the ship, a clinker-built vessel made of oak, 21.6 metres long by 5.1 metres broad and 1.6 metres deep, with twelve strakes a side, each riveted to the one below it. Propulsion was by fifteen pairs of OARS and a single square sail. The ship has an elegant appearance and is decorated with elaborate wood carvings of the highest quality. It is thought that it is an early example of a karve, a chieftain's private transport ship. Sea trials with a replica have shown that it was not very seaworthy, and it was probably used only for short voyages in sheltered waters. Radiocarbon dating has recently shown that it was built *c*.820, making it the earliest Scandinavian sailing ship known, and was buried about fifteen years later. The skeletal remains of two females were found in the ship, one was aged fifty to sixty years, the other, twenty to thirty. Both had been placed in beds in a burial chamber hung with tapestries of fine wool and Byzantine silk. Local traditions held that the burial mound was that of queen Ása, the mother of king HARALD FAIRHAIR. This is unlikely on chronological grounds – the burial is too old – but the richness of the grave goods certainly suggests that the deceased was a member of the Vestfold royal family. The grave goods that were placed in the ship are representative of most of the activities that would have taken place on a prosperous farm or royal manor. There was a wealth of wooden objects, many of them finely carved, including sledges, a wagon, FURNITURE, buckets, troughs, storage chests and

The restored Oseberg ship. Elegant and richly decorated, the original ship was built for show rather than seaworthiness.

boxes, and ladles and other kitchenware. There was a full range of farm hand tools, such as a hoe and a pitchfork, axes and spades, and all the equipment necessary for producing woollen textiles, from sheep shears to a WEAVING frame. Many vessels in the burial contained token quantities of foodstuffs and other useful plants, including wild apples, wheat, oats, cress, hazelnuts, walnuts, hemp and woad. There were also baskets, leather shoes, horse gear and dog chains.

Ostmen A name used from the 11th century to describe the long-established Christianized Norse settlers in IRELAND, especially of DUBLIN. The name, meaning 'men of the east [of Ireland]' served to distinguish them from both the Irish and the native Scandinavians. The Ostmen became increasingly assimilated to Irish culture, some becoming Gaelic-speaking, others speaking a Norse dialect heavily influenced by Gaelic syntax and vocabulary. Following Henry II's conquest of Ireland in 1171, the Ostmen were promised equal rights with the incoming English settlers, but they did not always receive them because of the difficulty of distinguishing them from the native Irish. The Ostmen sought the aid of Håkon IV of NORWAY against the English in 1263, but the collapse of Norse power in the Scottish isles following his death in the same year ended any possibility of their recovering their independence. By c.1300 the Ostmen had become completely assimilated into either the native or the English communities in Ireland.

Ottar In Scandinavian mythology, the son of Hreidmar and the brother of FAFNIR and REGIN. Ottar, a shape-shifter, was killed by the malicious god LOKI while fishing for salmon in the form of an otter.

Hreidmar held ODIN and THOR captive until Loki raised the RANSOM by blackmailing the DWARF ANDVARI.

outlawry In Viking Age Scandinavia physical penalties were rarely imposed by courts as punishments for freemen. Though thieves could be hanged, the penalties for most offences, including homicide, were financial, the amount of compensation to be paid being laid down by LAW on a scale related to the severity of injury and the social rank of the victim. If an offender refused to pay compensation he could be sentenced to outlawry: in NORWAY and GOTLAND it was possible to force someone into outlawry even if they were willing to pay compensation, as victims had the right to refuse payment to protect their honour. Outlawry literally placed the offender outside the protection of the law and meant that he could be killed with impunity by anyone.

There were two kinds of outlawry. 'Lesser outlawry' could be compounded by payment of compensation and the outlaw retained some legal rights. In ICELAND, if the offender paid RANSOM for his life (usually a heavy silver ring), the sentence to outlawry was limited to three years exile, and the outlaw continued to enjoy legal protection in specified places for up to three years while he tried to arrange passage out of the country. If, however, he failed to leave after three years he was sentenced to 'full outlawry'. Full outlawry was for life and involved total rejection from society. It was illegal to feed or to harbour a full outlaw, or to help him in any way: even abroad he was not safe. He lost all his property and his CHILDREN were declared illegitimate and lost their inheritance rights. The fugitive nature of the full outlaw was reflected in the common name given

Heroic warriors slain in battle enter Valhalla. Odin is seen in the centre on his eight-legged stallion Sleipnir.

P

him, *skógarmaðr* ('forest man'). Full outlawry was normally irredeemable, although in the Scandinavian monarchies, the king had the right to issue a pardon. In DENMARK, if the offender had been outlawed for homicide, this could be done only with the consent of the victim's FAMILY. In Iceland, a full outlaw could earn remission on his sentence by killing another outlaw. This was a calculated measure to create distrust among outlaws and to discourage them from forming bands.

pagan religion Until as late as *c.*1000 most Scandinavians were pagans. Scandinavian paganism was unlike CHRISTIANITY in that it had no systematic theology, no absolute concept of good and evil, and vague and conflicting ideas about the afterlife. Pagan religion was not much concerned with personal spirituality but was primarily a matter of winning the favour of the gods by the correct observance and performance of rituals, sacrifices and festivals. As there was no professional pagan priesthood, it was the responsibility of the king or local chieftain to ensure that festivals were observed. Contemporary European writers refer to pagan temples, though none has so far been identified. Stone SHIP SETTINGS were also used for performing religious rituals.

A cycle of cosmological myths described the CREATION of the world and predicted its ultimate destruction at RAGNAROK. Fate was the greatest cosmological force; even the gods were powerless to avert their destruction at Ragnarok along with the rest of creation. In common with other polytheistic religions, the pagan gods presided over different aspects of human life. There were two families of gods, both of which dwelt in ASGARD. The larger family of the Æsir were gods of the sky and war; the smaller family of the VANIR were gods of fertility and sensual pleasure. The most important of the Æsir were the high god ODIN, the god of kings, warriors and poets, and THOR, the god of strength, thunder and lightning. The beautiful sun-god BALDER, the watchman HEIMDALL, the malicious god LOKI, FRIGG, the wife of Odin and goddess of childbirth, and the war-god TYR were also numbered among the Æsir. The chief gods of the Vanir were the sea-god NJORD and the fertility-god FREYR and his sensual sister FREYJA. Freyja was the leader of the *DÍSIR*, a

Weapons and everyday
objects from a male burial
at Birka, Sweden, intended
for the deceased to use
in the afterlife.

race of supernatural female beings who presided
over fertility. Pagan Scandinavians also believed in
many other supernatural beings, including the races
of DWARVES, GIANTS and ELVES; the VALKYRIES, or
warrior maidens; the NORNS, who ruled over fate;
and, of course, ghosts.

Central to the worship of the gods was the
sacrificial FEAST, called a *blót* ('blood-offering'). At
one *blót*, held in Trondelag in the mid-10th century,
the local peasants dedicated a meal of horseflesh to
the gods Odin, Njord, Freyr and BRAGI in the hope
of ensuring a good harvest. Human sacrifice was
also a feature of Scandinavian paganism. At the
major cult centre at Gamla UPPSALA in SWEDEN nine
of every kind of male creature, including humans,
were hanged in a sacred grove as a sacrifice to Odin,
Thor and Freyr once every nine years. At the cult
centre at LEJRE in DENMARK ninety-nine humans,
the same number of horses, and unknown numbers
of cocks and dogs were sacrificed in a festival held
every nine years.

Pagan beliefs offered little comfort to the dying.
For most people, that is, those who died of illness
and old age, there was only the daunting prospect of
a twilight existence in the freezing fogs NIFLHEIM,
the realm of the dead ruled over by the hideous
goddess HEL. The souls of heroic warriors killed in
battle were shared by Odin and Freyja. Odin's
warriors were taken by the valkyries to feast and
fight in his hall of VALHALLA; Freyja's went to dwell
in her hall of Folkvangr. Freyja also claimed the souls
of unmarried girls, while the souls of righteous men
went to a hall in Asgard called Gimli. Alongside
these beliefs was the belief that the dead in some
way lived on in the grave. The widespread BURIAL
CUSTOM of placing everyday objects, such as
WEAPONS, tools, wagons, and SHIPS, and sacrificed

animals and humans in graves is evidence that
pagan Scandinavians believed that the afterlife
would resemble this life. Grave offerings were
sometimes deliberately broken, perhaps because it
was believed that they had to be 'killed' if they were
to be used by the deceased in the afterlife. With the
richest burials, such as the lavish SHIP BURIALS at
OSEBERG and GOKSTAD, the grave goods were
probably intended to impress the living as much as
to benefit the dead. Despite the attention they paid
to the afterlife, pagan Scandinavians did not believe
that the soul was immortal: come Ragnarok all
would face extinction with the gods.

Though pagan beliefs and practices persisted in
Scandinavia into the 12th century, the institutional
and doctrinal weaknesses of paganism made its
decline inevitable once CHRISTIANITY had become
established in the ruling class.

Paris, siege of (885–6) Indirectly, one of the decisive
events in the breakup of the CAROLINGIAN EMPIRE.
Paris was first attacked and plundered by the Vikings
in 845. Further attacks took place in 857, 861 and
865. The construction of a fortified BRIDGE at PONT
DE L'ARCHE gave Paris some respite after this until
it was destroyed by an exceptionally large Danish
ARMY in 885. This army continued up the River
Seine and laid siege to Paris in late November.
Paris at the time was still largely confined to the Île
de la Cité. The island was linked to the north bank
of the Seine by a stone bridge defended at both ends
with fortified towers. A wooden bridge, also fortified
with towers at each end, linked the island to the
south bank. The siege is vividly described in verse
by Abbo, a monk of Saint-Germain-des-Prés, who
was present throughout. The defence was led by
Joscelin, abbot of Saint-Germain, and count ODO of

One of the finest Gotland picture stones, from Lärbro. The stone, dating from the 8th century, shows mythological scenes, including a human sacrifice (*top left*).

Paris. Their garrison of 200 was certainly outnumbered by the Danes, but Abbo's estimate that the besieging army was 40,000 strong with 700 ships is almost certainly a gross exaggeration: such a large force could hardly have been kept together for a year-long siege in early medieval conditions. In January, a Danish offer to leave Paris in peace in return for a free passage upstream was contemptuously rejected. Viking attacks destroyed the wooden bridge in February, opening the river to passage upstream, but the city was kept under siege. An attempt by Henry of Saxony to relieve the city failed in March. Despite this, the Danish leader Sigfred decided that the siege was an unprofitable waste of time and in April he agreed to withdraw for only 60 pounds of silver, but his army refused to follow him. Joscelin died soon after, and it was only in October that the siege was finally lifted by the arrival of the emperor Charles the Fat with a large army. But instead of attacking the Danes, Charles gave them the free passage upstream they had sought, so that they could plunder his rebellious subjects in Burgundy. In the spring of 887 he paid them a further 700 pounds of silver. After the heroic defence of Paris, Charles's actions looked like cowardice to the Franks. His authority was fatally undermined and his consequent deposition in 888 was followed by the final breakup of the Carolingian Empire.

Paviken Viking Age trading place on a sheltered lagoon near Västergarn on Gotland. Paviken was in use from the 8th century to the 11th, when it was abandoned, probably because its harbour had silted up. Excavations have uncovered evidence of shipbuilding, ironworking, bead-making, goldsmithing and other industries. Fishing was

an important activity. Arabic coins and weights indicate contacts with the east. As there are no graves nearby, Paviken was probably occupied only on a seasonal basis.

Pechenegs (Patzinaks) Turkic nomad people that migrated to the Ukrainian steppes in the 9th century. They posed a considerable threat to Rus merchants hauling their boats around the impassable rapids on the lower River Dniepr: prince Svyatoslav I of Kiev was killed during one of their raids on the rapids in 972. During the 11th century they raided Byzantine and Kievan territory, but they declined into obscurity after defeat by the Byzantines in 1090–1.

picture stones Unique tombstones or memorial stones erected for the dead on the Swedish island of Gotland from the 5th century to the 11th: most date from *c.*600–800. The picture stones are covered with inscribed and low-relief patterns, pictures of mythological scenes and runic inscriptions, and they were originally brightly painted. They are the single most important iconographic source for the later periods of the Scandinavian Iron Age and the early Viking Age, particularly as regards the development of shipbuilding and the adoption of the sail. The earliest stones (*c.* AD 400–600) were roughly rectangular in shape with a slightly rounded top. Most are around 1 metre in height, but some are more than 3 metres high. Geometrical patterns, such as sun symbols, are important motifs on these stones. Mythological animals, human figures and rowing ships also appear. After *c.*600 the stones have a horseshoe-shaped top and average around 2 metres in height. The stones have decorative borders of interlace patterns and are completely covered with dramatic

Runic memorial to the Swede Osten, who died in Greece while returning from a pilgrimage to Jerusalem.

mythological scenes of gods, VALKYRIES welcoming slain warriors into VALHALLA, human sacrifices, sailing ships and occasional runic inscriptions. Following the introduction of CHRISTIANITY in the 11th century the mythological scenes are replaced by elegant animal interlace patterns, long runic inscriptions and Christian symbols.

E. Nylén and J. P. Lamm, *Stones, Ships and Symbols: The Picture Stones of Gotland from the Viking Age and Before* (Stockholm, 1988).

pilgrimage Pilgrimages – religious journeys to holy places to acquire spiritual merit or to perform penance – were an important part of the popular religion of medieval Christendom. The custom was introduced into Scandinavia along with CHRISTIANITY, and the first pilgrimages by Scandinavians are recorded soon after 1000. The earliest Scandinavian pilgrim was probably OLAF HARALDSSON (St Olaf), who may have visited the popular shrine of St James at Santiago de Compostella in Spain *c*.1013. King CNUT journeyed from ENGLAND to Rome in 1027, though perhaps his main object was to attend the coronation of the emperor Conrad II. The poet SIGHVATR THÓRÐARSON became the first pilgrim to travel from ICELAND to Rome in 1030. Jerusalem also became a destination for Scandinavians after its capture by crusaders in 1099. The Danish king Erik the Evergood set out for Jerusalem via RUSSIA, but died *en route* in 1103. King Sigurd Magnusson ('Sigurd the Crusader') sailed from NORWAY to the Holy Land in 1107–10, and Rognvald Kali, earl of ORKNEY followed in his footsteps fifty years later. Both took well-armed retinues and fought against the Saracens. Although it was the later Middle Ages before pilgrimage became fully established as part of

popular religious practice in Scandinavia, various pilgrimages by the common people are recorded from the second half of the 11th century, for example, to the tomb of St Olaf at TRONDHEIM. The guest book of the German abbey of Reichenau records the names of some 40,000 pilgrims who stayed there on their way to Rome in the 11th and 12th centuries. They included nearly 700 Scandinavians, mostly DANES but also a few Norwegians and Icelanders.

Pippin II of Aquitaine (823–64) Frankish leader, grandson of LOUIS THE PIOUS, son of Pippin I, king of Aquitaine. On his father's death in 839 Pippin was disinherited by Louis, who made his own son, CHARLES THE BALD, king of Aquitaine. Pippin governed Aquitaine briefly in the 840s, but his failure to defend Bordeaux against a Viking attack led the Aquitainians to expel him in 848, and Charles forced him to join a monastery. Escaping, in 857 he allied with the Loire Vikings in an attempt to win back his inheritance, and with them he sacked Poitiers. It was said that Pippin adopted the Viking way of life and was even accused of becoming a pagan. Captured in 864, he was sentenced to death by Charles for treason and apostasy, and executed.

Pont de l'Arche Fortified BRIDGE built by the FRANKS near Pîtres, upstream from Rouen, to block the River Seine to Viking FLEETS. CHARLES THE BALD ordered the construction of the bridge in 862, but work was slow and the unfinished structure was captured by the Vikings in 865. Work was finally completed in 870. The bridge is thought to have been built of wood and was protected by garrisons stationed in forts at either end. Excavations of the fort on the north bank have shown that it had substantial earth ramparts reinforced with stone revetments, topped

A portage: Scandinavian merchants drag their ship overland from one river system to another.

Left: The German missionary Poppo undergoes an ordeal to prove the power of Christianity, from the Tamdrup altarpiece, Jutland.

with a wooden palisade. The outer faces of the ramparts were protected by a forest of projecting *chevaux de frises*. For fifteen years after the completion of the bridge, the upper Seine was free of Vikings, but it did not stop a large Danish fleet from sailing up river and laying siege to PARIS in 885. The excavations have found that the defences were burned around this time, presumably as a result of a Viking attack. Other bridges were built by Charles at Auvers on the Oise, Charenton and Isles-le-Villenoy on the Marne, and at Les Ponts-de-Cé on the Loire.

Poppo, St (*fl. c.*960) German missionary bishop, closely associated with the official conversion of DENMARK to CHRISTIANITY. Probably sent to Denmark by emperor Otto I, Poppo convinced HARALD BLUETOOTH to convert to Christianity in 965 by carrying red-hot irons in his bare hands without suffering injury, thus demonstrating the superior power of the Christian God (in later medieval iconography, the irons had become red-hot iron gloves). Poppo's exact identity is unclear, as there were several bishops of the same name in late-10th-century Germany: bishop Poppo of Würzburg (961–84) is thought to be the most likely candidate.

portage A place where a SHIP or boat is transported overland from one stretch of navigable water to another. Place-names with the elements -*drag*, -*dræ*, *ed*- and *bor*- show that there were many such places in Viking Age and medieval Scandinavia. Portages were found on both inland waterways and on the coast, where they could save sailing time or avoid dangerous headlands by cutting across promontories. It has been suggested that there was a portage across the neck of the Jutland peninsula between the rivers Eider or Rheide,

which flow into the North Sea, and the port of HEDEBY on Schlei Fjord, an inlet of the Baltic Sea, but no evidence for this has been found. Portages also formed essential links on the TRADE route through RUSSIA between the headwaters of the rivers Lovat, Dvina, Volga and Dniepr, and around the rapids on the lower Dniepr. Merchants negotiating the latter were vulnerable to ambushes by Slav and PECHENEG raiders. Those in Russia continued to be used into modern times. A section of a roughly 200-metre-long portage at Södertälje in Sweden, linking the Baltic with Lake Mälaren and the port of BIRKA, has been excavated. It was constructed by digging a shallow trench and lining it with timber to make a smooth passage along which a boat could be dragged easily.

Portland According to the *ANGLO-SAXON CHRONICLE*, the location of the first Viking raid on ENGLAND. The attack is also recorded in a Latin chronicle by Æthelweard, an ealdorman under ALFRED THE GREAT. Three ships of 'Northmen' arrived at Portland, now in Dorset but then in the kingdom of WESSEX, from Hordaland in NORWAY. Believing them to be traders, the reeve BEADUHEARD went to order them to the royal manor at Dorchester nearby and was killed for his trouble, along with his men. Unfortunately, the raid is not precisely dated in the chronicle. Though it is recorded under the year 789, the chronicle actually says only that it took place during the reign of king Beorhtric (r. 786–802). This section of the chronicle is not a contemporary record of events – it was written a century later, in Alfred's reign – and it is possible that the raid was given precedence to the attack on LINDISFARNE in 793 to emphasize the leading role Wessex had always played in fighting the Vikings. Nevertheless, a late

A late-9th-century York ware cooking pot.

copy of a charter of the Mercian king Offa to the Church of Kent, dated to 792, makes reference to military obligations 'against the pagans', suggesting that Viking raids were already a problem around the English coast before Lindisfarne was attacked. Portland was attacked again by Vikings in 840.

pottery Pottery was little used in Viking Age Scandinavia: only at the Danish TOWN of HEDEBY has evidence of large-scale pottery manufacture been identified. SOAPSTONE pots were generally preferred for cooking, and wooden vessels were widely used for storage. The potter's wheel was not used in Scandinavia until *c*.1200, so most pottery was made crudely by hand, usually by building up the vessel from coils of clay. The clay was tempered with grit, which often protrudes, giving the pots an uneven surface. Pottery was usually fired at low temperatures on a fire or in an earth clamp. A variety of regional styles are known; decoration, if there is any, is simple. Round-bottomed vessels were preferred in Jutland; flat-bottomed, elsewhere in Scandinavia. After 1000, Slav-inspired pottery styles became popular in Scandinavia. Fine-quality pottery was imported into Scandinavia from the Rhineland throughout the Viking Age.

Quentovic Frankish emporium near Visemarest on the River Canche, inland from the modern TOWN of Étaples, France, and a major centre for cross-Channel TRADE from the 7th century to the 10th. Quentovic has not been extensively excavated, but evidence of a wide range of craft activities has been discovered, including iron-smelting and WEAVING. Similarities in POTTERY styles suggest close links with Hamwih, an Anglo-Saxon port near modern Southampton. Quentovic covered approximately 45 hectares, making it comparable in size with DORESTAD on the Rhine. Among the signs of Quentovic's importance are the presence of a mint from the late 6th century and its supervision by high royal officials. Quentovic was plundered and burned by the Vikings in a surprise dawn attack in 842. Loss of life was heavy and many of the inhabitants were taken captive; others, however, managed to save their property by paying protection money. The raid appears to have had no long-term impact on the town's prosperity, for Quentovic was not abandoned until the 10th century, most probably because silting of the river was making access from the sea increasingly difficult.

A page from *Ragnars saga loðbrókar*, the saga of the legendary Viking Ragnar Lodbrok.

R

Ragnald (d. 921) Viking king of YORK (r. *c*.911, 919–21). Ragnald was a grandson of IVAR I, king of DUBLIN. Nothing certain is known of Ragnald's early career, though he was probably among the 'grandsons of Ivar' who ravaged SCOTLAND in 903–4. Around 911 he briefly held power in York, as COINS were issued in his name there. In 914 he invaded the earldom of NORTHUMBRIA, defeating CONSTANTINE II of Scotland and the Northumbrians at Corbridge on the River Tyne. Later in the same year, he defeated a rival Norse leader, Bárdr Óttarsson, in a naval battle off the Isle of MAN. For the next four years Ragnald campaigned in Munster from his base at WATERFORD. After his brother SIHTRIC CÁECH captured Dublin in 917, Ragnald left Waterford to ravage in Scotland, sacking Dunblane. The following year, he was back in Northumbria and was once again brought to battle by the Scots and Northumbrians at Corbridge. The outcome this time was indecisive and he moved on, recapturing York from the DANES in 919 and making himself king. He was succeeded by Sihtric Cáech.

Ragnar (Reginherus) (d. *c*.845?) Viking leader in FRANCIA. Ragnar was established by CHARLES THE BALD at Turholt in Flanders *c*.840, probably to help guard the area against other Vikings. For some reason Ragnar fell out of favour with Charles, and he is next heard of entering the River Seine with a FLEET of 120 SHIPS in March 845. Charles prepared to stop him, but unwisely divided his ARMY into two forces, positioning one on either side of the river. Ragnar attacked and defeated the smaller of the two forces, hanging 111 prisoners in full view of the other Frankish army, which was helpless to intervene. Ragnar then plundered Paris and the nearby monastery of Saint-Germain-des-Prés on Easter

Sunday (28 March). A demoralized Charles paid Ragnar 7,000 pounds of silver to withdraw. Ragnar returned to DENMARK, where he is said to have died from an epidemic of dysentery that broke out in the army while it was at Saint-Germain-des-Prés (this was, of course, the saint's revenge). Ragnar has often been identified with the legendary RAGNAR LODBROK.

Ragnar Lodbrok ('hairy breeches') Famous legendary Viking leader whose exploits are the subject of Book Nine of Saxo Grammaticus's *GESTA DANORUM* (in which he is called Regner Lothbrog), the 12th-century Icelandic poem *Krákumál* and the 13th-century *Ragnars saga loðbrókar* ('The Saga of Ragnar Lodbrok'). Ragnar Lodbrok is probably a composite figure, incorporating elements of the careers of several historical Viking leaders – including the Danish king Reginfred (d. 814), the RAGNAR who sacked Paris in 845, and Ragnall (a Viking leader active in IRELAND and SCOTLAND in the 860s) – and Loðbrók/Loðbróka, the father or mother of IVAR, HALFDAN, Ubba and BJORN IRONSIDE, who were historical Viking leaders active in ENGLAND and FRANCIA in the mid-9th century. In addition, a great many purely legendary exploits have been credited to Ragnar. According to Saxo, Ragnar was the son of Sivard, the historical Sigfred, a nephew of king GODFRED mentioned in the *Royal Frankish Annals* and by ADAM OF BREMEN. In Icelandic traditions he is the son of Sigurd Hringr, a king of DENMARK. Ragnar is said to have become king of Denmark himself while still a youth. He had to fight against rival claimants to keep his throne, and made conquests across almost the whole of the Vikings' known world. Ragnar won the hand of his wife, the princess Thora, from a grateful Swedish king as a

A fragment of Thorwald's cross, Andreas, Isle of Man, depicting Odin being devoured by Fenrir at Ragnarok, symbolizing in this context the triumph of Christianity over paganism.

reward for slaying two giant serpents. The shaggy trousers he wore during the fight to protect himself from the serpents' venom gave Ragnar his nickname. In Icelandic versions, Ragnar marries Áslaug, the daughter of SIGURD FAFNISBANE and BRYNHILD, after the death of Thora. In Saxo's version, Ragnar's first wife was the VALKYRIE-like Lathgertha, whom he eventually divorced because of his love for Thora. Ragnar was finally captured by Ella (ÆLLE), king of NORTHUMBRIA, and put to death by being thrown into a pit of adders. While waiting to die he consoled himself by composing a heroic death-song. Ragnar's sons IVAR THE BONELESS, Sivard (or Sigurd Snake-eye) and Bjorn Ironside invaded England, captured Ella and, in revenge for their father's death, killed him by cutting a BLOOD EAGLE in his back.

Saxo Grammaticus: *History of the Danes, Books I–IX*, ed. H. E. Davidson, trans. P. Fisher (Woodbridge, Suffolk, 1996).

Ragnarok In Scandinavian mythology, the doom of the gods and destruction of the world: it is the equivalent of the Germanic *Götterdämmerung* ('twilight of the gods'). The major accounts of Ragnarok are found in the Eddic poem *VOLUSPÁ* and in SNORRI STURLUSON's *Gylfaginning* in his *Prose EDDA*. Ragnarok is in some way caused by ODIN's failure to save BALDER from death. Ragnarok will be preceded by three years in which there will be acts of great greed and treachery in the world of humans. The bonds of kinship, so important in the Viking world, will come to count for nothing. Then there will be three mighty winters with no summers between them. The wolf FENRIR will then break free from its bonds and swallow the sun. The moon and stars will disappear. Then the enraged MIDGARD SERPENT will emerge from the sea, throwing huge waves over the land and spewing venom everywhere. The GIANT Hrym and a crew of frost-giants will sail over the land in NAGLFAR, a ship made from the untrimmed nails of dead people. The fire realm of MUSPELL will open and its ruler Surt will lead the sons of Muspell out. Hrym and Surt with their followers, LOKI with HEL's people, Fenrir and the Midgard Serpent will converge in a mighty battle on the field of Vigrid. HEIMDALL will sound his horn to awaken the gods to their peril. The gods will arm themselves and Odin will lead his chosen warriors out of VALHALLA to do battle. Odin will be swallowed by Fenrir, but will be avenged by his son Vidar, who will tear the wolf's jaws apart. Thor will triumph over the Midgard Serpent, only to die at once from its venom. Surt will kill FREYR; the evil hound GARM and TYR will die fighting one another, as will Loki and Heimdall. Finally, Surt will fling fire across the earth and burn it entirely before it sinks beneath the waves.

However, YGGDRASIL, the world-tree, will not fall, and its branches will shelter a man and woman called Life and Leifthrasir, who will repopulate the earth when it rises again, cleansed and purified from the waters. Odin's sons Vidar and Vali, and Thor's sons Modi and Magni will also survive. Balder and HOD will escape from Hel and a daughter of the sun will light the heavens. Thus, after the cataclysm, a new cycle of the universe will begin.

Scenes from Ragnarok frequently appear in Norse Christian art, where it symbolized the overthrow of paganism by CHRISTIANITY: one of the finest examples is the 10th-century sculpted cross at Gosforth in Cumbria, ENGLAND.

Snorri Sturluson, *Edda*, trans. A. Faulkes (London, 1987); H. R. Ellis Davidson, *Gods and Myths of Northern Europe* (Harmondsworth, 1964).

An Anglo-Saxon gospel book, the *Codex Aureus*. An inscription in the book records that it was ransomed from the Vikings in the 9th century by the ealdorman Alfred of Surrey and his wife Werburg.

Ragnhild (d. *c.*970) Daughter of ERIK BLOODAXE, king of NORWAY and YORK. After Erik's death in 954, Ragnhild went with her mother Gunnhild and brothers to ORKNEY, where she was married to Arnfinn, the son of the Orkney earl THORFINN SKULLSPLITTER. Ragnhild is portrayed in *ORKNEYINGA SAGA* as ruthless and manipulative. Soon after Arnfinn had succeeded his father, Ragnhild had him murdered in Caithness so that she could marry his brother and successor Havard. Ragnhild soon became dissatisfied with Havard and incited his nephew Einar to murder him too. Afterwards, she denied complicity in the murder and betrayed Einar to his death. She subsequently married the new earl, Havard's brother Ljot, suggesting that her complicity in the murders of Arnfinn and Havard was not as obvious to contemporaries as it was to the later SAGA writers. Ragnhild was apparently satisfied with Ljot, for she is not heard of again. Ljot himself died of wounds received in battle with the Scots.

ransom Contemporary sources frequently note the importance to Viking raiders of holding captives to ransom. This was the case right from the beginning of the Viking Age: ALCUIN tells us that the emperor CHARLEMAGNE made efforts to ransom the monks carried off following the raid on LINDISFARNE in 793. Vikings could demand a small fortune for releasing nobles or senior churchmen. For example, abbot Louis of St-Denis was ransomed in 858 for the enormous sum of 686 pounds of gold and 3,250 pounds of silver. Quite ordinary people could also be held to ransom. FRANKS who had gone to trade with the Vikings were captured at Ascloha in 882, and in 866 the Vikings on the Seine even held serfs to ransom. The experience of Findan, a 9th-century

Irishman, shows that ransoming captives could be a complicated and risky business. Sent to ransom his sister, he was clapped in irons by her Viking captors while they debated what to do with him. Fortunately for Findan, the Vikings decided that it was not ethical to kidnap people who had come to pay ransom money. No doubt many unransomed prisoners finished up on the slave market, but the consequences if negotiations broke down could be more serious. When archbishop ÆLFHEAH refused to allow anyone to ransom him in 1012, his enraged captors battered him with animal bones before finishing him off with an axe. Nor did the Vikings always keep their word. In FRANCIA in 884 the Vikings killed their hostages even though ransom had been paid.

Property could also be held to ransom. When the Vikings sacked QUENTOVIC in 842 some people were able to save their property from destruction by paying ransom. The monastic buildings of St-Wandrille were ransomed for 6 pounds of silver in 841; the monastery's 68 monks fetched 26 pounds. The Vikings also found that sacred vessels were often worth more in ransom than as bullion. In 854, the Breton count Pascwathen ransomed church plate worth 60 solidi in gold and 7 solidi in silver. In Ireland the relics of St Adomnan were held to ransom in the 840s.

rape Although the Vikings are popularly supposed to have been addicted to rape and pillage, evidence of rape (if not of pillage) is remarkably difficult to find. While killing, looting, burning, captive-taking and extortion are commonplace in contemporary accounts of Viking activity, rape is conspicuous by its absence. It is significant in this context that in the 9th-century Frankish *Annals of St-Bertin*, covering 830–81, while there are two references to Christians

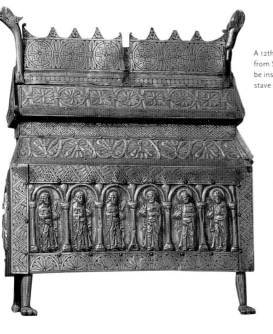

A 12th-century brass reliquary from Sweden. The design may be inspired by contemporary stave churches.

A small Byzantine reliquary from Valbo, Sweden.

committing rape (in one case of nuns), there is not a single instance of Viking raiders doing so. It may be that contemporary writers took it so much for granted that the Vikings raped their female captives that they simply did not think it worth mentioning, but it is more likely that the Vikings were not regarded, in this respect at least, as being worse than anyone else at the time. Of course, slave WOMEN had little choice in the matter if their owners decided to use them for sexual gratification. In Scandinavia itself, rape was severely punished. Writing in the 11th century, ADAM OF BREMEN reported that the rape of virgins was punishable by death.

Regin Mythological character. Regin was the son of Hreidmar, the brother of FAFNIR and OTTAR and foster-father to SIGURD FAFNISBANE. Regin told Sigurd about Fafnir's hoard of gold and how he had turned himself into a dragon. A skilled smith, Regin forged the sword Gram for Sigurd and urged him to kill Fafnir and take his gold. After Fafnir was killed, Regin drank his blood and instructed Sigurd to roast his heart. Accidentally consuming some of the dragon's blood, Sigurd learned the language of birds. Advised by four nuthatches that Regin intended to betray him, Sigurd decapitated him. *See also* VOLSUNGA SAGA.

religion *see* BURIAL CUSTOMS; CHRISTIANITY, CONVERSION TO; PAGAN RELIGION

reliquary A receptacle for storing and exhibiting holy relics, especially the remains of saints. The veneration of relics, which were frequently credited with miraculous powers, was an important expression of popular religious devotion in medieval Europe, and reliquaries were to be found in many

CHURCHES and monasteries by the beginning of the Viking Age. Because of the religious importance of their contents, reliquaries were frequently richly ornamented with precious metals and jewels, and so were obviously attractive to Viking raiders. The normal fate of a reliquary falling into Viking hands was to be broken up and then melted down or converted into JEWELRY. Many small pieces of ornamental Anglo-Saxon and Celtic metalwork found in 9th-century Scandinavian metal hoards and graves were originally parts of reliquaries looted by Vikings. Some reliquaries that made their way to Scandinavia survived intact. One such is Ranvaik's casket (so-called because the name Ranvaik is inscribed in RUNES on its base), a late-8th-century reliquary of Scottish or Pictish origin. This may have survived because it was used as a jewel box, but its use in medieval NORWAY as a reliquary suggests that it may have been acquired by an early Scandinavian convert to CHRISTIANITY. Once Christianity had become firmly established there, reliquaries began to be made in Scandinavia itself, two of the finest being the 11th-century caskets from Kamien in Poland (now lost) and Bamberg in Germany. Both feature exuberantly carved panels in the Mammen ART STYLE.

Repton Viking winter camp. It is known from literary sources that Viking ARMIES campaigning in ENGLAND and FRANCIA built fortified winter camps, but Repton in Derbyshire is the only one that has so far been identified with certainty and excavated. The camp consisted of a D-shaped enclosure, opening onto the banks of the River Trent, defended by a massive earth bank and ditch about 200 metres in length. An Anglo-Saxon stone CHURCH (which still stands) was incorporated into the defences as a

Mass burial of Vikings at
their winter camp at Repton,
Derbyshire, apparently
victims of an epidemic.

fortified gateway. A slipway was dug into the steep
riverbank, suggesting that the Vikings' SHIPS were
kept within the fort for safety. To the west of the fort
was a mass burial of at least 249 individuals, eighty
per cent of them robust males of non-local physique
aged between fifteen and forty-five. The bones were
arranged around a central burial of a high-status
male Viking, presumably one of the leaders of the
Viking army surrounded by his followers. As none
had apparently died of battle injuries, it is likely that
the army had been ravaged by an epidemic during
the winter. Several scattered Viking burials were also
found on the site, including one of a warrior who
had been killed by a blow to the hip. COINS found on
the site date the fort to 873–4, the same years that
the ANGLO-SAXON CHRONICLE tells us the Danish
GREAT ARMY wintered at Repton.
M. Biddle and B. Kjølbye-Biddle, 'Repton and the Vikings', in
Antiquity 66 (1992), pp. 36–51.

Reric An emporium on the Baltic coast of Germany,
known from early 9th-century Frankish sources.
Although the emporium was in the territory of the
Slavic Abodrites, it paid dues to the Danish king
GODFRED. Godfred burned Reric in 808 after a
costly campaign against the Abodrites, presumably
to stop it falling into enemy hands, and removed the
merchants to 'Sliesthorp' (i.e. HEDEBY, at the neck of
the Jutland peninsula). Reric apparently survived
Godfred's attentions, for an Abodrite chief was
murdered there in 809, but it disappears from the
sources thereafter. Alt Lübeck is commonly cited as
the location of Reric, but excavations have recovered
no evidence of occupation before 817. A more likely
location is Mecklenburg, near Wismar. Numerous
finds of Arabic COINS point to this site having been a
TRADE centre in the early 9th century. A third

possibility is Dierkow on the River Warnow near
Rostock, where occupation deposits, harbour
installations, cemeteries and artefacts of
Scandinavian origin have been found.

Rhodri Mawr (Rhodri the Great) (d. 878) King of
Gwynedd (r. 844–77). Rhodri's expansionist policy
made Gwynedd the dominant Welsh principality.
From 852 onwards, Anglesey and the coasts of
Gwynedd frequently suffered Viking raids. Rhodri
defeated the Danish leader Horm (Gorm) in 856,
and successfully prevented any large-scale Viking
settlement in his realms. However, a major Viking
attack eventually forced him briefly to seek refuge in
IRELAND in 877. Returning the following year, he was
killed in battle against the Mercians.

Ribblehead Viking Age farmstead in North
Yorkshire, consisting of a longhouse similar to those
found in NORWAY, a smithy and a small bakery,
grouped around a central courtyard. The farm stood
at the centre of a system of field enclosures. COINS,
including a bronze *styca* of archbishop Wulfhere of
YORK (*c*.862), found in the longhouse suggest that
the farm was occupied in the 9th century. The few
surviving artefacts from the site, most notably a
bronze bell and a quernstone, are not distinctively
Scandinavian in character, so the ethnic identity of
its occupants cannot be identified with certainty.

Ribe Probably the earliest TOWN to develop in
Scandinavia. Ribe is situated on the west side of the
Jutland peninsula on the River Ribe, about 5
kilometres inland from the North Sea. The Viking
town was on the north bank of the river, at the point
where it ceased to be tidal. A small seasonal market
centre developed here, north-west of the river, at the

A hoard of silver *sceattas* from Ribe, minted in Frisia or, possibly, locally.

Coin of Richard the Fearless. Under his rule, Normandy became a French feudal principality.

beginning of the 8th century, with wooden booths (dated to *c.*710) in which craftsmen in leather, ANTLER, GLASS, AMBER and bronze made and sold their goods. So many spindle-whorls and loom weights have been found that there must have been a large number of WOMEN on the site engaged in spinning and WEAVING. Sheep bones from the site are exclusively from older animals, showing that they were kept for wool to supply the local textile industry, rather than for meat. Thick layers of cattle dung suggest that one of Ribe's most important exports may have been hides. Large numbers of silver COINS – Frisian *sceattas* or, possibly, local imitations of them – show Ribe's importance as a TRADE centre. Ribe was well placed to make trading connections south along the North Sea coast, and a permanent settlement soon developed. The town's boundary was demarcated by a ditch in the 9th century, and in the next century an earth rampart was built as protection. Ribe is first mentioned in literary sources in the *Life of St* ANSGAR by Rimbert. Ansgar was given permission by king Horik II to build a CHURCH there in the 850s. By 948 Ribe had become a BISHOPRIC. Around 1000 the settlement shifted to the south side of the river, where the modern town centre lies today. Ribe remained an important trade centre until the late Middle Ages, when the river began to silt up, making access from the sea increasingly difficult.

Richard the Fearless (Richard I) (*c.*932–96) The third ruler of Normandy (r. 942–96). Richard, the illegitimate son of WILLIAM LONGSWORD, was about ten years old when he became count of Rouen after his father's murder in 942. Because of his youth, Richard had great difficulty establishing control over Normandy in the face of attempts by both king Louis

IV of the West FRANKS and count Hugh the Great to seize power. The situation was further complicated by the arrival at Bayeux of a new Viking warband under Sihtric, an exile from YORK. Louis IV took Richard into protective custody at Laon. When Louis was captured by Vikings in 945, Richard escaped, and by 946 he had recovered control of Rouen. It took Richard several years to recover control of western Normandy, however. Gradually, he abandoned the aggressive policies of his predecessors and began to take part in the mainstream of French feudal politics. Church organization and monasticism, badly disrupted by Viking activity in the 9th century, recovered under his stable rule. Richard formed a close alliance with Hugh the Great, whose daughter Emma he married. In 987 Richard played an important part in securing the French throne for his brother-in-law Hugh Capet. Richard's marriage to Emma was childless, but he had several children by Gunnor, his Danish concubine, including his successor RICHARD THE GOOD.

Richard the Good (Richard II) (d. 1026) The fourth ruler of NORMANDY (r. 996–1026) and the first to use the title duke (from 1006). He was the son of RICHARD THE FEARLESS by a Danish concubine. Richard put down a peasant rebellion that followed his accession, supported the French king Robert II in his wars with Burgundy, and encouraged the reform of the Norman Church. By marrying Judith, sister of the count of Rennes, he began to bring BRITTANY within the Norman orbit. Richard was the last Norman ruler to maintain close links with Scandinavia. He allowed king SVEIN FORKBEARD to use Normandy as a base for his attacks on ENGLAND, and in 1000 he beat off an Anglo-Saxon retaliatory raid on the Cotentin peninsula. This support

The modern village of Oost-Souburg preserves the layout of the 9th-century ring-fort built to protect Frisia against Viking attack.

continued despite Richard marrying his sister EMMA to ÆTHELRED II in 1002. In 1003 Svein agreed to give Richard a share of the plunder in return for his support, but he also gave Æthelred a safe refuge when he fled England in 1013. A Viking ARMY took part in Richard's attack on Chartres in 1013–14, and Norman soldiers fought with the Viking contingent in the battle of CLONTARF in 1014. After CNUT established his Anglo-Scandinavian empire, relations with the north quickly faded, the last vestige of Scandinavian influence in Normandy being the presence of a Norwegian poet at Richard's court in 1025. Richard was succeeded by his sons Richard III (r. 1026–7) and Robert the Magnificent (r. 1027–37).

ring-forts, Frankish A chain of eight circular forts on the North Sea coast of the Low Countries between Flanders and Texel. None of the sites have been extensively excavated and cannot be dated precisely. Excavations of the fort at Oost-Souburg on the island of Walcheren (The Netherlands) in the Rhine Estuary have produced evidence of occupation during the 9th century. Oost-Souburg has a diameter of about 130 metres, four equally spaced gateways and regularly laid-out roads and buildings. The ramparts were protected by a wide moat. The poor dating evidence makes it impossible to say with certainty who was responsible for building the forts. Frankish sources tell us that CHARLEMAGNE built coastal FORTIFICATIONS against the Vikings, but not where. His son LOUIS THE PIOUS is known to have ordered the construction of coastal defences in 835 and in 837. While Louis was nearby at Nijmegen, the Vikings stormed a fort on Walcheren, causing him to order even more forts to be built. According to a history of the abbey of St-Bertin written c.890, count

Baldwin II of Flanders (d. 918) also built forts in the area. The shape and layout of the forts has led to speculation that they were the model for the 10th-century circular TRELLEBORG FORTS in DENMARK.

roads Except in TOWNS, man-made roads were rare in Viking Age Scandinavia. Even major roads, such as the *Hærvej* (the 'Army Road' or 'Ox Road'), the ancient route from northern Jutland to the German border, were simply broad bands of parallel ruts worn by cartwheels in the earth. Such roads followed natural routes, keeping to watersheds and avoiding marshy valleys wherever possible. In SWEDEN, roads frequently followed eskers, long well-drained gravel ridges laid down by subglacial streams during the Ice Age. True road-building occurred only in marshy areas that would otherwise be completely impassable to wheeled vehicles. At its most basic, road-building involved simply laying branches on boggy ground to create a stable surface, but more sophisticated techniques were also used. The kerbs of some roads, such as the late-Viking Age road at Risby in Sjælland, DENMARK, were defined by rows of upright stones, and the roadway between was built up of gravel and paved with stones. In NORWAY, many kilometres of timber-paved bridle-paths were laid in marshy areas c.1000–1200. Timber paving with split logs or planks was also the usual method of road-building in towns: good examples have been excavated in DUBLIN, HEDEBY and YORK. Footpaths were made of woven wooden wattles. Fords could also be paved to make the crossing easier: one such is a 50-metre-long ford over the River Nyköping at Släbro in Sweden. Timber BRIDGES over rivers were also being built by the late Viking Age. After the introduction of CHRISTIANITY, roads, bridges and causeways in Sweden were frequently marked by

A late-Viking Age stone paved road from Risby in Sjælland, Denmark.

commemorative rune-stones. These show that road-building was not a public responsibility but a pious charitable act that was performed by the builder for religious reasons. One such builder was Livsten, who built two causeways at Näs for 'his soul's sake and for that of Ingerun his wife and of his sons'. Rune-stones also had the entirely practical function of marking the line of the road in winter when the ground was covered in snow.

Robert, count of Angers (d. 866) Robert was one of the more effective Frankish military leaders, campaigning energetically against the Vikings on the Loire during the 860s. He was appointed count of Angers by CHARLES THE BALD in 843. Despite being in rebellion against Charles 856–61, Robert held Angers until 865, when he was transferred to the county of Autun. In 862 he captured twelve Viking ships on the Loire and slaughtered their crews. Shortly afterwards, he hired a Viking ARMY from the Seine to fight against the Bretons for 6,000 pounds of silver. In 864 he fought two Viking bands on the Loire, annihilating one but being defeated and wounded in the battle with the second. The following year Robert defeated another Viking force killing, according to the contemporary *Annals of St-Bertin*, 500 Vikings for no Frankish losses, but early in 866 his army ran away rather than join battle with the Vikings on the Seine. Later in the year Robert and count Ranulf of Poitiers intercepted 400 Vikings and their Breton allies at Brissarthe, near Le Mans. In the ensuing battle Ranulf was wounded and fled; Robert was killed.

Rognvald (*fl. c.*919–25) Viking leader who conquered BRITTANY. Nothing is known of Rognvald's career until he captured Nantes at the mouth of the River Loire in 919: he had probably been active previously on the Seine but had moved on following ROLLO's settlement of NORMANDY. Rognvald led ferocious attacks on the Bretons and gained control of the whole of Brittany by the end of 920. In 921 count Robert of Neustria formally ceded Nantes to Rognvald after he had unsuccessfully laid siege to the city, but, unlike Rollo, Rognvald was not interested in peaceful settlement. In 923 he raided Poitou, Aquitaine and the Auvergne. Returning to the area in 924–5, Rognvald was defeated by king Raoul I and count Hugh the Great, and had to make a fighting retreat to Nantes. There is no reliable information about the end of Rognvald's career, but he probably died soon after his defeat by Raoul: the terror he inspired in his lifetime is reflected in the stories of the dreadful portents, lights in the sky, moving rocks and apparitions which, according to the later medieval *Miracles of St Benoit*, marked his death.

Rognvald of Møre (*fl. c.*870) Jarl (earl) of Møre in western NORWAY, Rognvald was remembered as a close ally of king HARALD FAIRHAIR. Rognvald is generally considered to have been the founder of the earldom of ORKNEY. Irish sources suggest that this happened at about the same time as the DANES captured YORK (866). Rognvald was content to remain in Norway and handed Orkney over to his brother SIGURD THE MIGHTY, who consolidated the authority of the earldom. Rognvald was killed in a dispute with king Harald's son Halfdan Halegg and was succeeded by his son Thore as jarl of Møre. His illegitimate son TORF-EINAR later became earl of Orkney. Another of his sons was Göngu-Hrolf, who is probably to be identified with ROLLO, the founder of NORMANDY.

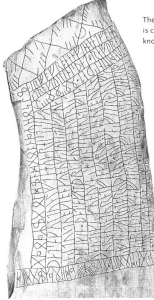

The 9th-century Rok stone is covered with the longest known runic inscription.

Duke Rollo lands at Jumièges, from the 15th-century *Chroniques de Normandie*.

Rök stone Rune-stone at Rök in Östergötland, SWEDEN. The stone is 4 metres high by 1.5 metres wide and 1.5 metres thick and is completely covered with RUNES on all four sides and on the top. With a total of 750 characters, it is the longest known runic inscription. Dating from the early 9th century, the inscription was written in short-twig runes by Varin in memory of his dead son Væmod. The inscription includes an eight-line verse and cryptic allusions to lost poems and legends.

Rollo (French Rollon) (d. *c.*928) Viking leader who founded the duchy of NORMANDY. Although regarded in Norman sources as a Dane, Rollo was probably a Norwegian: late Icelandic sources identify him with Göngu-Hrolf, a son of ROGNVALD OF MØRE, who turned to piracy after he was outlawed by king HARALD FAIRHAIR. According to the Norman chronicler DUDO OF ST-QUENTIN, Rollo arrived on the Seine in 876. In 911 he led a band of Danish Vikings in an unsuccessful attack on Chartres. In peace talks at ST-CLAIRE-SUR-EPTE, king CHARLES THE SIMPLE of the West FRANKS granted Rollo the county of Rouen and other districts on the lower Seine in return for his homage and defence of the area against other Viking raiders. Rollo was baptized in 912, though he did not give up worshipping the pagan gods. Rollo was granted further territories around Bayeux in 924, but broke the treaty in 925, attacking Amiens, Arras and Noyon, before he was defeated at Eux by the counts of Flanders and Vermandois. Rollo was succeeded by his son WILLIAM LONGSWORD.

Roman Iron Age (*c.* AD 1–400) Period of Scandinavian prehistory that saw the appearance of chieftain dwellings, cult centres, richly furnished warrior graves and votive hoards of WEAPONS. These developments point to the emergence of a warrior aristocracy and the beginnings of political centralization. The impetus for this is thought to have been competition to control wealth generated by contacts with the Roman Empire.

Roric (*fl.* mid-9th century) Viking leader in FRISIA. It is unclear whether he was the brother or nephew of HARALD KLAK, an exiled Danish king who had received Frisia as a fief from LOUIS THE PIOUS in 826. After Louis's death, Roric was denounced as a traitor to the new emperor, Lothar, and imprisoned. Escaping, he fled to Saxony and entered the service of Lothar's brother, king Louis the German. In 850 Roric raised a Danish ARMY and sailed down the Rhine and captured DORESTAD. Unable to defeat him, Lothar granted him the TOWN and other counties in Frisia as a fief in return for his allegiance and on condition that he would defend the area against other Danish pirates and hand over the TAX revenues to the royal fisc. In the mid-850s Roric returned briefly to Denmark to make an unsuccessful bid for the throne. Roric probably collaborated with a Danish Viking raid on Dorestad in 863 because he was driven into exile for a year by the Frisians in 866. Roric agreed a treaty with CHARLES THE BALD in 870 and proved to be a loyal ally. He disappears from the sources after 873, and presumably died before 882, by which time his lands were in the hands of Godafrid, another Dane.

Roskilde Situated at the head of the long, sheltered Roskilde Fjord in Sjælland, DENMARK, Roskilde developed as a royal and ecclesiastical centre in the late 10th century. Soon after 1000, the sea route to Roskilde was protected with a SEA BARRIER near

A runic memorial from the Isle of Man.

Below: Short-twig, or Norwegian-Swedish, runes.

Bottom: Long-branch, or Danish, runes.

ᚠᚢᚦᚨᚱᚲ	ᚼᚾᛁᛅᛋ	ᛏᛒᛘᛚ ᛦ

f u þ a r k   h n i a s   t b m l R

ᚠᚢᚦᚨᚱᚲ	ᚾᚾᛁᛏᚤ	ᛐᛒᛕᛚᛣ

f u þ a r k   h n i a s   t b m l R

SKULDELEV. King HARALD BLUETOOTH (r. 958–87) was buried there in a CHURCH he had built to the Holy Trinity, and *c*.1020 Roskilde became the seat of a BISHOPRIC. Soon after 1026, work began on a stone church, the first known in Scandinavia, to replace Harald's church. A second stone church was built in the TOWN *c*.1040. Roskilde grew rapidly in the 11th century and became one of the most important cities of medieval Denmark.

Roskilde ships The wrecks of six late-Viking Age and medieval SHIPS discovered in 1996–7 during excavations for an extension of the Viking Ship Museum in ROSKILDE, DENMARK. Five of the wrecks were merchant ships of post-Viking date. The sixth (Roskilde 6), dating from the 11th century, has the proportions of a large warship, being originally 20 metres or more in length by 3.4 metres broad with a hull 1.5 metres deep. These wrecks should not be confused with the SKULDELEV ships, which are displayed in the Viking Ship Museum itself.

runes The individual letters of the runic alphabet, the oldest and only indigenous system of writing used by the early Germanic peoples. The alphabet is known as the *futhark*, after its first six letters (th = þ). In Viking times, ODIN was credited with the invention of runes; they are now thought to be derived from Latin and Etruscan letters. Runes were probably originally designed to be carved on wood as they avoid horizontal lines, which could not be clearly distinguished from the grain. The earliest known runic inscriptions date from *c*. AD 150, so it is presumed that they had developed in the previous century. The Latin alphabet, introduced along with CHRISTIANITY, gradually replaced runic writing. Because of its late conversion to Christianity, Scandinavia kept runic writing far longer than northern Germany, FRISIA and ENGLAND, continuing into the 15th century. In Dalarna, SWEDEN, a tradition of runic writing survived into the 20th century.

The earliest *futhark*, in use *c*.150–750, had twenty-four characters. This was replaced in Viking Age Scandinavia by a *futhark* of 16 letters. Two versions are known: the long-branch runes (also known from their distribution as Danish runes) and the simpler short-twig runes (also known, again from their distribution, as Norwegian-Swedish runes). About 2,500 runic inscriptions are known from the Viking Age: 1,300 from Sweden, 350 from Denmark and rather fewer from NORWAY. The remainder are to be found in the areas colonized by the Vikings, chiefly RUSSIA, ORKNEY, Shetland and the Hebrides, the Isle of MAN, IRELAND and England. Viking graffiti are even known from Istanbul (Constantinople), and Piraeus in Greece. Surprisingly, no runic inscriptions are known from ICELAND or NORMANDY, though both were settled by Vikings. Runic inscriptions were used as marks of ownership on everyday objects and WEAPONS, for charms and curses, on memorial stones and for sending short messages carved on twigs. The longest known runic inscription, comprising 750 characters, is on an early 9th-century memorial stone at RÖK in Östergötland, Sweden. Many inscriptions were made by professional rune-masters, some of whom signed their work. One, Øpir, carved eighty memorial stones in Uppland, Sweden. However, the public nature of many runic inscriptions implies that literacy in runes was fairly widespread in Viking Age Scandinavia. The early 9th-century Swedish king Björn gave a runic message 'written by his own hand' to St ANSGAR to deliver to the emperor LOUIS THE PIOUS.

Romantic 19th-century portraits of the semi-legendary founders of the Rus state, the Vikings Rurik (*left*) and Oleg (*right*).

The Viking *futhark* does not have enough letters to represent all the sounds of speech; there are no letters for the vowels 'e' and 'o', for example. As a result, runic inscriptions are often difficult to interpret. Despite this, as the only form of written evidence to come from Viking Age Scandinavia itself, their importance as historical evidence is of the first order. It is the longer inscriptions on memorial stones that are most valuable, giving information about social and FAMILY relationships, TRADE and military expeditions, running a farm or a great household, road-building and WOMEN's activities.

R. I. Page, *Runes* (London, 1987).

Rurik (Ryurik, Roric) (d. *c*.879?) Semi-legendary founder of the Rus state. According to the RUSSIAN PRIMARY CHRONICLE, *c*.860–2 the Slavs became weary of their internecine warfare and decided to appeal to the VARANGIAN Rus to send them a leader to rule them according to LAW. They chose three brothers. The eldest, Rurik, established himself as the ruler of NOVGOROD; the second brother, Sineus, was established at Beloozero; and the third, Truvor, at Izborsk. When Rurik's brothers died two years later, he became the ruler of all north-west RUSSIA. He was succeeded by his kinsman OLEG, who fostered Rurik's young son IGOR. Modern historians regard the *Chronicle*'s account as mostly legendary, intended primarily to establish the legitimacy of the Kievan RYURIK DYNASTY, which claimed Rurik as its founder.

Rus A term used to describe Scandinavians living in RUSSIA, which is named after them. Rus is generally thought to be derived from *Ruotsi*, the Finnish name for the Swedes, the Scandinavians who were most active in eastern Europe during the Viking Age. *Ruotsi* itself probably derives from the Scandinavian *roðr*, meaning 'a crew of oarsmen'. A credible alternative to this view is that the term is of Greek origin, derived from literary references to the Rosomones (*rusioi*, or 'blondes'), an alternative name for the Heruls, a Scandinavian tribe that was active in the Eastern Roman Empire as pirates and mercenaries between the 3rd and 6th centuries. Particularly in the Soviet period, an influential school of Russian historians inclined to the view that the Rus were Slavs rather than Scandinavians. Although by the 11th century, if not before, the Rus had become assimilated to the native Slavs, the evidence for their Scandinavian origins is strong. Archaeological evidence for Scandinavian settlement in Russia during the Viking Age is plentiful, and contemporary written sources confirm the original Scandinavian identity of the Rus. The contemporary *Annals of St-Bertin* relate that a group of men described as 'Rhos' visited the court of the Frankish emperor LOUIS THE PIOUS with a Byzantine delegation in 839. Enquiries on behalf of the emperor revealed that they 'belonged to the people of the Swedes'. Louis feared that they might be Viking spies. Liudprand of Cremona, recording an account by his stepfather, who was an eyewitness, identified the Rus who attacked Constantinople in 941 as *nordmanni* ('northmen'). The well-travelled Arab writer al-Ya'qubi identifies the Vikings who attacked Seville in 844 with 'the pagans who are called *ar-Rus*'. It is also clear that the Rus spoke a different language from the Slavs. In his work *De administrando imperio*, the Byzantine emperor Constantine VII Porphyrogenitos (r. 913–59) gives both the Rus and Slavic names for the rapids on the River Dnieper: the Rus names (e.g. *Baruforos*,

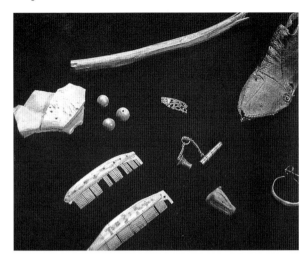

Scandinavian artefacts from Staraja Ladoga, Russia, including a rune stick and typical Viking antler combs.

A typical Viking sword, from a male burial at Zaozere near Ladoga, north-east Russia.

'wave-force') are Old Scandinavian. Finally, the names of the earliest rulers of the Rus state – RURIK (Roric), OLEG (Helgi) and IGOR (Ingvar) – are also clearly of Scandinavian rather than Slavic origin. From the mid-10th century, Scandinavians were sometimes called VARANGIANS by the Greeks, ARABS and Slavs.

Russia, Vikings in Evidence from Scandinavian merchant graves at the trading centres of GROBIN and ELBLAG show that Viking expansion east of the Baltic Sea began *c*.650, more than a century before the outbreak of raiding in the west. The main motive was probably to collect furs for the western European market. At the end of the 8th century, Arab merchants began to penetrate the Volga, introducing high-quality silver COINS (*DIRHEMS*) into circulation and encouraging the Scandinavians to press inland along Russia's many navigable rivers to discover their source. Because of their geographical proximity, it was the Swedes who took the lead. By the 830s the RUS, as Scandinavians were known in the east, were trading directly with the ARABS on the Volga and with the Byzantines at Constantinople. Judging by the number of female Scandinavian graves in Russia, some Rus merchants travelled in FAMILY groups. Vast amounts of Arab silver, received in exchange for furs and slaves, began to find its way back to SWEDEN. The TRADE routes flourished until the exhaustion of the Islamic world's silver mines between 965 and 1015 caused their decline and eventual abandonment.

During the course of the 9th century the Rus took over existing Slav settlements, such as NOVGOROD and KIEV, and used them as bases to subjugate the surrounding countryside. According to the *RUSSIAN PRIMARY CHRONICLE*, Novgorod, under its semi-

legendary ruler RURIK, had emerged as the capital of a Rus state by *c*.860–2. Around 882 OLEG (r. *c*.879–913), Rurik's kinsman and successor (another semi-legendary character), captured Kiev and made it the capital of the Rus state. By the reign of IGOR (r. 913–45) the state stretched from the Gulf of Finland to the lower River Dnieper. Though the Scandinavian presence in Russia is well attested by archaeological evidence – for example, the 187 Viking oval brooches found there far exceeds the number found in western Europe – it is clear from the evidence of Viking Age cemeteries that the Rus were a minority among a Slavic population, even in the TOWNS. From the countryside there is almost no evidence at all of Scandinavian settlement. The Rus were therefore a warrior and merchant élite. Although memorial inscriptions on rune-stones in Sweden attest that Scandinavian immigration continued into the 11th century, the Rus became increasingly assimilated to the Slav majority with whom they intermarried and allied. A sign of this is the adoption of Slavic names by the ruling dynasty. The first Rus ruler to have a Slav name was Igor's son SVYATOSLAV I (r. 945–78), as did all his successors. His son VLADIMIR I (r. 978–1015) worshipped the Slavic thunder-god Perun before his conversion to CHRISTIANITY in 988. By this time most of the ruling élite must have been Slavic speakers, because Slavic became the language of the Church. By the time Kiev reached the height of its power in the reign of JAROSLAV THE WISE (r. 1019–54), the Rus were entirely Slavic in character, though there remained close dynastic ties to Scandinavia.

Before the Viking expansion in eastern Europe, many of the Slavs' fortified settlements in the region had already started to develop into true towns, but

ДЛ ПОЧХНИ СЕДОШАПОД ЕСНІБ ИПОСЕМН. ИПОСѠЛІБ ИИАРЄ

there can be no doubt that the arrival of Scandinavian merchants gave the process enormous impetus, turning small settlements like Novgorod into flourishing cities in less than a century. Apart from this, however, the Viking contribution to Russian civilization was slight. The Slavic peoples were at a similar social and technological level to the Vikings and had little to learn from them. A sign of this is that there are only half a dozen Scandinavian loan words in the Russian language. The most important outside influence on the cultural development of early Russia was in fact Byzantium, a consequence of Vladimir's decision to convert to Orthodox rather than Roman Christianity. Kievan Russia's alphabet, architecture, art, LAW, music and political ideologies were all essentially Byzantine in origin.
H. R. Ellis Davidson, *The Viking Road to Byzantium* (London, 1976); P. M. Dolukhanov, *The Early Slavs: Eastern Europe from the Initial Settlement to the Kievan Rus* (London, 1996); S. Franklin and J. Shepard, *The Emergence of Rus 750–1200* (London and New York, 1996).

Russian Primary Chronicle (Russian *Povest Vremennykh Let*, literally the 'Chronicle of Past Years'). The most important indigenous source for the early history of RUSSIA. The chronicle was compiled at KIEV in the early 12th century using lost earlier annals, KHAZAR sources and oral traditions, some of them certainly mythical. It describes the coming of the Scandinavians to Russia and the establishment of a Scandinavian kingdom at Kiev and its subsequent history. The chronicle was compiled for dynastic purposes, such as establishing favourable territorial and familial connections for the RYURIK DYNASTY, and its account of the establishment of the Kievan state is now

regarded as being mostly, if not entirely, legendary. The attribution of the chronicle to the 11th-century Kievan monk Nestor is no longer widely accepted.
Russian Primary Chronicle: Laurentian Text, ed. and trans. S. H. Cross and O. P. Sherbowitz-Wetzor (Cambridge, Mass., 1953).

Ryurik dynasty Ruling dynasty of RUSSIA from the 10th century until 1598. It took its name from the semi-legendary Viking RURIK (d. *c.*879?) who, from the 12th century onwards, was claimed by the dynasty as its founder. Prior to the 12th century, Russian rulers regarded IGOR, prince of KIEV (r. 913–45) and the first historically attested member of the dynasty, as its founder.

Ryurikovo Gorodisce Ninth-century fortified settlement on an island in the River Volkhov, 2 kilometres upstream from the centre of modern NOVGOROD. Many of the artefacts discovered in excavations on the site are of Scandinavian character. It is highly likely that Ryurikovo Gorodisce is the Novgorod mentioned in the *RUSSIAN PRIMARY CHRONICLE* as the capital of RURIK's early RUS state. It is also likely that the Viking name for Novgorod, Holmgarð ('island town'), was also originally applied to this location.

Pages from the *Flateyjarbók*, a sumptuously illustrated collection of Norse kings' sagas.

Saami *see* LAPPS

Sæmundr Sigfússon, 'the learned' (1056–1133). Icelandic churchman and scholar. Sæmundr is regarded as the founder of historical writing in ICELAND. He studied for some years in FRANCIA, returning to Iceland in 1076 to be ordained as a priest. Sæmundr's works, which included a history of the kings of NORWAY and a collection of Eddic poetry, are no longer extant, but are frequently cited as a source in later works.

saga Saga is a term used to describe medieval Icelandic prose narrative literature. In Icelandic, *saga* means 'what is said', or 'told,' a derivation that indicates the importance of the tradition of oral storytelling in the development of the form. The saga developed in the 12th century and died out in the 14th. The oldest examples, dating from *c.*1150, are exclusively religious texts – mainly anonymous translations of Latin biographies of saints and apostles – which served as models for four later subgenres.

The *konungasögur* ('kings' sagas') are historical biographies of rulers, most of which were written between 1190 and 1230. SKALDIC VERSE was an important source for these works and is often quoted at length in them. The most important *konungasaga* is SNORRI STURLUSON's mighty *HEIMSKRINGLA*, a history in saga form of the kings of NORWAY to 1177. The best-known sagas are the anonymous *Íslendingasögur* ('sagas of the Icelanders'). These are essentially historical novels, in the form of FAMILY histories, based on the personalities and events of Viking Age ICELAND, but written in the 13th century. Iceland was increasingly troubled by political violence in this period, and the *Íslendingasögur*

probably catered for an escapist desire to re-create a 'golden age' of the past. A common theme in these sagas is the working out of a blood feud, sometimes over several generations. In *NJÁLS SAGA*, for example, ties of kinship, personal loyalty and friendship inexorably draw Njal, a good and peaceable man, into other people's disputes, leading to his own violent death. Though the authors of these sagas are much concerned with the workings of fate, their characters control their own destinies and meet their ends as a result of their own failings. Compared with the chivalric romances then fashionable in Europe, the *Íslendingasögur* are strikingly modern-seeming works, written in a compelling, terse style and featuring psychologically realistic characters. The finest of them, *Njáls saga*, *EGILS SAGA* and *LAXDÆLA SAGA*, rank with the greatest works of European literature.

Riddarasögur ('sagas of knights') are adaptations of the chivalric romances of western Europe for an Icelandic audience: most are regarded as mediocre works of literature. The *fornaldarsögur* ('sagas of ancient times') are heroic legends and fantastic adventure tales. The most important example of the first type is *VOLSUNGA SAGA*, the story of SIGURD FAFNISBANE, the dragon-slayer. *GÖNGU-HROLFS SAGA*, about the eponymous hero's romantic and magical journey to RUSSIA, is typical of the second type. Most *fornaldarsögur* were written in the 14th century.

sails Viking sailing SHIPS, in common with most of those used elsewhere in northern Europe at the time, were driven by a single square sail. A few fragments of Viking Age sails are known from the Norwegian OSEBERG and GOKSTAD ship burials: these were made of wool. Rope for rigging was made

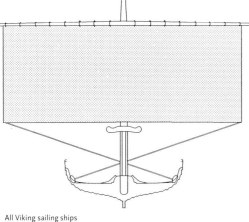

All Viking sailing ships carried a single 'square' sail.

Penannular brooches from the Viking silver hoard discovered at Skail, Orkney, the largest in Scotland.

of lime bast or walrus hide. The date of the adoption of the sail by Scandinavian seafarers is controversial and still uncertain. A letter written by the 5th-century Gallo-Roman aristocrat Sidonius Apollinaris makes reference to the use of sailing ships by the Saxons, a Germanic people whose territory bordered on southern DENMARK. The earliest certain evidence of the use of the sail in Scandinavia itself comes from PICTURE STONES on the Baltic island of GOTLAND dating from the 7th and 8th centuries. These show a number of experimental rigs in use, as might be expected during the early stages of the adoption of a new technology. There is also a tiny engraving of a sailing ship on a pebble from Karlby in Jutland. This was not found in a datable context, but it is also thought to be from the 7th century on the basis of the style of animal ornament also incised on the stone. A 4th-century side rudder discovered at Nydam in Denmark has a design well suited to sailing, but the earliest indisputable sailing ship that is known from Scandinavia is the Oseberg ship, built c.820, which also had fifteen pairs of OARS. The earliest known Scandinavian ships to rely entirely on sail are the late-10th-century ships from ÄSKEKÄRR and KLÅSTAD. *See also* SHIPS AND SHIPBUILDING.

St Brice's Day Massacre Mass killing of DANES living in ENGLAND, on St Brice's Day (13 November) 1002, ordered by king ÆTHELRED II after he had been informed of a Danish conspiracy against his life. It is known from charter evidence that Danes living in Oxford were killed, but it is not known where other killings took place, nor how many casualties there were. Among the slain was said to be Gunnhild, the sister of king SVEIN FORKBEARD of DENMARK, who was being held in England as a HOSTAGE. If true, it is

possible that Svein's invasion of England in 1003 was motivated by a desire for revenge.

St-Claire-sur-Epte, treaty of (911) Agreement between the Viking leader ROLLO and king CHARLES THE SIMPLE of the West FRANKS that led to the establishment of the duchy of NORMANDY. Charles granted Rollo the city of Rouen and other districts on the lower Seine, including Talou, Caux and Roumois, in return for homage and defence of the area against other Viking raiders. It is generally accepted that Charles also gave Rollo the title count of Rouen and the right to take over royal lands and to represent royal authority in his territory. The earliest reference to the agreement dates from 918.

Sandwich, battle of (851) The first recorded naval battle in English history. A Viking FLEET lying in Sandwich harbour was attacked and defeated by an Anglo-Saxon fleet under king Athelstan of Kent and ealdorman Ealhere, losing nine SHIPS. The survivors withdrew, but the battle was no more than a temporary setback for the Vikings, who attacked Kent again the following year, defeating and killing Ealhere in battle at Thanet.

Saucourt, battle of (881) Fought between a Viking ARMY and king Louis III of the West FRANKS near Abbeville, north-west France. Contemporary Frankish sources give conflicting accounts of the battle. The *Annals of St-Bertin* record that despite inflicting heavy casualties on the Vikings, the Frankish army suddenly broke and fled. The *Annals of Fulda* record a major Frankish victory, claiming that 9,000 Viking horsemen were killed. The account of the *Annals of St-Bertin* is probably closer to the truth, since the Vikings went on in the same

A Viking Age canal on the Isle of Skye.
It was built to take ships from the sea
to the shelter of an inland loch.

year to sack Cambrai, Utrecht, Cologne, Bonn,
Prüm, Cornelimünster, Stavelot, Malmedy and
the imperial palace at Aachen, whose chapel
they are said to have used as a stable. The battle
is the subject of the medieval German praise-poem
the *Ludwigslied*.

Saxo Grammaticus (*c*.1150–*c*.1220) Danish historian
and poet. Saxo was given the title Grammaticus
('the learned') because of his great knowledge.
Almost nothing is known of Saxo's life. He was
born into a warrior family, probably from
Sjælland. His familiarity with Church business
suggests that he was a cleric, though probably
not a monk. Sometime before 1185, Saxo joined
the household of Absalon, bishop of Roskilde
(later archbishop of Lund), who encouraged him
to write his great history of the DANES, the Latin
GESTA DANORUM.

Scotland, Vikings in The first recorded Viking raid
in Scotland was on the monastery on IONA in 795.
Pirate raids like this continued up to the early 13th
century, but by the middle of the 9th century most
Vikings coming to Scotland were more interested
in winning lands for settlement. By 900, settlers
from NORWAY were well established in ORKNEY,
Shetland and the Hebrides, and on the mainland
in Caithness, parts of the west coast and in
Galloway in the far south-west. DANES also
settled in Galloway and neighbouring Dumfries.
In Orkney and Shetland, the native Celts were
either exterminated or, more likely, assimilated to
Norse culture and language. In the Hebrides and
Galloway, the Norse intermarried with the Celtic
population, becoming partially assimilated to
Celtic culture and language. This distinct hybrid

population was known to the Irish as the
Gall-Gaedhil ('foreign Gael'), from which Galloway
gets its name. One result of Celtic influence was
that many of the Norse in these areas had become
Christians by 900. In Orkney and Shetland the
Norse remained pagan until the 11th century.

The political organization of the Norse
settlements is uncertain, but as in ICELAND, they
were probably led by aristocrats such as KETIL
FLATNOSE, who ruled in the Hebrides in the 850s.
By 900 an earldom had become established in
Orkney under loose Norwegian sovereignty. The
Orkney earldom had greatly expanded by the time of
earl SIGURD THE STOUT (r. *c*.985–1014), when it
controlled most of the Norse-settled areas of
Scotland. In the late 11th century the Orkney earls
lost control of the Hebrides to a rival Norse state to
the south, the kingdom of MAN. King MAGNUS
BARELEGS brought both the Orkney earldom and the
kingdom of Man under effective Norwegian control
in 1098. This was the high point of Norse power in
Scotland: in 1156 the kingdom of Man lost control of
much of the Hebrides to SOMERLED, a chieftain of
Argyll of mixed Norse and Scottish ancestry, while
the Scots conquered Galloway *c*.1160 and Ross,
Caithness and Sutherland in 1199–1202. King
Håkon IV (r. 1217–63) of Norway tried to arrest the
decline of Norse power in Scotland when he
descended on the western isles with the 'Great Fleet'
in 1263. After an indecisive skirmish with the Scots
at Largs, Håkon, now ailing, withdrew to Orkney,
where he died. His successor Magnus VI had
problems at home, and ceded Man and the Isles to
Scotland in 1266 in return for 4,000 marks and an
annuity. The Scandinavian character of Orkney and
Shetland was being undermined by Scots' influence
even before they were ceded by DENMARK in 1469.

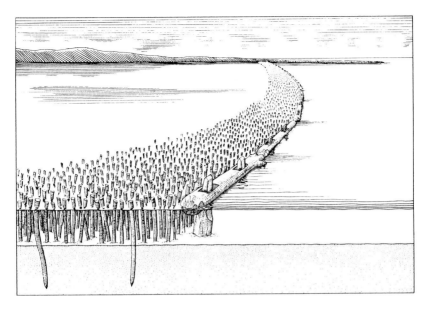

A reconstruction of a sea barrier built at Hominde, Lolland, Denmark, at the end of the Viking Age.

The Viking impact on Scottish history was considerable. As in ENGLAND, the arrival of the Vikings in the 9th century broke up the existing power structures. In 800, what is now Scotland was divided between four ethnic groups: the Picts of the Highlands, the Scots of Dalriada (Argyll), the Britons of STRATHCLYDE and the ANGLO-SAXONS of NORTHUMBRIA. The southern Pictish kingdom of Fortriu was severely weakened after its defeat by the Vikings in 839, while the northern Picts of Moray came under attack from Vikings based in the northern isles. The power of Strathclyde was broken after its capital at Dumbarton was captured by the DUBLIN Vikings under OLAF and IVAR in 870–1. Northumbrian power likewise declined after its capital at YORK was captured by the Danes in 866. Although they lost control of Dalriada to the Vikings, the Scots were able to benefit from the weakness of their neighbours, beginning in the 840s when their king Kenneth macAlpin (r. c.840–58) took over Fortriu. His successors completed the absorption of the Picts and won control over Strathclyde and Lothian (part of Northumbria) in the 10th century to create the kingdom of Scotland. The Viking presence in Scotland is attested by excavated settlements such as The UDAL in the Hebrides, BIRSAY in Orkney and JARLSHOF in Shetland, and by place-name evidence. In Orkney, Shetland and Caithness almost all place-names are of Norse origin, evidence of dense Scandinavian settlement. There is also strong Norse influence on place-names on the west coast and Hebrides. Typical Norse elements here include -staðir, as in Grimista ('Grim's place'), -bólstaðr, as in Isbister ('Eastern farm'), -dalr, as in Papadil ('Priest's valley') and -fjall, as in Askival ('Ash-tree hill'). In Dumfries and Galloway in south-west Scotland there are concentrations of place-names that show both Norse and Danish influences.

B. E. Crawford, *Scandinavian Scotland* (Leicester, 1987); J. Graham-Campbell and C. E. Batey, *Vikings in Scotland* (Edinburgh, 1998); A. Ritchie, *Viking Scotland* (London, 1993).

sea barriers Many areas of Scandinavia were vulnerable to attack by the sea. Important sites were, therefore, often defended with sea barriers to prevent sudden landings. The earliest known sea barrier dates from c.200 BC, but the majority were built in the period 1000–1200, when pirate raids by the WENDS were at their peak. More than forty sea barriers are known from DENMARK, and nearly a dozen from SWEDEN. One of the most impressive sea barriers was at Hominde on Lolland, Denmark. Dating from the early 12th century, this barrier consisted of a broad belt of stakes driven into the seabed. Behind the stakes was a further barrier of horizontally laid logs. The harbours at HEDEBY and BIRKA were protected with single rows of wooden stakes and, at Birka, sunken rocks. At SKULDELEV in Denmark a stake barrier across Roskilde Fjord was reinforced by block-ships filled with stones, and fascines. Most barriers were maintained for only relatively short periods, but one, at Gudsø Vig, Jutland, was periodically renewed from the mid-7th century to the 15th. *See also* FORTIFICATIONS.

A. Nørgård Jørgensen, 'Sea defence in Denmark AD 200–1300', in A. Nørgård Jørgensen and B. L. Clausen (eds), *Military Aspects of Scandinavian Society in a European Perspective, AD 1–1300* (Copenhagen, 1997).

Serkland Term used in Viking Age Scandinavia to describe the Muslim lands of the Middle East. The name means either Silkland (i.e. the land where

A small ship burial at Westness on Ronsay, Orkney. The deceased was a warrior, and was buried with his sword, shield and arrows, as well as farm tools. His shield showed signs of having been used in battle.

silk could be obtained, from Latin *sericum*) or Saracenland. The former is the more widely accepted explanation.

Sermon of the Wolf to the English (*Sermo lupi ad Anglos*) Written by archbishop Wulfstan II of YORK in 1014 after king ÆTHELRED II had been forced into exile by SVEIN FORKBEARD of DENMARK, the sermon calls on the thoroughly demoralized English to repent and reform, explaining their defeats by the DANES as the result of God's anger with a sinful people. The title is a pun on Wulfstan's name.

D. Whitelock, *English Historical Documents c.500–1000*, vol. 1 (revised edition, Oxford, 1979).

sex, attitudes to Sexual double standards were the rule in Scandinavia, both before and after the conversion to CHRISTIANITY. Male sexuality could be indulged with suitably available WOMEN (usually of lower social status); female sexuality was seen as a possession of her FAMILY and was, as far as possible, controlled. This does not mean that women's sexual needs counted for nothing. Sex was regarded as central to marriage, and a man's failure to live up to his wife's sexual expectations was grounds for divorce.

Viking Age Scandinavian men were certainly regarded by contemporary Europeans as having a relaxed sexual morality. In the 11th century the German historian ADAM OF BREMEN complained of king SVEIN ESTRITHSON's serial infidelities but was inclined to be forgiving, since he saw this as an inbred fault of the DANES and their Swedish neighbours. Slave girls, and free-born women who lacked male guardians, were seen as fair game for casual sex or long-term extramarital relationships.

The Arab writer Ibn Fadlan, who visited the RUS *c.*920, recorded that casual sexual relationships with slave girls were common, even being conducted in public, while Icelandic LAWS from the end of the Viking Age show that attractive slave girls were bought and sold for sexual purposes at premium prices. However, sexual latitude did not extend to relations with other men's wives, daughters, foster-daughters, sisters, mothers and foster-mothers, as this impugned family honour, and the consequences for a man could be fatal if caught *in flagrante delicto*. Direct advances by a man to a single woman were frowned upon and, if they were not followed up by a formal proposal of MARRIAGE, the girl's father or guardian was likely to seek blood vengeance if it was suspected that sexual intercourse had taken place. It is clear that single women were expected still to be virgins on marriage, but the Viking saying 'praise a virgin when she is married' is a recognition that this was inevitably not always going to be the case, and, according to SAGA accounts, paternity suits were not uncommon, in Viking Age ICELAND at least. Male and female homosexual acts, incest and bestiality were all punishable offences.

ship burial A burial in which a boat or ship is used as a container for the body of the deceased and for the grave goods. Though the use of SHIPS as grave offerings is not completely unknown in other cultures, for example in ancient Egypt, ship burial was a north European custom, practised by the pagan ANGLO-SAXONS and Scandinavians. There are a few examples of dug-out boats being used as coffins in Scandinavia as early as the Mesolithic period, but the custom of ship burial developed around the beginning of the first millennium AD and continued until the introduction

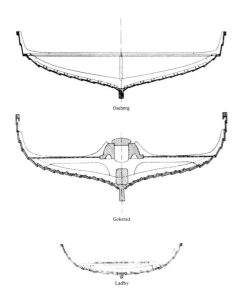

Oseberg

Gokstad

Ladby

of CHRISTIANITY c.1000. The majority of known ship burials date from the Viking Age. Both male and female ship burials are known, but the custom was always restricted to a minority of the population. For instance, at the ROMAN IRON AGE cemetery at Slusegård on the Danish island of Bornholm, dated to AD 100–250, only 43 of 467 burials included boats. The use of stone SHIP SETTINGS as a symbolic substitute for a real ship was a widespread alternative, though rarely were ship burials and ship settings combined. The appearance of richly furnished ship burials, such as those at VENDEL and VALSGÄRDE in SWEDEN, in the 6th and 7th centuries is among the most telling evidence of the process of centralization of power and of the emergence of royal dynasties that preceded the Viking Age in Scandinavia.

Viking Age ship burials are known not only from NORWAY, Sweden and DENMARK but also from Scandinavian-settled areas in Finland, SCOTLAND, the Isle of MAN and northern RUSSIA. There is also one isolated Viking ship burial on Île de GROIX off the coast of BRITTANY. Though one settler, Ásmund Atlason, is said in literary sources to have been buried in a ship, no ship burials have ever been discovered in ICELAND. It may be that in that treeless land, ships were far too valuable to be buried.

In Viking Age ship burials the deceased was laid out in the centre of the ship and surrounded with grave goods, which might be exceptionally rich and sometimes included human sacrifices. In some cases, such as the famous burials from GOKSTAD, OSEBERG and TUNE in Norway and LADBY in Denmark, the ship and its contents were simply buried beneath an earth barrow, but it was also a common practice to burn them before burial. In such cases, the only way to recognize a grave as a

ship burial is from the hundreds of iron rivets that were used to fasten the planking of the ship's hull. Probably the best-known example of a cremated ship burial is that from Île de Groix. The 10th-century Arab traveller Ibn Fadlan witnessed this type of burial on the River Volga when, after an elaborate funeral ceremony, a dead RUS chieftain was placed in his ship and cremated along with a sacrificed slave girl. A variation of the ship burial is described in the 8th-century Anglo-Saxon poem *Beowulf*. The body of the Danish king Scyld Scefing was taken to the seashore and laid to rest by the mast of his ship and surrounded by WEAPONS, armour and treasure. Then the ship was launched and 'bequeathed to the sea'. In the *Ynglinga saga*, SNORRI STURLUSON describes a similar funeral for the legendary Swedish king Haki, except that here the ship was set on fire before being launched on the waves. For obvious reasons, it is unlikely that archaeological evidence will be found to verify this custom.

The religious and symbolic significance of ship burial is unclear: the practice may have embodied different beliefs and customs at different times and places. One obvious interpretation is that the ship was a symbol of the soul's journey to the realm of the dead or, even more literally, a ferry to take the soul of the deceased there. No Norse myth embodies this belief, however. It has also been suggested that ship burial was related to cults of the fertility-gods NJORD and FREYR, both of whom are associated with ships and the sea. The practice of burning the ship and its contents before burial has parallels with the myths associated with the murdered god BALDER, who was cremated in his ship *Hringhorni*. At another level, a ship may have been simply a status symbol, a public demonstration of the wealth and power not only of the deceased but of his surviving relatives. In this

Opposite, far left: Cross-sections of three Viking ships: top, the Oseberg ship (c.820); centre, the Gokstad ship (c.895–900); and bottom, the Ladby ship (mid-10th century).

Opposite, left: A small merchant ship, Skuldelev 3 in the Viking Ship Museum at Roskilde, Denmark.

Constructing a Scandinavian clinker-built boat.

case, it may be that the ship was just another luxury object, like the weapons, armour and JEWELRY that were placed in the grave, for the deceased to use in the realm of the dead. Apart from the information they have yielded about pagan BURIAL CUSTOMS, ship burials have also been a major source of knowledge about Viking SHIPS AND SHIPBUILDING.

ships and shipbuilding All Viking ships shared certain common characteristics: they were built of overlapping planks ('clinker-built') fastened together with iron rivets; they had double-ended hulls with the bow and stern both built in the same way; they were steered by a single side rudder, which was always fitted onto the right-hand side of the ship (hence 'starboard') and they carried a single mast and square SAIL. Within this basic pattern, there were many different types of Viking ship, each built for a particular environment and function.

Viking warships, usually loosely described as longships, were first and foremost personnel transport ships for carrying ARMIES and raiding parties. Warships were always galleys, for they had to be able to manoeuvre independently of the wind. Their masts could be lowered before going into battle or to make the ship less conspicuous. Typical longships may be represented by the long and narrow LADBY and SKULDELEV 5 ships from Denmark, with thirty-two and twenty-four/twenty-six OARS respectively. Sea trials with a replica of Skuldelev 5 have shown it to have been swift under sails or oars, while its shallow draft (less than half a metre fully loaded) made it ideal for raiding in the shallow waters of the Baltic Sea or southern North Sea, as well as for penetrating far inland along rivers. The ship was not very seaworthy; because of its low freeboard, it would have been easily swamped in a rough sea. In the later Viking Age a type of 'super-longship', called a *drakkar* ('dragon'), came into use. These were ships of thirty benches (i.e. sixty oars) or larger, built, with sea fighting very much in mind, with high prows and sides to allow their crews to shoot down onto smaller enemy ships and to make boarding more difficult. Ships of this size were usually the preserve of kings. Famous examples include OLAF TRYGGVASON'S *LONG SERPENT* and OLAF HARALDSSON'S *VISUNDEN*; the largest, and last, known was Håkon IV's *Kristsuden*, built at BERGEN in 1262–3, which had thirty-seven benches. Skuldelev 2 is probably an example of a *drakkar*.

TRADE ships were shorter and broader than warships, with deeper and heavier hulls for maximum cargo-carrying capacity. Apart from carrying a few oars for manoeuvring into and out of harbour, trade ships relied entirely on sail for propulsion, and their masts were permanently fixed. The most important type of Viking trade ship was the *knarr*, a sturdy, broad and deep-hulled sailing ship. Shown from sea trials with modern replicas to have been very seaworthy, the *knarr* was in all probability the type of ship used for the voyages of settlement and exploration in the North Atlantic. The largest known *knarr*, discovered in the harbour at HEDEBY, was 25 metres long, 5.7 metres broad and 2.5 metres deep, and had a cargo capacity of 38 tonnes. Other examples of *knarrs* have been discovered at Skuldelev and ÄSKEKÄRR. The large cargo-carrying capacity of the *knarr* demonstrates that Viking Age trade was not simply concerned with high-value, low-bulk products.

The karve (ON *karfi*) was a type of ship built as the private travelling vessels of chieftains and their households. The term is probably derived from

A large group of small
Viking Age ship settings
in the cemetery at
Lindholm Høje, Jutland.

korabi, a Slavic word used to describe the ships of
the Rus and Varangians. The Viking ships from
Oseberg and Gokstad are thought to be karves.
Though these ships had full crews of oarsmen, their
proportions are closer to those of Viking trading
ships than those of the longships from Ladby and
Skuldelev. As a result, they would have been able to
carry a large retinue plus all the tents, portable
furniture and supplies that would have
accompanied a chieftain travelling in style.

Unlike modern wooden ships and boats, where
the hull is built by laying planks onto a pre-erected
skeleton of frames, Viking ships were built hull first
and the frames were added later. Viking shipbuilders
started by laying the keel and adding the bow and
stern posts. The hull was built up gradually using
planks, which were carefully shaped by eye to
produce a hull with the desired lines. The hull was
made watertight by pressing wool, cattle hair, cloth
or plant fibres and moss into the spaces between the
planks and then by tarring the outside. Internal
strengthening frames were fitted in stages as the
hull was completed. The single mast was fitted in a
mast-step, a long, heavy timber designed to spread
the load of the mast and sail over a large area of
the keel and hull. Decking, side rudder, sail and
rigging completed the ship's fitting out. Viking Age
Scandinavian shipbuilders used only unseasoned
wood since it was easier to work. Planks were split
radially from logs, never sawed, and finished with an
ordinary axe. Radially split planking utilized the
natural strength and flexibility of wood to its best
advantage and minimized the shrinkage as the
new wood seasoned. Evidence of shipbuilding
and ship repair has been found at many Viking
Age settlements, and a shipyard has been excavated
at Fribrødre Å in Denmark.

Except for the replacement of the side rudder by
the more efficient stern rudder in the 13th century,
ships very similar to those built by Viking Age
Scandinavians continued to dominate the northern
seas until the beginning of the 14th century. By this
time the cog, a type of sturdy, flat-bottomed sailing
ship, which probably originated in Frisia or the Low
Countries, was beginning to take over as the main
type of ship for trade and war. Cogs were slow and
had poor sailing characteristics, but they could carry
large cargoes in their capacious holds and, as their
decks were much higher above the water, they
made better fighting platforms than the sleek
longships. Fishing boats and coastal traders built
in Scandinavia and Scotland continued to show
the influence of Viking shipbuilding traditions into
the modern age.

A. E. Christensen (ed.), *The Earliest Ships: The Evolution of Boats
into Ships* (London, 1996); R. W. Unger (ed.), *Cogs, Caravels and
Galleons: The Sailing Ship 1000–1650* (London, 1994); A. W.
Brøgger and H. Shetelig, *The Viking Ships: Their Ancestry and
Evolution* (London, 1971).

ship settings Settings of stones arranged in the
outline of a ship were built in Scandinavia,
especially in Sweden and Denmark, from the
Bronze Age to the introduction of Christianity
*c.*1000. During the Viking Age larger ship settings
were probably used as places of worship. These
often have small pits containing burnt offerings
and charcoal. The largest known ship setting, at
Lejre on Sjælland in Denmark, is about 80 metres
long. Large ship settings sometimes contain burials.
A 60-metre-long setting at Glavendrup, on Fyn in
Denmark, enclosed a small Viking Age cremation
cemetery. Its prow was marked by a runic memorial
stone. Smaller ship-shaped settings of stones were

A graceful Bronze Age ship setting on the Baltic island of Gotland.

used for individual burials – always cremations – most probably as a symbolic substitute for a real ship, as at LINDHOLM HØJE, near Ålborg in Jutland, although in two Viking Age burials from Mølen and Ølbør in Rogaland, NORWAY, a stone ship setting was used to outline a cremated SHIP BURIAL.

Sigfred (*fl.* 882–7) Viking leader in FRANCIA. Sigfred first appears as one of the leaders of the Vikings who were besieged by emperor CHARLES THE BALD at Ascloha on the River Meuse (exact location uncertain) in 882. With his fellow leaders Godfred and Orm, he successfully negotiated their withdrawal for a payment of 2,400 pounds of silver and gold and his conversion to CHRISTIANITY. In 885 Sigfred led a Viking force up the Seine, destroying the fortified BRIDGE at PONT DE L'ARCHE and unsuccessfully laying siege to PARIS when its inhabitants refused his force safe passage up stream to attack Burgundy. Sigfred was killed in 887 while raiding in FRISIA.

Sighvatr Thórðarson (d. c.1043) SKALDIC poet from ICELAND, born probably around 1000 into a family with a strong poetic tradition: he was said to have acquired his gift for poetry by eating a magical fish. While still in his teens, Sighvatr became skald to OLAF HARALDSSON and fought with him at the battle of Nesjar in 1015. In 1017–18 Olaf sent Sighvatr on an embassy to jarl Rognvald of Västergötland, and in the 1020s Sighvatr went to ENGLAND to gather intelligence on CNUT's intentions towards NORWAY. After Olaf was exiled in 1028, Sighvatr went on a PILGRIMAGE to Rome. On his return, he refused to serve Cnut's son SVEIN ALFIVASON, the nominal ruler of Norway, and

went with Olaf's widow to SWEDEN. Though none of his poems survive complete, more of Sighvatr's poetry has come down to us than that of any other skaldic poet. The largest body of Sighvatr's work is recorded in SNORRI STURLUSON's *Óláfs saga helga* ('The Saga of St Olaf'), which is also the main source of information about the poet's life. Sighvatr's verses are notable for their spontaneity and humour; he rarely used mythological allusions in his poems, reflecting the Christian beliefs of his patrons.

Sigmund Legendary king and warrior, the eldest son of Volsung and his wife Liod. By his second wife Hjordis, Sigmund was the father of SIGURD FAFNISBANE. Sigmund was fatally wounded after ODIN broke his sword in battle shortly before Sigurd's birth.

Sigtuna Founded *c.*970 on the northern shores of Lake Mälaren in central SWEDEN as a royal, administrative, ecclesiastical and commercial centre, Sigtuna was the successor to BIRKA, which was abandoned around this time. The TOWN was laid out on a regular plan along a central street. Around 100 long narrow tenements fronted the street on either side; at the centre was an enclosure for the royal residence. Sigtuna was the site of Sweden's earliest mint, and a centre for high-status craftworking. The town's function as an ecclesiastical centre is emphasized by COINS issued by king OLOF SKÖTKONUNG *c.*995 bearing the legend 'God's Sigtuna', and by its seven CHURCHES – the pagan cult centre at nearby UPPSALA was still flourishing a century later. For a short period in the 11th century Sigtuna was the seat of a BISHOPRIC.

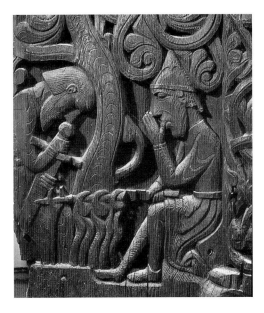

Sigurd Fafnisbane (Sigurd the Volsung) A popular legendary hero and the central character of *VOLSUNGA SAGA*. Sigurd was the posthumous son of the hero SIGMUND. His foster-father REGIN told Sigurd the story of OTTAR'S RANSOM and encouraged him to kill the dragon FAFNIR, who guarded the gold, plotting to murder him afterwards. After killing Fafnir, Sigurd learned of Regin's treacherous intentions and killed him too, acquiring the gold for himself. But the gold had been cursed by its original owner, the DWARF ANDVARI, and Sigurd was now doomed. Having proved himself a great warrior, Sigurd became betrothed to the VALKYRIE BRYNHILD. After drinking a magic potion administered by queen Grimhild, Sigurd forgot about Brynhild and married the queen's daughter Gudrun instead. Gudrun's brother Gunnar then sought Sigurd's help in winning the hand of Brynhild because he was unable to ride through the magic fire that surrounded her hall. Sigurd and Gunnar exchanged shapes by magic, and Sigurd successfully wooed Brynhild for his brother-in-law. Brynhild later learned that she had been deceived, and in her anger ordered Gunnar to kill Sigurd. Gunnar persuaded his brother Guttorm to do the deed and he fatally injured Sigurd, though only at the cost of his own life. Heartbroken, Brynhild immolated herself on Sigurd's funeral pyre. Scenes from the story of Sigurd were popular subjects for wood- and stone-carvers in the late Viking Age, featuring on the 10th-century MANX CROSSES, the 10th-century Norse cross at Halton in Lancashire, several Swedish rune-stones and, in wood, the portals of the 12th-century stave CHURCH at Hylestad in NORWAY.

Sigurd the Mighty (d. *c.*892) Earl of ORKNEY. According to Icelandic SAGA traditions, HARALD FAIRHAIR of NORWAY granted ROGNVALD OF MØRE an earldom in SCOTLAND's northern isles in compensation for the death of his son. Rognvald, who wished to concentrate on his own earldom of Møre, immediately passed the title on to his brother Sigurd. Sigurd allied with THORSTEIN THE RED, a Viking ruler from the Hebrides, to conquer Caithness and Sutherland on the Scottish mainland. Suspecting treachery of the Scots at a peace meeting, Sigurd killed 'earl' Maelbrigte, cut off his head as a trophy, and strapped it to his saddle. While riding home a tooth sticking out of Maelbrigte's head is said to have scratched Sigurd's leg and he died soon afterwards from blood-poisoning. He was succeeded by his son Guttorm, who ruled for only one year before dying without issue.

Sigurd the Stout (d. 1014) Earl of ORKNEY (r. *c.*985–1014). Sigurd was the son of earl Hlodver of Orkney and his wife Eithne, an Irish princess. His grandfather was THORFINN SKULLSPLITTER. Apart from Orkney and Shetland, Sigurd controlled Caithness and Sutherland, and in 989 he raided the Hebrides and the Isle of MAN, killing Godfred, a Norse king of Man, and laying a tribute on the islands. Sigurd successfully defended his mainland possessions against Scottish attack, defeating Finnlaech, the ruler of Moray, at Skitten Mire in Caithness. He strengthened his position with marriage alliances, marrying the daughter of 'king Malcolm of Scots' (Malcolm II?) himself and marrying his sister Svanlaug to earl Gilli, the Norse ruler of the Hebrides who became his tributary. When OLAF TRYGGVASON visited Orkney in 995, he forced Sigurd to submit to baptism at swordpoint and to surrender his son Hvelp as a HOSTAGE to guarantee his loyalty. Hvelp died soon afterwards

Coin of Sihtric Silkbeard, king of Dublin, the first ruler in Ireland to issue coinage.

Opposite, left: A scene from the legend of Sigurd Fafnisbane, from Hylestad stave church, Norway, showing Sigurd roasting Fafnir's heart; when Sigurd licks the blood from his fingers, he learns to understand the speech of birds; when two birds tell him of Regin's treacherous intentions, Sigurd kills him (*right*).

and Sigurd withdrew his allegiance and renounced CHRISTIANITY. In 1014 SIHTRIC SILKBEARD of DUBLIN persuaded Sigurd to join the alliance with Leinster against the high king BRIAN BORU and was killed at the battle of CLONTARF. According to the Icelandic saga traditions, Sigurd owned a magic raven banner, which brought victory from ODIN but also guaranteed death for whoever carried it. At Clontarf, as none of his men were willing to carry it, Sigurd carried the banner himself and fell with it wrapped around his body. Sigurd's lands were divided after his death between his sons Sumarlidi, Einar and Brusi.

Sihtric Cáech ('squinty') (d. 927) King of DUBLIN (r. 917–21); king of YORK (r. 921–7). Sihtric was a grandson of IVAR I of Dublin. With his brother RAGNALD, he was one of the leaders of the great FLEET that arrived at WATERFORD in 914 to re-establish Viking power in IRELAND. In 917 Sihtric recaptured Dublin from the Irish, and in 919 he defeated an Irish counter-attack at Islandbridge, killing the Uí Néill king NIALL GLÚNDUBH and five other kings. In 921, Sihtric succeeded Ragnald as king of York, giving up Dublin to his brother GUTHFRITH. At Tamworth in 926, Sihtric agreed a treaty with ATHELSTAN of WESSEX, accepted baptism and was given the king's sister Eadgyth in marriage. The following year Sihtric died and Athelstan annexed York, driving out Sihtric's young son OLAF SIHTRICSSON and Guthfrith, who had arrived from Dublin to take up the KINGSHIP.

Sihtric Silkbeard (Sihtric Olafsson) (d. 1042) King of DUBLIN (r. 989–1036). An astute ruler, Sihtric struggled, ultimately unsuccessfully, to maintain the political autonomy of Dublin against increasingly

powerful Irish kings. The son of OLAF SIHTRICSSON, Sihtric succeeded to the KINGSHIP of Dublin as an underking of the Uí Néill high king Maél Sechnaill II in 989. In 997 BRIAN BORU of Munster and Maél Sechnaill divided IRELAND between them, and Dublin came under the overlordship of Brian. Fearing a loss of autonomy, Sihtric allied with Leinster in 999, only to be soundly defeated by Brian, who then occupied Dublin. Sihtric submitted, was reinstated as a tributary king, and married one of Brian's daughters (Brian had recently married Sihtric's mother Gormflaith, so he was already his step-father). In 1012 Sihtric rebelled with Maél Mórda of Leinster, and the following year Brian unsuccessfully laid siege to Dublin. In 1014 Sihtric engineered the coalition between Maél Mórda and SIGURD THE STOUT of ORKNEY, which was defeated by Brian at CLONTARF. Brian's death in the battle and the collapse of the Munster hegemony in Ireland brought little benefit to Sihtric, for in 1015 Maél Sechnaill reasserted his lordship of Dublin. Sihtric continued to play a full part in the internecine struggles of the Irish kingdom, but his forces were defeated as often as they won, and by the time he abdicated in favour of his nephew Echmarcach mac Ragnaill in 1036 Dublin was a minor power. In 997 Sihtric became the first ruler in Ireland to issue coinage (based on English COINS). A devout Christian, he visited Rome in 1028 and is credited with founding Christ Church cathedral in Dublin in 1030; one of his daughters became a nun. He was murdered in the course of a second journey to Rome in 1042.

skaldic verse Skaldic verse is Old Norse poetry that is not mythological (*see* EDDAS); the name is derived from the Old Norse word *skald*, meaning poet. Skaldic verse was composed and transmitted orally,

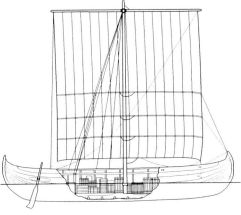

Skuldelev 1, a deep-sea trader.

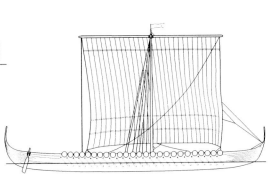

Skuldelev 2, a *drakkar*.

and only one verse, on a rune-stone at Karlevi on the Swedish island of Öland, has survived in a written form from the Viking Age itself. The majority of skaldic verse is preserved in the form of quotations in SAGAS and other prose literature written after the end of the Viking Age. Skaldic verse was typically composed in eight-line stanzas and used ornate metres, the most important of which are *dróttkvætt* ('court measure') and *hrynhent* ('accentuated verse'), both of which involved internal rhymes and consonances in alternate alliterative lines. Skaldic verse also makes extravagant use of kennings, conventional metaphorical compound names for something, for example *benregn* ('bone-rain'), meaning 'blood'. Most skalds were male, but a few female ones (*skáldkonur*) are known. Skalds enjoyed considerable prestige in Scandinavian society and several, including EGIL SKALLA-GRÍMSSON and Kormák Ogmundarson (d. 970), were considered worthy subjects for sagas. There are several subgenres of skaldic verse. The most important are panegyrics (*drápur*) composed from the 9th century through to the 13th by court poets, such as SIGHVATR THÓRÐARSON, in honour of kings and chieftains. These poems catalogue the victories and heroic deeds of the subject, often (to modern taste) in gratuitously bloodthirsty detail, and praise him for his generosity and valour. Most panegyrics were composed to be recited in the presence of the subject at FEASTS and other public occasions. Others are funeral lays, composed after the subject's death as an indirect way of praising his descendants. From a purely historical point of view, the panegyrics are the most important skaldic poetry, as they are often the only contemporary accounts of events in Viking Age Scandinavia. However, due allowance has to be made for the possibility, even

likelihood, of bias and exaggeration as the poet sought to present his patron's achievements in the best possible light. There is also the question of the reliability of oral transmission, sometimes over several centuries, until the poems were committed to writing. Other forms of skaldic verse include shield-poems (describing painted shields), love poems, heroic narratives and *lausavísur*, occasional verses on everyday subjects. Love poems were illegal in ICELAND because of the possibility that they might contain spells.

L. M. Hollander (trans.), *The Skalds: A Selection of Their Poems, with Introduction and Notes* (2nd edition, Ithaca, 1968); E. O. G. Turville-Petre, *Scaldic Poetry* (Oxford, 1976).

Skien A small Viking Age settlement west of KAUPANG, Skien stands on an isthmus between two lakes and can be reached easily by ship from Oslo Fjord. It probably served as an export harbour for iron and hone stones brought from the interior of Telemark.

Skrælings The Norse name used to describe the native peoples of North America and GREENLAND, whether American Indian or ESKIMO. The name may be related to the modern Norwegian *skræla*, meaning 'scream', or to the Icelandic *skrælna*, meaning 'shrink' (the Eskimo are described in Norse sources as being short). In modern Icelandic, *skræling* has come to mean 'churl' or 'surly ill-bred person'.

Skuldelev ships Five 11th-century Viking SHIPS discovered at Skuldelev in Roskilde Fjord, DENMARK. The ships had been filled with boulders and deliberately sunk to form a blockage in the fjord. Discovery of the ships in the 1960s revolutionized knowledge of Viking shipbuilding, showing that

Skuldelev 3, a small trade ship.

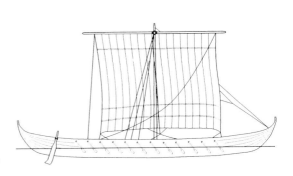

Skuldelev 5, a small warship.

there had been a far greater diversity of ship types than had previously been suspected. All the ships were clinker-built using iron rivets, with double-ended hulls, side rudders, a single mast and curved stems. Two of the wrecks were warships, two, trading ships, and one, a large multi-purpose boat.

Wreck 1 is a sturdy broad-beamed seagoing trader, thought to be an example of a type known from SAGA literature as a *knarr*. The ship measured 15.9 metres in length, 4.8 metres broad and 2.2 metres deep and had a cargo capacity estimated at 24 tonnes. The ship is made of a mixture of pine, oak and lime woods, suggesting that it was built in NORWAY. A replica of Skuldelev 1 circumnavigated the world in 1984–6.

Wreck 2 is a large longship (initially thought to be two ships) around 30 metres in length by 3.7 metres broad and 1.6 metres deep. It probably had thirty pairs of OARS. The mast-step was constructed so that the mast could be lowered at sea, in preparation for joining battle, for example. As the ship was made of oak that had grown in eastern IRELAND, it was probably built at DUBLIN, but repairs using Danish-grown oak show that it had spent much of its working life in Scandinavia. Dendrochronology dates the ship to *c*.1060. Skuldelev 2 is probably an example of the largest class of Viking warship, known in the saga literature as a *drakkar*.

Wreck 3 was a small trading ship, built of oak, 13.85 metres long, 3.6 metres broad and 1.3 metres deep, with a cargo capacity of 4.5 tonnes. The ship had provision for seven oars, which would have been used for manoeuvring in harbour. This was the most complete of the Skuldelev wrecks, around seventy-five per cent of the original timbers having survived. Sea trials with a replica of Skuldelev 3 have shown it to have been a seaworthy and relatively swift vessel.

Wreck 5 (wreck 4 was found to be part of wreck 2) was a small longship of twelve or thirteen pairs of oars, 17.2 metres long by 2.6 metres broad and 1.1 metres deep. The ship was built mostly of oak but with some hull planks of ash and pine. Dendrochronology shows that the oak grew in Denmark and was felled *c*.1030–40. Skuldelev 5 had a long service life and had been repaired many times: it is thought to have been maintained by a local chieftain for coastal defence. Sea trials with a replica show that Skuldelev 5 drew only 50 centimetres of water, even when fully loaded, making it an ideal ship for raiding in the shallow Baltic Sea or up rivers like the Seine or Rhine, but, because of its narrow hull and low freeboard, it was very vulnerable to swamping in rough seas. In good conditions Skuldelev 5 could have reached about 9 knots under sail, and about 5 under oars.

Wreck 6 was a large boat, 11.6 metres long, 2.5 metres broad and 1.16 metres deep. The boat was originally built with only six strakes a side, but a seventh was added later to increase the freeboard and to improve its seaworthiness. The hull planks were made of pine, the keel, of oak, and the frames, of alder, pine and birch. The boat may have been a small TRADE ship or fishing boat and was built in Sognefjord, NORWAY. *See also* SEA BARRIERS; SHIPS AND SHIPBUILDING.

O. Olsen and O. Crumlin-Pedersen, *Five Viking Ships from Roskilde Fjord* (Copenhagen, 1978).

slavery Slavery was common in Viking Age Scandinavia and in areas overseas that were settled by Scandinavians during that period, such as the Scottish Hebrides. Most slaves were either captives from overseas or, as slavery was hereditary, their descendants. Scandinavians could also be enslaved

Odin's eight-legged horse Sleipnir,
depicted on a Gotland picture stone.

for crime or debt, or if they were captured in war. Debt slavery was usually for a fixed term only. In LAW, a slave or thrall (ON *thræll*) was simply property. Like livestock, they could be bought and sold or offered as payment for debts. Until the Christian period it was not a crime for an owner to injure or kill a slave, and it was not uncommon for slaves, especially female ones, to be sacrificed and included as grave offerings. Arab accounts of RUS merchants indicate that slave girls were frequently used for the sexual gratification of their masters. Someone who killed another person's slave paid the owner compensation linked to the market value of the slave. Owners were liable to pay compensation for crimes committed by their slaves. Slaves appear to have been engaged on the same kind of work as free labourers and craftsmen and WOMEN. Slaves on their way to market were not treated especially well – the missionary St ANSGAR saw slaves chained together by the neck when he visited HEDEBY in the 9th century – but skilled or loyal slaves could live well and enjoy respect, and be allowed to work for their freedom. After the introduction of CHRISTIANITY, some efforts were made to improve the legal position of slaves. For example, in ICELAND it was forbidden for an owner to kill a slave during Lent. The Church encouraged manumission of slaves as an act of piety, but never condemned the institution itself. Slavery died out in Scandinavia between the 12th and 14th centuries. *See also* SLAVE TRADE.

R. Karras, *Slavery and Society in Medieval Scandinavia* (New Haven, Connecticut, 1988).

slave trade Slaves were one of the major commodities of Viking commerce. Viking involvement in the slave trade is well documented in contemporary Irish, Icelandic and Arabic sources, though there is little evidence for it from English and Frankish sources. Major slave raids are recorded on Armagh in 869, 895, 921 and 933. A 9th-century monk called Findan was captured by Vikings at a FEAST, sold and resold, before making his escape in the ORKNEY Islands. Another Irish source gives a humorous account of an Irishman called Murchad, who was captured by Vikings and sold to a nunnery in NORTHUMBRIA. After seducing all the nuns, he was recaptured by Vikings and sold to a widow in Saxony, whom he also seduced! After many adventures Murchad eventually returned home to be reunited with his family. More typical of the experience of Irish (and Scottish) slaves captured by Vikings were the many who, according to the *LANDNÁMABÓK* and other Icelandic sources, finished up living permanently in NORWAY and ICELAND. Slaves captured by Vikings in other areas were also taken to IRELAND, though it is not clear how they were marketed. Moorish slaves, described as 'blue men', were taken to Ireland in the 860s by Vikings following a raid in the MEDITERRANEAN, and English, Welsh and Pictish prisoners were taken as slaves to DUBLIN after raids in Britain in 870. Slave raiding also took place in the Baltic. Around 1075 ADAM OF BREMEN records that the DANES of Sjælland were licensed by king Harald III to raid the WENDS for slaves and plunder. Adam notes that the Sjællanders abused their licences, capturing and selling Danes as well. To judge from the detailed 10th-century accounts of the Arab Ibn Fadlan and the Persian Ibn Rusta, it was in eastern Europe where Viking slave-trading was most intense. Along with furs, the RUS exchanged large numbers of slaves with Arab and Bulgar merchants at markets on the River Volga in return for silver. Quantities of

Snorri Sturluson, the greatest
literary figure of medieval Iceland.

both slaves and furs may have been acquired by peaceful TRADE from the Slavs and FINNS, but others were acquired from them as tribute by the Scandinavian rulers of KIEV and NOVGOROD, and by slave raiding. The relative lack of evidence for Viking slave raiding in FRANCIA and ENGLAND may be a consequence of the greater wealth of these areas compared with Ireland and RUSSIA: it may often have been more lucrative to RANSOM prisoners than sell them as slaves. *See also* SLAVERY.

Slavs *see* WENDS

Sleipnir A mythological eight-legged horse owned by the Scandinavian high god ODIN. He was the fastest horse alive and could surmount any obstacle, being able to run as well on air and water as he could on land. Sleipnir was sired by the stallion Svadilfari on the god LOKI, who had turned himself into a mare to entice the stallion away from his master, a GIANT working on the walls of ASGARD. As a result, the giant completed his work late and the gods refused to pay him. Odin's son HERMOD rode Sleipnir to HEL to try to obtain BALDER's restoration to life.

Snæbjorn Galti (*fl. c.*978) Icelandic navigator who led the first, unsuccessful attempt to settle GREENLAND in *c.*978. Snæbjorn's party attempted to settle on the bleak Gunnbjorn Skerries, discovered more than fifty years previously by Gunnbjorn Ulf-Krakuson, off Greenland's ice-bound east coast. The settlers fell out with one another almost immediately, and after a desperate winter Snæbjorn was murdered and the settlement abandoned.

snekke ('snake') A common term used rather imprecisely in Norse literature and poetry to describe a longship. The term serves not so much to classify a particular type or size of longship as to convey an image of a slim, fast war galley, but it is not used to describe the great royal ships – the *drakkars* – of the late Viking Age. A similar term *esnecca*, probably derived from Old Norse, was used to describe war galleys in ENGLAND after the Norman Conquest.

Snorri Sturluson (*c.*1179–1241) The most outstanding medieval Icelandic poet and historian, Snorri was the author of two major works, *HEIMSKRINGLA*, a monumental SAGA history of the kings of NORWAY, and the *Prose EDDA*, a handbook for poets that contains a wealth of information about pagan Scandinavian mythology. He was possibly also the author of *EGILS SAGA*, about the life of the 10th-century Icelandic SKALDIC poet EGIL SKALLA-GRÍMSSON. Snorri was a member of one of the wealthiest and most influential Icelandic FAMILIES of his day, and he played an active, if reluctant, part in the political power struggles that eventually destroyed the Icelandic Commonwealth. He served three terms as LAWSPEAKER at the ALTHING, and was not above abusing his legal expertise to further his ambitions and those of his friends. Early in his career, Snorri courted the approval of Norwegian rulers and magnates by sending them praise-poems, and he visited the Norwegian royal court in 1218–20 and 1237–8. Unfortunately for Snorri, his close friendship with the treasonous jarl Skúli earned him the enmity of king Håkon IV, at whose instigation he was murdered in his home at Reykjaholt on 22 September 1241.

soapstone Soapstone, or steatite, is a compact form of talc, a magnesium-silicate mineral. Veins of

Soapstone bowls, from
Jarlshof, Shetland.

soapstone are common in NORWAY, western
SWEDEN and the Shetland Islands, where they were
extensively exploited in the Viking Age. Soft and
easily carved, soapstone was used to make cooking
pots and lamps, spindle-whorls, loom weights,
fishing-net sinkers and moulds for casting metals.
Soapstone vessels were exported throughout
Scandinavia and Scandinavian-settled areas to the
west, where they were preferred to POTTERY for
cooking because they were tough, easy to clean,
distributed heat well and did not taint the flavour of
FOOD as unglazed pottery can. Soapstone bowls were
also exported to Poland and Germany. After the
introduction of CHRISTIANITY, soapstone was widely
used in Norway for decorative sculptures in
CHURCHES, especially at TRONDHEIM.

social classes Scandinavian society in the Viking
Age was divided into the free and the unfree (*see*
SLAVERY). Freemen shared the right to bear arms and
to speak at the local THING, and had the protection of
the LAW. But Scandinavian society was by no means
egalitarian. This social inequality was reflected in the
scale of compensation paid to compound a murder:
the wealthier and more influential the victim, the
greater the amount paid to his FAMILY by the guilty
party. Only in ICELAND were all freemen treated
equally in this respect. As legal judgments had to
be enforced by the individuals concerned, poorer
freemen were at a disadvantage unless they had the
support of a powerful chieftain who could force the
guilty party to comply. Such support always came
at a price, of course. Status also had other legal
implications. In DENMARK and SWEDEN only
landowners could serve as jurymen, for example,
while in NORWAY a landowner's oath was taken
more seriously than a landless man's. Though there

were notable exceptions, WOMEN's status depended
on their husbands': they had fewer legal rights
than men and no political rights. Viking society
was hierarchical, but it was far from static: the
ambitious, able or daring could increase their
wealth and status by means of piracy or trading,
or by entering royal service.

The most numerous class of freemen were
farmers, the *bóndi*. Freeholders were distinguished
from tenant farmers by the name *óðalsbóndi* (from
ÓÐAL, or 'allodial land') or, in Norway, *hauldr*. There
was also a class of farm managers called *bryti*.
These were probably originally slaves, but by the
end of the Viking Age *bryti* in royal or aristocratic
service could enjoy high status and wealth.
Respected freemen of higher, but less than
aristocratic, rank were described as *drengr* (literally
'lad') or *thegn* ('thane' or 'gentleman'). Some
freemen who neither owned nor tenanted land
were employed as farm labourers. Others made
a living as full-time craftsmen in house-building,
shipbuilding and metalwork, but these were few
in number in an overwhelmingly agrarian society
where most people had to be jacks-of-all-trades.
Poets, lawyers, doctors, priests, stone-carvers and
most warriors and merchants were all part-timers
whose main occupation was farming.

The hereditary aristocracy exercised considerable
local influence, playing a leading role at the local and
regional *things*. Its power came from landownership
and from offering protection to less-powerful men in
return for their political and military support. Local
chieftains, such as the *hersar* in Norway, formed the
lowest rank of the aristocracy. Later known as *lendr
maðr* ('landed men'), they exercised authority on the
king's behalf, had high rank in the HIRÐ, and acted
as local military commanders in wartime. Higher

A soapstone mould used by an opportunistic metal-caster to make both Christian and pagan (Thor's hammer) amulets.

sums of compensation had to be paid to their families if they were killed or injured. In pagan times the chieftains saw to the correct observance of religious festivals, and after the conversion to CHRISTIANITY they built and maintained the local CHURCH. In Iceland, the local chieftains (GOÐAR) remained the leaders of society until the 13th century, but in Scandinavia they lost much of their autonomy during the Viking Age due to the growth of royal power. Elsewhere in Scandinavia there was a small class of great magnates who bore the title *jarl* ('earl'), which probably originally meant simply 'prominent man'. In Norway, the compensation payable for the killing or injuring of a jarl was twice that of an ordinary chieftain and half that of a king. The greatest jarls, those of HLAÐIR in Norway and ORKNEY, were considerable rulers in their own right who exercised virtually royal powers over wide territories. Resistance by the jarls of Hlaðir to the centralization of royal power proved a serious obstacle to the creation of a unified Norwegian kingdom. *See also* KINGSHIP.

Somerled (d. 1164) A chieftain of Argyll of mixed Gaelic and Norse descent, he married Ragnhild, the daughter of king Olaf of MAN *c.*1140. In January 1156 he defeated Olaf's son and successor Godred II in a naval battle off Islay to win control of the southern Hebrides. In 1158 he seized Man, and Godred fled to NORWAY. Somerled acknowledged the sovereignty of the Norwegian king over his possessions, bringing him into conflict with the Scots king Malcolm IV: he was killed near Renfrew in 1164 while raiding lowland Scotland. Godred recovered control of Man a year later, but the southern Hebrides remained in the possession of Somerled's descendants until

1249. Somerled's career is a sign of the gradual assimilation of the Norse settlers of Man and the Hebrides into the native Gaelic population.

Stamford Bridge, battle of (25 September 1066) The last major battle of the Viking Age in ENGLAND. Following the death of king Edward the Confessor, HAROLD GODWINSON was elected king by the English, but the throne was also claimed by WILLIAM THE CONQUEROR of NORMANDY and HARALD HARDRADA, king of NORWAY. Supported by Harold's exiled brother Tostig, Harald invaded England with 300 SHIPS, and defeated the earls Edwin and Morcar at Fulford Gate near York on 20 September. Harold was already hurrying north by forced marches, and on 25 September he surprised the Viking ARMY camped at Stamford Bridge, 6 miles east of York. The Viking army was annihilated. Both Harald and Tostig were killed and, according to the ANGLO-SAXON CHRONICLE, only twenty-four ships were needed to take the survivors home. The losses were so severe that it would be the end of the century before a Norwegian king could again take a major force overseas. Two days later, Harold heard that William had invaded, and he marched his exhausted army south to defeat at Hastings on 14 October. Hastings was not an easy victory for the Normans: had William invaded before Harald he would have met the full might of Harold's army and quite probably lost. Stamford Bridge therefore had decisive consequences for English and European history.

Staraja Ladoga Known to the Vikings as Aldeigjuborg, Staraja Ladoga was a market and craft centre on the River Volkhov, within easy reach of Lake Ladoga, north-west RUSSIA. Staraja Ladoga was founded in the mid-8th century and was the main

centre of Viking TRADE in northern Russia until the rise of NOVGOROD and KIEV in the later 9th century. From the outset, the TOWN had a mixed population of Scandinavians, Slavs and FINNS. Evidence from the many cemeteries surrounding the town suggest that the different ethnic groups were segregated. Excavations have revealed evidence of a wide range of craft production: jewelry- and glass-making, blacksmithing, bronze-casting, amber- and bone-working. Some of these manufactured products were traded with the Finns for furs, which in turn were sold on to Arab merchants. Connections with the Muslim world were established early: one hoard of silver DIRHEMS dates from the 780s. Much of the town was destroyed by fire in the 860s, perhaps as a result of a violent attack.

steatite *see* SOAPSTONE

Stiklestad, battle of (29 July 1030) In 1028 the leading Norwegian chieftains accepted CNUT as king, forcing OLAF HARALDSSON into exile. In 1030 Olaf raised an ARMY of 480 men in SWEDEN and returned to NORWAY, where he was joined by around 3,000 supporters. The Norwegian chieftains raised an army of 14,000 peasant levies, and brought Olaf to battle at Stiklestad, about 80 kilometres north-east of TRONDHEIM. Olaf's smaller army was overwhelmed and he himself was killed. Miracles, reported to have taken place both before and after the battle, were attributed to Olaf, whose sanctity was soon proclaimed.

stone-carving Scandinavians had no strong traditions of stone-carving or sculpture before the end of the Viking Age. Patterns and pictures portrayed on stone were either simply inscribed

on a flat surface, such as those on 10th- and 11th-century runic memorials in SWEDEN, or carved in a low relief, as on the 7th- and 8th-century PICTURE STONES from GOTLAND and the spectacular 10th-century royal memorial stones at JELLING in DENMARK. In both cases, brightly coloured paint was used to highlight the design. True three-dimensional sculpture did not appear in Scandinavia until the 12th century.

Scandinavians who settled in the British Isles came into contact with peoples that had long-established traditions of stone sculpture. As the settlers converted to CHRISTIANITY, they became patrons of native stone-sculptors, who produced for them grave memorials and crosses incorporating both native and Scandinavian, Christian and pagan, motifs and figures. It is not clear to what extent Scandinavian settlers themselves took up the art of stone sculpture, but the name of one 10th-century Norse stone sculptor, Gaut Björnsson, is known from the Isle of MAN (*see* MANX CROSSES). The greatest concentrations of Scandinavian-inspired Viking Age stone sculptures in the British Isles are found in Yorkshire and north-west ENGLAND. Among the finest of these is the cross from Gosforth in Cumbria, which symbolically contrasts scenes of the Crucifixion and Resurrection with pagan scenes from RAGNAROK. Also of note are the distinctive and widespread HOGBACK tombstones, which were shaped like Viking longhouses. Scandinavian ART STYLES continued to influence English sculpture, even in areas that had not seen Viking settlement, into the early 12th century.

Stöng Viking Age farmstead in south-east ICELAND. Stöng was occupied from the earliest stages of the settlement of Iceland until it was buried in layers of

Opposite: Reconstruction of the prosperous Viking Age farm at Stöng in Iceland.

The religious centre of the pagan Svear, Gamla Uppsala, central Sweden.

volcanic ash from an eruption of Mount Hekla in 1104 and abandoned. Because the turf-and-stone walls were preserved by the ash, it has been possible to reconstruct the farmstead in some detail. The farmhouse was a long two-roomed hall with stone foundations; its turf walls and roof were lined with wood for insulation, a common feature of later medieval Icelandic housing. Each room had sleeping benches arranged around a central hearth. Two small annexes were used for processing wool. There was a separate byre with cattle stalls, a smithy for working local bog iron, a barn and a livestock enclosure.

Storhaug ship burial The oldest known Norwegian SHIP BURIAL, discovered in 1885 in Avaldsnes on Karmøy, western NORWAY. Thought to date from the 9th century when excavated, radiocarbon dating of the ship's timbers has shown that the burial probably took place in the 7th century. The burial's rich furnishings, which included a gold arm ring, WEAPONS and gaming pieces of GLASS and AMBER, were appropriate for a powerful chieftain. The vessel itself was poorly preserved, but it was probably a large rowing ship, 20 metres or more in length.

strandhögg A small-scale beach raid specifically to seize cattle and other provisions, practised widely by pirates and other seafarers throughout the Viking Age in Scandinavia. Though neither economically ruinous nor inevitably violent, such raids were always an annoyance for the victims, and as royal authority increased in the 10th and 11th centuries the practice was gradually suppressed.

Strathclyde British (i.e. Welsh-speaking) kingdom of south-west SCOTLAND, founded in the 5th century following the Roman withdrawal from Britain. The kingdom survived attacks by NORTHUMBRIA in the 7th century, but after OLAF, the Norse king of DUBLIN, sacked its capital Dumbarton in 870–1 it fell increasingly under the domination of the Scots. Strathclyde's last Welsh-speaking king, Owain the Bald, was killed in 1018, and the kingdom was finally absorbed by the Scots in 1124; the Welsh language died out there a few decades later.

sun stone (*sólarsteinn*) A navigational device mentioned in *Hauksbók* and several other medieval Icelandic sources. It has been suggested that it was made from feldspar or calcite, common minerals in ICELAND and NORWAY, which polarize light, so allowing the position of the sun to be located even when it is covered by cloud. However, the polarizing effect can be seen only if the sky overhead itself is cloudless, so the sun stone would have been useless on overcast days and unnecessary on clear ones. There is only one record of a sun stone being used, in a legendary story about OLAF HARALDSSON. *See also* NAVIGATION.

Svear The major people of central SWEDEN, known from the 1st century AD when the Roman historian Tacitus recorded that they were well known for their large FLEETS of rowing SHIPS. The heartland of the Svear was around Lake Mälaren and UPPSALA. Spectacular royal and aristocratic burials at VALSGÄRDE, VENDEL and Uppsala are evidence of the emergence of a powerful royal dynasty among the Svear in the 6th and 7th centuries. This is probably to be identified with the semi-legendary YNGLING DYNASTY, which is known from Anglo-Saxon and later Scandinavian sources. Little is known about the political development of the Svear during the Viking

Coin of Svein Forkbeard,
king of Denmark and, for
a few weeks of England.

Age, but they had a close, probably dominant,
relationship with the neighbouring GÖTAR. The
Svear king OLOF SKÖTKONUNG (r. 995–1022)
became the first known also to have ruled the Götar,
and thereafter the two peoples usually shared the
same king until they were formally united in 1172.

Svein Alfivason (*c*.1014–36) King of NORWAY
(r. 1030–5). Svein was a son of CNUT by his English
concubine ÆLFGIFU (Alfiva). When Cnut married
EMMA of NORMANDY in 1018, Svein was sent with
his mother to DENMARK. In 1030 Cnut appointed
Svein king of Norway, under the regency of his
mother. Svein's rule was unpopular on account of
new TAXES and the preferment of DANES over
Norwegians, although his mother got most of the
blame because of Svein's youth. When OLAF
HARALDSSON's son MAGNUS THE GOOD returned
from exile in RUSSIA in 1035, Svein fled to Denmark,
where he died early in 1036.

Svein Asleifarson (d. 1171) One of the last old-
fashioned Viking freebooters. Svein raided widely in
the Hebrides, IRELAND and WALES with a band of
around eighty warriors, which he kept at his hall on
Gairsay in the ORKNEY Islands. According to the
ORKNEYINGA SAGA, Svein led two Viking raids a year,
which he fitted into the quiet periods of the farming
year: a 'spring trip', between sowing and the
beginning of haymaking in midsummer, and an
'autumn trip', between the grain harvest and
midwinter. Svein began his lawless career after he
was outlawed *c*.1136 for his part in a FAMILY blood
feud. He was sometimes useful to the Orkney
earls as a 'hit man' and was killed in 1171 during
a failed attempt to recapture DUBLIN from
the Anglo-Normans.

Svein Estrithson (Svein Ulfsson) (d. 1074)
King of DENMARK (r. 1047–74). Svein was the last
reigning Scandinavian king to lead a full-scale
invasion of ENGLAND. A nephew of CNUT (his
mother was Cnut's sister Estrith), Svein was
appointed regent of Denmark by MAGNUS THE
GOOD in 1042. He rebelled almost immediately,
but was driven into exile in SWEDEN. There, in
1044, he allied with HARALD HARDRADA, who had
returned from the east to seek a share of Magnus's
Norwegian-Danish kingdom. Magnus broke up
the alliance by offering Harald a share of NORWAY,
but Svein continued to resist. On Magnus's death,
Svein immediately seized power in Denmark. For
the next sixteen years Harald, now sole king of
Norway, inflicted defeat after defeat on Svein, but
he continued to resist doggedly. In the end Harald
gave up and recognized Svein as king of Denmark in
1064. In 1069–70 Svein and his son Cnut (CNUT II)
supported an English rebellion against WILLIAM THE
CONQUEROR, but despite committing a force of
more than 200 SHIPS they were unwilling to face
William in battle and achieved little. Svein was
succeeded by his son Harald III.

Svein Forkbeard (Svein Haraldsson) (d. 1014) King
of DENMARK (r. 987–1014) and, for five weeks in
1013–14, king of ENGLAND. Svein seized power from
his father HARALD BLUETOOTH in 987. Svein's reign
saw a resurgence of Viking raids against England
and he himself led raids in 991 (probably) and 994.
For the next five years Svein was distracted by OLAF
TRYGGVASON's seizure of power in NORWAY. He
allied with his stepson, the Swedish king OLOF
SKÖTKONUNG, to support the pro-Danish jarl ERIK
of HLAÐIR against Olaf. Svein's policy was crowned
with success when Erik defeated Olaf at the battle

Rus cavalry under Svyatoslav I invade Bulgaria in 971, from a Byzantine manuscript.

of Svöld in 1000. Svein led new raids to England in 1003–4, according to later medieval sources, to avenge the death of his sister, who was killed in 1002 during the St Brice's Day Massacre, and in 1006–7. On both occasions he was bought off with huge payments of Danegeld. When Svein next returned to England in 1013 it was not Danegeld he had in mind but conquest. English defences had been getting increasingly disorganized in the previous four years under the impact of continuous attacks by Thorkell the Tall, and it may be that Svein's timing was simply opportunistic. However, it is just as likely that Svein was anxious as to what a skilled military leader like Thorkell, who was becoming enormously rich on Danegeld, might do when he finally came home. Despite the support of Thorkell, English resistance collapsed quickly after Svein's arrival. By the end of the year the English king Æthelred II had fled into exile in Normandy and Svein had been accepted as king of England. Svein's triumph was short-lived: in February 1014 he fell ill and died at Gainsborough in Lincolnshire, and the English called Æthelred back from exile.

Svein's frequent campaigns abroad were made possible by his unquestioned authority in Denmark, and he was able to allow the fortifications that his father had built in the country to decay. Svein was the first Scandinavian ruler to issue coins bearing his own name. He was succeeded in Denmark by his son Harald II (r. 1014–18), and a younger son, Cnut, inherited his claim to England.

Svein Håkonsson (d. 1015) Jarl of Hlaðir (r. 1015). Svein was the brother of jarl Erik of Hlaðir. When Erik joined Cnut in England in 1015, Svein was left in charge of Norway. He was defeated at the battle of Nesjar in April that year by Olaf Haraldsson and fled into exile. After a summer leading a Viking raid in Russia, he went to Sweden, where he fell ill and died.

Svyatoslav I (d. 972) The last pagan ruler of the Kievan Rus state (r. 945–72) and the first to bear a Slavic name. The son of prince Igor and his redoubtable wife Olga, Svyatoslav was above all a great warrior leader. Svyatoslav succeeded as ruler while still a child, after his father was killed on a tribute-gathering raid, but his mother was the effective ruler until he came of age. Even then he continued to rely on her to manage the internal affairs of the Kievan state until her death in 969, while he concentrated on an aggressive foreign policy. In 964–5 he defeated the Khazars, destroying their capital Itil on the lower River Volga. Probably as a prelude to this campaign, he also attacked the Volga Bulgars, sacking their capital Bulgar. Encouraged by the Byzantines, Svyatoslav attacked the Danube Bulgars in 967, conquering them by 969. His declared intention to establish a new capital for his empire at Pereyaslavets (now Pereyaslav-Khmelnytsky) on the River Danube led inevitably to war with the Byzantines, who were not about to allow a Bulgar threat to their empire be replaced by one from the Rus. In 971, Svyatoslav was defeated by a Byzantine army under emperor John I Tzimisces in a ferocious battle at Pereyaslavets, and he was forced to abandon his claim to Bulgar territory. In the spring of 972, while he was returning to Kiev with a small retinue, Svyatoslav was ambushed and killed near the River Dnieper rapids by the Pechenegs, who made his skull into a drinking cup. He was succeeded by his son Vladimir. Most of Svyatoslav's conquests were lost soon after his death.

Sweden, kingdom of Sweden was the last of the Scandinavian kingdoms to develop as a unified state. There were two main peoples in Viking Age Sweden: the SVEAR, from whom Sweden (Sverige) takes its name, centred in the region around Lake Mälaren and UPPSALA; and the GÖTAR, to the south around lakes Vänern and Vättern. The relationship between the two peoples was already close at the beginning of the Viking Age. Some kings of the Götar, such as Alrik, who ruled Västergötland c.800, were members of the Svear royal family, while some kings of the Svear may have originated among the Götar. The first king who is known for certain to have ruled both the Svear and the Götar was OLOF SKÖTKONUNG (r. 995–1022), but the two peoples were not permanently united as a single kingdom until 1172. CHRISTIANITY was slower to become established in Sweden than the other Scandinavian countries. The religion was first actively promoted in Sweden by Olof Skötkonung, who founded the country's first BISHOPRIC at Skara in 1014, but the pagan cult centre at Uppsala continued to flourish until the end of the 11th century, and Sweden was not fully Christianized until the end of the 12th century.

tax and tribute There is no evidence of general taxation in Scandinavia during the Viking Age, though by its end, if not before, kings enjoyed the right to hospitality and supplies from their subjects as they travelled around their kingdoms. TOWNS and TRADE were the most lucrative source of taxes for kings. In the late 11th century, many Danish towns paid the *arnegæld* ('hearth tax') to the king as their 'protector'. Kings exacted tolls and taxes on merchants and travellers such as the *LANDAURAR*, a toll of 5 ounces of silver introduced in the late 9th century by king HARALD FAIRHAIR of NORWAY. Institutionalized tribute-gathering was an important source of wealth for chieftains, as well as for kings. A late-10th-century Anglo-Saxon source tells how the Norwegian chieftain-merchant OHTHERE led annual expeditions to northern Norway to collect tribute in furs from the LAPPS, while, according to contemporary Arab writers, the RUS regularly exacted tribute in slaves and other products from the Slavs. In the 9th century, kings of the SVEAR raided the BALTS for tribute. Probably the most successful tribute-gathering exercises were the expeditions against ENGLAND in the late 10th and early 11th centuries, led by OLAF TRYGGVASON and SVEIN FORKBEARD, which forced enormous payments of DANEGELD. Olaf used his takings to finance a successful bid for the Norwegian throne; Svein, to raise further ARMIES to conquer England.

Tettenhall, battle of (5 August 910) In 909 king EDWARD THE ELDER sent forces from WESSEX and MERCIA to ravage the kingdom of YORK. In retaliation, the DANES invaded Mercia in 910. The levies of Mercia and Wessex brought the Danes to battle at Wednesfield near Tettenhall, Staffordshire, on 5 August, inflicting a crushing defeat on them.

A visit to the tax collector, from the Icelandic *Jomsbók*.

A figurine of Thor, the most popular of the Norse pagan gods, from Iceland *c*.1000.

Among the Danish dead were three kings – Eowils, Halfdan and Ivar – and eleven jarls. The disaster paralysed the Danish leadership and left York open for takeover by RAGNALD, brother of king SIHTRIC CÁECH, king of DUBLIN.

things The most important governmental institutions of Viking Age Scandinavia were the assemblies of freemen, or *things*. Every district had its assembly, called the *héraðsthing* ('district *thing*') or alternatively the *allthing*, so-named because all freemen had the right to attend and speak. Issues of more than local concern were debated at regional assemblies such as the Danish *landsthings* ('provincial *things*') or the Norwegian *lögthings* ('law *things*'). These were attended by chosen representatives of the district assemblies. The assemblies had many functions. They made new LAWS, were courts of law, and were the places where public declarations, about inheritance, land transactions or the freeing of slaves, could be made before witnesses. They also provided a forum for political discussion, socializing, business and, in pagan times, religious festivals. The more important assemblies had the right to approve or reject new laws proposed by the king. Meetings were held in the open air, often on a low earth platform surrounded by a ditch. The local chieftains or the king presided over proceedings and the assembly showed its approval for a decision by brandishing WEAPONS (*vápnatak*, 'weapon-taking'). *Things* were also established by Scandinavian settlers overseas. The sites of former assemblies in Scandinavian-settled areas can often be identified by place-names such as TYNWALD (Isle of MAN), Dingwall (Sutherland), Thingwall (Cheshire) and the best known, THINGVELLIR, the seat of the Icelandic national assembly, the ALTHING.

Thingvellir (Thingvöllr) 'Parliament Plain', the spectacular meeting place of the Icelandic ALTHING, in the valley of the River Öxará, 48 kilometres east of Reykjavik. Meetings were held in the open air; people attending the Althing built temporary booths or lived in tents. The main business of the Althing was conducted from two different locations, the *Lögberg* ('Law Rock') and the *Lögrétta* ('Court of Legislature'). The Althing was moved to Reykjavik in 1799.

Thjazi A mythological GIANT. Disguised as an eagle, Thjazi kidnapped LOKI, setting the apples of eternal youth as the price of his RANSOM. Loki arranged for Thjazi to capture IDUN and the apples, but without their rejuvenating powers the gods began to age. Threatened with death by the gods, Loki disguised himself as a falcon, rescued Idun from Thjazi's abode and returned her to ASGARD. When Thjazi discovered his loss he flew after Loki, but the gods burned his wings and killed him when he fell to earth.

Thor The god of physical strength, oaths, thunder and lightning, rain and good weather, Thor was the most popular of the Scandinavian pagan gods during the Viking Age, revered in particular by farmers and sailors: Thor's hammer pendants were commonly worn by Viking Age Scandinavians as good-luck talismans. Using his mighty hammer MJÖLLNIR, Thor defended both gods and humans against the destructive power of the GIANTS. Thor also possessed a magic belt, which doubled his strength, and a pair of iron gloves. He travelled in a chariot that was drawn by goats. Thor was married to Sif, whose hair was made of gold. Unlike the high god ODIN, who was in many ways a frightening and

Gotland picture stone showing
scenes from the stories of Thor
fishing for the Midgard Serpent
(*top and bottom left*) and Tyr
binding Fenrir (*bottom centre*).

unpredictable deity, Thor was unambiguously well disposed towards humans and though quick-tempered he was easily pacified. Thor was thought to be somewhat of an oaf, and many of the myths associated with him highlight in a humorous way the limitations of brute strength.

Many of Thor's exploits involved battles with giants or giantesses. On one occasion the giant Thrym stole Thor's hammer and refused to return it unless he was given the beautiful goddess FREYJA in marriage. To recover the hammer, Thor reluctantly disguised himself as Freyja, covering his face with a bridal veil, and travelled to Thrym's hall in JOTUNHEIM. As soon as the hammer was handed over at the wedding FEAST, Thor threw off his disguise and slaughtered Thrym and his guests. One of the few giants to get the better of Thor was UTGARD-LOKI, who deceived him with magic into believing that his strength had failed him. Thor's most deadly adversary was the mighty MIDGARD SERPENT. Thor went fishing at sea for the serpent with the giant Hymir, using an ox's head for bait. Though Thor hooked the serpent, Hymir panicked at its fearsome appearance and cut the line, so letting it escape. In his anger, Thor threw the giant overboard to drown. At RAGNAROK, Thor will finally kill the Midgard Serpent, but will himself be fatally poisoned by its venom.

Thorfinn Karlsefni (*fl.* early 11th century) A wealthy Icelandic merchant, Karlsefni visited GREENLAND some time after LEIF ERIKSSON had discovered VINLAND. While in Greenland, he married Gudrid, the widow of Leif's brother Thorsteinn, who had been killed on an expedition to Vinland. Karlsefni led a major expedition to Vinland, but returned to Greenland after two winters because of the hostility of the native Indians. While there, Gudrid gave birth to a son, Snorri, the first European to be born in the Americas. Following their return to Greenland, Karlsefni and Gudrid went on a trading voyage to NORWAY, before finally settling in the north of ICELAND.

Thorfinn Skullsplitter (d. *c.*963) Earl of ORKNEY. The son of earl TORF-EINAR, Thorfinn shared the earldom of Orkney with his brothers Arnkel and Erlend, until they were killed alongside ERIK BLOODAXE at Stainmore after his expulsion from YORK in 954. Erik's widow Gunnhild and their sons fled to Orkney, where for a time they took over control of the earldom from Thorfinn. After a few years Gunnhild and her sons moved on to DENMARK, seeking HARALD BLUETOOTH'S support for a bid to win power in NORWAY, and Thorfinn was returned to power. His son and eventual successor Arnfinn was married to Gunnhild's daughter RAGNHILD. Though he was remembered as a great warrior, Thorfinn died in bed and was buried on the island of North Ronaldsay.

Thorfinn the Mighty (*c.*1009–65) Remembered in Norse tradition as the greatest earl of ORKNEY (r. *c.*1020–65). Thorfinn was about five years old when his father SIGURD THE STOUT, earl of Orkney, was killed at the battle of CLONTARF in 1014. The earldom was divided between Sigurd's elder sons, Sumarlidi, Brusi and Einar Falsemouth, while Thorfinn was fostered by Thorkell Amunderson of Sandwick under the protection of the king of Scots. When Sumarlidi died, Einar and Brusi reluctantly granted his share of the earldom to Thorfinn. The relationship between Einar and Thorfinn was always tense, and it ended in violence when Thorkell

The Orkney island of
North Ronaldsay, home
of Thorfinn Skullsplitter.

Amunderson murdered Einar *c.*1020. Thorfinn and
Brusi then shared the earldom peaceably until
Brusi's death *c.*1030–5, after which Thorfinn took
control of the whole earldom. Thorfinn made great
efforts to extend the power of the Orkney earldom
over the Hebrides, and defeated an attempt by the
Scots, under the otherwise unknown Karl
Hundison, to recover control of Caithness and
Sutherland from the Norse at the battle of Torfness
(Tarbat Ness, Easter Ross) *c.*1030–5. After the battle,
Thorfinn ravaged widely in SCOTLAND and probably
also gained control of Ross. In 1042 he raided in
north-west ENGLAND.

In 1037–8 Brusi's son Rognvald returned from
exile in NORWAY to claim a share in the earldom
from Thorfinn. Thorfinn granted Rognvald a
third-share, and the two ruled peacefully for eight
years until Rognvald demanded another third
of the earldom. Despite being supported by king
MAGNUS THE GOOD, Rognvald was defeated by
Thorfinn in a sea battle in the Pentland Firth and
fled back to NORWAY. Thorfinn narrowly escaped
with his life when Rognvald returned with a hand-
picked force in the dead of winter and burned his
hall in a surprise attack. Thorfinn soon had his
revenge, surprising and killing Rognvald on Papa
Stronsay shortly before Christmas 1046. Thorfinn
subsequently ruled as sole earl until his death. Now
that his power in Orkney was unchallenged,
Thorfinn gave up raiding and concentrated on
providing his domains with a unifying
administrative and ecclesiastical structure. The first
Orkney earl to be brought up a Christian, Thorfinn
actively encouraged the conversion of the still largely
pagan Norse settlers in Orkney, founding a
BISHOPRIC at his palace at BIRSAY *c.*1050 after his
return from a PILGRIMAGE to Rome.

Thorkell the Tall (d. after 1023) The leader of a great
Viking ARMY that invaded ENGLAND in 1009 and
ravaged the south-east for the next three years: he
was joined by contingents under OLAF HARALDSSON
and Eilaf. Most of Thorkell's army came from
DENMARK, but there were also Swedes and probably
Norwegians. In May 1010 Thorkell won a major
victory over Ulfcytel, ealdorman of EAST ANGLIA,
at Ringmere (location unknown) in Norfolk: the
English dead included king ÆTHELRED II's son-in-
law. In 1011 Thorkell sacked Canterbury, capturing
many nobles and important churchmen, including
archbishop ÆLFHEAH. Thorkell seems to have been
opposed to the subsequent killing of Ælfheah, and in
1012 he took forty-five SHIPS into king Æthelred's
service, for which he was paid (in 1014) 12,000
pounds of silver in addition to the 48,000 pounds
of DANEGELD he had already extorted. Thorkell
helped the Londoners beat off SVEIN FORKBEARD's
attack in 1013, and later took Æthelred into exile in
NORMANDY. Following Æthelred's death, Thorkell
joined CNUT and, after the latter became king of
England in 1016, he was rewarded with the earldom
of East Anglia. Thorkell quarrelled with Cnut,
however, and was outlawed. Reconciled in 1023,
Cnut appointed Thorkell regent of Denmark, after
which he is not heard of again.

Thorstein the Red (*fl.* late 9th century) A Norse
king in SCOTLAND, known only from later Icelandic
sources. Thorstein was said to be the son of king
OLAF THE WHITE and AUD THE DEEP-MINDED.
Thorstein allied with earl SIGURD THE MIGHTY
of ORKNEY to conquer Caithness and Sutherland
from the Scots. After Thorstein was treacherously
killed by the Scots in Caithness, his family emigrated
to ICELAND.

Left and below: Fine Arabic vessels of bronze, silver and pottery, from Scandinavian settlements in Russia, brought back from trading expeditions to the Black and Caspian seas.

Thyre (*fl. c.*950) Danish queen, the wife of king GORM THE OLD, who erected a runic memorial to her at JELLING, and the mother of king HARALD BLUETOOTH. Little is known about the historical Thyre, but she enjoyed a posthumous reputation for beauty, chastity, wisdom and saintliness. She was also credited, erroneously, with building the DANEVIRKE.

Timerovo (Bolsoe Timerovo) Late-10th-century settlement and cemetery of 485 graves near Jaroslavl, RUSSIA, on the upper River Volga, with a mixed Finnish, Scandinavian and Slav population. FINNS formed the largest group of inhabitants. Imports from the MEDITERRANEAN and Middle East show that some of the population were engaged in international TRADE. Both male and female Scandinavian burials have been found, including a few warrior graves, perhaps of the bodyguards of a local chieftain.

Tomrair erell (Thórer jarl) (d. 848) Viking leader in IRELAND, described in Irish sources as 'heir of the king of Laithlinn', a Norse kingdom in the Hebrides, Northern Isles or western NORWAY. He was apparently intent on creating a kingdom for himself in Ireland, but was defeated and killed at the battle of Sciath Nechtain (near Castledermot, County Kildare) in 848 by the kings of Munster and Leinster, along with up to 1,200 of his men.

Torf-Einar (d. *c.*910) Earl of ORKNEY (r. *c.*895–910). The illegitimate youngest son of ROGNVALD OF MØRE in western NORWAY, Einar became earl of Orkney when his brother Hallad abdicated after failing to protect local Norse farmers against pirates. Einar's control of Orkney was challenged by

Halfdan Highleg, described in *ORKNEYINGA SAGA* as a son of king HARALD FAIRHAIR of Norway and the murderer of Einar's father. Einar defeated and captured Halfdan in a sea battle, making a BLOOD EAGLE sacrifice of him to ODIN. He gained his nickname *Torf*-Einar because he was the first Norse settler in the northern isles to use peat ('turf') as a fuel, wood being very scarce in the area.

towns The development of towns in Viking Age Scandinavia is closely linked to the growth of royal power. The first towns were deliberate royal foundations intended to encourage, control and profit from TRADE through tolls and TAXES. By the late 10th century, towns were also being founded as royal administrative and ecclesiastical centres. It was not until the 12th century that there was any spontaneous self-sustaining urban development in Scandinavia.

There were no towns in Scandinavia before the Viking Age, but there were several flourishing seasonal market-places. Some of these, such as HELGÖ in SWEDEN, seem to have developed at religious cult centres; others were probably royal foundations. KAUPANG in NORWAY was adjacent to a royal estate, while RIBE in DENMARK was a carefully planned foundation, possibly the work of the early 8th-century king ANGANTYR. Ribe went on to develop into a town in the 9th century, but the only other two towns in Scandinavia by this time were founded on virgin sites. HEDEBY in Denmark owed its existence to the decision of king GODFRED to settle merchants there in 808. BIRKA in Sweden developed a little earlier on an island close to royal estates, and the town is known to have been under close royal control in the 9th century. These early

Above: A fragment of red taffeta on silk, excavated at Lund, an expensive luxury, probably imported from the Byzantine Empire.

A wine jug and glass beaker from the Rhineland, exported to Birka, Sweden.

towns were small: Hedeby, the largest, had a population of only 1,000–1,500.

After these foundations, there was no further urban development in Scandinavia until *c*.948, when Århus in Jutland was founded as a heavily fortified craft centre. The rapid growth of royal power that followed the introduction of CHRISTIANITY in the late 10th century stimulated a new period of urbanization. SIGTUNA and LUND in Sweden, TRONDHEIM and Oslo in Norway, VIBORG, ODENSE and ROSKILDE in Denmark were all founded around this time as royal or ecclesiastical centres. Predictably, urban development was slowest in Sweden, where the growth of royal power lagged behind that in Denmark and Norway. While there were eight towns in Norway by 1100, and fifteen in Denmark, there were still only four in Sweden, and urban life was not securely established there until the 13th century. Because they played host to so many foreign visitors, by the end of the Viking Age Scandinavian towns often had separate LAWS, known in Norway as the *BJARKEYJAR RÉTTUR*, from the surrounding countryside. Viking settlers also stimulated urban growth overseas, particularly in IRELAND and RUSSIA.

H. Clarke and B. Ambrosiani, *Towns in the Viking Age* (2nd revised edition, Leicester, 1995).

trade Archaeological evidence indicates that trade contacts between Scandinavia and eastern and western Europe began to increase in the 8th century, and may have played a role in encouraging the Viking expansion. Scandinavians on trading voyages would have become familiar with the western European coast and its rich, unguarded monasteries and TOWNS, while the growing fur trade gave the Swedes the incentive to settle in northern RUSSIA

and explore its river systems, ultimately to make contact with the ARABS and the Byzantine Empire. The flow of wealth that followed, from plunder and tribute as well as from commerce, led to a general increase in economic activity in Viking Age Scandinavia. While the exhaustion of the Muslim world's silver mines caused the trade routes to the Middle East to fall out of use before the end of the Viking Age, trade between Scandinavia and western Europe continued to increase throughout the Middle Ages.

Most long-distance trade was probably in high-value luxuries and slaves, but Viking Age Scandinavians did build merchant SHIPS that were capable of carrying bulk cargoes of lower-value commodities. For the Icelanders, Faroe Islanders and Norse Greenlanders, who were not self-sufficient in grain, timber or iron, such trade in basic commodities was essential. The line between Viking piracy and trade was often a fine one, as many of their most valuable commodities were obtained by the use or threat of violence. Much of the silver circulating in Scandinavia had been obtained originally as plunder or tribute. The flourishing Viking SLAVE TRADE was supplied with captives from pirate raids in IRELAND and other parts of western Europe, or extorted as tribute by the RUS from the Slavs. The Slavs also paid tribute in wax and honey. Furs were obtained by the Norwegians, Swedes and Rus on tribute-gathering expeditions against the LAPPS and FINNS. Other important commodities dealt in by Scandinavian merchants included walrus IVORY and hide, seal skins, SOAPSTONE, falcons, and salted and dried fish. In return, the Vikings sought silver and silks from the east, and WEAPONS, silver, GLASS, wine and fine POTTERY from western Europe. While some Viking Age Scandinavians may have

made a full-time living from trade, most merchants, like OHTHERE, a Norwegian who visited king ALFRED THE GREAT's court c.890, were part-timers who also engaged in farming, crafts or piracy.

It is easy to exaggerate the importance of the Vikings' long-distance trading expeditions – some Scandinavian merchants did reach Baghdad, others, the Canadian Arctic – but most trade was actually over short distances, conducted to and from dozens of small ports and trading places around the Scandinavian and Baltic coasts. Exotic objects could travel long distances simply by being passed from one trader to another. For this reason, for example, the thousands of Arabic COINS discovered on the Baltic island of GOTLAND cannot be taken as evidence that Gotlanders were trading directly with the Middle East: they are more likely to have been obtained by trading with intermediaries such as the Rus and Slavs across the Baltic. A small number of international trading centres, such as HEDEBY and BIRKA, attracted foreign merchants from ENGLAND, FRISIA, Germany, and even Baghdad and Spain. Kings sought to encourage and control trade by establishing towns and protecting merchants from piracy in exchange for tolls and TAXES. In this way, trade was an important factor in the growth of royal power in Viking Age Scandinavia.

transport, land In Viking Age Scandinavia, as almost everywhere in early medieval Europe, travel overland on unmade ROADS and tracks was far slower than travel by water, and it was quite uneconomic to transport heavy loads for long distances. Most Viking Age Scandinavians travelled on foot; those who could afford it, on horseback, where the country was not too rough. No doubt pack-horses were widely used to transport merchandise, but there is no firm

evidence of this. Scandinavian horses of the Viking Age were small and stocky, about the size of a modern Icelandic pony. Saddles, stirrups, spurs and bridles were used for riding and are relatively common finds in rich male pagan burials; horseshoes are not known to have been used before the end of the Viking Age. Four-wheeled wagons were used in DENMARK, southern NORWAY and SWEDEN for transporting heavy loads, luggage and WOMEN of high social rank, but wheeled vehicles were not used at all farther north, and possibly not in ICELAND. The only complete wagon to have survived from Viking Age Scandinavia was discovered in the OSEBERG SHIP BURIAL. The elaborately decorated wagon's wheels were spoked and were the same diameter front and rear. As the front axle could not be steered, and the wheels show no signs of wear, the wagon was probably made specially for the burial. Part of a wheel made in the same way as those on the Oseberg wagon has been discovered at LINDHOLM HØJE in Denmark, and other fragments of wagons, including axles, have been found at several other sites in the country. Pictures of wagons are also known from a tapestry from the Oseberg burial and on PICTURE STONES from GOTLAND. From these it appears that wagons were usually drawn by one horse, more rarely by two. Using the breast harness, which was introduced into Scandinavia during the Viking Age, it is estimated that a horse could have hauled a wagon load of up to 500 kilograms on a good surface. Hand barrows, carried by two men like a stretcher, were used to carry loads over short distances: examples have been excavated at JELLING, HEDEBY and the DANEVIRKE rampart in Denmark.

In some respects, travel overland was easier in winter, especially in the north, when the bogs and

Ceremonial sledge (*opposite*) and wagon (*left*) from the Oseberg ship burial, and iron stirrups (*below*) from a Norwegian burial – a sign of the high status of the deceased, as few people could afford to ride horses.

rivers were frozen. Sledges, skis and skates were all used for winter transport. The commonest type of sledge was the 'ski-sledge', a low, hand-drawn device with upturned runners to push through snow drifts. The best-preserved sledges are from the Oseberg burial. This contained three richly carved sledges for personal transport, and a small ski-sledge used for transporting goods. Sledges were also among the goods in the later GOKSTAD SHIP BURIAL. Large sledges were drawn by horses shod with iron crampons to secure a grip in icy conditions. Skis, which originated among the Lapp and Finnish peoples of northern Scandinavia more than 5,000 years ago, were widely used in Norway and Sweden. Skiing is mentioned in SKALDIC poetry, and a carving of a Viking Age skier appears on a stone from Böksta in Uppland, Sweden. Skis were commonly made of pine, because of its elasticity, and because the resin enhanced its gliding potential. The skis were fastened to the feet with straps, which passed through holes cut horizontally through the ski. Viking Age skiers normally used only one pole, or none at all: skiing with two sticks is a modern development. In central Scandinavia skis were made in unmatched pairs, the shorter ski being used for propulsion, the longer, for gliding. Skates, known as 'ice legs', have been found in large numbers throughout Scandinavia. They were usually made from the metatarsals (long foot-bones) of horses or cattle and were fastened to the feet with leather straps. The straps were threaded through a hole at the front of the skate and were hooked around a wooden plug inserted in the back. This type of skate did not cut the ice as metal-bladed skates do, so modern-style skating was not possible. Instead, Viking Age skaters propelled themselves over the ice using iron-tipped sticks.

Trelleborg forts Five 10th-century circular fortresses located at Trelleborg in Sjælland, Fyrkat and Aggersborg in Jutland, Nonnebakken on Fyn, and Trelleborg in Skåne (southern SWEDEN). The forts are the strongest evidence we have of the emergence of a centralized royal power structure in DENMARK in the late 10th century. It is possible that the forts were modelled on the 9th-century Frankish RING-FORTS in the Low Countries. All the forts are precisely circular, with four equally spaced covered gateways placed on the four points of the compass. Axial streets divide the interiors into four equally sized quadrants. At Fyrkat and Trelleborg (Sjælland) each quadrant contained four bow-sided, three-roomed wooden buildings arranged in a square; at Aggersborg – which at 240 metres was twice the diameter of the other forts – there were twelve buildings arranged in three squares. At the centre of each square was a smaller wooden building. A ring road ran around the inside of the earth ramparts, which were faced with timber to make them more difficult to climb. The forts were encircled by a ditch. The striking similarities in the plans of the forts is compelling evidence that they were all built by a single central authority that controlled Jutland, the Danish islands and southern Sweden.

The regular layout of the forts has a military appearance, and they were originally believed to have been built as barracks for the ARMY raised by SVEIN FORKBEARD for his invasions of ENGLAND at the beginning of the 11th century. However, dendrochronology has shown that the timbers used for the buildings at Fyrkat and Trelleborg were felled *c.*980, during the reign of HARALD BLUETOOTH. Further investigation of the buildings at Fyrkat has shown that while some were used as dwellings, most were workshops, stables and stores. WOMEN and

Trelleborg fort, Sjælland, Denmark, built by Harald Bluetooth as part of his programme to consolidate royal power.

The old centre of Trondheim and the cathedral of St Olaf.

CHILDREN, as well as adult males, were found buried in a cemetery outside the ramparts. Because of this, it is now thought that the forts were centres for royal administration, where TAXES were collected, and strong points for controlling the local population. The forts were occupied for no more than twenty or thirty years. Once centralized royal government had become accepted, they were no longer needed.

Trondheim According to the Icelandic SAGAS, Trondheim was founded by king OLAF TRYGGVASON in 997: archaeological excavations have not discovered any evidence of settlement on the site before this date. In the 11th century, Trondheim became an important royal and ecclesiastical centre, becoming the seat of a BISHOPRIC in 1029 and, after his death in 1030, a cult centre for St Olaf (king OLAF HARALDSSON). The first CHURCH was built on the site of St Olaf's grave in 1075; the present magnificent Gothic cathedral was begun in the 12th century with the help of masons from Lincoln in ENGLAND. The bishopric was elevated to an archbishopric in 1152. Trondheim had a mint c.1050. From the late 11th century the TOWN was an important centre for the stockfish TRADE until this was undermined by the German Hanseatic League in the 14th century. Until the 16th century, Trondheim was known as Nidaros.

Truso *see* ELBLAG

Tune ship burial Early 10th-century SHIP BURIAL discovered in a mound at Tune near Haugen, Rolvsøy in Østfold, NORWAY, in 1867. The ship in the Tune burial is less well preserved than those from OSEBERG and GOKSTAD: only the lower parts of the hull, the keelson and a short section of the mast remain. The ship shows many structural similarities to the contemporary Gokstad ship, but had a shallower, widely flared hull and a lower freeboard. The ship's overall dimensions are estimated at 20 metres long by 4.5 metres broad and 1.3 metres deep. Grave goods found in the ship included a sword, shield and saddle, all poorly preserved. Dendrochronology has shown that the ship was built of timber felled c.910; the burial chamber, of timber felled c.910–20.

Turgeis (Thórgestr or Thórgils) Viking leader active in IRELAND in the 840s. Turgeis was probably one of the leaders of the Viking FLEET that sailed up the River Shannon in 844 and established a base on Lough Ree, in the heart of Ireland, from there ravaging Connacht and Meath. In 845 Turgeis was captured by the high king Maél Sechlainn and drowned in Lough Owel (County Westmeath). Posthumously, Turgeis acquired semi-legendary stature as a symbol of everything that was wicked about the pagan Vikings, and many colourful stories became attached to his name. Said to be a leader of the Vikings who founded DUBLIN in 841, he became king of all the Vikings in Ireland. He captured Armagh, the centre of Irish CHRISTIANITY, drove out the abbot, and set himself up as a pagan high priest. His wife Ota (Auðr) even performed acts of witchcraft on the high altar at Clonmacnoise. But Turgeis's life came to an appropriately bad end: he was lured to his death by his lust for the daughter of Maél Sechlainn. The king agreed to send the girl to meet Turgeis, accompanied by fifteen beautiful maidens. The delighted Viking attended the rendezvous accompanied by fifteen of his nobles. But the Irish maidens were really young men, shaven of their beards and dressed in women's

Tynwald Hill, the meeting place of the *thing* of the kingdom of Man.

clothing. They stabbed Turgeis and his companions to death with hidden daggers as they embraced.

Tynwald (ON Thingvöllur) The open-air meeting place of the THING of the Norse kingdom of MAN and the Isles at St Johns in the Isle of Man. The modern Manx parliament, the House of Keys, still meets at Tynwald annually on 5 July to promulgate LAWS passed during the previous year.

Tyr A Scandinavian war-god, regarded variously as the son of either the high god ODIN or the sea-giant Hymir. Only Tyr was brave enough to feed the wolf FENRIR. When the gods decided to chain Fenrir, Tyr placed his hand in his mouth as a pledge that he would be released again. When Fenrir realized that he would not be unchained, he bit off Tyr's hand. At RAGNAROK, Tyr will kill the evil hound GARM, but will die from wounds inflicted by its claws. Tyr is a shadowy figure in Scandinavian mythology, far less important than his Germanic equivalent Tiwaz. It is likely that by Viking times Tyr's attributes were being assimilated by Odin, who was also a god of war.

Udal, The A Viking settlement on the Hebridean island of North Uist. The Udal (from ON ÓÐAL) has a complex history, being first settled by the Celtic Picts *c.* AD 300–400; another settlement only 100 metres away was occupied from the Neolithic period to the early Iron Age. Scandinavian settlers took over the site in the 9th century and built a small but substantial stone-and-turf enclosure, interpreted as a 'mini-fort', and a number of Norse-type turf houses. Artefacts such as POTTERY and bone pins and COMBS show no native influences, suggesting that the Pictish population was completely displaced by the newcomers. By the 13th century, the population of The Udal was Gaelic-speaking: the village was finally abandoned in the 1690s after it was buried by blown sand.

Ulf (d. *c.*1027) Danish jarl, the son of Thorgils Sprakaleg and the brother-in-law of CNUT, whose sister Estrith he married. Although he was in ENGLAND in 1022, Ulf appears never to have held land or office there. After the death of THORKELL THE TALL *c.*1023, Cnut appointed Ulf regent of DENMARK for his young son HARTHACNUT. Ulf apparently tried to forge documents proclaiming Harthacnut king of Denmark, and in 1026 he fought with OLAF HARALDSSON of NORWAY and ÖNUND JACOB of the SVEAR against Cnut at the battle of Helgeå. Though Cnut was defeated, their victory brought the allies no lasting advantage. Shortly after an official reconciliation, Cnut had Ulf murdered in church at ROSKILDE. Because of his treason, Ulf's sons were usually known by their mother's name: SVEIN ESTRITHSON, a future king of Denmark, and Beorn Estrithson, later an earl in England.

Uppsala, Gamla (Old Uppsala) Royal cemetery and pagan cult centre, a few kilometres north of the

Burial mounds of the
Yngling kings at
Gamla Uppsala.

Opposite: Odin's great hall
Valhalla, from a 17th-century
Icelandic copy of the *Edda*.

modern city of Uppsala in central Sweden. Three
vast burial mounds at Gamla Uppsala are
traditionally associated with the 6th-century Svear
kings Aun, Egil and Adils of the semi-legendary
Yngling dynasty. Two of the mounds that have
been excavated have been dated to the 5th and 6th
centuries AD, and each contained the cremated
remains of a high-ranking male. Hundreds of
smaller burial mounds surround the great mounds.
A flat-topped mound to the east of the larger
mounds, traditionally known as the 'Thing-mound',
may have served a ceremonial purpose. According to
the German historian Adam of Bremen, pagan
festivals, including human sacrifices, were still
being celebrated at Gamla Uppsala in a wooden
temple dedicated to Thor, Odin and Freyr at the
end of the 11th century. Adam records that nine of all
kinds of living males were hanged in sacred grove
near the temple as sacrifices to the gods every nine
years. A church was built on the site of the temple
in the 12th century.

Utgard-Loki A mythological giant, the king of
Utgard in Jotunheim. Disguised as the giant
Skrymir, Utgard-Loki met with the gods Loki and
Thor, and Thor's fleet-footed servant Thialfi, and
played various magic tricks on them as they were
travelling through a forest on their way to Utgard.
When they finally reached Utgard, Utgard-Loki
challenged Loki and Thor to a number of feats of
strength. In every case the gods apparently failed,
but only because their senses had been deceived by
Utgard-Loki's magic.

Valhalla 'The Hall of the Slain', the great hall of the
high god Odin in Asgard. Valhalla is home to the
souls of the brave warriors who have died in battle.
Chosen by Odin, the warriors were led to Valhalla by
the valkyries and welcomed by Bragi, the god of
poetry. Valhalla has a roof of spears, is filled with
shields and coats of mail, and has 640 doors
through which Odin's warriors pour out to do battle
with one another every day. The fallen are restored to
life in time to spend the night feasting on pork and
mead with Odin. This everlasting battle will end only
at Ragnarok, when the warriors will sally forth with
the gods to do battle with the giants. The exact
significance of Valhalla in pagan times has been lost,
but it seems to have been a symbol of the grave
rather than a warrior paradise.

valkyries (ON *valkyrja*, 'choosers of the slain')
Maiden warriors who dwelt with the high god Odin
in Valhalla. Odin, who was the bringer of victory in
battle, decided who was to fall in battle and chose the
souls of the bravest to join him in Valhalla. At Odin's
bidding, the valkyries rode into battle to carry the
chosen warriors to Valhalla and to give them their
welcoming cups of mead. Odin might 'marry'
valkyries to warrior kings who worshipped him as
their supernatural protectors. Valkyries feature in
many Scandinavian legends, sometimes as fearsome
supernatural beings, other times in more human
guise, such as Brynhild, the lover of the hero
Sigurd Fafnisbane. Valkyries are sometimes
also called shield-maidens (*skjaldmær*), but that
term is also applied in legendary literature to
human female warriors.

Valsgärde A major pagan cemetery near Uppsala,
central Sweden, used from the beginning of the

The Byzantine emperor Basil II, founder of the élite Varangian Guard of Scandinavian mercenaries.

VENDEL PERIOD (*c*.550) to the end of the Viking Age (11th century). The richest burials were the earliest. The bodies were laid in boats, perhaps symbolizing the journey to the realm of the dead, and supplied with FOOD, cooking utensils, GLASS, horse gear, and fine armour and WEAPONS. The burials were covered with low mounds. A replica of one of the boats, a small clinker-built rowing boat with five pairs of OARS, has been reconstructed and tested. The richness of the grave goods at Valsgärde and the poverty of grave goods in other contemporary cemeteries in the area indicate the high rank of the people buried there. Valsgärde was presumably close to a power centre of an early royal dynasty of the SVEAR.

Vanir The smaller of the two families of gods that made up the pagan Scandinavian pantheon, the larger being the ÆSIR. The chief gods of the Vanir were NJORD, a god of the sea, the fertility-god FREYR and his sister FREYJA, a fertility-goddess. The Vanir frequently fought the Æsir until they were admitted into ASGARD.

Varangian Guard An élite unit of Scandinavian mercenaries serving as part of the Byzantine emperor's imperial guard. Scandinavian mercenaries were recruited into the imperial guard as early as the reign of Michael III (r. 842–67), but there was no specifically Scandinavian unit until the Varangian Guard itself was founded in 988 by Basil II with recruits supplied by prince VLADIMIR I of KIEV. Regarded as being outstandingly loyal, Varangians fought with traditional Scandinavian WEAPONS and were described as 'the emperor's axe-wielding barbarians'. Varangian guardsmen were the highest-paid mercenaries in Byzantine service,

receiving the equivalent of 1 $\frac{1}{3}$ to 2 $\frac{1}{2}$ pounds of gold a year, plus an enhanced share of war booty. Not surprisingly, service in the Varangian Guard was regarded as highly prestigious in Scandinavia, even for a king. The most famous member of the guard was HARALD HARDRADA, who served as an officer from 1034–43, making enough money to finance his bid for the Norwegian throne in the process, but the careers of many others are recorded in Icelandic SAGAS. A returning veteran could cut quite a dash on his homecoming. *LAXDÆLA SAGA* describes Bolli Bollasson on his return to ICELAND (*c*.1026–30) as being dressed in fine silks – a gift from the emperor himself – a scarlet cloak, a gilded helmet, richly decorated shield and a gold-hilted sword. Members of the guard are also commemorated on several Swedish rune-stones, for example Ragnvald from Uppland, who was a commander in the guard in the 11th century. After 1066 many English exiles joined the guard, diluting its Scandinavian character. The guard survived until 1204, when Constantinople was taken by the Fourth Crusade. On this occasion, the guard showed that its loyalty was not absolute by refusing to fight the crusaders unless given an exorbitant pay rise.

S. Blöndal, *The Varangians of Byzantium: An Aspect of Byzantine Military History*, translated, revised and rewritten by B. S. Benedikz (Cambridge, 1978).

Varangians (ON *Væringjar*, Slavic *Variazi*, Greek *Varaggoi*, Arabic *Warank*) A term used by Greeks, ARABS and Slavs from the mid-10th century to describe Scandinavians. Though the RUS are sometimes described as Varangians, indicating their Scandinavian origins, the term is more usually reserved for Scandinavian merchants and mercenaries newly arrived in the east from their

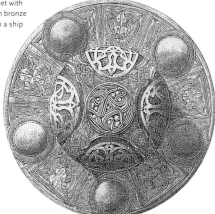

Left: An iron helmet with mail skirt and rich bronze decorations, from a ship burial at Vendel.

Above: A bronze-plated iron shield boss from a ship burial at Vendel, showing the distinctive style of animal ornament named after the site.

homelands. In English and the Scandinavian languages, the term is generally used more narrowly to describe members of the Byzantine emperor's élite bodyguard, the VARANGIAN GUARD. The word 'Varangian' is probably derived from Old Norse *vár*, meaning 'pledge', possibly because bands of Scandinavian merchants and warriors customarily formed sworn fellowships (*see* FÉLAG).

Vendel A major pagan cemetery, north of UPPSALA in central SWEDEN, in use from the beginning of the VENDEL PERIOD to the early Viking period. The burials, the richest in Sweden for this time, are most probably of members of a royal dynasty: traditionally Vendel is regarded as the burial place of the 6th-century king Ottar of the semi-legendary YNGLING DYNASTY. The bodies were interred, without cremation, in large boats 10 metres or more in length, perhaps symbolizing the journey to the realm of the dead. The bodies were surrounded with valuable grave goods: FOOD and cooking gear for the journey, GLASS, superb WEAPONS AND ARMOUR, including a justifiably famous bronze-decorated iron helmet, hunting dogs, horses and saddles, and, in one grave, a falcon. A distinctive metalwork style of animal ornament is named after the site.

Vendel period (*c.* AD 550–800) The last period of Swedish prehistory before the Viking Age, roughly equivalent to the Late GERMANIC IRON AGE in DENMARK and the MEROVINGIAN PERIOD in NORWAY. The richly furnished cemeteries at VENDEL (after which the period is named), UPPSALA and VALSGÄRDE are evidence of the emergence of wealthy royal dynasties in SWEDEN in this period.

Viborg The TOWN of Viborg in Jutland developed in the late 10th century around the old site of the Jutland THING and near the end of the *Hærvej* ('Army Road'), the ancient north–south track through Jutland to Germany. The Viking town lay a little to the south of the medieval and modern town centre. The layout of the settlement was extensively reorganized in the mid-11th century, and it had become the seat of a BISHOPRIC by 1060. The town is one of the earliest in Scandinavia to have developed inland with only overland communications (i.e. not on a navigable river).

Viking (ON *víkingr*, OE *wicing*) The word 'Viking' has come to be used to describe all early medieval Scandinavians, but as originally used by contemporaries the term *víkingr* applied only to someone who went *í víking*, that is, plundering. Only a minority of early medieval Scandinavians were, therefore, Vikings in the strict sense of the word. Various explanations of the origin of the word have been proposed. The commonest explanations are that 'Viking' is derived either from Viken in southern NORWAY, and therefore means simply 'the men from Viken', or that it comes from the Scandinavian word *vík* ('bay' or 'cove'), and means 'the men of the bays'. Another possibility is that it derives from the Old Scandinavian verb *vikya*, meaning 'to turn away' and so came to be used to describe Scandinavians who were travelling away from home. However, a Scandinavian origin for the word seems unlikely, as its use in Old English predates the Viking Age. It was used to describe any band of pirates, not simply those from Scandinavia. In the 8th-century poem *Exodus*, the seafaring sons of Reuben are described as *wicingas*, for example. In this case, it seems likely that *wicing* is derived from

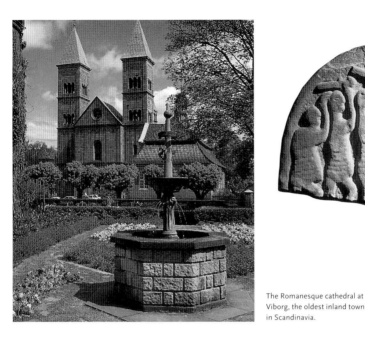

The Romanesque cathedral at Viborg, the oldest inland town in Scandinavia.

This gravestone from the Northumbrian monastery of Lindisfarne may show Viking raiders.

Old English *wic* ('port of trade') and means 'the men who frequent (or attack) ports', and that it was only later adopted by the Scandinavians themselves. After falling into disuse in the central Middle Ages, the use of 'Viking' was revived by the 19th-century Romantic movement.

villages and rural settlement The pattern of rural settlement in Viking Age Scandinavia was largely determined by environmental conditions. In DENMARK and the far south of SWEDEN, which have the largest areas of fertile arable land in Scandinavia, nucleated settlement in villages was normal even at the beginning of the Viking Age. In the larger pockets of fertile land in Västergötland and Uppland in central Sweden, villages were also beginning to develop by the end of the Viking Age as a result of the subdivision of existing farms. In the rest of Sweden and in NORWAY fertile land was confined mostly to small pockets in rough country, making nucleated settlement impossible: in these areas the settlement pattern was one of dispersed individual farmsteads. The population of Scandinavia was rising throughout the Viking Age, and the period saw an expansion of the area under cultivation and the foundation of new farms and settlements where enough fertile land could be claimed between existing villages and farms. Settlements founded during the Viking Age can often be identified by the place-name elements -*thorp* ('outlying farm') in Denmark and -*ryd* ('clearing') in Sweden and Norway. In Denmark, village sites were periodically abandoned as the inhabitants moved to a new site a few hundred metres away. Only in the 11th century did villages become fixed permanently in one location. For example, the village of VORBASSE in Jutland moved seven or eight times

in the first millennium AD, becoming established on its present site only *c*.1100. The main factor in the stabilization of settlement may have been a change from pastoral to arable farming in the 11th century, thought to be a consequence of the introduction of the mould-board plough. Village sites before 1000 were close to water meadows; those after that date were close to good soils for arable farming. The 'filling up' of the landscape as the population increased and the growth of royal government and ecclesiastical organization were also probably factors in the stabilization of settlement. In ICELAND, the FAROES, the Scottish islands and north-west ENGLAND, Norse settlers reproduced the dispersed settlement pattern typical of Viking Age Norway, but it is not clear how Scandinavian settlers fitted into the more densely populated regions of NORMANDY and the DANELAW of eastern England.

Vinland The wooded land in North America visited by LEIF ERIKSSON and other Norsemen *c*.1000. The location of Vinland remains uncertain. One possibility is that Vinland was Newfoundland, where a Norse settlement dating to Leif's time has been discovered at L'ANSE-AUX-MEADOWS. However, the bleak local environment is quite unlike the descriptions of Vinland recorded in the 13th-century VINLAND SAGAS. Apart from the abundant wild grapes after which Leif named Vinland ('Vine land'), according to the *Grænlendinga saga*, there were maple trees, rivers teeming with salmon, frost-free winters and midwinter days that were much longer than those in GREENLAND, the sun being above the horizon from before nine in the morning to after three in the afternoon. The astronomical information places Vinland south of the latitude

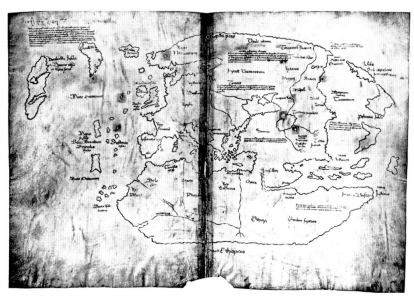

The Vinland map – unique medieval world map or modern forgery?

50° north, that is south of the mouth of the Gulf of St Lawrence. Wild grapes do not grow north of the Gulf of St Lawrence, and salmon are not found on the Atlantic coast of North America south of the Hudson River. This would seem to make New England or Nova Scotia the most likely location for Vinland, but no one who had been there would be likely to describe their winters as frost-free. There must, therefore, be a distinct possibility that Leif deliberately exaggerated the attractions of his new-found land, just as his father ERIK THE RED had already done to attract settlers to Greenland. Perhaps the story of the grapes is also an invention, but it is not certainly so. Though no evidence of Norse settlement has ever been found south of L'Anse-aux-Meadows, finds of butternuts on the site show that the Norse must have sailed at least as far south as the Gulf of St Lawrence, the northern limit of their range (a COIN of king OLAF THE PEACEFUL found on an Indian site at Godard Point in Maine could have been obtained by TRADE with the ESKIMOS of the Canadian Arctic, who were in direct contact with the Norse Greenlanders).

The attractions of Vinland led to several attempts at settlement in the years following Leif's voyage, but misunderstandings between the Norse and the SKRÆLINGS, as they called the native American Indians, soon led to violence. Despite their superior iron WEAPONS, there was no way that such small numbers of Norse could hope to establish a permanent presence on a hostile shore so far from their home bases. An attempt to rediscover Vinland was made in 1121 by bishop Eiríkr Gnúpsson, but it is not known if he ever returned from his voyage. Icelandic sources record voyages to 'new lands' in the 13th century; their location, however, is unknown

and thereafter Vinland came to be regarded as a semi-legendary land.

G. Jones, *The Norse Atlantic Saga* (2nd edition, Oxford, 1986).

Vinland map A map on parchment of unknown provenance and date, probably a forgery, which first came to light in the late 1950s. The Vinland map purports to be a late medieval map of the world (*c.*1440) and portrays VINLAND as a large island in the Atlantic Ocean. Latin annotation on the map says that this was the land discovered by 'Byarnus' (BJARNI HERJOLFSSON) and 'Leiphus' (LEIF ERIKSSON). If the map is genuine, it is the earliest known cartographic representation of the New World. The map was declared a forgery in 1974 after tests showed that the ink contained a large amount of titanium dioxide, a chemical not manufactured until 1917. However, new tests conducted in the 1990s have found only minute traces of the chemical in the ink. As a result, the map's authenticity is once again a matter of acrimonious debate. Those who claim that the Vinland map is genuine still have to explain how these traces of a 20th-century substance got into supposedly medieval ink.

Vinland sagas The name applied to the two Icelandic SAGAS, *Grœnlendinga saga* ('The Saga of the Greenlanders') and *Eiríks saga rauða* ('ERIK THE RED's Saga'), which describe the Norse discovery and exploration of GREENLAND and North America in the late 10th and early 11th centuries. *Grœnlendinga saga* was written *c.*1200; the shorter *Eiríks saga*, not until *c.*1265. Generally considered to be the more reliable account, *Grœnlendinga saga* describes six voyages to North America, beginning with the accidental sighting of an unknown land by BJARNI

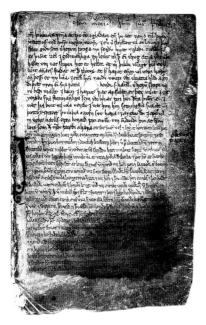

Eiríks saga rauða, the shorter and later of the two Vinland sagas.

Vladimir I is baptized by a Byzantine missionary, from the 15th-century *Radziwill Chronicle*.

HERJOLFSSON and the subsequent voyage of LEIF ERIKSSON that led to the discovery and naming of Helluland ('Slab Land' = Baffin Island?), MARKLAND ('Forest Land' = Labrador?) and VINLAND ('Vine Land' = New England or Nova Scotia). The saga continues with an account of a voyage by Leif's brother Thorvaldr that ended with his death in Vinland from an arrow shot by a SKRÆLING. A fourth voyage by Thorsteinn, another of Leif's brothers, failed to reach Vinland. THORFINN KARLSEFNI, an Icelandic merchant, led a fifth expedition of three ships with sixty-five would-be settlers, including five women. After two winters, Karlsefni gave up the attempt at settlement after fighting broke out with the *Skrælings*. The final expedition was led by Leif's half-sister Freydis and two brothers called Helgi and Finnbogi. Ill feeling arose between the partners, and Freydis eventually murdered Helgi, Finnbogi and their followers, before returning to Greenland. The historicity of this final voyage has often been questioned. *Eiríks saga* is a more sophisticated work of literature than *Grænlendinga saga*, and it is regarded as a skilful rewriting of the history of the Vinland voyages to place more emphasis on the role of Thorfinn Karlsefni in the venture. The saga describes Erik the Red's settlement of Greenland and three voyages to North America. The first has Leif discover Vinland accidentally after being blown off course on a voyage from NORWAY to Greenland: there is no mention of Bjarni Herjolfsson. The saga then describes Thorsteinn's unsuccessful voyage. Finally, the saga describes the expedition of Thorfinn Karlsefni, which in this version comprises 160 men and women. On reaching the North American coast, the party splits up to search vainly for Vinland. After a battle with the *Skrælings*, in which Freydis plays an improbably heroic role, Karlsefni decides to return

to Greenland. Demonstrably unhistorical elements, such as an encounter with a uniped, a mythical one-legged beast, also suggest that *Eiríks saga* is a less reliable account of the Norse voyages to North America than *Grænlendinga saga*.
The Vinland Sagas, trans. M. Magnusson and H. Pálsson (Harmondsworth, 1965).

Visunden ('The Ox') The famous *drakkar* built at TRONDHEIM in NORWAY in 1026 for king OLAF HARALDSSON. *Visunden* had thirty pairs of OARS and a gilded ox's (or bison's) head for a figurehead. It was probably one of the largest Viking SHIPS built, and was compared favourably with OLAF TRYGGVASON's near-legendary LONG SERPENT.

Vladimir I (St Vladimir, Vladimir the Great, ON Valdemar) (*c*.956–1015) Grand prince of KIEV (r. 978/80–1015). The first Christian ruler of the Kievan RUS, Vladimir's decision to convert to Orthodox CHRISTIANITY in 988 had a lasting influence on the development of Russian civilization. The son of SVYATOSLAV I of Kiev, Vladimir became prince of NOVGOROD in 970. On his father's death in 972, Vladimir's brother Jaropolk seized power, forcing him into exile in SWEDEN, where he raised an ARMY. Helped by an uncle and a Slav chief called Blud, Vladimir returned to Kiev in 978/80, killing Jaropolk by treachery and seizing power. The early years of his reign were occupied with campaigns against the Volga BULGARS and the overthrow of the Swedish ruler of Polotsk, whose daughter Ragnheid he married.

Though Christianity had been established in Kiev since the 940s, Vladimir had been brought up as a devotee of the Slavic god Perun. Later stories tell how Vladimir considered converting to several

Volsunga saga –
the inspiration for
Wagner's opera the
Ring des Nibelungen.

Vorbasse, Jutland, the site of a
prosperous farming village from
100 BC to AD 1100. Excavations can
be seen in the foreground.

religions, including Islam, before settling on
Orthodox Christianity because of the unmatched
beauty of its liturgy. In reality, Vladimir's decision to
convert to Orthodox Christianity was probably taken
primarily for political reasons. The Byzantine
emperor Basil II (r. 976–1025) began to negotiate an
alliance with Vladimir, offering his sister Anna in
marriage in exchange. Anna was less than
enthusiastic about the prospect of marriage to a
barbarian ruler who was reputed to keep hundreds
of concubines and to take part in human sacrifices,
but a pact was finally agreed in 988 when Vladimir
consented to convert to Orthodox Christianity. The
following year, Vladimir captured the rebellious
Byzantine city of Cherson in the Crimea, handing
it over to Basil. Vladimir ordered the forcible
conversion of his subjects to Christianity, the
destruction of pagan idols, and the building of many
CHURCHES. A sign of the degree to which the Rus
had been assimilated to the Slavs by Vladimir's reign
is that he made the LANGUAGE of the Church Slavic,
not Scandinavian. Vladimir's decision to accept
Orthodox Christianity opened RUSSIA to a strong
Byzantine culture, which exercised a profound
influence over the development of its own
civilization. Later in his reign Vladimir built
close diplomatic and dynastic links with the Holy
Roman Empire and Poland. He was succeeded
by his sons Svyatopolk I (r. 1015–19) and JAROSLAV
THE WISE (r. 1019–54).

Volsunga saga ('The Saga of the Volsungs') Probably
the most famous and influential of the legendary
SAGAS, written in Iceland *c.*1260–70 but
incorporating legendary traditions dating back to
well before the Viking Age. The saga includes heroic
figures from the MIGRATION PERIOD, including
Jormunrek (Ermanaric), a 4th-century king of
the Goths, and Atli (Attila), the 5th-century king of
the Huns, but they bear little resemblance to their
historical selves. The central character of the saga
is SIGURD FAFNISBANE, the slayer of the dragon
FAFNIR and the lover of the VALKYRIE BRYNHILD.
The saga owes much of its fame in the modern
world to its use by the composer Richard Wagner
as a major source of inspiration for his epic opera
cycle the *Ring des Nibelungen.*
*The Saga of the Volsungs: The Norse Epic of Sigurd the
Dragon Slayer,* trans. J. L. Byock (Berkeley, Los Angeles and
London, 1990).

Voluspá ('The Prophecy of the Seeress') One of the
major mythological poems in the *Poetic* EDDA,
Voluspá was one of the main sources for SNORRI
STURLUSON's *Prose Edda.* The poem is recited by a
seeress who can remember back to before the
CREATION of the world and can see into the future
beyond RAGNAROK, the inevitable doom of the gods.
Interrogated by the high god ODIN about the future,
the seeress recounts the creation of the world, the
golden age of the gods, the creation of the DWARVES
and that of the human race. She continues with an
account of the war between the two families of gods,
the ÆSIR and the VANIR. The seeress then tells Odin
how the death of the beautiful god BALDER will
signal the onset of Ragnarok and describes the
terrible last battle in which the gods and GIANTS
will destroy one another and the world with them.
Finally, a mysterious unnamed supreme deity,
possibly Christ, appears in a reborn and purified
world, but has evil really been banished? Almost at
once, a shadow falls across the new world with the
appearance of the dreadful corpse-eating dragon
Niðhoggr from NIFLHEIM, the realm of the dead.

Voluspá was probably composed in ICELAND – though NORWAY and the DANELAW in ENGLAND have also been proposed – around the year 1000, just as PAGAN RELIGION was being supplanted by CHRISTIANITY. The author was a pagan who clearly regretted the passing of the old gods, but the poem shows Christian influences in its moral concepts, its idea of reward for merit and punishment for sin in the afterlife, and its apocalyptic vision, perhaps inspired by The Book of Revelations.
The Poetic Edda, trans. C. Larrington (Oxford, 1996).

Vorbasse Vorbasse in Jutland is the only complete Viking Age farming village to have been excavated. The site has a complex history of occupation, lasting from around 100 BC until AD 1100, when the village moved to its present location about 750 metres to the south. In the period 700–1000 there were seven farms in the village, six of roughly the same size and one substantially larger than the rest, which must have belonged to a wealthy farmer or lord who probably owned the whole village. The farms consisted of a longhouse – divided into living room, byre and hay barn – and several sunken-floored buildings that were used for WEAVING and pottery-making. Every farm had its own well, and one had a smithy. The main occupation was stock-rearing: the smaller farms had byres to accommodate between 20 and 30 cows each; the larger farm, up to 100. Grain was also grown. The village must have produced a surplus of FOOD and other products, such as hides, which were traded for the necessities that it could not provide for itself: good building timber, iron, whetstones and SOAPSTONE pots from NORWAY, and good-quality POTTERY and lava quernstones from the Rhineland. *See also* HOUSES; VILLAGES AND RURAL SETTLEMENT.

wagons *see* TRANSPORT, LAND

Wales, Vikings in There is no evidence that Wales suffered any serious Viking raids until *c.*855, when Anglesey was ravaged by Irish-based Vikings. Stiff Welsh resistance led by RHODRI MAWR (r. 844–77), king of the leading Welsh kingdom of Gwynedd, prevented any attempts by the Vikings at colonization. Raids from IRELAND tailed off in the 870s, reflecting the decline of Viking power there, but Wales was often affected by the 'overspill' of raids that were directed primarily at ENGLAND. The Welsh and ANGLO-SAXONS sometimes cooperated against the Vikings. In 893 they joined forces to defeat a Viking ARMY at Buttington in mid-Wales, and it was king EDWARD THE ELDER of WESSEX who ransomed Cyfeiliog, bishop of Llandaff, after he had been captured by a Viking force from BRITTANY in 914.

The expulsion of the Vikings from DUBLIN in 902 was followed by an attempt by INGAMUND to settle in Anglesey: driven out by the Welsh, he eventually settled in England. The re-establishment of Viking power in Ireland in 914 was immediately followed by renewed raiding, beginning with an attack on Anglesey in 915. But that year also brought another strong ruler to the throne of Gwynedd, Hywel Dda (r. 915–50), during whose reign Wales was almost untroubled by Viking activity. The civil war that broke out on Hywel's death was a signal to the Vikings of Ireland and the Scottish islands to launch a new onslaught, and the second half of the 10th century was the worst period of the Viking Age as far as Wales was concerned. It was probably in this period that the Vikings created permanent settlements in Pembrokeshire, along the south coast, and in the far north-east on the Dee Estuary. A king 'Sigferth' (Sigfrid?), who attested a charter of king

Below: Viking silver arm rings, buried at Red Wharf Bay, Anglesey *c.*910.

Right: Excavations of St Peter's Church, Waterford, built at the end of the Viking Age, when the city had come under the domination of Irish kings.

EADRED of England in 955 in the company of Welsh princes, may have been the leader of one of these settlements. In 989, Maredudd, king of the south Welsh kingdom of Dyfed, was reduced to buying off the Vikings, but the raids continued, culminating in 999 with the sack of the cathedral of St David's, during which its bishop was killed. Raids, mainly from Ireland and the Scottish islands, continued throughout the 11th century – St David's was sacked at least six more times before 1100. Despite the destruction caused by the Vikings, many Welsh rulers saw them as potential allies against the English. In 992 Maredudd of Dyfed hired Irish Vikings to fight the English, as did Gruffudd ap Llywelyn of Gwynedd in 1055–6 and 1058. The last major Viking intervention in Wales was king MAGNUS BARELEGS' brief occupation of Anglesey in 1098, when he defeated a Norman army, but raids by Viking pirates from the Scottish islands, such as SVEIN ASLEIFARSON of ORKNEY, continued well into the 12th century.

Overall, the Vikings had only a slight impact on Wales. Viking raids may have weakened Welsh resistance to the English in the 11th century, but there is no conclusive evidence that this was the case. The small Viking settlements were confined mainly to the coast and had no discernible political influence. Nor is there any evidence that they exercised any cultural influence, such examples of Viking ART STYLES as there are in Wales probably being the work of Scandinavian settlers. The many coastal features with Scandinavian names are, however, a lasting reminder of the Viking dominance of the seas around Wales in the period 800–1100.

H. R. Loyn, *The Vikings in Wales* (London, 1976).

wapentake (ON *vápnatak*, OE *wæpentac*) A local division for the administration of justice in the DANELAW of eastern ENGLAND, roughly equivalent to the English hundred (a division based on a unit of 100 hides of land, i.e. the area needed to support 100 peasant FAMILIES). In Scandinavia the term *vápnatak* (weapon-taking) was applied only to the symbolic clashing of WEAPONS that confirmed judgments made by the local THING, the assembly of freemen. Only in Scandinavian-settled areas of England did the term come to be applied both to the assembly and its district.

'War of the Irish with the Foreigners' *see* COGADH GAEDHEL RE GALLAIBH

Waterford (ON Vethrafjörthr) Norse TOWN that developed from a mid-9th-century Viking LONGPHORT in a deep inlet on the south-east coast of Ireland. Excavations suggest that the layout of the Viking town was similar to that of DUBLIN, with rectangular wattle-walled buildings set in plots surrounded by wattle fences. Part of the street plan and the remains of a massive defensive earthen bank and ditch, larger than any known elsewhere in the Viking world, have been uncovered. There is literary evidence that some of the town's defences were built of stone by the 12th century. Waterford was the base from which SIHTRIC CÁECH recaptured Dublin in 917. Later in the 10th century, Waterford came under the overlordship of the kings of Munster, and in 984 and 988 it placed its FLEET at the disposal of BRIAN BORU. Ragnall, the last king of Waterford, died in 1035.

weapons and armour Viking Age Scandinavian warriors fought with weapons that were little different from those used by other early medieval Europeans. The most favoured weapon in NORWAY and DENMARK was the double-edged longsword,

The kite-shaped shield was adopted by the Vikings in the 11th century, even though it was developed for cavalry warfare and gave poorer protection to an infantryman's legs than the traditional round shield.

A mail shirt, effective protection in battle for those who could afford it, from Trøndelag, Norway, 11th century.

which was used for hacking at the enemy rather than for thrusting. Though Frankish swords were particularly prized for their high quality, Scandinavian smiths were also highly skilled and able to produce swords with pattern-welded cores to give greater strength and flexibility. Hilts and scabbards were often intricately decorated with silver inlaid patterns and gilded bronze. As war was the most prestigious activity in Viking Age Scandinavia, beautifully finished weapons were an important way for a warrior to display his wealth and status. Such was the prestige attached to fine swords that they were often given their own names. Spears were common weapons in Viking Age Scandinavia, and in SWEDEN they appear to have been the weapon of preference. Viking spears were usually around 2–3 metres long including the socketed iron spearhead, which was 20–60 centimetres in length. Shafts were made of ash wood. Lighter, narrower spearheads were made for throwing; heavier broader ones, for stabbing. In the later Viking Age there was a trend towards the use of heavier spearheads with thicker shafts. Though spears were less prestigious weapons than swords, great care was taken with their manufacture. Pattern-welded blades are common, and the sockets of spearheads were often decorated with silver inlaid patterns. Frankish winged spearheads or *angons* were also imported into Scandinavia in the early Viking Age. In order to prevent spears that had missed their mark being returned by the enemy, the pins that attached the head to the shaft were removed before throwing. Thus, any attempt to pull the spear out of the ground would result in the head and shaft separating. According to the *EYRBYGGJA SAGA*, it was customary to start a battle by throwing a spear right over the enemy ARMY to claim it for ODIN. The battleaxe is the weapon most often associated with

the Vikings in the popular imagination. Several different types of axe were made, including the light *handøx*, which could be wielded effectively with one hand, and the popular heavy broad-bladed *breiðøx*, which was wielded with two hands. Although axes were perhaps most often seen as a cheap alternative to the sword, some were decorated with silver inlaid patterns. Bows of yew or elm were often used, especially in sea battles, even by aristocratic warriors such as the Norwegian EINAR TAMBARSKELVE, who made his reputation as an archer. A variety of barbed and leaf-shaped iron arrowheads were used. In the course of their campaigns in FRANCIA, the Vikings learned to make and use siege-warfare weapons, such as battering rams and catapults.

The most important defensive weapon in Viking Age Scandinavia was the shield. Vikings used flat circular shields, approximately 1 metre in diameter, designed to protect the body from chin to kneecap. Shields were often brightly painted, like the yellow-and-black shields found in the 10th-century GOKSTAD SHIP BURIAL, or the shield painted with mythological scenes described in the late-9th-century SKALDIC poem *Ragnarsdrápa*. Shields were made of wood and reinforced with leather or, occasionally, iron around the rim. The hand-grip in the centre of the shield was protected by a protruding iron boss, which could also be used as a weapon in its own right. In the 11th century, the kite-shaped shield, as portrayed in the Bayeux Tapestry, also came into use in Scandinavia, though it was not ideally suited to Viking-style infantry warfare. Armour was probably too expensive for most warriors, who had to make do with a tough leather jerkin and a hardened leather cap. A chieftain might turn out for battle wearing an iron helmet with face-guard (but *never* any horns, alas) and a coat of chain-mail, painstakingly made from thousands

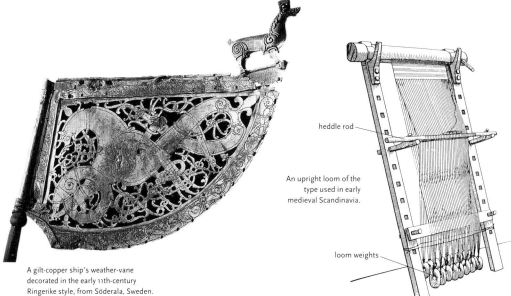

A gilt-copper ship's weather-vane decorated in the early 11th-century Ringerike style, from Söderala, Sweden.

An upright loom of the type used in early medieval Scandinavia.

heddle rod

loom weights

of interlinked iron rings, each one of which had to be individually riveted together by hand. Chain-mail coats had short, wide sleeves and were long enough to protect the thighs. Scale armour, probably imported from Byzantium, is known from Sweden.

weather-vanes, ships' The SAGAS frequently mention the use of gilded weather-vanes on Viking warships. Two types of vane were in use, the *veðrviti*, which was mounted on the prow, and the *flaug*, which was mounted on the mast. Four *veðrviti* from the late Viking Age have survived, thanks to their being reused as weather-vanes on CHURCH towers. The three oldest, from Söderala and Källunge in SWEDEN and Heggen in NORWAY, are decorated in the Ringerike style, which dates them to the first half of the 11th century. The fourth, from Tingelstad in Norway, dates from *c.*1100. All the vanes are made of gilded copper and had holes drilled along their leading edges, to which streamers were attached. The outer ends are decorated with animal figures. A 13th-century *flaug* is preserved at Höyjord church in Norway. *Flaug* were hinged at 90 degrees to the vertical; *veðrviti*, at 110 degrees. Weather-vanes are also known from late-Viking Age graffiti and from boat-shaped candle holders, which were popular in medieval Scandinavia.

M. Blindheim, 'The Gilded Vikingship Vanes: Their Use and Technique', in R. T. Farrell (ed.), *The Vikings* (London, 1982), pp. 116–27.

weaving Artefacts associated with weaving, such as spindle-whorls and loom weights, are common finds in archaeological excavations of Viking Age Scandinavian settlements, indicating that it was an important domestic activity. Until the late Middle Ages, spinning and weaving was a female occupation in

Scandinavia. Most housewives probably made their own cloth, and weaving was not seen as being beneath the dignity of even a queen, as the inclusion of a loom in the OSEBERG SHIP BURIAL suggests. Wool was the most important textile woven, but linen was also used in DENMARK. Wool was combed to untangle it before spinning. Spindle-whorls, used to create a fly-wheel effect to make the spindle spin faster, were usually conical in shape and made of fired clay, though stone, ANTLER, bone, GLASS, lead and AMBER were also used. The finished thread was woven to make cloth on an upright loom. Doughnut-shaped clay loom weights were used for weighting the warp (i.e. the vertical thread on an upright loom) to keep it taut during weaving. Loom weights begin to disappear in southern Scandinavia in the 11th century when the horizontal loom came into use, but the upright loom continued to be used in NORWAY and the FAROE ISLANDS until modern times.

Wedmore, treaty of (878) The name sometimes given to the peace agreement between ALFRED THE GREAT and GUTHRUM, the leader of the Danish GREAT ARMY, following Guthrum's defeat at EDINGTON. He agreed to withdraw from WESSEX and to accept baptism. Guthrum was baptized at Aller near Athelney, and the ceremonial removal of his baptismal costume took place a few days later at nearby Wedmore, from which the agreement gets its name.

weights and measures Scales and weights are relatively common finds from Viking Age sites in Scandinavia and in Scandinavian settlements overseas. Their main use was for weighing silver, the most important medium of exchange in Viking Age Scandinavia: though COINS were in circulation, they were treated merely as another form of bullion, and

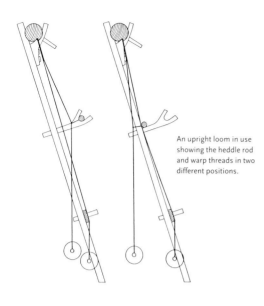

An upright loom in use showing the heddle rod and warp threads in two different positions.

Merchant scales from Birka, Sweden, used for weighing silver.

their value depended entirely on their weight and purity. By the late Viking Age, a standard system of weights had come into use on the basis of 1 *mörk* ('mark') equalling 8 *aurar* (singular *eyrir*, 'øre'), which equalled 24 *ertogar*, which in turn equalled 240 *penningar* ('pennies'). The oldest element of the system was the *eyrir* (from Latin *aureus*, 'of gold'), which developed in the ROMAN IRON AGE (AD 1–400). This weight was originally based on a gold standard and weighed around 26.4 grams (approximately 1 ounce) at the beginning of the Viking Age, gradually reduced to 24.5 grams by its end. The *ertog* of around 8 grams came into use after the *eyrir* and was based on a silver standard from the outset, and probably derived from a late-4th-century Roman coin called the *tremissis*. The *penning* was roughly the same weight as the standard Anglo-Saxon coin of the same name, the Frankish *denier* and the Arabic half-DIRHEM. Because coins could be underweight or debased, weighed *penningar* came to be differentiated from counted *penningar*. The most recent element of the system was the *mörk*, which is first heard of as a measure of weight in the late 9th century. Originating in Scandinavia, the measure spread to ENGLAND and later to Germany. The name is derived from the mark on the bar of the steelyard-type of scales. It is not known whether standard units of measurement of length and volume were used by Viking Age Scandinavians. The late-10th-century Danish TRELLEBORG FORTS, were built to a measure nearly equivalent to the Roman foot (29.5 centimetres) but, as no yardsticks have ever been discovered, it is not known how widespread its use was. Nothing at all is known about measures of volume.

Weland (d. 863) Viking leader in FRANCIA. He was probably a member of the Danish ARMY that was active on the River Somme in 859. In return for a payment from CHARLES THE BALD of 5,000 pounds of silver, plus livestock and grain supplies, Weland took his army up the Seine to besiege the Viking fort on the island of Oissel. Reduced to desperation by hunger, the besieged Vikings bribed Weland with 6,000 pounds of gold and silver to let them escape. Joined by many of the Vikings he had been paid to fight, Weland spent the winter of 861–2 at Melun, but in the spring he lost control of his army. When it withdrew down the Seine, Weland, with his family, joined king Charles, becoming his vassal and accepting baptism. In 863 Weland was accused by a Viking of converting in bad faith. Challenged by his accuser to single combat, Weland was killed in the presence of the king.

Wends The collective name given to the West Slavic peoples of the south Baltic coast in the Viking Age and the central Middle Ages: they included the Wagrians, Polabians, Abodrites, Rugians, Liutzians and Pomeranians. At the beginning of the Viking Age, Wendish territory extended from the mouth of the River Vistula in modern Poland west to the vicinity of modern Kiel in Germany. The Wends were at a very similar level of social and technological development to the Viking Age Scandinavians. The Wends had many trading TOWNS along the Baltic coast, and finds of large quantities of Arabic COINS show that they were involved in an important way with the Russian TRADE routes to the east. The Wends were skilled fortress builders and had a warlike aristocratic society. Though the DANES and Swedes might occasionally take control of a coastal town, such as RERIC in the early 9th century or Jumne (WOLIN) in the late 10th, they made no conquests or settlements inland. According to later SAGA accounts

The murder of William Longsword of Normandy, from the 15th-century *Chroniques de Normandie.*

many great Vikings, such as OLAF TRYGGVASON began their careers raiding the Wends. There was a certain amount of cultural interchange between the Wends and the Scandinavians. The Scandinavians may have learned bridge-building and adopted styles of JEWELRY and POTTERY from the Wends. In return, the Wends learned shipbuilding from the Scandinavians. The Wends had the better part of this exchange, and in the 11th century they turned to piracy. The Danish islands suffered worst from Wendish attacks, but some raids reached as far north as southern NORWAY and GOTLAND. Not until the Wends were conquered and forcibly Christianized by German and Danish crusaders in the early 13th century did their piracy cease.

Wessex The only Anglo-Saxon kingdom to survive the Viking invasions of the late 9th century intact. Wessex, the kingdom of the West Saxons, is traditionally considered to have been founded by Cerdic *c.* AD 500, and by the 9th century it covered most of ENGLAND south of the River Thames. Its main TOWNS were Winchester and Hamwic (Southampton). The victory of king Egbert (r. 802–39) over the rival kingdom of MERCIA at Ellandun in 825 established Wessex as the strongest Anglo-Saxon kingdom, and in 829 he was recognized as *Bretwalda* ('high king of Britain'). Viking attacks on Wessex began during the reign of Egbert's predecessor Beorhtric (r. 786–802) with a raid on PORTLAND, probably in 789. Later tradition in Wessex held that this was the first Viking raid in Britain. Large-scale Viking attacks on Wessex began only in 836 when Egbert was defeated by thirty-five SHIPS' companies at Carhampton in Somerset. The scale of raids escalated dramatically in the 850s when the Vikings wintered at Thanet in the Thames

Estuary, but generally the West Saxons gave the Vikings as good as they got.

With the arrival of the Danish GREAT ARMY in East Anglia in 865 the Viking threat escalated yet again, but its first foray into Wessex five years later was defeated by king ÆTHELRED I and his brother ALFRED after bitter fighting. The DANES, under GUTHRUM, Oscetel and Anund, invaded again in 875 and Alfred, now king (r. 871–99), was hard pressed, driving them out only after his decisive victory at EDINGTON in 878. Alfred successfully defended his kingdom against a second Viking onslaught in 892–6.

Alfred was followed by a succession of able kings who progressively brought the rest of England under their control. Alfred's son EDWARD THE ELDER worked closely with his sister ÆTHELFLÆD, wife of the Mercian ealdorman ÆTHELRED, to conquer the DANELAW of eastern England in 912–18. A year after Æthelflæd's death in 918, Edward annexed Mercia, taking West Saxon control to the Humber and the Mersey. When Edward's son ATHELSTAN captured YORK from the Norse in 927, all the Anglo-Saxons and all the Scandinavian settlers in England came under a single ruler for the first time and Wessex was transformed into the kingdom of England.

Wexford (ON Veigsfjörthr) Norse TOWN that developed from a LONGPHORT founded on a fine natural harbour in south-east IRELAND in the mid-9th century. Excavations have revealed rectangular buildings of the 10th and 11th centuries in plots flanking streets, similar to those in DUBLIN and WATERFORD. According to literary sources, Wexford also had substantial defences. The Wexford Vikings frequently raided in south-east Ireland, but by *c.*1000 the town was under the control of native Irish lords.

William the Conqueror giving arms to Harold Godwinson during Harold's visit to Normandy (*left*) and riding off on a campaign against the Bretons (*right*).

William Longsword (d. 942) Son of Rollo, William, count of Rouen (r. *c*.928–42), was the second ruler of Normandy. William continued the expansionist policy of his father and was granted the Cotentin peninsula in 933 and attempted to establish his protection over Brittany. In 935 William invaded Flanders but was defeated at Thérouanne. William also consolidated his authority over the Scandinavian settlers in Normandy, putting down a rebellion led by a Viking called Rioul in 933–4. In 939 he allied himself with Hugh the Great in a rebellion against king Louis IV. The war was ended through the mediation of the pope, and Louis confirmed William's investiture of Normandy in 940. William's murder, on the orders of Arnulf I, count of Flanders, during a meeting on an island in the River Somme in 942, threw Normandy into chaos. He was succeeded by his illegitimate son Richard I (Richard the Fearless).

William the Conqueror (*c*.1027–87) Duke of Normandy (1035–87); king of England (r. 1066–87). William was the last ruler of England to face a major Scandinavian invasion. The illegitimate son of Robert the Magnificent, William succeeded his father as duke of Normandy while still a child. On attaining his majority *c*.1042, he successfully established his authority in the face of baronial opposition. It is likely that the pro-Norman king Edward the Confessor had promised William the English throne, but on his death in 1066 the English chose Harold Godwinson as their king instead. Invading England, William defeated and killed Harold at Hastings (14 October 1066). William was fortunate that Harold's army had not had time to recover from its victory over a third claimant to the English throne, Harald Hardrada

of Norway, at Stamford Bridge less than three weeks before. He was crowned king of England on Christmas Day 1066. William faced many uncoordinated rebellions during the early years of his reign, prompting interventions by the Danish king Svein Estrithson, who had inherited Harald Hardrada's claim to the English throne. In October 1069, a fleet of 240 Danish ships under Svein's son Cnut (Cnut II) allied with English rebels and took York. William recaptured York in December and spent the winter engaged in the infamous 'Harrying of the North'. As well as punishing the locals for supporting the rebels, this scorched-earth campaign was intended to make the area unattractive to further Danish intervention. Svein met his son on the Humber in spring 1070, and in June they joined Hereward the Wake in sacking Peterborough. But English resistance was collapsing and William was able to negotiate Svein's withdrawal. A second Danish intervention came in 1075, when Cnut was invited to take the English throne by rebel Norman barons. William had crushed the rebellion by the time Cnut arrived. William faced the threat of a third Danish intervention in 1085, when Cnut, now king of Denmark, began to prepare an expedition to conquer England. The attack never materialized because Cnut was assassinated the following year. It was partly in response to this threat that William ordered the famous Domesday survey in 1086. He was killed the following year while fighting in France.

Although William was of Scandinavian descent, the Norman conquest of England can in no way be considered as an extension of Viking activity: William and his followers were culturally and linguistically completely French. The conquest led to a decline of cultural and political links between

A selection of woodworking tools from Mästermyr on Gotland.

England and Scandinavia as English institutions were Normanized and English culture was exposed to powerful French influences.

Willibrord, St (St Clement) (658–739) Leader of the first Christian mission to Scandinavia. Born in NORTHUMBRIA, Willibrord joined a mission to FRISIA in 690. In 695 he became archbishop of Utrecht. Though Willibrord was driven out of Utrecht by the pagan Frisian leader Radbod between 714 and 719, his missionary activity was outstandingly successful. Around 725 he led a mission to king ANGANTYR in DENMARK. He was politely received, but, although he was allowed to buy thirty slave boys to bring up as Christians, he won no converts. Willibrord's *Life* was written by ALCUIN.

Wolin Port near the mouth of the River Oder in Poland. Known in the late Viking Age as Jumne, Wolin is probably to be identified with Jomsborg, the headquarters of the semi-legendary JOMSVIKINGS in the 10th century. Wolin developed from a fishing village in the 7th century. By *c.*700 there is evidence that it had become a craft centre. In the 9th century Wolin was fortified with an earth rampart; a northern suburb, Silberberg, was also fortified. In the late 9th century the TOWN was laid out in regular square blocks, each containing four houses. The population in the Viking Age was several thousands. The harbour had a regularly laid-out quay built of halved oak logs, with jetties projecting at right angles. There was also a beacon site near the town and a pagan temple. Tools associated with IRONWORKING, shipbuilding, WEAVING, leather-working, amber-working and comb-making have been found. Many of these artefacts were similar to ones found in the Scandinavian ports of HEDEBY and BIRKA. THOR'S

hammer amulets, SOAPSTONE bowls and runic inscriptions, among other items, point to the presence of Scandinavians, but because POTTERY was of an exclusively Slavic style, they were probably only a minority. Writing in the late 11th century, ADAM OF BREMEN describes Wolin as a Slav town, but says it played host to merchants from as far away as Greece.

women Viking Age Scandinavian society was dominated by men, but women enjoyed higher status than in other areas of Europe at the time. Men and women had clearly defined social and economic roles. Men ploughed, hunted, fished, traded and fought. Most crafts were also the preserve of men. Women's lives were usually confined to the home and family farm: they ground flour and baked bread, brewed ale, spun woollen thread, wove cloth, made and mended clothes, milked the cows, churned butter, nursed the sick, and looked after the CHILDREN. In pagan times these distinctions were expected to continue in the afterlife. Men were buried with their WEAPONS or the tools of their trade; women, with JEWELRY, needlework, WEAVING equipment and other household utensils.

A single woman's MARRIAGE was usually arranged by negotiation between the prospective husband and her father or guardian, but widows had greater freedom in this respect. A married woman retained property rights after marriage. Both her dowry and the 'bride-price' paid by the husband remained her property, and she had the right to a divorce if the marriage was unsuccessful. Women could also inherit property, though they could not expect an equal share if there were also surviving male heirs. Women had no formal role in public life, nor is there any evidence that they could take part in legal procedures but, as Icelandic SAGA accounts show, a

High-quality wood-carving from the Oseberg ship burial – a mythological scene from a wagon (*below*) and a 'gripping beast' motif from the stem of the ship (*right*).

strong-minded woman could enjoy a great deal of practical influence and authority. In the home, a married woman exercised authority over slaves and hired hands, had custody of the keys to the house and the strongbox, and would expect her husband to involve her with any major decisions affecting the welfare of the family. If her husband was away from home, a wife had full responsibility for running the household and family farm until he returned. If she was widowed, a woman had to take her husband's place, unless she decided to remarry. Women were no less zealous in defending family honour than men. In Icelandic saga literature, for example NJÁLS SAGA, women were often among the instigators of blood feuds. Pagan graves from DENMARK suggest that a woman's status increased with age. While young men were likely to be buried with more-valuable grave goods than older men, the reverse was true for women.

Though VALKYRIES and other supernatural maiden warriors feature in Scandinavian pagan mythology, there is no reliable historical evidence that merely mortal women ever fought as warriors. However, it is certain that at least some of the warriors who joined the great Viking ARMIES that ravaged ENGLAND and FRANCIA in the 9th century took their wives and even children with them. These women gave valuable support to the army, cooking and tending the sick and injured. As their presence was essential from the very start, women played a more prominent role in the settlement of ICELAND and GREENLAND. The presence of women on the voyages to VINLAND is attested not only by saga accounts but also by the discovery of spindle-whorls (used in spinning thread for weaving) in excavations of the Norse settlement at L'ANSE-AUX-MEADOWS in Newfoundland. Finds of typically Scandinavian

female artefacts in Viking Age graves in RUSSIA indicate that the RUS were accompanied by Scandinavian women on their journeys in the east; but contemporary Arab sources suggest that most of them took local women, perhaps speeding their assimilation into the native Slav population.

J. Jesch, *Women in the Viking Age* (Woodbridge, Suffolk, 1991); J. Jochens, *Women in Old Norse Society* (Ithaca and London, 1995).

wood-carving Viking Age Scandinavia had a rich tradition of decorative wood-carving. Until the introduction of CHRISTIANITY, Scandinavia lacked traditions of stone architecture, sculpture and manuscript illumination, so wood-carving attracted the best artistic talent and enjoyed considerable prestige. Almost any wooden object could be decorated with carvings: buildings, SHIPS, FURNITURE, wagons, sledges, skis and everyday objects. Oak and pine were the most common woods used by carvers. The most skilled could execute complex designs in relief with two or more horizontal planes (i.e. with layers of motifs superimposed one on another, with the deepest motifs visible only by peering through gaps in the upper layers of decoration). The simplest designs were just incised on a wooden surface. At least some carvings were painted to highlight the design or decorated with metal studs. The motifs used in decorative wood-carving reflect the fashionable ART STYLES of the period in which they were carved. Figurative carvings with a narrative content are known but are rare. The most important collection of Viking Age wood-carving was found in the early 9th-century OSEBERG SHIP BURIAL, which included a richly decorated ship and animal-headed posts with designs of amazing complexity. The wood-carving of

the late Viking Age is also well represented thanks to the survival of several carved portals from Norwegian stave CHURCHES, such as Urnes, Hylestad and Ulvik: it is likely that the halls of Viking Age kings and chieftains were decorated with similar exuberance.

Wulfstan (*fl. c.*890) A Scandinavian or Anglo-Saxon merchant based at the Danish port of HEDEBY. Around 890, Wulfstan visited the court of ALFRED THE GREAT and gave the king a description of his journey from Hedeby to Truso (probably modern ELBLAG on the River Vistula in Poland), an account that was included in the *Old English OROSIUS*. Wulfstan's description of the customs of the Slav and Baltic peoples is one of the earliest written sources for the region.

Wulfstan I (d. 955) Archbishop of YORK (931–52). Appointed archbishop by king ATHELSTAN, Wulfstan collaborated with a succession of Viking rulers. He accompanied OLAF GUTHFRITHSSON on his campaign against the FIVE BOROUGHS in 940 and helped negotiate peace with the English king EDMUND. Wulfstan later supported ERIK BLOODAXE in his struggle for control of York with OLAF SIHTRICSSON of DUBLIN and Edmund's successor EADRED. As a result, he was arrested by Eadred in 952 and not allowed to return to his see, even after Erik's expulsion from York and death in 954.

Yggdrasil In Scandinavian mythology, the 'world-tree', a vast ash tree that supported the universe. Yggdrasil grew from three roots, one each in NIFLHEIM, the realm of the dead, JOTUNHEIM, the land of the GIANTS, and ASGARD, the realm of the gods. Beneath its root in Jotunheim was the spring of Mimir, whose waters were the source of wisdom and understanding. Beneath its root in Asgard was the spring of fate, where the gods daily held court. Near the spring dwelled the NORNS ('fates'), who watered and tended the tree. At the same time, Yggdrasil was constantly threatened by a host of creatures that gnawed its leaves, branches and roots. Yggdrasil is a timeless eternal tree; its origin is unknown and it will survive RAGNAROK. *See also* CREATION MYTH.

Yngling dynasty Semi-legendary dynasty of kings that ruled the SVEAR from UPPSALA from the end of the third century AD to the mid-9th century. The dynasty was named after the god FREYR (Yngvi-Freyr), from whom the Yngling kings were believed to be descended. King HARALD FAIRHAIR (r. *c.*880–930), the first unifier of NORWAY, and his successors claimed descent from the Ynglings through a marriage between Hild, daughter of king Erik Agnarsson of the Vestfold in southern Norway, and Eystein, the son of the Yngling king Halfdan Hvitbein, which probably took place sometime in the late 8th century. As king Erik had no sons, he was succeeded as king of Vestfold by Eystein. The main source for the historical traditions surrounding the Ynglings is the poem *Ynglingatal* ('List of the Ynglings'), composed *c.*900 by the Norwegian skald Thjóðólfr of Hvin in honour of king Harald's cousin Rognvald, which traces the descent of the dynasty from its mythical origins.

Intricate carvings from Urnes stave church, Norway, representing Yggdrasil. In the centre, a deer gnaws at the tree's branches.

Yngvars saga víðforla ('The Saga of Yngvar the Widefarer') Based loosely on historical events and persons, *Yngvars saga* is a translation into Old Icelandic, made *c.*1200, of a lost 12th-century Latin work by the Icelandic monk Odd Snorrason. The SAGA recounts the life and adventures of YNGVAR THE WIDEFARER, a historical character known from independent sources, but with so many fantastic elements and chronological inconsistencies that it must be regarded primarily as a work of fiction. The Yngvar of the saga is a warrior in the service of the Swedish king OLOF SKÖTKONUNG. When the king refuses to grant him a royal title, Yngvar raises an expedition to go to the east in search of a kingdom for himself. He goes first to the court of king JAROSLAV THE WISE in RUSSIA before pressing on by ship along an unnamed river into the east. From this point onwards, Yngvar's adventures become increasingly fantastic, with encounters with GIANTS, dragons, witches and, of course, a beautiful queen, Silkisif of Gardariki, who falls in love with him. Finally, Yngvar dies in an epidemic that decimates his expedition, and his body is returned to Silkisif, who orders the survivors home with instructions to send missionaries to convert her country to CHRISTIANITY. According to the saga, Yngvar died 'eleven years after the fall of king OLAF HARALDSSON' (i.e. 1041), aged twenty-five, which would have made him just six when he left the service of king Olof.

Vikings in Russia: Yngvar's Saga and Eymund's Saga, trans. H. Pálsson and P. Edwards (Edinburgh, 1989).

Yngvar the Widefarer (d. 1041) Swedish adventurer who led a disastrous expedition to south-east RUSSIA or the Caspian Sea region in the mid-11th century, in the course of which he died. The expedition is known from a group of thirty rune-stones in central SWEDEN that commemorate men who fell 'in the East with Yngvar', references to Yngvar's death in 1041 in two near-contemporary Icelandic annals, and the highly fictionalized account in YNGVARS SAGA VÍÐFORLA. The purpose of Yngvar's expedition is not known, but it may be that he was trying to re-establish trading contacts with the Muslim world, which had virtually ceased around the end of the 10th century.

York (OE *Eoforwic*, ON *Jórvík*) For most of the period 866–954, York was the capital of a Viking kingdom that controlled most of northern ENGLAND between the rivers Humber and Tees. York originated as a legionary fortress in Roman times, was abandoned in the 5th century, and was reoccupied in the 6th century as a royal, ecclesiastical and merchant centre of the Anglo-Saxon kingdom of NORTHUMBRIA. The city was captured by the Danish GREAT ARMY under HALFDAN in 866, and an attempt by the Northumbrians to recapture it was beaten off with heavy losses the following year. At first, the DANES ruled through an Anglo-Saxon puppet king, but in 876 Halfdan returned to rule in person and settled his followers on lands around York. Halfdan was probably killed in IRELAND in 877; of his successors, little is known apart from their names. Danish rule was threatened by the influx of Irish-Norse settlers to north-west England that followed the Irish victory over the DUBLIN Vikings in 902. The death of three Danish kings and numerous chieftains in a disastrous defeat by the combined forces of WESSEX and MERCIA at the battle of TETTENHALL in 910 paralysed the kingdom, and York fell easily to the Irish-Norse Viking RAGNALD in 911. Ragnald did not hold power for long, but he returned to York in 919

Excavations of Viking Age
deposits at Coppergate, York.

and ruled there until his death in 921. The Irish-Norse hold on York was precarious, and in 927 they were driven out by king ATHELSTAN of Wessex. An attempt to recapture the city by OLAF GUTHFRITHSSON, king of Dublin, in alliance with the Scots and Britons of STRATHCLYDE, was crushingly defeated by Athelstan at the battle of BRUNANBURH in 937. Following Athelstan's death in 939, however, Olaf returned and not only recaptured York but conquered Northumbria and the FIVE BOROUGHS of the DANELAW as well. His victory was short-lived: York was back in English hands by 944. The city was returned to Scandinavian rule for the last time by the exiled Norwegian king ERIK BLOODAXE in 948. For the next six years, he fought a losing battle for control, first with king OLAF SIHTRICSSON of Dublin and then with king EADRED of England, who finally engineered Erik's overthrow and permanently restored English rule in 954. Because of its Scandinavian links, 10th- and 11th-century English kings were wary of York's loyalty, and, as a precaution against the development of local particularism, the earls and archbishops they appointed to the city came from the south of England. York was briefly occupied by the Norwegian king HARALD HARDRADA in 1066, and by the Danes during the English rebellions against the Normans in 1069 and 1075.

Archaeological excavations have shown that about thirty years after the arrival of the Vikings, York began a period of rapid urban growth, and by 1000 its population had reached 10,000, making it a large city by the standards of early medieval Europe and second only to London in the British Isles. The division of much of the city into regular tenement blocks and streets at the beginning of the 10th century is a sign of deliberate town planning, either by the Scandinavian kings or a city council of leading citizens. The Roman city walls were also restored and extended during the Viking period.

The Scandinavian kings increased the silver content of York's coinage (which typically carries both pagan and Christian symbols) and encouraged TRADE as a source of revenue. York developed strong commercial links with Ireland and Scandinavia to add to its longer-standing links with FRISIA and the Rhineland. Exotic products such as Byzantine silk also reached York, probably through a series of middlemen. Viking York was also a thriving manufacturing centre. Excavations have provided evidence of glass-making, metallurgy, textiles and wood-, leather-, bone-, antler- and jet-working. Most of the Scandinavian (mainly Danish) settlement lay to the south of the old Roman legionary fort, which was the Northumbrian administrative and ecclesiastical centre. This continued to function undisturbed by the Vikings, and York's archbishops, especially WULFSTAN I, enjoyed close and friendly relations with their kings. The final English capture of York was not followed by an expulsion of its Scandinavian population: they had already begun to become assimilated with the native ANGLO-SAXONS, but the city retained an Anglo-Scandinavian character until after the Norman Conquest.

R. A. Hall, *Viking Age York* (London, 1994); A. P. Smyth, *Scandinavian York and Dublin* (2 vols, Dublin, 1975–9).

Chronology AD 1–1500

c. AD 1–400	Emergence of a warrior aristocracy in southern Scandinavia.
c.400–800	The first kingdoms develop in Denmark, Norway and Sweden.
c.425–500	Anglo-Saxon migrations from Denmark and Germany to Britain.
c.516–34	Hygelac leads a Scandinavian pirate raid on the lower Rhine.
c.725	St Willibrord leads the first Christian mission to Scandinavia.
737	The first phase of the Danevirke rampart is completed.
c.750	Swedes established at Staraja Ladoga in Russia.
c.789	Norwegian Vikings sack Portland in Wessex.
793	Vikings plunder the Northumbrian monastery of Lindisfarne.
795	First recorded Viking raids on Scotland and Ireland.
799	Vikings raid Aquitaine.
800	Charlemagne organizes coastal defences against the Vikings.
810	Danish king Godfred ravages Frisia.
822–3	Archbishop Ebo of Rheims undertakes a mission to Denmark.
c.825	First Danish coins are minted at Hedeby; Irish monks driven out of the Faroe Islands by the Vikings.
826	Danish king Harald Klak is baptized at Mainz; St Ansgar's first mission to Denmark.
829–30	St Ansgar's first mission to the Svear at Birka.
832	Armagh in Ireland is raided by Vikings three times in one month.
834–7	Dorestad on the Rhine is raided annually.
c.835	The Oseberg ship burial in Norway.
839	The Rus reach Constantinople.
841	Viking base is established at Dublin.
843	Treaty of Verdun partitions the Carolingian Empire.
844	Viking army in Spain is defeated near Seville.
845	The Danes sack Hamburg and Paris.
851–2	St Ansgar's second mission to Denmark and Sweden.
859–62	Hastein and Bjorn Ironside raid in the Mediterranean.
860	The first Rus attack on Constantinople is driven off.
c.860	Gardar the Swede explores the coast of Iceland.
862	Charles the Bald, king of the West Franks, orders the construction of fortified bridges against the Vikings.
c.862	Rurik becomes ruler of Novgorod; Askold and Dir seize Kiev.
865	Danish Great Army invades England.
866	The Danes capture York.
869	The Danes conquer East Anglia.
c.870–930	The Vikings settle in Iceland.
c.870	The earldom of Orkney is established by Rognvald of Møre.
873–914	The 'Forty Years Rest' in Ireland.
876–9	The beginning of Danish settlement in eastern England.
878	Alfred the Great of Wessex defeats the Danes at Edington.

c.882	Oleg unites Novgorod and Kiev.
885–6	Unsuccessful Viking siege of Paris.
c.885–90	Harald Fairhair wins the battle of Hafrsfjord, uniting most of Norway.
891	Arnulf, king of the East Franks, defeats the Vikings at the Dyle.
c.900	Norwegian settlement begins in north-west England.
c.900–5	The Gokstad ship burial in Norway.
902	Irish expel the Vikings from Dublin.
907	After their attack on Constantinople is defeated, the Rus agree a trade treaty with the Byzantine Empire.
911	Rollo is made count of Rouen, founding Normandy.
912–18	Wessex conquers the Danelaw as far north as the Humber.
912–36	Vikings occupy Brittany.
917	Vikings under Sihtric Cáech recapture Dublin.
c.930	Foundation of the Icelandic Althing.
934	Henry the Fowler leads a German invasion of Denmark.
937	English defeat a Scottish-Norse alliance at Brunanburh.
948	First Scandinavian bishoprics founded at Ribe, Århus and Schleswig.
954	Erik Bloodaxe, last Viking king of York, is killed at Stainmore.
964–71	Svyatoslav of Kiev campaigns against the Bulgars, Khazars and Byzantines.
965	Harald Bluetooth of Denmark is converted to Christianity.
c.965	Exhaustion of Muslim silver mines leads to the decline of Viking trade routes to the east.
974–81	Germans occupy Hedeby.
c.980	Harald Bluetooth constructs the Trelleborg forts in Denmark.
986	Erik the Red leads the Norse settlement of Greenland.
988	Byzantine emperor Basil II founds the Varangian Guard; Vladimir, prince of Kiev, converts to Orthodox Christianity.
991	Olaf Tryggvason defeats the English at Maldon.
995	Olaf Tryggvason wins control of Norway and adopts a policy of forcible Christianization; Olof Skötkonung becomes the first king to rule both the Svear and Götar.
1000	Olaf Tryggvason is killed at the battle of Svöld; the Icelanders accept Christianity.
c.1000	Voyages to Vinland begin.
1002	St Brice's Day Massacre of Danes living in England.
1013	Svein Forkbeard of Denmark conquers England.
1014	Brian Boru, high king of Ireland, defeats Norse-Leinster alliance at Clontarf.
1016	Olaf Haraldsson becomes king of Norway; Cnut becomes king of England.
c.1027	First stone church built in Denmark at Roskilde.
1030	Olaf Haraldsson killed at the battle of Stiklestad.
c.1030–5	Battle of Tarbat Ness: Thorfinn the Mighty, earl of Orkney wins control of northern Scotland.
1042	End of Danish rule in England.
1043	Magnus the Good defeats the Wends at the battle of Lyrskov Heath.
1066	Harald Hardrada killed at the battle of Stamford Bridge; battle of Hastings.
1075	Last Danish invasion of England.
1079	Battle of Skyhill; Godred Crovan unites the Isle of Man and the Hebrides.
1086	Cnut II of Denmark is murdered after abandoning a planned invasion of England.
1098	Magnus Barelegs establishes Norwegian authority in the Scottish isles.
1103–4	Lund becomes the first Scandinavian archbishopric.
1107–11	Norwegian king Sigurd 'the Crusader' leads an expedition to the Holy Land.
1122–32	Ari Thorgilsson writes Íslendingabók ('The Book of the Icelanders').
1147	The Danes join a crusade against the pagan Wends.
1156	Somerled wins the southern Hebrides from Godred II of Man.
1171	Asgall, last Norse king of Dublin, captured and executed by the Anglo-Normans.
1241	The Icelandic poet and historian Snorri Sturluson is murdered.
1261	Norse Greenland colony comes under direct rule from Norway.
1263	Iceland comes under Norwegian rule; Scots defeat Håkon IV of Norway at Largs.
1266	Norway cedes Man and the Hebrides to Scotland.
1341	Eskimos occupy the Western Settlement in Greenland.
1397	Union of Kalmar unites Denmark, Norway and Sweden.
1469	Denmark cedes Orkney and Shetland to Scotland.
c.1500?	Extinction of the Norse Greenland colony.

Viking Kings and Rulers 700–1100

Capitals indicate entry in the encyclopaedia
Italics indicate rulers from dynasties of non-Norse origin

Kings of Denmark

THE EARLY KINGS

*c.*720	Angantyr
*c.*777	Sigfred
*c.*804–10	Godfred
810–12	Hemming
812–13	Harald Klak (deposed)
812–13	Reginfred (deposed)
813–54	Horik
819–27	Harald Klak (restored, deposed)
854–63	Horik II
*c.*873	Sigfred
*c.*873	Halfdan
d. *c.*900	Helgi (possibly legendary)
*c.*900–36	Swedish Olaf dynasty (Olaf, Gnupa, Gerd, Sigtryg)
*c.*936	Hardegon

THE JELLING DYNASTY

*c.*936–58	Gorm the Old
958–87	Harald Bluetooth (deposed)
987–1014	Svein Forkbeard (king of England 1013–14)
1014–18	Harald II
1019–35	Cnut the Great (king of England 1016–35)
1035–42	Harthacnut (king of England 1040–2)
1042–7	Magnus the Good (king of Norway 1035–47)

THE DYNASTY OF SVEIN ESTRITHSON

1047–74	Svein Estrithson
1074–80	Harald III
1080–6	Cnut II
1086–95	Olaf Hunger
1095–1103	Erik the Evergood

Kings of Norway

d. *c.*880	Halfdan the Black
*c.*880–*c.*930	Harald Fairhair
*c.*930–6	Erik Bloodaxe (deposed; king of York 948, 952–4)
*c.*936–60	Håkon the Good
*c.*960–70	Harald Greycloak
995–1000	Olaf Tryggvason
1016–28	Olaf Haraldsson (deposed)
1030–5	Svein Alfivason (deposed)
1035–47	Magnus the Good (king of Denmark 1042–7)

1046–66	HARALD HARDRADA	1052–70	*Murchad mac Diarmata*
1066–9	Magnus II	1070–2	*Domnall mac Murchada* or
1067–93	OLAF THE PEACEFUL		*Diarmit mac Máel*
1093–5	Håkon Magnusson	1072–4	Gofraid
1093–1103	MAGNUS BARELEGS		(deposed)
	(king of Man 1098–1103)	1074–86	*Muirchertach ua Briain*
		1086–9	*Enna* or *Donnchad*
		1091–4	GODRED CROVAN

Kings of the Svear

*c.*829	Björn
*c.*850	Olaf
980–95	ERIK THE VICTORIOUS
995–1022	OLOF SKÖTKONUNG
1022–50	ÖNUND JACOB
1050–60	Emund the Old
1060–6	Stenkil Ragnvaldsson
1066–70	Halsten
	(deposed)
1070–?	Håkon the Red
?–1080	Inge I
	(deposed)
1080–3	Blot-Sven
1083–1110	Inge I
	(restored)

Godred Crovan (expelled; king of Man 1079–95)

1094–1118 *Domnall mac Muirchertaig ua Briain* (deposed; king of Man 1096–8)

Kings of York

876–7	HALFDAN
*c.*883–95	Guthfrith
*c.*895–901	Sigfrid
*c.*900–2	Cnut
d. 903	*Æthelwold*
902–10	Halfdan II
902–10	Eowils
902–10	Ivar
*c.*911, 919–21	RAGNALD
921–7	SIHTRIC CÁECH
	(king of Dublin 917–21)
927	GUTHFRITH
	(expelled; king of Dublin 921–34)
927–39	ATHELSTAN
	(king of Wessex 924–39)
939–41	OLAF GUTHFRITHSSON
	(king of Dublin 934–41)
941–4	OLAF SIHTRICSSON
	(expelled; king of Dublin 945–80)
943–4	Ragnald Guthfrithsson
	(expelled)
944–6	EDMUND I
	(king of England 939–46)
946–8	EADRED
	(king of England 946–56)
948	ERIK BLOODAXE
	(expelled; king of Norway *c.*930–6)
949–52	Olaf Sihtricsson
	(restored, expelled)
952–4	Erik Bloodaxe
	(restored, expelled)

Kings of Dublin

853–*c.*871	OLAF
863–7	Auisle
*c.*871–3	IVAR I
873–5	Eystein Olafsson
877–81	Bardr
883–8	Sigfred
888–93	Sihtric I
	(deposed)
893–4	Sigfred jarl
894–6	Sihtric I
	(restored)
896–902	IVAR II
	(expelled)
917–21	SIHTRIC CÁECH
	(king of York 921–7)
921–34	GUTHFRITH
	(king of York 927)
934–41	OLAF GUTHFRITHSSON
	(king of York 939–41)
941–45	Blacaire
945–80	OLAF SIHTRICSSON
	(abdicated; king of York 941–4, 949–52)
980–9	Járnkné Olafsson
989–1036	SIHTRIC SILKBEARD
	(abdicated)
1036–8	Echmarcach mac Ragnaill
	(deposed)
1038–46	Ivar Haraldsson
	(deposed)
1046–52	Echmarcach mac Ragnaill
	(restored, deposed; king of Man 1052–64)

Kings of Man

*c.*971	Maccus mac Arailt (Magnus Haraldsson)
d. 989	Gofraid mac Arailt (Godfred Haraldsson)
d. 1004–5	Ragnall
d. 1014	Brodir?

1052–64	Echmarcach mac Ragnaill (abdicated; king of Dublin 1036–8, 1046–52)
c.1066–75	Godred Sihtricsson
c.1075–9	Fingal Godredsson (deposed)
1079–95	GODRED CROVAN (king of Dublin 1091–4)
1095–6	Lagmann Godredsson (abdicated)
1096–8	*Domnall mac Muirchertaig ua Briain* (deposed; king of Dublin 1094–1118)
1098–1103	MAGNUS BARELEGS (king of Norway 1093–1103)

Jarls of Hlaðir (Lade)

c.900	Håkon Grjotgarðson
d. c.963	Sigurd Håkonsson
c.963–95	HÅKON SIGURDSSON
1000–15	ERIK OF HLAÐIR
1015	SVEIN HÅKONSSON (deposed)

Earls of Orkney

c.870	ROGNVALD OF MØRE
d. c.892	SIGURD THE MIGHTY
c.893	Guttorm
c.894	Hallad (abdicated)
c.895–910	TORF-EINAR
d. 954	Arnkell
d. 954	Erlend
d. c.963	THORFINN SKULLSPLITTER
	Arnfinn Thorfinnsson
	Havard Thorfinnsson
	Ljot Thorfinnsson
	Hlodver Thorfinnsson

c.985–1014	SIGURD THE STOUT
1014–18	Sumarlidi
1014–20	Einar Falsemouth
1014–c.1030	Brusi
c.1020–65	THORFINN THE MIGHTY
1037–46	Rognvald (deposed)
1065–93	Paul (deposed)
1065–93	Erlend (deposed)
1093–1103	Sigurd (king of Norway 1103–30)

Dukes of Normandy

911–c.928	ROLLO
c.928–42	WILLIAM LONGSWORD
942–96	RICHARD I
996–1026	RICHARD II
1026–7	Richard III
1027–35	Robert the Magnificent
1035–87	WILLIAM THE CONQUEROR (king of England 1066–87)

Princes of Kievan Rus

c.860–c.879	RURIK (semi-legendary ruler of Novgorod)
c.879–913	OLEG
913–45	IGOR
945–72	SVYATOSLAV I
972–78/80	Jaropolk I
978/80–1015	VLADIMIR I
1015–19	Svyatopolk I
1019–54	JAROSLAV THE WISE

Kievan dynasty survives until 1271

Further Reading

Primary Sources in Translation

ANNALS, CHRONICLES, LIVES AND LETTERS

Adam of Bremen, *History of the Archbishops of Hamburg-Bremen*, trans. F. J. Tschan (New York, 1959)

Allott, S. (trans.), *Alcuin of York: His Life and Letters* (York, 1974)

Chronicles of the Kings of Man and the Isles, ed. and trans. G. Broderick (Douglas, Isle of Man, 1995)

Dudo of St-Quentin: History of the Normans, trans. E. Christiansen (Woodbridge, Suffolk, 1998)

Encomium Emmae Regina, ed. and trans. A. Campbell, Camden Society 3rd Series 72 (London, 1949, reprint 1998)

Keynes, S. and M. Lapidge (trans.), *Alfred the Great: Asser's Life of King Alfred and Other Contemporary Sources* (Harmondsworth, 1983)

King, P. D. (trans.), *Charlemagne: Translated Sources* (Lambrigg, Cumbria, 1987)

Rimbert, *Life of St Ansgar*, in C. H. Robinson (trans.), *Anskar, Apostle of the North, 801–65: Translated from the Vita Anskarii by Bishop Rimbert, his fellow Missionary and Successor* (London, 1921)

Russian Primary Chronicle: Laurentian Text, ed. and trans. S. H. Cross and O. P. Sherbowitz-Wetzor (Cambridge, Mass., 1953)

Scholz, B. W. and B. Rogers (trans.), *Carolingian Chronicles* (Ann Arbor, 1972)

The Anglo-Saxon Chronicle, trans. N. Garmonsway (London, 1953)

The Annals of Fulda, trans. T. Reuter (Manchester, 1992)

The Annals of St-Bertin, trans. J. L. Nelson (Manchester, 1991)

The Annals of Ulster, trans. S. Mac Airt and G. Mac Niocaill (Dublin, 1983)

The Book of the Icelanders (Íslendingabók) by Ari Thorgilsson, ed. and trans. H. Hermannsson (New York, 1930)

The Book of Settlements: Landnámabók, trans. H. Pálsson and P. Edwards (Winnipeg, 1972)

The War of the Gaedhil with the Gaill, ed. and trans. J. H. Todd (London, 1867)

Whitelock, D. (ed. and trans.), *English Historical Documents, Vol. 1 c.500–1042* (revised edition, London, 1971)

SAGAS

Egil's Saga, trans. H. Pálsson and P. Edwards (Harmondsworth, 1977)

Eyrbyggja Saga, trans. H. Pálsson and P. Edwards (Edinburgh, 1973)

Göngu-Hrolf's Saga: A Viking Romance, trans. H. Pálsson and P. Edwards (Edinburgh, 1980)

Heimskringla: History of the Kings of Norway, trans. L. M. Hollander (Austin, Texas, 1964).

King Harald's Saga: Harald Hardradi of Norway, trans. M. Magnusson and H. Pálsson (Harmondsworth, 1966)

Laxdæla Saga, trans. M. Magnusson and H. Pálsson (Harmondsworth, 1969)

Njal's Saga, trans. M. Magnusson and H. Pálsson (Harmondsworth, 1960)

Orkneyinga Saga, trans. M. Magnusson and
  H. Pálsson (London, 1978)
The Faroe Islanders' Saga, trans. G. Johnston
  (Ottawa, 1975)
The Saga of Grettir the Strong, trans. G. A. Hight,
  edited and introduced by Peter Foote
  (London, 1965)
The Vinland Sagas, trans. M. Magnusson and
  H. Pálsson (Harmondsworth, 1965)
*Vikings in Russia: Yngvar's Saga and Eymund's
  Saga*, trans. H. Pálsson and P. Edwards
  (Edinburgh, 1989)

POETRY, LEGEND AND MYTHOLOGY

Hollander, L. M. (trans.), *The Skalds: A Selection
  of Their Poems, with Introduction and Notes*
  (2nd edition, Ithaca, 1968);
*Saga of the Volsungs: The Norse Epic of Sigurd the
  Dragon Slayer*, trans. J. L. Byock (Berkeley,
  Los Angeles and London, 1990)
*Saxo Grammaticus: The History of the Danes,
  Books I–IX*, ed. H. Ellis Davidson, trans.
  P. Fisher (Woodbridge, Suffolk, 1996)
Snorri Sturluson, *Edda*, trans. A. Faulkes
  (London and Rutland, Vermont, 1987)
The Battle of Maldon, ed. and trans. B. Griffiths
  (Hockwold-cum-Wilton, Norfolk, 1995)
The Poetic Edda, trans. C. Larrington (Oxford,
  1996)

Secondary Sources

The following is a selective list for the general
reader, concentrating on recent works in English
only. Readers of the Scandinavian (and other)
languages are referred to the extensive
bibliographies in Roesdahl and Wilson (1992).

GENERAL SURVEYS

Brønsted, J., *The Vikings* (Harmondsworth,
  1960)
Foote, P. G. and D. M. Wilson, *The Viking
  Achievement* (2nd revised edition,
  London, 1980)
Graham-Campbell, J., *The Viking World*
  (2nd revised edition, London, 1989)
Haywood, J., *The Vikings* (Stroud,
  Gloucestershire, 1999)
Jones, G., *A History of the Vikings* (Oxford,
  1968)
Roesdahl, E., *The Vikings* (London, 1991)
Roesdahl, E. and D. M. Wilson (eds), *From
  Viking to Crusader: Scandinavia and Europe
  800–1200* (Copenhagen, 1992)
Sawyer, P. H., *The Age of the Vikings* (London,
  1962)
Sawyer, P. H., (ed.), *The Oxford Illustrated
  History of the Vikings* (Oxford, 1997)

Wilson, D. M., *The Vikings and their Origins*
  (3rd revised edition, London, 1989)

HISTORICAL ATLASES

Graham-Campbell, J. (ed.), *Cultural Atlas of
  the Viking World* (London and New York,
  1994)
Haywood, J., *The Penguin Historical Atlas of the
  Vikings* (London, 1995)
Hill, D., *An Atlas of Anglo-Saxon England*
  (Oxford, 1981)
Hooper, N. and M. Bennett, *Cambridge
  Illustrated Atlas – Warfare: The Middle Ages
  768–1487* (Cambridge, 1996)

VIKING AGE SCANDINAVIA

Hagen, A., *Norway* (London, 1967)
Lund, N., 'Scandinavia, c.700–1066', in
  The New Cambridge Medieval History Vol. 2,
  ed. R. McKitterick (Cambridge, 1995),
  pp. 202–27
Pulsiano, P. (ed.), *Medieval Scandinavia:
  An Encyclopedia* (New York and London,
  1993)
Randsborg, K., *The Viking Age in Denmark*
  (London, 1980)
Roesdahl, E., *Viking Age Denmark* (London, 1982)
Sawyer B. and P. H. Sawyer, *Medieval Scandinavia*
  (Minneapolis, 1993)
Sawyer, P. H., *Kings and Vikings* (London,
  1982)

THE NORTH ATLANTIC

Batey, C. E., J. Jesch, and C. D. Morris, *The
  Viking Age in Caithness, Orkney and the
  North Atlantic* (Edinburgh, 1993)
Byock, J. L., *Medieval Iceland: Society, Sagas and
  Power* (Berkeley, Los Angeles and London,
  1988)
Dahl, S., 'The Norse Settlement of the Faroe
  Islands', in *Medieval Archaeology 14* (1970),
  pp. 60–73
Ingstad, A. S., *The Discovery of a Norse
  Settlement in America: Excavations at
  L'Anse-aux-Meadows, Newfoundland 1961–68*
  (Oslo, 1977)
J. Jóhannesson, *A History of the Old Icelandic
  Commonwealth: Íslendinga Saga* (Winnipeg,
  1974)
Jones, G., *The Norse Atlantic Saga* (2nd edition,
  Oxford, 1986)
Krogh, K. J., *Viking Greenland* (Copenhagen,
  1967)

THE CELTIC WORLD

Batey, C. E., J. Jesch, and C. D. Morris, *The Viking
  Age in Caithness, Orkney and the North
  Atlantic* (Edinburgh, 1993)

Clark, H. B., M. Ní Mhaonaigh, and R. Ó Floinn, (eds), *Ireland and Scandinavia in the Early Viking Age* (Dublin and Portland, Oregon, 1998)

Crawford, B. E., *Scandinavian Scotland* (Leicester, 1987)

Davies, W., *Wales in the Early Middle Ages* (Leicester, 1982)

Fell, C. E., P. Foote, J. Graham-Campbell, and R. Thomson (eds), *The Viking Age in the Isle of Man* (London, 1983)

Fenton, A. and H. Pálsson (eds), *The Northern and Western Isles in the Viking World* (Edinburgh, 1984)

Graham-Campbell, J. and C. E. Batey, *Vikings in Scotland* (Edinburgh, 1998)

Loyn, H. R., *The Vikings in Wales* (London, 1976)

Ó Corráin, D., *Ireland before the Normans* (Dublin, 1972)

Ó Cróinín, D., *Early Medieval Ireland 400–1200* (London, 1995)

Price, N., *The Vikings in Brittany*, Viking Society for Northern Research, Saga Book 22 (1986–9), pp. 319–440

Ritchie, A., *Viking Scotland* (London, 1993)

Smyth, A. P., *Scandinavian York and Dublin* (2 vols, Dublin, 1975–9)

Smyth, A. P., *Warlords and Holy Men: Scotland AD 400–1000* (London, 1984)

ENGLAND

Abels, R., *Alfred the Great* (London and New York, 1998)

Biddle, M. and B. Kjølbye-Biddle, 'Repton and the Vikings', in *Antiquity* 66 (1992), pp. 36–51

Brooks, N. P., 'England in the Ninth Century: the Crucible of Defeat', in *Transactions of the Royal Historical Society*, 5th Series, 29, pp. 1–20

Hall, R. A., *Viking Age Archaeology in Britain and Ireland* (Princes Risborough, 1990)

Hall, R. A., *Viking Age York* (London, 1994)

Hart, C., *The Danelaw* (London, 1992)

Lawson, M. K., *Cnut* (London and New York, 1993)

Loyn, H. R., *The Vikings in Britain* (London, 1977)

Richards, J. D., *Viking Age England* (London, 1991)

Roesdahl, E. et al, *The Vikings in England* (London, 1981)

Scragg, D. G. (ed.), *The Battle of Maldon AD 991* (Oxford, 1991)

Smyth, A. P., *Scandinavian York and Dublin* (2 vols, Dublin, 1975–9)

Stenton, F. M., *Anglo-Saxon England* (3rd edition, Oxford, 1971)

Wainwright, F. T., *Scandinavian England* (Chichester, Sussex, 1975)

FRANCIA

Bates, D., *Normandy before 1066* (London, 1982)

Logan, F. D., *The Vikings in History* (London, 1983)

McKitterick, R., *The Frankish Kingdoms under the Carolingians 751–987* (London, 1983)

Nelson, J. L., *Charles the Bald* (London and New York, 1992)

Wallace-Hadrill, J. M., 'The Vikings in Francia', in *Early Medieval History* (Oxford, 1975)

RUSSIA AND THE EAST

Brisbane, M. A. (ed.), *The Archaeology of Novgorod, Russia* (Lincoln, 1992)

Dolukhanov, P. M., *The Early Slavs: Eastern Europe from the Initial Settlement to the Kievan Rus* (London, 1996)

Ellis Davidson, H. R., *The Viking Road to Byzantium* (London, 1976)

Franklin, S. and J. Shepard *The Emergence of Rus 750–1200* (London and New York, 1996)

SHIPS AND SEAFARING

Brøgger, A. W. and H. Shetelig, *The Viking Ships: Their Ancestry and Evolution* (London, 1971)

Christensen, A. E. (ed.), *The Earliest Ships: The Evolution of Boats into Ships* (London, 1996)

Crumlin-Pedersen, O., *Aspects of Maritime Scandinavia AD 200–1200* (Roskilde, 1990)

Haywood, J., *Dark Age Naval Power* (2nd revised edition, Hockwold-cum-Wilton, Norfolk, 1999)

McGrail, S., *Ancient Boats in North-West Europe* (London, 1987)

Unger, R. W. (ed.), *Cogs, Caravels and Galleons: The Sailing Ship 1000–1650* (London, 1994)

MILITARY

Griffith, P., *The Viking Art of War* (London, 1995)

Harrison, M., *Viking Hersir* (London, 1993)

Lund, N., 'Danish Military Organisation', in J. Cooper (ed.), *The Battle of Maldon, Fiction and Fact* (London, 1993)

Nørgård Jørgensen, A. and B. L. Clausen (eds), *Military Aspects of Scandinavian Society in a European Perspective, AD 1–1300* (Copenhagen, 1997)

MYTH AND RELIGION

Crossley-Holland, K., *The Norse Myths* (London, 1980)

Ellis Davidson, H. R., *Gods and Myths of Northern Europe* (Harmondsworth, 1964)

Page, R. I., *Norse Myths* (London, 1990)

Sawyer, B., P. H. Sawyer, and I. Wood (eds), *The Christianization of Scandinavia* (Alingsås, 1987)

Turville-Petre, E. O. G., *Myth and Religion of the North: The Religion of Ancient Scandinavia* (2nd edition, Greenwich, Conn., 1977)

VIKING LIFE AND CULTURE

Anker, P. and A. Andersson, *The Art of Scandinavia* (2 vols, London, 1970)

Bailey, R. N., *Viking Age Sculpture in Northern England* (London, 1980)

Clarke, H. and B. Ambrosiani, *Towns in the Viking Age* (2nd revised edition, Leicester, 1995)

Graham-Campbell, J., *Viking Artefacts: A Select Catalogue* (London, 1980)

Jesch, J., *Women in the Viking Age* (Woodbridge, Suffolk, 1991)

Jochens, J., *Women in Old Norse Society* (Ithaca and London, 1995)

Karras, R., *Slavery and Society in Medieval Scandinavia* (New Haven, 1988)

Page, R. I., *Runes* (London, 1987)

Turville-Petre, E. O. G., *Scaldic Poetry* (Oxford, 1976).

Sources of Illustrations